ROYAL HISTORICAL SOCIETY

STUDIES IN HISTORY

New Series

VICTORIAN RADICALS
AND ITALIAN DEMOCRATS

VICTORIAN RADICALS
AND ITALIAN DEMOCRATS

Marcella Pellegrino Sutcliffe

THE ROYAL HISTORICAL SOCIETY
THE BOYDELL PRESS

First published 2014

A Royal Historical Society publication
Published by The Boydell Press
an imprint of Boydell & Brewer Ltd
PO Box 9, Woodbridge, Suffolk IP12 3DF, UK
and of Boydell & Brewer Inc.
668 Mt Hope Avenue, Rochester, NY 14620–2731, USA
website: www.boydellandbrewer.com

ISBN 978–0–86193–322–8

ISSN 0269–2244

A CIP catalogue record for this book is available
from the British Library

AI MIEI GENITORI

Publication of this volume was aided by a generous grant
from the Scouloudi Foundation, in association with
the Institute of Historical Research

Contents

List of Figures

The author and publisher acknowledge with thanks the following for permission to reproduce material from their collections: Toynbee Hall, London, for the cover illustrations and for figures 6–12; the Bishopsgate Foundation and Institute for figures 1 and 4; the Brotherton Library Special Collections, University of Leeds, for figure 2; the Senate House Library, University of London, for figure 3; the British Library, for figure 5; and the Archivio Romussi, Milan, for figure 13.

List of Tables

Acknowledgements

The research that underpins this book was made possible by the generous support of the University of Newcastle: in 2008 the School of Historical Studies and the Faculty of Humanities and Social Sciences awarded me a maintenance grant and a scholarship. I was also fortunate to benefit from the support of a travel grant offered to me by the Royal Historical Society in 2009. Thanks to this project, I have had the pleasure of meeting numerous people to whom I am immensely grateful and whom I wish to thank. At Newcastle, I was able to draw on the considerable expertise of Joan Allen and Claudia Baldoli, who provided me with guidance and advice at various stages. Rachel Hammersley was equally important: her enthusiasm, trust and gentle coaxing strengthened my determination to write this book. As a member of the editorial board of the Royal Historical Society Studies in History series, Rachel introduced me to Sue Carr and Christine Linehan, whose expert editorial support ensured that my manuscript could be turned into a book. I am, of course, the only one responsible for any errors contained in these pages.

Throughout these years discussions with a number of distinguished historians have inspired me and helped me clarify my own thoughts: Eugenio Biagini and John Davis, who both read and provided detailed comments on the first draft of this book, have been an invaluable source of advice. Their feedback enabled me to sharpen the focus of my argument. I was also inspired to learn about the work carried out by one of John Davis's former mature students, Joan Browne, who died only a few months after I had come across some of her unpublished papers. This book is, in part, also a legacy of her work. Informal conversations with historians who were interested in my research helped to boost my confidence at critical times: I am grateful to Roland Sarti, David Laven, Giuseppe Monsagrati and Pietro Finelli for encouraging me in different ways and to Edoardo Romagnoli for his assistance in Milan.

Finding my way around unfamiliar archives was sometimes a daunting task: in Italy I was met by the assistance of helpful archivists, such as David Bidussa and Francesco Basile. In the UK, I was always heartened by Stefan Dickers's enthusiastic and efficient reception whenever I entered the Bishopsgate Institute archive; at the London Library, Andrea Del Cornò was a very precious guide around the Italian collection.

During my research trips I could also count on the unstinting support of loyal friends, including Gae Gagliano, whose house was always open to me, and my sister, Simona Pellegrino, who never flinched at the thought of my arriving on her doorstep at the most untimely hours. My extended family and friends in England were equally supportive: in particular, Mark Sutcliffe was a tremendous assistant, reading drafts of some chapters and helping me to improve my style; Sophie Forgan, a fellow historian and a much valued neighbour and friend, supported me with her advice and inspired me with her example. But, as ever, it is the closest and dearest who have borne the brunt of my commitment; and it is thanks to Johnny's selfless, unlimited availability, Francesca's intrigued marvelling at my enthusiasm, Edward's forgiving tolerance and, foremost, Ceci's kind, generous and unfaltering patience, that I was able to write this book. To them especially, I want to say thank you.

Marcella Pellegrino Sutcliffe
July 2013

Abbreviations

AGF	Archivio Giangiacomo Feltrinelli, Milan
FL	Fondo Linton
AISSH	International Institute of Social History, Amsterdam
AP	W. E. Adams papers
BCAB	Biblioteca Comunale dell'Archiginnasio, Bologna
FS	Fondo Saffi
HHM	Co-operative Archives, Holyoake House, Manchester
HP	Holyoake papers
LMA	London Metropolitan Archives
MCCR	Museo Centrale del Risorgimento, Rome
JWM	Jessie White Mario papers
MRM	Museo del Risorgimento, Milan
FC	Fondo Curatulo
FH	Fondo Holyoake
TWAS	Tyne and Wear Archives Service, Newcastle-upon-Tyne
CP	Cowen papers

NR	*The National Reformer*
NS	*The Northern Star*
NWC	*Newcastle Weekly Chronicle*
WR	*The Westminster and Foreign Quarterly Review* or *The Westminster Review*

AHR	*American Historical Review*
BDM	*Bollettino della Domus Mazziniana*
BSM	*Bollettino Storico Mantovano*
EHQ	*European History Quarterly*
EJPT	*European Journal of Political Theory*
HJ	*Historical Journal*
HS	*Historical Studies*
HT	*History Today*
IHR	*International History Review*
JBS	*Journal of British Studies*
JIH	*Journal of Interdisciplinary History*
JMH	*Journal of Modern History*
JMIS	*Journal of Modern Italian Studies*
LHR	*Labour History Review*
NA	*Nuova Antologia*
NRS	*Nuova Rivista Storica*

NT	*Northern Tribune*
RSR	*Rassegna Storica del Risorgimento*
RST	*Rassegna Storica Toscana*
SS	*Studi Storici*
TLS	*Times Literary Supplement*
VS	*Victorian Studies*
WH	*Women's History*

DBDI	M. Caravale (ed.), *Dizionario biografico degli italiani*, Rome 1960
DMBR	J. O. Baylen, and N. Gossman (eds), *Biographical dictionary of modern British radicals*, ii–iii, Brighton, Hemel Hempstead, 1984, 1988
DNCJ	L. Brake and M. Demoor (eds), *Dictionary of nineteenth-century journalism*, Ghent–London 2009
ODNB	H. C. G. Mathew and B. Harrison (eds) [online Lawrence Goldman], *Oxford dictionary of national biography*, Oxford 2004
SEI	G. Mazzini, *Edizione nazionale: scritti editi ed inediti*, ed. M. Menghini, Imola 1906–90

Note on the Text

All translations are the author's unless otherwise indicated.

Introduction: Victorian Visions
of a Radical Risorgimento

'We still need to understand and analyse the Risorgimento – not ignore it! Indeed, we must counter the official Risorgimento, Piedmontese and written for schools, with the popular, revolutionary Risorgimento, still unknown to too many, and tear off the vested veils of the official historiography.'[1]

Republican Italy was a nineteenth-century transnational dream. This 'imagined nation' galvanised and united Risorgimento democrats in Italy and Victorian radicals in Britain, who called themselves Mazzinians.[2] It was Giuseppe Mazzini's vision of a unified, republican Italy, combined with his promotion of the universal principles of individual freedom, equality and emancipation within democratically-governed nation states, which drew Victorian radicals to support the ideal of a 'popular Risorgimento'.[3] While they condemned both Britain's imperial politics and the government's 'non-interventionist' stance in European revolutions, Victorian radicals endorsed the establishment outside Britain of a new model of a republican nation which would lead the way towards a fully-realised form of democracy across all nations.[4] By embracing the 'transnational turn' in the context of the new history of nineteenth-century Italy, this book adds a novel dimension specifically to the so-called 'popular Risorgimento', reconstituting the historical fragments and tracing the continuities of a forgotten, *longue durée*

[1] 'Altro che ignorare! Noi dobbiamo, il Risorgimento, ancora conoscerlo e studiarlo. *Contro* il Risorgimento ufficiale, scolastico, piemontese; *per* il Risorgimento popolare, rivoluzionario, ignoto ancora a troppi, stracciando gli interessati veli della storiografia ufficiale': C. Rosselli, 'Discussione sul Risorgimento', *Giustizia e Libertà*, 26 Apr. 1935, in A. Castelli (ed.), *L'unità d'Italia: pro e contro il Risorgimento*, Rome 1997, 40–6.

[2] B. Anderson, *Imagined communities: reflections on the origins and spread of nationalism*, London 1991.

[3] These concepts are discussed in S. Recchia and N. Urbinati (eds), *A cosmopolitanism of nations: Giuseppe Mazzini's writings on democracy, nation building, and international relations*, Princeton–Oxford 2009.

[4] Salvo Mastellone's work focused on the years between 1836 and 1857: *Mazzini e Linton: una democrazia europea (1845–55)*, Florence 2007; *La nascita della democrazia in Europa: Carlyle, Harney, Mill, Engels, Mazzini, Schapper: addresses, appeals, manifestos (1836–55)*, Florence 2009; *Mazzini scrittore politico in inglese: democracy in Europe, 1840–55*, Florence 2004; *Il progetto politico di Mazzini: Italia–Europa*, Florence 1994; 'Mazzini's International League and the politics of the London Democratic Manifestos, 1837–50', 93–104, in C. A. Bayly and E. F. Biagini (eds), *Giuseppe Mazzini and the globalisation of democratic nationalism*, Oxford 2008, 93–104; and, as editor, *Mazzini e gli scrittori politici europei (1837–57)*, Florence 2005.

process.[5] This spanned national boundaries from Mazzini's arrival in London, in 1837, to the death, in 1890, of his most loyal disciple, Aurelio Saffi, a Risorgimento democrat exiled in Britain from 1851 to 1860, who, in the aftermath of Italy's unification in 1861, continued to pursue the republican dream.

Writing in 1935, Carlo Rosselli famously asserted that there had been 'two Risorgimenti: the official one, first neoguelph, then sabaudian, and always moderate which [triumphed] with the intervention of Piedmont and the ridding of the popular movement; and the popular Risorgimento … which bowed under the very skilful pincer movement of Cavour'.[6] Claiming that the latter was too often forgotten, he appealed to historians to speak up against the official Risorgimento and to study the popular one.[7] Yet, to this day, the historiography on the relationship between the British and Italy's struggle for nationhood has been reluctant to engage with the 'popular Risorgimento', no doubt due to the consensus which has highlighted British support for the moderates' solution for Italy and neatly overshadowed the 'unofficial history' of the 'losers'.[8] Notwithstanding a number of important studies focusing on the significant role which Mazzini played while exiled in

---

[5]   Oliver Janz and Lucy Riall have identified the signs of a transnational 'turn' in the new history of the Risorgimento which focuses on 'the process of transfers, the role of entanglements and the impact of associations outside and across Italy's borders': 'Introduction: the Italian Risorgimento: transnational perspectives', *Modern Italy*, special issue xix/1 (2014), 1–4 at p. 2.

[6]   Rosselli, 'Discussione sul Risorgimento'. The 'neoguelph' movement wished for an internal Catholic reform capable of re-establishing the moral authority of the pope and leading the national movement in Italy. The Sabaudian dynasty reigned in the Kingdom of Sardinia (1720–1861), including the Savoy, Nice, Liguria, Piedmont and Sardinia. Its capital was Turin. With the unification of Italy and the establishment of the new Kingdom on 17 March 1861 the Sabaudian monarch was crowned king of Italy as Victor Emanuel II.

[7]   While Rosselli's historiographical distinction between the 'popular Risorgimento' of democrats and the 'official Risorgimento' of moderates has been overshadowed by the 'cultural turn' of the 'new history of Risorgimento nationalism' (A. M. Banti and P. Ginsborg [eds], *Storia d'Italia*, Turin 2007), Alberto Banti's construction of the Risorgimento as a 'cultural project' has the limitation of virtually excluding the ideological and political sphere. This critique is cogently argued in M. Isabella, 'Emotions, rationality and political intentionality in patriotic discourse', *Nations and Nationalism* xv/3 (2009), 396–401.

[8]   D. Beales, *England and Italy (1859–60)*, London 1961; J. Parry, *The politics of patriotism: English liberalism, national identity and Europe, 1830–86*, Cambridge 2006; E. F. Biagini, *Gladstone*, London 2000, 79. On Cavour's popularity in Britain see J. A. Davis, 'L'immagine di Cavour in Inghilterra', in U. Levra (ed.), *Cavour, l'Italia e l'Europa*, Bologna 2011, 225–40, and H. Hearder, *Cavour*, New York 1994. See also A. Viarengo, *Cavour*, Rome 2010. On Palmerston's policy see S. Matsumoto, 'Palmerston and Italy', in D. Brown and M. Taylor (eds), *Palmerston studies*, ii, Southampton 2007, 79–96.

Britain, the official narrative on the 'English' and the Italian Risorgimento has remained unchallenged.[9]

Indeed, despite the emergence of new historiographical perspectives on the attitudes of nineteenth-century radicals to global order and empire, the reservations of mid- to late-Victorian radicals concerning the establishment of the kingdom of Italy have attracted little attention.[10] Echoing the predominant historiographical view, Jonathan Parry has reiterated that, following the unification of Italy under the Piedmontese monarchy, the consensus in Britain was that, with Cavour, the 'English of Italy' had won: Italian unification 'seemed to mark a victory for English political values'.[11] The connection between the victory of the Italian moderates and reaffirming the British monarchical constitution as a model for all nations is a constant which weaves its way through decades of historiographical interpretations, leaving little opportunity to test whether some British observers were in fact disappointed with the turn that events took in 1860. Indeed, the whiggish approach has so dominated the literature on the British and Italy that, while revisionist historians of the Risorgimento have paid increasing attention to the resentment of the Italian losers, warding off teleological representations, it has become difficult to frame the connection between Victorians and the Risorgimento in terms other than of overwhelming satisfaction with the outcome.[12] Challenging this myth, this book contends that the claim that, by supporting the Italian cause, the British simply reaffirmed their national

---

[9] E. Morelli, *L'Inghilterra di Mazzini*, Rome 1965, and *Mazzini in Inghilterra*, Florence 1938. In addition to Salvo Mastellone's studies (see n. 3 above) see E. Biagini, 'Mazzini and anticlericalism: the English exile', and C. Duggan, 'Giuseppe Mazzini in Britain and Italy: divergent legacies (1837–1915)', in Bayly and Biagini, *Mazzini*, 145–66, 187–210, and D. Laven, 'Mazzini, Mazzinian conspiracy and British politics in the 1850s', *BSM* ii (2003), 267–82. Earlier studies included G. Claeys, 'Mazzini, Kossuth, and British radicalism, 1848–54', *JBS* xxviii/3 (1989), 225–61; A. Campanella, 'Joseph Cowen, Garibaldi e Mazzini', *NRS* i–ii (1966), 201–18; D. Mackay, 'Joseph Cowen e il Risorgimento', *RSR* li (1964), 5–26; P. Onnis, 'Battaglie democratiche e Risorgimento in un carteggio inedito di Giuseppe Mazzini e George Jacob Holyoake', *RSR* xxii (1935), 883–927; and L. Gasparini, 'Una nuova fonte di documenti sul movimento mazziniano nei rapporti coi patrioti inglesi, e specialmente con G. J. Holyoake', *RSR* iv (1933), 767–79.

[10] On radical and Chartist views on empire see G. Claeys, *Imperial sceptics: British critics of empire (1850–1920)*, Cambridge 2010; G. Vargo. ' "Outworks of the citadel of corruption": the Chartist press reports the empire', *VS* liv/2 (2012), 227–53; and E. Biagini, 'The politics of Italianism: *Reynolds's Newspaper*, the Indian mutiny, and the radical critique of liberal imperialism in mid-Victorian Britain', in T. Crook, R. Gill and B. Taithe (eds), *Evil, barbarism and empire: Britain and abroad. c. 1830–2000*, Basingstoke 2011, 99–125.

[11] Parry, *The politics of patriotism*, 231–2, 242; A. Howe, '"Friends of moderate opinions": Italian political thought in 1859 in a British liberal mirror', *JMIS* xvii/5 (2012), 608–11.

[12] Eva Cecchinato and Mario Isnenghi have highlighted the presence of a resentful parallel Italy ('rancorosa Italia parallela'): *Gli italiani in guerra: conflitti identità, memorie dal Risorgimento ai nostri giorni*, i, Turin, 2008, 717.

identity and political beliefs does not reflect the full picture. Indeed, it does not do credit either to the part that Victorian radicals played in the 'popular Risorgimento' or to the feelings of disappointment and resentment which were experienced across national boundaries.[13] It expunges both.

Following decades of nationalist struggles by Italian democrats in which the cry for emancipation, unity and liberty had often been combined with the call for republicanism, the decision taken by Italy's 'liberator', Giuseppe Garibaldi, to hand Italy over to the Sabaudian monarch was disappointing, a result which left radicals across national boundaries dismayed.[14] In 1861 the unification of Italy under the Piedmontese king was perceived by the Mazzinian 'international' not as a triumph of liberalism, but as a blow: Italy not only became a monarchy rather than the republic for which Mazzinians had hoped, but its political system, although based on the representative principle, was distorted by a high, undemocratic political qualification for the parliamentary franchise. As John A. Davis suggested in 1982, Garibaldi's decision to support Victor Emmanuel, had come 'as a shock for English radicals'.[15] Yet, no further studies have treated this assertion with the seriousness that it deserves.

Mazzini was unique amongst early exiled democrats in his ability to disseminate his ideas on Italy across Britain; his writings were published across a broad range of English radical papers and journals read by self-improving workers beyond the metropolis. The long connection between Victorian radicals and Risorgimento democrats which was to ensue would extend well beyond the achievement of political unification by Italy and the liberation of Rome in 1870: indeed, the resilience of these links quietly outlived the popular clamour expressed at the zenith of British Garibaldimania, between 1859 and 1860. Yet, to this day, accounts of the relationship between Britain and Italy, in privileging the role played by Garibaldi in enthusing the British of all ranks and political beliefs, completely obscure the disappointment, frustration, and in some cases resentment, that Victorian radicals – and republicans – shared when learning of Italy's unification under a monarch.[16]

Transnational history has a way of privileging the shared positive emotions of enthusiasm: episodes like fund-raising subscriptions for Italy or volunteering for Garibaldi are often referred to in this context. Disappointment in other nations, conversely, is more likely to be associated with disillusionment, estrangement and closure.[17] Yet the 'losers' of the 'popular

---

[13] M. Isabella, 'Italian exiles and British politics before and after 1848', in S. Freitag (ed.), *Exiles from European revolutions: refugees in mid-Victorian England*, New York–Oxford 2003, 59–87 at p. 78.

[14] For 'Sabaudian' see n. 2 above.

[15] J. A. Davis, 'Garibaldi and England', *HT* xxxii (1982), 21–6 at p. 24.

[16] Duggan, 'Giuseppe Mazzini', 187–210. This is particularly evident in public history: see, for example, M. Isabella, 'Garibaldi, re di Londra', *Il Sole 24 Ore*, 28 Feb. 2010.

[17] D. Beales, 'Garibaldi in England: the politics of Italian enthusiasm', in J. A. Davis

Risorgimento' maintained their cross-Channel connections, sharing flickering hopes, as well as feelings of dismay, resentment, disappointment and, finally, nostalgia across borders.[18]

The 'Garibaldi moment', underlined by Lucy Riall, for all its flamboyance and its media manipulation was mainly a depoliticised mass phenomenon, a short-lived aspect of British support for Italy.[19] Yet it is still the liberal propaganda for Italy which attracts scholars interested in Victorian support for the unification process.[20] By focusing overwhelmingly on the endorsement of Garibaldi's monarchical turn, historians interested in the widening of British popular support for Italy have contributed towards relegating to obscurity the long-lasting links between British and Italian Mazzinians, which weaved the threads of a veritable 'Mazzini epoch'.[21] Eugenio Biagini, Gregory Claeys and Derek Beales have variously stressed the extraordinary popularity achieved by Mazzini in mid-Victorian Britain: yet it is the *longue durée* of his influence which is examined here.[22] Indeed, it is argued that British Mazzinians continued to believe in the historic mission of Mazzini's 'Third Rome' (the Rome of the people replacing Imperial Rome and the 'Popes' Rome'), trusting in the value of supporting Italian republican democrats until the death of their leader, Aurelio Saffi. As Risorgimento patriot, triumvir in Mazzini's

and P. Ginsborg (eds), *Society and politics in the age of the Risorgimento*, Cambridge 1991, 184–216.

[18] On the emotions of British volunteers for Garibaldi see M. P. Sutcliffe, 'L'amore per Garibaldi: consumante passione o prodotto di consumo', in P. Morris, F. Ricatti and M. Seymour (eds), *Politica ed emozioni nella storia d'Italia*, Rome 2012, 53–70.

[19] L. Riall, *Garibaldi: invention of a hero*, New Haven–London 2007, 294–305; M. P. Sutcliffe, 'Marketing "Garibaldi panoramas" in Britain (1860–1864)', *JMIS* xviii/2 (2013), 232–43.

[20] See E. Bacchin, '"Italy for the Italians": l'opinione pubblica britannica di fronte al Risorgimento (1859–60)', *Annali della Scuola normale superiore di Pisa* ii/2 (2010), 463–88.

[21] Idem, 'Il Risorgimento oltremanica: nazionalismo cosmopolita nei meeting britannici di metà Ottocento', *Contemporanea: rivista di storia dell'800 e del 900* xiv (2011), 173–203; D. Raponi, 'Gran Bretagna', in F. Cammarano and M. Marchi (eds), *Il mondo ci guarda: l'unificazione italiana nella stampa e nell'opinione pubblica internazionali (1859–61)*, Florence 2011, 141–52; K. Windland, 'Garibaldi in Britain: reflections of a liberal hero', unpubl. DPhil. Oxford 2002; Beales, 'Garibaldi in England', 184–216; M. O'Connor, *The romance of Italy and the English political imagination*, Basingstoke 1998, 149–85; M. Finn, *After Chartism*, Cambridge 1993, 203–26; Davis, 'Garibaldi and England'; D. Mack Smith, 'Garibaldi e l'Inghilterra', *NA* cxvii (1982), 415–32; F. Conti, 'I riflessi del viaggio di Garibaldi in Inghilterra: la sinistra fiorentina fra opposizione e alternative di governo', *RST* xxviii (1982), 219–36; L. E. Funaro, 'Il viaggio di Garibaldi in Inghilterra e la crisi della democrazia italiana dopo l'unità', *SS* vii (1966), 129–57. For a more chequered picture of Garibaldi's popularity in England in the early 1860s, and a regional approach, see M. P. Sutcliffe, 'Negotiating the "Garibaldi moment" in Newcastle-upon-Tyne (1854–61)', *Modern Italy* xv/2 (2010), 129–44.

[22] E. F. Biagini, *Liberty, retrenchment and reform: popular liberalism in the age of Gladstone, 1860–80*, Cambridge 1992, 48; Claeys, 'Mazzini', 228, 259–61; Beales, *England and Italy*, 31–3.

short-lived Roman Republic, defender of republican values in liberal Italy and former exile, Saffi stood for continuity between the shared ideals of the past, the challenges of the present and the hopes for the future.

Since it may seem surprising that a book devoted to the long British connection with the Risorgimento pays only marginal attention to Garibaldi, the chosen approach will need some qualifying. As John A. Davis percep- tively pointed out, not only was Mazzini's image and influence in Britain 'immeasurably greater and more lasting' than Garibaldi's, but British radi- cals in particular 'looked on Garibaldi as Mazzini's partner but subordinate'. According to Davis, Garibaldi's impact in the country was 'more ambiguous and more superficial', than that of Mazzini: it was G. M. Trevelyan's trilogy, written on the eve of the First World War, which crucially contributed towards reversing perceptions of the popularity of the two men in Britain, posthumously inflating Garibaldi's aura and elevating him as a universal symbol of nineteenth-century heroism.[23] Viewed in this light, Trevelyan's contribution to reinforcing the whiggish interpretation of the relationship between Britain and the moderate Risorgimento cannot be underestimated.

Garibaldi's aura as national 'hero' – with all the qualities of manliness and gentleness attributed to him by the popular press – was also emphasised by the romantic image of Italy as a gendered nation, a beautiful woman who had been wronged and violated by invaders and who needed to be rescued.[24] Italy's landscape, literature, history and woes were familiar to the educated classes.[25] As travellers witnessed clear signs of oppression on their journeys around the peninsula, they associated themselves more closely with the Ital- ians' calls for revolution than with the plight of other oppressed nations: as Maura O'Connor has stated, 'the "romance of Italy" played in English support for the Italian nationalist cause'.[26] The 'English' 'love of Italy' had its roots in the romantic allure that the peninsula's natural beauty, its exotic attraction and its artistic treasures traditionally had for the elites and the well-travelled Victorian bourgeoisie.[27]

Although these travellers constituted a minority social group – hardly representative of the British 'nation' – the *Grand Tour* master-narrative, with its combination of high culture and travel, had successfully made an appre- ciation of Italy the preserve of the established, educated classes – equally keen to admire the Mediterranean landscapes and observe their inhabitants,

---

[23] J. A. Davis, 'The many English lives of Giuseppe Garibaldi', in S. Bonanni, *Garibaldi: cultura e ideali*, Rome 2008, 339–62.

[24] Riall, *Garibaldi*.

[25] S. Patriarca, 'Indolence and regeneration: tropes and tensions of Risorgimento patriotism', *AHR* cx (2005), 380–408.

[26] This view is shared by Trevelyan, Beales and O'Connor: G. M. Trevelyan, 'Englishmen and Italians: some aspects of their relations past and present' (1919), in his *Clio, A muse and other essays* (1930). Freeport 1968, 104–23, and O'Connor, *Romance of Italy*, 4, 65.

[27] Beales, *England and Italy*; O'Connor, *Romance of Italy*.

cast according to the 'picturesque' stereotype.[28] Reversing this literary *topos* would prove challenging. Indeed, post-colonial readings of the northern Europeans' 'gaze' on the Italians, which largely attempted to deconstruct the constituents of the romance of the South, did little to shift the object of historical enquiry away from the conventional upper-class and bourgeois protagonists attracted by the romance of Italy: rather, paradoxically, post-colonial interpretations, by focusing on the 'othering' of the Italians, further increased the attention paid to the perspective on Italy of socially privileged Britons.[29]

This book shifts the focus of the enquiry to the British people.[30] It builds on the approach taken by Ross McKibbin, who underlined that Britain before the First World War was one of the most working-class countries in the world, with an upper-class population of only 0.1%. As recent studies have shown, however, historical research on the working classes has many pitfalls: although E. P. Thompson claimed to have written the history of the 'English working class', critics have highlighted that even he entirely neglected domestic workers.[31] When analysing working-class protagonists the focus of this book is therefore defined by the workers' aspirations: it concentrates on radical, working-class individuals who were guided by the desire to self-improve through education.[32]

By looking at transnational connections through the prism of the adult education movement, so central to the progress of social and political reforms in nineteenth-century Britain, this book engages with an array of artisans, skilled workers, co-operators and also, in the latter stages, school board

[28] On the relationship between the 'English' and Italy see H. W. Rudman, *Italian nationalism and English letters: figures of the Risorgimento and Victorian men of letters*, London 1940, and C. P. Brand, *Italy and the English romantics: the Italianate fashion in early nineteenth century England*, Cambridge 1957. The literature on the tradition of travel in Italy is vast and beyond the scope of this study. Amongst many works see O'Connor, *Romance of Italy*; M. Pfister, *The fatal gift of beauty: the Italies of British travellers: an annotated anthology*, Amsterdam–Atlanta 1996; H. Fraser, *The Victorians and Renaissance Italy*, Oxford 1993; R. S. Pine-Coffin, *Bibliography of British and American travel in Italy to 1860*, Florence 1974; and J. Buzard, *The beaten track*, Oxford 1993, 187. On Italy as a destination for cultured travellers see E. Chaney, *The evolution of the Grand Tour: Anglo-Italian cultural relations since the Renaissance*, London 2000, and A. Brilli, *Il viaggio in Italia: storia di una grande tradizione culturale*, Bologna 2008, and *Un paese di romantici briganti: gli italiani dell'immaginario del Grand Tour*, Bologna 2003.

[29] Patriarca, 'Indolence and regeneration'; O'Connor, *Romance of Italy*; N. Moe, *The view from the Vesuvius*, Berkeley 2002; J. Schneider, *Italy's southern question: orientalism in one country*, Oxford 1998; J. Pemble, *The Mediterranean passion: Victorians and Edwardians in the South*, Oxford 1987; J. Urry, *The tourist gaze: leisure and travel in contemporary societies*, London 2002.

[30] R. McKibbin, *Classes and cultures: England, 1918–51*, Oxford 1998.

[31] E. P. Thompson, *The making of the English working class*, New York 1964; C. Steedman, *Labours lost: domestic service and the making of modern England*, Cambridge 2009.

[32] J. Rose, *The intellectual life of the British working classes*, New Haven–London 2001, 62.

teachers, who were female and middle-class, whose lives were shaped by the extensively circulated theories of 'self-improvement' and whose collective imagination of Italy was defined not by travel, but by their access to the popular press and co-operative literature. Jonathan Rose has demonstrated how the intellectual life of the working classes in Britain had been shaped by the books read by autodidacts; following this approach, this book highlights how the reading of radical literature shaped the understanding of the world of British self-improving workers and, in particular, helped them to imagine Italy as a new, republican nation.[33]

Within the broad groupings of skilled workers (artisans or 'mechanics'), semi-skilled factory workers (the manufacturing or operative classes) and unskilled workers (the labouring population), it was primarily skilled workers who frequented educational institutes, often mixing with lower-middle-class clerks and constituting, as J. F. C. Harrison puts it, 'a point of contact with middle-class ideals'.[34] Yet a closer analysis of such institutions located across England – mechanics' institutes, mutual improvement clubs, working men's colleges and, later, university extension classes – also signals that the political, social and indeed gender traits of the workers examined could vary from one local institution to another, according to whether that institution had a reputation for being politically neutral or radical and was frequented mainly by the lower middle classes or by the lower social ranks.

In mapping support for Mazzini's radical project across regions, and noting how it varied, the centrality of the adult education movement is therefore pivotal: Lancashire, Yorkshire and the North-East, as seedbeds for radical experiments, whether within Chartism, republicanism or in the context of the co-operative movement, were the hub of Mazzini's provincial support. Not only London, therefore, but localities across the length and breadth of England, where the number of mechanics' institutes outnumbered in quantity and efficacy those in Wales, Scotland and Ireland, offer a privileged perspective for analysing Mazzini's influence in his country of exile.[35] The other significant laboratory for discussing and elaborating Mazzinian ideas was reformed Oxford, where men like Arnold Toynbee, T. H. Green and Bolton King, committed to the university extension movement, planned to set up a university settlement in the East End of London.[36] It is not, therefore,

---

[33] Ibid.

[34] J. F. C. Harrison, *Learning and living, 1790–1960: a study in the history of the English adult education*, London 1961, 44.

[35] W. J. Hudson, *The history of adult education: in which is comprised a full and complete history of the mechanics' and literary institutions*, London 1851. The total returns indicated in 1851 were 610 mechanics' institutes in England, 55 in Scotland, 25 in Ireland and 12 in Wales. More recent studies confirmed the regional distribution: M. Tylecote, *The mechanics' institutes of Lancashire and Yorkshire before 1851*, Manchester 1957.

[36] In Cambridge a group of Liberal Anglicans, including Frederic Maurice and John Robert Seeley, formed a reading group to discuss Mazzini's *Duties of man*.

so much on the public platform, in 'public meetings' and lectures – where most of the liberal philo-Italian propaganda took place – that the majority of radical, republican discourses here analysed were located.[37] Rather they were part of a diffused *sociabilité* which saw workers and social reformers come together in forms of associations which included co-operative societies, republican clubs, secular societies, educational institutions and university settlements.

For the geography of Mazzinian support within Scotland interpersonal connections were more significant. Evidence for Scottish support for the Mazzinian project lies not within worker's associations, but in the agency of particular individuals, such as John McAdam in Glasgow, whose political activities were often organised in conjunction with the Newcastle magnate, Joseph Cowen, in view of the close association of the 'borders' with the radical North-East. A further later link between Scotland and Italy is the cross-fertilisation between nationalism and family connections which recent studies on intimacy and migration have highlighted.[38] In the 1870s reports on Italian republican affairs in radical Scottish papers were mainly the result of the efforts of Saffi's Scottish in-laws, the Craufords, to disseminate news about the continuing republican struggles in liberal Italy. No doubt more could be said about the links that Scottish or indeed Welsh sympathisers established with Italian exiles during the Risorgimento.[39] However this book argues that the popular dissemination amongst English workers' educational associations of Giuseppe Mazzini's vision for Italy, including his theories on republicanism, education and association, constituted the linchpin of the enduring ties between Victorian radicals and Italian democrats.

Italian democrats and Victorian radicals: perspectives old and new

Revisiting the intellectual framework first introduced by Franco Venturi in his seminal essay 'La circolazione delle idee' (1954), recent studies have situated Italy's national struggle in its transnational, European and global dimension, highlighting the international intellectual exchanges, the phenomenon of volunteering across boundaries and the emergence of the participatory

---

[37] Bacchin, "'Italy for the Italians'".

[38] R. Pesman, 'The marriage of Giorgina Saffi and Aurelio Saffi: Mazzinian nationalism and the Italian home', in L. Baldassar and D. Gabaccia (eds), *Intimacy and Italian migration: gender and domestic lives in a mobile world*, New York 2010, 25–35.

[39] Although the Mazzinian Gwylim. O. Griffith, mentioned in this book, was Welsh, he had first come across Mazzini's readings in Birmingham. On the relationship between Italian revolutionaries and Wales see K. Windland, 'Garibaldi and the Welsh political imagination', in M. Cragoe and C. Williams (eds), *Wales and war: society, politics and religion in the nineteenth and twentieth centuries*, Cardiff 2007. On the Ruffini brothers' exile in Scotland see C. Cagnacci, *Giuseppe Mazzini e i fratelli Ruffini*, Porto Maurizio 1893, and J. Fyfe, 'Scotland and the Risorgimento', unpubl. Phd diss. Guelph 1976.

role of a cross-national public whose opinions on Italy were shaped by the explosion of press culture.[40] This book contributes to the analysis of transnational European networks of democracy by widening the field geographically – taking a regional and 'peripheral' approach, rather than focusing on the exchanges which occurred in Britain within the metropolis.[41] De-centring narratives and integrating the pluralism of connected histories is indeed one of the new directions of transnational history, which aims to include the geographical 'margins', with their local variants, within the discourses and networks which crossed national boundaries.[42]

A survey of the latest interpretative directions on the Italian Risorgimento will help to situate the specific contribution that the transnational perspective of this book makes to the revisionist approach to the history of nineteenth-century Italy.[43] The rhetoric of tensions between Risorgimento 'democrats' and 'moderates' is laced with the legacy of a burdensome historiographical debate, centred on shared responsibilities in the making of the nation and the 'difficult modernisation' which followed.[44] Recent historiography has endeavoured to distance itself from the long shadow of Gramsci's post-war interpretation of the Italian Risorgimento as a 'failed revolution', allegedly responsible for the 'exceptionalism' of Italy's nation-building process and for its subsequent failed modernity. The deconstruction of Gramsci's legacy has been one of the main challenges which revisionist, cultural historians of the Risorgimento have encountered. According to Gramsci, the inability of Italian democrats to engage the majority of Italians – and the peasantry in particular – in the making of Italy had confined patriotism to the intellectual elites and had ultimately handed the national revolution to the moderates. Associating the peasantry with Italy's South, Gramsci had further contributed towards linking the responsibilities of the

---

[40] F. Venturi, 'La circolazione delle idee', *RSR* xli (1954), 223–42; M. Isabella, *Risorgimento in exile: Italian emigrés and the liberal international in the post-Napoleonic era*, Oxford 2009; Bayly and Biagini, *Giuseppe Mazzini*; M. Ridolfi (ed.), *La democrazia radicale nell'ottocento europeo: forme della politica, modelli culturali, riforme sociali*, Milan 2005; M. Gottardi (ed.), *Fuori d'Italia: Manin e l'esilio*, Venice 2009; G. Pécout, (ed.), 'International volunteers and the Risorgimento: introduction', *JMIS* xiv/4 (2009), 413–26.

[41] Bacchin also included the provinces in her analysis of the liberal philo-Italian propaganda and the support for Garibaldi.

[42] For a discussion on the Risorgimento in global context see M. Isabella, 'Il movimento risorgimentale in un contesto globale', in A. Roccucci, *La costruzione dello stato-nazione in Italia*, Rome 2012, 87–107.

[43] For a comprehensive review of recent historiographical debates see M. Isabella, 'Review article: rethinking Italy's nation-building 150 years afterwards: the new Risorgimento historiography', *Past & Present* ccxvii/1 (2012), 247–68. See also S. Patriarca and L. Riall (eds), *The Risorgimento revisited: nationalism and culture in nineteenth-century Italy*, Basingstoke 2012.

[44] On Italy's 'difficult modernisation' see J. A. Davis (ed.), *Italy in the nineteenth century*, Oxford 2000, 1–24.

democrats with the failed agrarian revolution and the emergence of the 'Southern Question'.

Revisionist historians have gone some way towards reframing the myth that common Italians – or the 'masses' – had not participated in the project of the nation. Alberto Banti's anthropological reading of the Italian 'nation' as a 'deep' biological bond has aimed to question the overriding historiographical consensus on the polarised divide between the elites and the people and there have been a number of studies which have pointed to greater popular involvement in the national revolution, albeit predominantly engaging urban Italian workers.[45] If Gramsci argued that the revolutions of 1848 had constituted the turning point for the moderates' appropriation of the Risorgimento process, recent studies have shown that, on the contrary, between 1848 and 1860 a new popular nationalist culture emerged. Moreover, new studies on the *Mezzogiorno* have also questioned the cultural construction of Southern Italy as backward, uncivilised and passive, pointing rather to long-standing tensions within Southern society between liberalism and tradition.[46]

The transnational perspective on the 'popular Risorgimento' offers a further opportunity for revising the Gramscian narrative and identifying the traces of low culture within the Risorgimento experience, particularly between 1849 – coinciding with the international reverberations of the crushing of the Roman Republic – and the 1860s, when Mazzinians across national boundaries endeavoured to re-ignite the republican momentum. The experience of exile and the spread of reading practices had given Italian democrats, republicans, and their undisputed leader, Mazzini, an audience amongst the working classes beyond the confines of nation, reaching scores of workers in Britain. While in Italy occasional readers hardly reached 20 per cent of the population at the time of unification, in Britain literacy levels were around 60 per cent; by the end of the 1860s 75 per cent of British working-class adults were readers.[47]

Through Mazzini's writings, British 'common readers' were able to 'imagine' a 'nation' other than their own. Yet the 'nation' that they imagined was not necessarily modelled on contemporary Britain, nor was Italy's new nation expected to be a 'hybrid of their own' constitutional monarchy.[48]

---

[45] A. M. Banti, *La nazione del Risorgimento: parentela, santità e onore all'origine dell'Italia unita*, Turin 2000; Banti and Ginsborg, *Storia d'Italia*; G. L. Fruci, 'Il Sacramento dell'unità nazionale: linguaggi, iconografia e pratiche dei plebisciti risorgimentali (1848–70)', in Banti and Ginsborg, *Storia d'Italia*, 567–605.

[46] J. A. Davis, *Naples and Napoleon: southern Italy and the European revolutions, 1780–1860*, Oxford 2006; C. Pinto, '1857: conflitto civile e guerra nazionale nel mezzogiorno', *Meridiana* lxix (2011), 171–200, and 'La rivoluzione disciplinata del 1860: cambio di regime ed elite politiche nel mezzogiorno italiano', *Contemporanea* 1 (2013), 39–68. See also S. Lupo, *L'unificazione italiana: mezzogiorno, rivoluzione, guerra civile*, Rome 2011.

[47] These comparative data are taken from M. Meriggi, 'Il Risorgimento rivisitato: un bilancio', in Roccucci, *La costruzione dello stato-nazione*, 48. See also Biagini, *Liberty*, 195.

[48] O'Connor, *Romance of Italy*, 3.

Rather, radical workers were mindful of Britain's republican past and Cromwell's Commonwealth. Having read Mazzini's works, they were enthused by the vision of a republican Italy, and, in some cases, they signed up as transnational volunteers in the hope that by establishing the model nation in Rome a renewed 'English Republic' would follow.[49]

Moreover, their political activism was not totally removed from the agency of Italian workers. Indeed, traces of the connections which Victorian workers sought and established with their Italian counterparts occasionally bring to the surface the active part that some Italian urban operatives – in the North (Genoa) and in the South (Naples) – played in the struggle for unity and for democracy in Italy. Insofar as it may be possible to piece together the history of the Risorgimento from a 'nationhood from below' perspective, the transnational approach provides a further viewpoint which shores up the recent Italian historiography on popular support for the Risorgimento.

The faith of Victorian Mazzinians in the imminence of the Italian republic would repeatedly defy the blows of fortune, as Mazzini's attempts to realise unification under the republican banner ran into difficulties rooted in the lack of political education among Italians. In fact, Mazzini's miscalculated attempts at insurrection, which increasingly alienated sympathisers on both sides of the Channel, found in Victorian republicans and co-operators a particularly resilient minority, prepared to forgive the blunders of the present in the hope of realising Mazzini's vision for Italy and for humanity. While some Italian republicans, guided by Saffi, did continue to uphold Mazzini's ideals, it is well-known that the majority of democrats who had joined the Mazzinian movement in the early 1830s deserted him for the moderate route. Recent readings of this shift have abandoned the Gramscian theory of the prevailing hegemony of the moderates, favouring instead the view that the juvenile, emotional enthusiasm, which had mobilised the first generation of Mazzinians to take part in the early insurrections, gave way to a more mature approach: patriots had become fathers and breadwinners and were less prone to embrace sacrifice with the passion of youth.[50] As Lucy Riall and Silvana Patriarca have argued, the emotion of commitment to the national-patriotic discourse was particularly evident amongst Mazzinian radicals; indeed, the

---

[49] On the hopes of British Mazzinian volunteers following Garibaldi see M. P. Sutcliffe, 'British red shirts: a history of the Garibaldi volunteers (1860)', in B. Collins and N. Airelli, *Transnational soldiers: foreign military enlistment in the modern era*, Basingstoke 2013, 202–18.

[50] A. Arisi Rota, *I piccoli cospiratori: politica ed emozioni nei primi mazziniani*, Bologna 2010; A. Arisi Rota and R. Balzani, 'Discovering politics: action and recollection in the first Mazzinian generation', in Patriarca and Riall, *Risorgimento revisited*, 77–97. For a traditional history of the Italian democrats, which countered Gramsci's accusations of elitism see F. Della Peruta (ed.), *Giuseppe Mazzini e i democratici*, Milan–Naples 1969. See also C. M. Lovett, *The democratic movement in Italy, 1830–76*, Cambridge, MA 1982.

history of agency in the Risorgimento, and its mass appeal, must engage with the connection between emotions and politics.[51]

In this context transnational Mazzinian radicals need to be analysed within their own particular emotional register. Unlike first-generation Italian Mazzinians, who had been youths in the 1830s, most young Victorian radicals became Mazzinians following the news of the crushing of the Roman Republic in 1849. Amongst them, W. E. Adams, one of the most loyal republicans who read, copied and wrote Mazzinian texts as a young, working-class republican, was born in 1832; Charles Bradlaugh, the secular, republican editor who celebrated Mazzini in the *National Reformer*, was born in 1833. Still in their early youth when the Roman Republic fell, they, like other young radical labourers reading *Cooper's Journal*, were not easily disheartened by the failed insurrections of the 1850s: former Chartists, in the aftermath of the Kennington Common 'fiasco', participated enthusiastically in the Italian attempts at insurrection by dedicating impassioned poems to Mazzini. Adams's personal journal, written between 1848 and 1867 provides a valuable insight into the mentality, as well as the emotions, of a self-improving Victorian worker whose consumption of Mazzini's readings was a weekly, if not daily, routine and whose religious approach to life's mission was imbued with Mazzinian principles.

Despite the problems that historians have highlighted in the use of the term 'Victorian' – not least, the fact that it is monarchical – it is still valid when describing the communalities and continuities within the years here analysed.[52] The role that the Victorians in question – radicals and republicans – were able to play in shaping their own nation became increasingly peripheral in the second half of the nineteenth century, as the Gladstonian era of liberal reforms supplanted the age of Chartism and the appeal to 'physical force' gave way to the 'respectability' of the English working man.[53]

Moreover, Victorian republicans became progressively marginalised due to the undercurrents which divided and weakened them: asserters of classic 'republican' values within Victorian liberalism were not always antimonarchists, and indeed, amongst those who attacked the monarchy, many shunned the revolutionary language of French republicans. Yet despite dissonances and tensions, as Frank Prochaska has demonstrated, republicanism was still well represented in the provinces and in London in the 1870s. The *National Reformer*, as well as *Reynolds's Newspaper*, continued to use the language of

[51] Patriarca and Riall, *Risorgimento revisited*, 6.

[52] For a discussion of the term see F. O'Gorman, *The Cambridge companion to Victorian culture*, Cambridge 2010, 1–5. See also M. Hewitt, 'Why the notion of Victorian Britain does make sense', VS xlviii/3 (2006), 395–438.

[53] On the continuities and discontinuities of radicalism in Britain see K. Neville, *Change, continuity and class: labour in British society (1850–1920)*, Manchester 1998, and R. Harrison, *Before the socialists: studies in labour and politics*, London 1965.

radicalism and republicanism well into the 1880s.[54] Despite their resilience and the acknowledged influence of Charles Bradlaugh's charismatic politics, the success of nineteenth-century popular liberalism, has tended to overshadow the role that republicans played.[55] Indeed, traditionally, historians have hesitated to consider republicans as representative of 'Englishness': as Antony Taylor has stated, republicans are more likely to be constructed according to their 'anti-Englishness', as the 'peculiarities of the English' have traditionally been linked to plebeian support for the monarchy.[56]

Like Victorian radicals, Italian republicans played an increasingly peripheral role in the process of Italy's nation-building: they too operated on the margins of the parliamentary arena, moving within a web of associations and circulating ideas through the uneasy distribution of republican literature. In their common adherence to the values of education, association, citizenship and republicanism, both groups shared a transnational mental map which was resumed under Mazzini's doctrine. Indeed, as Francesco Crispi's grip on power steered liberal Italy towards increasingly authoritarian policies, Saffi, who, as Risorgimento patriot had enjoyed celebrity status while touring England and Scotland in 1857, would remain for Victorian radicals a favourite interlocutor, speaking from the heartland of Italian republicanism.[57]

Unlike Felice Orsini, also a romantic hero in Britain, whose life had ended dramatically; unlike Mazzini, who had died in 1872; unlike Garibaldi, who had eventually turned to socialism, an ideology unwelcome to British radicals, Saffi lived on within liberal Italy, yet remained committed to his Risorgimento ideals. Thanks to the reputation of moral integrity that he had earned during his exile in Oxford, Saffi, who relentlessly committed himself to educating the Italians and promoting social reform, would provide Victorian radicals with unique insights into the forces of democracy operating in liberal Italy. While the history of Italian Mazzinian democrats remains the history of the 'losers' of the Risorgimento, their political vision and moral integrity, albeit crippled in its efficacy by internal divisions, found some constructive common ground in initiatives subscribed to by radical Victorian educators and social reformers. Having shared the bitter disappointment of Italy's monarchical turn, the Victorian protagonists of this narrative underscored well into the late 1880s Mazzini's vision of a new, civil religion for Italy and for humanity.

---

[54] F. Prochaska, *The republic of Britain (1760–2000)*, London 2000.

[55] See Biagini's seminal *Liberty*, 2–8, 358–9.

[56] A. Taylor, *"Down with the crown": British anti-monarchism and debates about royalty since 1790*, London 1999, 14; E. P Thompson, 'The peculiarities of the English', in his *The poverty of theory and other essays*, London 1978, 245–301. For a more recent analysis of British monarchism and Englishness see R. Colls, *The identity of England*, Oxford 2002.

[57] On celebrities in history see S. Morgan, 'Historicizing celebrity', *Celebrity Studies* i/3 (2010), 366–8, and L. Riall, 'Garibaldi: the first celebrity', *HT* (2007), 57–8.

Victorians and Italy: a 'long connection'? The historiography

This book extends the analysis of Anglo-Italian connected histories to the 'long Risorgimento' by including the transnational networks that were established between Italian democrats and Victorian radicals in the period that spanned the nation-building phase. Looking at the Anglo-Italian connection in the 'long perspective' involves entering a historiographical debate which has seen a gradual shift in the boundary of periodisation traditionally associated with the British attraction for Italy. Studies have overwhelmingly concentrated on the period leading to 1861, occasionally stretching to 1870.[58] C. P. Brand's seminal study on Italy and the English romantics located the 'italomania' of fashionable literary London salons in the decades preceding 1830;[59] Paul Ginsborg extended this period into the 1860s by underlining the endurance of English political interest in Italy through the romantic myth of the Risorgimento – stopping short, however, of analysing the continuities which could be traced by including Italy's nation-building process, regarded by Ginsborg as entirely marginal to British history.[60] More recently Martin McLaughlin's book set out to expand further the period

---

[58] For studies focusing on British involvement with Italian affairs prior to 1861 see C. Duggan, 'Gran Bretagna e Italia nel Risorgimento', in Banti and Ginsborg, *Storia d'Italia*, 777–96; D. Mack Smith, 'Gli inglesi e l'amore per l'Italia', *NA* cxxi (1986), 144–53; N. Blakiston, *Inglesi e italiani nel Risorgimento*, Catania 1973; and Beales, *England and Italy*. On specific issues see Bacchin, 'Il Risorgimento oltremanica: nazionalismo, 173–202; N. Carter, 'Hudson, Malmesbury and Cavour: British diplomacy and the Italian question, February 1858 to June 1859', *HJ* xl/2 (1997), 389–423; and O. Barié, 'Il radicalismo inglese nel primo decennio dell'Italia unita', *RST* ix (1965), 117–40. Studies which cover the following decade, while more rare, have seen recent contributions: M. P. Sutcliffe, 'Italian women in the making: re-reading the *Englishwoman's Review* (ca. 1871–89)', in N. Carter (ed.), *Britain, Ireland and the Italian Risorgimento*, Basingtoke 2014, forthcoming; and O. J. Wright, 'British representatives and the surveillance of Italian affairs, 1860–70', *HJ* li/3 (2008), 669–87; 'British foreign policy and the Italian occupation of Rome, 1870', *IHR* xxiv/1 (2012) 161–76, xxxiv/1, 'Police "outrages" against British residents and travellers in liberal Italy (1867–77), *Crime Histories and Societies* xiv/1 (2010), 51–72; D. Raponi, 'An anti-Catholicism of free-trade? Religion and the Anglo-Italian relations of 1863', *EHQ* xl/4 (2009), 633–52, and 'Religious reformation and national unity: British Protestants and Italy, 1860–70', in R. Crone, D. Gange and K. Jones, *New perspectives in British cultural history*, Newcastle 2007, 78–89; J. C. Albisetti, 'Education for the poor Neapolitan children: Julie Schwabe's nineteenth-century secular mission', *History of Education* xxxv/6 (2006), 632–52; M. De Leonardis, *L'Inghilterra e la questione romana (1859–70)*, Milan 1980; and N. Blakiston (ed.), *The Roman question: extracts from the dispatches of Odo Russell from Rome (1858–1870)*, London 1962.

[59] Brand, *Italy and the English romantics*.

[60] P. Ginsborg, 'Il mito del Risorgimento nel mondo britannico: "la vera poesia della politica"', *Il Risorgimento* xliii/1–2 (1995), 384–99 at p. 385.

analysed by Brand, by including studies which surveyed the decades up to the early twentieth century.[61]

McLaughlin's approach has been at the forefront of the research for this book: in encompassing within the book decades when Italy had become accessible to the British lower classes, the new nation was shown to represent 'to the British imagination not so much a classical ruin as a new political reality'.[62] This suggested the need to shift the focus beyond the role played by the familiar Italophiles, 'known to have left Italian politics to the natives', and whom according to A. N. Wilson, Victorians regarded as the greatest English interpreters of Italy: most famously, Robert Browning, who, despite residing in Italy for fifteen years, had 'never established any lasting friendship with an Italian' and John Ruskin, who not only 'hated the republican movements in Italy' but also the railway, which had made Italy an accessible destination for 'tourists'.[63]

Contributors to McLaughlin's volume took an innovative look at Anglo-Italian relations, remapping the areas investigated by enlarging the field of enquiry to intellectual history. However, with the notable exception of Uberto Limentani, who referred to the remarkable career of the self-improved artisan, Thomas Okey, the relationship with Italy was still read through the eyes of the educated elites.[64] Indeed, Denis Mack Smith's essay on political history reiterated the idea that Italy 'was a country of predilection for the British political class and electorate, most of whom had an education that was weighted heavily towards classical history and literature': the 'political class' referred to was that of the 'politicians of London' while the 'electorate' was the small minority of the population that had access to suffrage prior to the 1867 Reform.[65] Yet, throughout these decades, Victorian sympathisers with Italy's national independence could also be found amongst the rank-and-file who had no access to suffrage and who lived in provincial England, often frequenting self-improving institutions.[66]

---

[61] M. McLaughlin (ed.), *Britain and Italy from romanticism to modernism: a Festschrift for Peter Brand*, Oxford 2000, 32–44

[62] Idem, 'Introduction: the centrality of Dante', in McLaughlin, *Britain and Italy*, 1–12 at p. 5.

[63] A. N. Wilson, *The Victorians*, London 2002, 87–90.

[64] U. Limentani, 'Leone and Arthur Serena and the Cambridge Chair of Italian: 1919–34', in McLaughlin, *Britain and Italy*, 154–77.

[65] D. Mack Smith, 'Britain and the Italian Risorgimento', in McLaughlin, *Britain and Italy*, 13–31. On this topic see also Beales, *England and Italy*.

[66] Scholars, who have recently widened the field of enquiry, have addressed other issues: A. French, *Art treasures in the north: northern families on the Grand Tour*, Norwich 2009; M. Pfister and R. Hertel, *Performing national identity: Anglo-Italian cultural transactions*, Amsterdam–New York 2008; B. Schaff, *Exiles, emigrés and intermediaries: Anglo-Italian cultural relations*, Amsterdam–New York 2010; and K. Sandrock and O. J. Wright, *Locating Italy: East and West in British-Italian cultural transactions*, Amsterdam–New York 2013.

More recent attempts to re-examine under a new light Victorian discourses on Italy have once again fallen into the trap of privileging texts which were produced for and consumed by the well-heeled, British middle class. *The Victorians and Italy*, edited by Alessandro Vescovi, Luisa Villa and Paul Vita, while promising to 'champion and challenge the understanding of self and other' in a collection gathering Victorian 'assumptions and their subversion' in the construction of Italy, only marginally succeeded in 'crossing national boundaries and prejudices', as the texts analysed were drawn from within Victorian bourgeois culture.[67] Focusing on this section of society the editors seemingly unwittingly underwrote an orientalist interpretation, by asserting that 'to the Victorians, Italy was what the Orient is to Europeans of the twentieth century, a mixture of attraction and repulsion'.[68] Such a view is clearly embraced by Annemarie McAllister, whose essay reiterates the centrality of the middle-class discourse, its anthropological and racial debate and the 'grammar of primitivism and savagery'. Indeed, McAllister claims that 'The power relations implicit in representation mean that although Italy was not in a colonial relationship with England, the strategies seen in colonial discourse of transforming foreign space into controlled, known, and therefore inferior space can also be seen operating (in the Italian context).'[69]

Not dissimilar language concerning the 'imperialist prerogative' of British women towards their Italian sisters was employed by Maura O'Connor in her critique of reports on liberal Italy in the *Englishwoman's Review*.[70] These readings on the constructions of Italy rely on neat applications of post-colonial theory and literature (from Edward Said to Homi K. Bhabha), and remain apparently indifferent to the substantial body of literature which has increasingly critiqued the interpretation of Said's position. That such 'mind-clamping schema' may not so comfortably fit all historical narratives of encounters between the West and the Orient has been recently affirmed in different contexts by a number of historians who reject the idea that the key to historical explanation may be found in any overarching structure.[71]

---

[67] A. Vescovi, L. Villa and P. Vita, *The Victorians and Italy: literature, travel, politics and art*, Milan 2009.

[68] Ibid. 9.

[69] A. McAllister, '"A pair of naked legs and a ragged scarf": an overview of Victorian discourses in Italy', in Vescovi, Villa and Vita *The Victorians and Italy*, 23.

[70] M. O' Connor, 'Civilizing southern Italy: British and Italian women and the cultural politics of European nation building', *Women's Writing* x/2 (2003), 253–68. For a critique see Sutcliffe, 'Italian women in the making'.

[71] The term 'mind-clamping schema' is borrowed from the review by R. Polonsky, 'Is this not paradise?', *Times Literary Supplement*, 9 Sept. 2011. Amongst examples which challenge the applicability of Said's model see R. Irwin, *For lust of knowing: the orientalists and their enemies*, London 2006, and I. Warraq, *Defending the West: a critique of Edward Said's orientalism*, Amherst 2007.

Yet it is one of the earliest challenges to the orientalist model which has provided the framework within which this narrative on radical Victorians' encounter with Italy has taken shape, namely, the inadequacy of Said's orientalist construct when reading popular texts, produced and consumed by working-class agents.[72] Chapter 6, which examines the ingredients of 'co-operative travel' against the stereotypes of the orientalist 'gaze', engages with the need to reframe this well-worn subject.

Re-framing the reception of Mazzini's ideas in Britain

While this book brings to the fore the views on Italy of radical, self-improving workers, it does not claim to frame the narrative from an exclusive 'class' perspective: British Mazzinians were a socially mixed group, which included enlightened bourgeois in the capital, reforming provincial radical manu-facturers, social reforming Oxford intellectuals as well as Chartist artisans and adult learners. Indeed, Victorian Mazzinism may best be framed within the wider context which defines 'English radicalism', a concept which was recently described as 'curiously weak'.[73]

Following the linguistic turn historians of Victorian popular political movements revisited the Marxist approach which established a direct link between the political and the social. As Gareth Stedman Jones has pointed out, radicalism 'could never be the ideology of a specific class'; rather, like Chartism, it identified with the political demands of the 'people' of a 'nation' to obtain political representation.[74] The word 'radicalism', coined in the 1820s, could be seen as having a variety of meanings and recent historians have underlined how in the course of the nineteenth century it became so diluted as to become an 'unspecific promise' or a loose 'abstraction', defined by its being 'on the side of the future'.[75]

Throughout the decades of the Victorian era the influence exercised by the thought of the radical philosopher, John Stuart Mill, paved the way towards political reforms which would address the amelioration of the people's condi-tions not by revolutionary means but by changes to be brought about within existing institutions. The reforms of 1832 and 1867 were the result of pres-sures exercised by petitions and town meetings demanding the extension of suffrage. There was no link however between political expression and social

---

[72] 'Interview', in M. Sprinker, *Edward Said: a critical reader*, Oxford 1992, 246.

[73] G. Burgess and M. Festenstein, *English radicalism, 1550–1850*, Cambridge 2007, 1.

[74] G. Stedman Jones, *Languages of class: studies in working-class history, 1832–1982*, Cambridge 1983, 104.

[75] J. C. D. Clark, 'Religion and the origins of radicalism in Britain', in Burgess and Festenstein, *English radicalism*, 241–84 at p. 247. See also C. Condren, 'Afterword: radicalism revisited', ibid. 313–14.

class, and no manifestation of what Marxist historians would have referred to as 'class consciousness'.

Within this frame of English radicalism Mazzini's political project found a receptive audience. As Gregory Claeys has shown, Mazzini's programme, in steering the working-classes away from materialism through his antisocialist republicanism, responded well to the aspirations of radicals, putting forward an agenda which appealed across class divisions to 'respectable' workers and social reformers alike.[76] Margot Finn has shown how Mazzini's ideals had found supporters amongst former Chartists, well into the 1850s.[77] By broadening chronologically the transnational perspective, this book shows how manifestations of support among Victorian radicals for Risorgimento democrats rested on their desire to witness the realisation of universal suffrage, beyond their national boundary, in a newly-unified Italy.

It is not, therefore, on the well-known episodes of support shown by radical MPs for the Italian revolutionaries that the book focuses. While episodes such as Thomas Duncombe's support for Mazzini in 1844, Thomas Milner Gibson's amendment to Palmerston's Conspiracy to Murder Bill (following Orsini's attack on Napoleon III) and James Stansfeld's resignation during the Greco-Mazzini affair provide the broad background in the context of the parliamentary debates, this book has focused on a narrative which unfolded outside political institutions, mostly far from the metropolis. While Derek Beales regarded the 1859 Italian crisis as a 'cardinal instance' in foreign policy and one of the few occasions when 'external factors' 'decisively affected the course of English policy' – causing the Whig-Liberal ministry of Lord Palmerston to succeed the Conservative ministry of Lord Derby in 1860 – the focus here lies not on the 'diplomacy of cabinets', but on the 'diplomacy of the people', which, as Gilles Pécout has highlighted, separated the dynastic Risorgimento from the popular.[78]

Of course, many of Mazzini's friends and admirers, who gravitated around his London Free School for Italian workers, were radical philanthropists and members of the established bourgeoisie. Indeed, historians studying English Mazzinians have overwhelmingly focused upon this particular group.[79] The Muswell Hill circle, which gathered in London around the solicitor William Ashurst and his four unconventional daughters, had provided Mazzini with loyal friends: Maura O'Connor, Ros Pesman and Anne Summers have analysed the role played by the Mazzinian women of this transnational network.[80] Well-known radical opinion-makers and politicians such as James

[76] Claeys, 'Mazzini'.

[77] Finn, *After Chartism*.

[78] Pécout, 'International volunteers', 414.

[79] O'Connor, *Romance of Italy*, ch. iii; Morelli, *L'Inghilterra di Mazzini*, ch. ii; D. Mack Smith, *Mazzini*, New Haven–London 1994, 89–96.

[80] O'Connor, *Romance of Italy*; R. Pesman, 'Mazzini in esilio e le inglesi', in I. Porciani (ed.), *Famiglia e nazione nel lungo ottocento italiano: modelli, strategie, reti di relazioni*, Rome

Stansfeld, Peter Taylor and Joseph Cowen Jr were also known to be strenuous supporters of republican Italy, contributing to the dissemination of Mazzini's political ideas beyond the confines of the capital.[81] However it is the geography of networks which ensured the capillary distribution of Mazzini's writings in mechanics' institutes, working men's colleges and the educational branches of co-operative societies, which provides an insight into how adult learners, self-improved working-class teachers and Oxford-educated social reformers found common ground in Mazzini's readings.

Research on the impact of Mazzini's ideas in Britain has identified two areas of particular resonance: his role in shaping the 'debate upon democracy' in the mid-nineteenth century, underlined by Salvo Mastellone, and the attraction of Mazzini's civic religion and 'democratic religiosity' within the puritan culture, highlighted by Eugenio Biagini.[82] While my own interest in evaluating the spread of Mazzini's ideas in working-class Britain intersects with such studies, as well as with those of Margot Finn and Gregory Claeys, it departs from them in extending the chronological period and focusing on how Mazzini's ideas permeated contemporary debates on republicanism and co-operation. Moreover, it is argued that once Italy had been united, faith in Mazzini's vision for the redemption of society and the desire to see his project realised in his country of origin would shape Victorian radicals' discourse on Italy's present and future in a way which defied negative British representations of liberal Italy.

Mastellone's reflections on Mazzini's influence in Britain harnessed his ideological contribution within the remit of the London manifestos on 'democracy' and 'nation' penned by political émigrés, concentrating on the constructions of the Risorgimento published in the Chartist press between 1837 and 1857. In Mazzini the 'nation' equated to affirming the liberty of the individual and of humanity, contrary to any form of despotism: the latter had found expression in Italy in both papal and royal rule. Capitalising on the fame that he acquired during the 'letter-opening affair', in 1844, Mazzini exposed to the 'English Nation' the political condition of Italy, highlighting the need for a revolutionary insurrection by its people.[83] The 'people' were the citizens, committed to their 'duty' as individuals, family members, contributors to 'associations' and inhabitants of the 'nation', realised in a democratic, non-confessional state.

If Mazzini's political project constituted an important voice in the chorus of democratic and socialist manifestos contributed by continental revolu-

2006, 55–82; A. Summers, 'British women and cultures of internationalism, c. 1815–1914', in D. Feldman and J. Lawrence (eds), *Structures and transformations in modern British history*, Cambridge 2011, 187–209.

[81] Duggan, 'Giuseppe Mazzini', 187–210.

[82] Biagini, 'Mazzini and anticlericalism', 145–66, and *Liberty*, 46–50.

[83] This was highlighted in Mazzini's *Italy, Austria and the pope*, published in the *Northern Star* as a series of eight extracts between 19 July and 27 September 1845.

tionary refugees within the capital, the brief episode of the Roman Republic in 1849, crushed by the intervention of the French and culminating in the re-establishment of papal rule, gave to the Italian exile a level of prestige in Britain which could not be matched by others. Gregory Claeys particularly underlined how Mazzini, returning as 'revolutionary hero', had acquired – as did Kossuth later but only briefly – particular leverage amongst the British working class, disoriented after the Chartist debacle.[84] Yet, even before the 'failure' of the Chartists' mobilisation on Kennington Common, Mazzini's entry onto the British political scene in 1844 had coincided with an important landmark in the history of nineteenth-century experiments in social reform: the collapse of Robert Owen's co-operative experiment. As Engels noted, Owen's ideas on co-operation versus competition had widened the divide between middle- and working-class radicals. Mazzini's ideas on association would render his ideological vision particularly appealing to both bourgeois reformers and provincial working-class radicals, at a time when English co-operators were embarking on co-operative experiments in Lancashire and Yorkshire.[85]

Mazzini's contribution to the debate on association would help to repair the split between the classes. As could be read in his *Duties of man*, which enjoyed wide circulation in Britain, 'association of labor, and division of the fruits of labor among the producers, in proportion to the amount and value of the work done by each' was the social future; however it was paramount that association should be 'free and voluntary', organised by men 'who know, respect and love each other'.[86] The religious tone employed by Mazzini resonated with the language which radicals understood, one that attracted not only 'respectable' Noncomformist workers, but Christian Socialists and middle-class reformers alike. Mazzini's theories on association and his social project for humanity as a whole were therefore embedded within contemporary debates which took place in his country of exile beyond the remit of the capital: not only did Mazzini contribute his vision, but, equally, he absorbed ideas shaped by the experience of co-operative stores in provincial England, the heartland of co-operation.

Mazzini's long legacy amongst British co-operators is a key aspect of his influence.[87] This book however focuses on how Mazzini's political vision of humanity helped co-operators to shape the English political imagination of Italy along new lines. Mazzini's early influence on Victorian co-operators

---

84 Claeys, 'Mazzini', 226.

85 Engels, as quoted in Stedman Jones, *Languages of class*, 122.

86 Giuseppe Mazzini, 'On the duties of man', in Recchia and Urbinati, *Cosmopolitanism*, 104.

87 M. P. Sutcliffe, 'Mazzini's transnational legacy amongst British co-operators (ca. 1885–1949)', *LHR* lxxvii/3 (2012), 267–88.

has attracted only anecdotal references.[88] Eugenio Biagini indicated in a footnote that in 1872 the *Beehive* had published a series of Mazzini's articles on co-operative alternatives to socialism,[89] but this did little to mitigate the impression that after 1844 it was primarily John Stuart Mill who provided English co-operators with the intellectual tools required to furnish co-operation with a model of respectability: the centrality of Mill's *Principles of political economy* (1848) to George Jacob Holyoake's *History of co-operation* (1875) was particularly remarked upon.[90] Yet, not only did Holyoake publicly acknowledge how Mazzini had contributed to shaping the debate on association in England when it was still in its infancy, but he had quiet reservations about Mill's utilitarian argument.[91] Significantly, in 1864 he wrote to Mazzini that 'I accept Mill's utilitarian doctrine as to the source of duty. But no one has taught as you have how paralyzed we are without principles which make duties the Precursors of Rights and lift us above the herd who gallop after Happiness.'[92]

Victorian republicans, Mazzini and the religious frame of mind

Holyoake's reference to Mill indicates that Mazzini's spiritual message appealed more powerfully to the religious mind-set of Victorian Mazzinians than the utilitarian argument.[93] As Roland Sarti suggested, Mazzini's concept of republicanism was rooted in the centrality of civil religion.[94] Although a secularist, Holyoake, was drawn to Mazzini by his religious, Unitarian sense of 'duty', an aspect of Christianity which, as Biagini and Bayly have argued, permeated all facets of mid nineteenth-century European thought, 'including secularism'.[95] Indeed, Mazzini's religious commitment to individual duty and progress and his belief in the powers of harmonious association equally

---

[88] P. Gurney, 'George Jacob Holyoake: socialism, association, and co-operation in nineteenth-century England', in S. Yeo, *New views on co-operation*, London–New York 1988, 52–72; Sutcliffe, 'Mazzini's transnational legacy'.

[89] Biagini, *Liberty*, 140–4 and at p. 140 n. 9.

[90] Ibid. 143. On Holyoake see J. McCabe, *Life and letters of George Jacob Holyoake*, London 1908, and L. R. Grugel, 'G. J. Holyoake', DMBR, ii. 242–4. See also Onnis, 'Battaglie democratiche', and Gasparini, 'Una nuova fonte'.

[91] G. J. Holyoake, 'The Bologna Congress', *Co-operative News*, 10 Nov. 1888, 1121.

[92] G. J. Holyoake to Mazzini, 13 Mar. 1864, FH, MRM, 12/63.

[93] For comparative studies of Mazzini and Mill see A. Bocchi and C. Palazzolo (eds), *Giuseppe Mazzini e John Stuart Mill*, BDM, special issue, I/1 (2004), and M. T. Pichetto, 'John Stuart Mill', in Mastellone, *Mazzini e gli scrittori politici*, i. 1–28.

[94] R. Sarti, *Mazzini: a life for the religion of politics*, Westport 1997. See also M. Ridolfi, 'Visions of republicanism in the writings of Giuseppe Mazzini', JMIS xiii/4 (2008), 468–79 at p. 469.

[95] C. Bayly and E. Biagini, 'Introduction', in their *Mazzini*, 2.

inspired Nonconformist and secular radicals.[96] Moreover, being intellectually and politically radical, secularists elected republicanism as the political doctrine of free thought: when embracing continental causes, they viewed the struggles for freedom 'in theological terms', equating, 'priestcraft' and 'kingcraft', according to Thomas Paine's teachings, to 'Old Corruption'.[97]

Anti-Catholic sentiments also united a broad spectrum of British sympathisers on the 'Italian question'.[98] On anticlericalism and 'No popery' propaganda, the paths of radicals and liberal conservative philo-Italians converged. Catholic emancipation, in 1829, and the influx of Irish immigrants, particularly to Lancashire and Scotland, had alarmed Protestants, who set up societies which revived the visceral hatred of superstition, dogma, tyranny and corruption which had eased at the beginning of the century: a network of organisations, such as the Reformation Society, targeting the middle classes, and the Protestant Association, aimed at workers, spread in mid-Victorian Britain.[99] The 'papal aggression' of 1850–1, and later the Syllabus of Errors in 1864 and the Vatican decrees of 1870, provided fresh stimuli.[100] Such sentiments were harnessed and variously channelled according to disparate creeds and missionary intents. The religious question also appeared central to the task of national moral resurgence in Italy: different solutions were put forward by men keen for the internal reform of the Catholic Church (Gioberti, Rosmini, Tommaseo, Campello), London exiles drawn to the Evangelical Church of Exeter Hall (Gavazzi, Salvatore Ferretti) and those who sympathised with the British established Church (Cavour, Garibaldi). Variants of religious reform associated with the Italian Risorgimento dovetailed with differing political solutions, from the moderate to the democratic. In the case of Mazzini and Saffi, anti-Catholicism was grounded in civil religion, or the religion of humanity. Hostility to the pope and British projects for moral renewal among the Italians were therefore abundant; yet the paths followed by radical and liberal-conservative philo-Italians in Britain diverged on constitutional grounds.

It is well known that British missionaries of various denominations, who welcomed Italy's unification under the Piedmontese monarch, set off for the

---

96   Biagini, *Liberty*, 143 n. 31. While Biagini has concentrated on Dissenters, he has not focused on secularists.

97   E. Royle, *Victorian infidels: the origins of the British secularist movement, 1791–1866*, Manchester 1974, 4, 252.

98   Beales, *England and Italy*, 22–5. On anti-Catholicism in mid-Victorian Britain see J. Wolffe, *The Protestant crusade in Great Britain, 1829–1860*, Oxford 1991, and M. Borutta, 'Anti-Catholicism and the culture of war in Risorgimento Italy', in Patriarca and Riall, *The Risorgimento revisited*, 191–213.

99   Wolffe, *Protestant crusade*, 149–74.

100 Still in 1883 Charles Bradlaugh told the National Secular Society that 'The fight between us and Rome must come one day. It may be far off; it may be tomorrow – the fight between Rome and Rationalism, between the fullest assertion of the right of private judgement and the most complete submission of authority': *NR*, 20 May 1883, 378.

peninsula hoping to participate in a spiritual renaissance – the so-called 'Protestant Risorgimento'.[101] Yet, there were also British radicals who set off for Italy inspired by Mazzini's republican projections for the new nation. David Nathan, imprisoned by the Italian authorities for attempting to spread Mazzini's Universal Republican Association, continued to hope for a republican turn, well after 1861. The heroes of these Victorian Mazzinians were Puritan revolutionaries like Cromwell, 'infidels' like Paine, and the popular leaders of medieval communes, such as Cola di Rienzo; their historical references were the Commonwealth or the English civil war; their myth was the Roman Republic; their congregation was the republican club; their language was Mazzini's rhetoric of 'brotherhood' and 'love'; their shared reading was the *Duties of man*, rather than the Bible of colporteurs. For these British Mazzinians, it was not so much a question of assuming the missionaries' 'civilisational' perspective to redeem the Italians' national character, as noted by Danilo Raponi. It was a question of the Italians connecting with their past tradition of civic virtue and taking responsibility for national education in the values of duty, family, co-operation, nation and harmonious humanity – teachings which would percolate through the peninsula thanks to the work of associations, co-operatives, evening classes and Mazzinian schools.[102] The latter were resonant of the Nonconformist tradition of self-improvement, which had bypassed educational institutions under the control of the Anglican hierarchy by setting up dissenting academies and Sunday schools.[103]

British Protestants, who had welcomed the establishment of the monarchical constitution in Italy and who promoted a religious awakening among the Italians, might have optimistically entrusted Garibaldi with the gargantuan task of redeeming the Italian 'character' in newly unified Italy.[104] But Victorian republicans who had dreamt of Mazzini's Third Rome as the revival of the civilisation of republican Rome, saw the liberal-moderate monarchy as an unsatisfactory compromise. Indeed, it was a compromise which, as Giorgio Spini laconically put it, would allow Mazzini's *Duties of man*, with its 'religious dimension of democracy', to be relegated to a dusty attic, opening the floodgates to mediocre slyboots, such as Italy's future prime ministers, Agostino Depretis and Giovanni Giolitti.[105]

---

[101] G. Spini, *Risorgimento e protestanti*, Turin 1998, and *Italia liberale e protestanti*, Turin 2002; D. Raponi, 'Risorgimento e virtù civiche: riflessioni dei protestanti britannici sull'identità nazionale italiana (1861–1875)', in S. Maghenzani, *Il protestantesimo italiano nel Risorgimento: influenze, miti, identità*, Turin 2012, 113–25.

[102] Raponi, 'Risorgimento e virtù civiche', 113, 115. The term 'civilizational perspective' is borrowed from P. Mandler, '"Race" and "nation" in mid-Victorian thought', in S. Collini, R. Whatmore and B. Young, *History, religion and culture: British intellectual history, 1750–1950*, Cambridge 2000, 224–44 at p. 226.

[103] Biagini, *Liberty*, 197.

[104] Raponi, 'Gran Bretagna', 150–2.

[105] G. Spini, 'Mazzini e la dimensione religiosa della democrazia', in G. Limiti (ed.),

As one of Mazzini's most stalwart republican supporters, W. E. Adams, would later recall: 'We had found a programme, but we wanted a religion. It came to us from Italy. The Republic, as [we] understood it was not so much a form of government as a system of morals, a law of life, a creed, a faith, a new and benign gospel.'[106] Biagini has underlined how Mazzini's belief in human progress as an expression of God's will was associated with a 'religious attitude to republicanism'.[107] Mazzini's religious republicanism, indeed his theism, as Edward Royle described it, summed up by the motto 'God and the People', was not only intensely powerful, but it remained a beacon for Victorian republicans for decades.[108] With the resurgence of republican values in England in the early 1870s, Mazzini's religious republicanism was still powerfully felt.[109]

Victorian Mazzinians, Italian republicans and liberal Italy

For many decades Italy could only be 'imagined' by self-improving Victorian adults. Even after Thomas Cook had made it accessible to a wider section of society in 1864, the groups considered here were still excluded from the experience of travel. They were skilled craftsmen or white-collar workers, united by similar earnings – between £50 and £100 a year – predominantly with no right to vote and meeting in adult education institutions or East London university settlements.[110] A small minority of them would, however, encounter Italy in the late 1880s, when joining one of the earliest 'co-operative tours'. Entering the political imagination of Italy of the English 'common reader', who encountered Italy by reading Mazzinian literature, has meant penetrating a world of transnational connections and practices which existed alongside the romantic myth of the Risorgimento of the educated English elites, indeed outliving such fascination by reaching out to the challenges faced by Italian workers in the aftermath of unification.[111]

While the British government became increasingly wary of liberal Italy's domestic and foreign policy, the intellectual circle that emerged out of the Oxford reform movement – which had abolished compulsory religious tests

Il mazzinianesimo nel mondo, iv, Pisa 2011, 249–58 at p. 258. Giolitti was Italian prime minister five times between 1892 and 1921.

106 W. E. Adams, *Memoirs of a social atom*, London 1903, i. 262.

107 Biagini, 'Mazzini and anticlericalism', 146.

108 'The Italian leaders held unorthodox religious views. Mazzini was a theist; Garibaldi a sentimental atheist': Royle, *Victorian infidels*, 252.

109 Idem, 'Bradlaugh, Charles (1833–91)', *ODNB*.

110 R. J. Morris, *Class, sect and party the making of the British middle class, Leeds, 1820–50*, Manchester–New York 1990.

111 R. D. Altick, *The English common reader: a social history of the mass reading public, 1800–1900*, Chicago 1957.

at matriculation – gathered together liberal, social-reforming academics who supported secular university settlements in the name of civic idealism and social duty. These men also followed the progress of democracy in liberal Italy. T. H. Green, James Bryce and Bolton King were amongst them. The support that Mazzini's republican model retained amongst two successive generations of Oxford dons and graduates was linked to Saffi's legacy: it was in Oxford that Saffi had spent most of his exile, and learning Italian from Saffi had been 'part of the ritual of cultured Liberalism in Oxford and an initiation into the spirit of the Risorgimento'.[112] When considering volunteering with Garibaldi, in 1860, Bryce had believed him to be 'Mazzinian nationalism incarnate'.[113] Inspired by civic idealism and Mazzini's vision, Oxford dons continued to support the building of the Mazzinian edifice in liberal Italy after the annexation of Rome, when British hopes of a Protestant Risorgimento waned.

Indeed, late nineteenth-century Victorians gravitating around university settlements, secular societies and workers' co-operatives continued to cultivate an interest in Mazzini's aims and in Italy's democratic progress. Links with co-operators were particularly strong in Milan, the hub of the democratic press, and in the Romagna, where Saffi personified the ideals for which the Risorgimento democrats had fought, pursuing them with moral integrity until his death.[114] In Rome, the vocal presence of the Nathans, Mazzini's close Anglo-Italian friends in whose home he had died, fostered further radical transnational links.[115] Italy's social problems, and the challenges of nation-building, may gradually have become a topic dear to only a minority of enlightened Victorian educators, but by disseminating their findings these resilient Mazzinians contributed to enlarging their audience.[116] In the 1870s, following Saffi's arrest, Victorian radicals laboured to bolster the activities of Italian republicans by supporting their clandestine networks, campaigning to raise awareness of their persecution by the police and the local authorities and regularly reporting on the establishment of new republican clubs – drawing information from the radical, republican press – *Il Dovere*, *l'Unità Italiana*, *l'Emancipazione* – which was wilfully ignored by the national press in Britain.

---

[112] H. A. L. Fisher, *Life of James Bryce, Viscount Bryce of Dechmont*, i, London 1927, 51. See also C. Harvie, *The lights of liberalism: university liberals and the challenge of democracy*, London 1976.

[113] W. A. Knight, *Memoir of John Nichol*, Glasgow 1896, 140.

[114] J. Usher, 'Okey, Thomas (1852–1935)', ODNB.

[115] A. M. Isastia, *Storia di una famiglia del Risorgimento: Sarina, Giuseppe, Ernesto Nathan*, Turin 2010. On the links between the Nathans and Josephine Butler see B. P. F. Wanrooij, 'Josephine Butler and regulated prostitution in Italy', *Women's Review* xvii/2 (2008), 157–71.

[116] Bolton King, 'England and Italy', *Macmillan's Magazine* lxxxii (July 1900), 216.

Marrying his commitment to adult education and his admiration for Mazzini, Bolton King introduced Toynbee Hall learners to Italy's newly-established democracy in a series of courses. Beginning in 1888, and aided by the self-improved artisan, Thomas Okey, he also organised a number of early 'co-operative tours' to Italy. These deconstructed the stereotypes of travel to Italy by challenging the paradigm of 'hegemony' which, according to James Buzard's Gramscian reading, had traditionally informed the continental encounters of elite travel.[117] Conversely, Okey and Bolton King guided adult learners through a journey across Italy which defied orientalist readings. After reading their book, *Italy today*, the philosopher and historian Benedetto Croce would ominously assert that the insight of such Englishmen into Italian society had the potential to show the Italians who they really were.[118]

Structure, methodology and scope

Part I of this book deals with the revolutionary years leading to the unification of Italy; part II concentrates on liberal Italy. The themes analysed in both parts are those which constituted the building blocks of Mazzini's vision for Italy's future and for 'humanity' as a whole: republicanism, education, suffrage and co-operation.

The approach chosen combines the transnational dimension with 'sociability'. The transnational reading of the earlier part of the Risorgimento has previously been studied by scholars interested in intellectual exchanges between individual exiles;[119] here the focus is rather on how the ideas developed by an exile, Mazzini, were debated, absorbed and elaborated by radicals who gathered in different forms of sociability, creating a network of transnational support for Italy's democratic project which survived in various forms after the exiled democrats returned home. The networks of associations that the democrats set up in liberal Italy, such as co-operative societies and educational institutions, and the debates that they opened up in the republican press, often subject to controls and censorship, constituted the vehicles which promoted the progress of Italian democracy outside the parliamentary arena. While the impact of associations on civil society, class, culture and nation has been highlighted in comparative studies focused on similarities within Europe, this book analyses the interconnections between forms of sociability which reached beyond national boundaries.[120]

---

[117] Buzard, *The beaten track*, 15.

[118] Bolton King and T. Okey, *L'Italia d'oggi*, Bari 1904, p. vi. In Italy two editions were printed between 1902 and 1903.

[119] See Isabella, *Risorgimento in exile*.

[120] G. Morton, B. de Vries and R. J. Morris, *Civil society, association and urban places: class, nation and culture in nineteenth-century Europe*, Farnham–Burlington, VT 2006.

Liberal Italy – balanced somewhat awkwardly between the epic battles for national unity and the emergence of the *fin de siècle* crisis, which solidified emerging nationalist, colonialist and authoritarian discourses – is only now attracting the closer scrutiny of historians: as Fulvio Cammarano has claimed, this historical period has critical relevance for understanding the fabric of Italian identity.[121] By analysing the period from a *histoire croisée* perspective, this book reaffirms the continuity of the language of radical democracy in the post-unification period, knitting together transnational historical fragments of democratic practices maintained between late nineteenth-century Victorian radicals and Italian protagonists of the republican and co-operative movement.

How Oxford intellectuals, social reformers and adult learners read and understood Mazzini's vision and legacy matters: it had a bearing on the way, in later years, Mazzinian historians like Bolton King and Gwilym O. Griffith, reached out to antifascist Italians, such as Gaetano Salvemini and Carlo Rosselli, because of their common adherence to Mazzinian principles of democracy.[122] When in 1935 Carlo Rosselli appealed for historians to study the 'popular Risorgimento' he was possibly not thinking of its transnational dimension.[123] In the light of the reiteration of the nationalist reading of Mazzini's democratic message in proto-fascist terms, which has still not abated in Italy, dwelling on outsiders' perspectives may help to consolidate the democratic stance of cosmopolitanism of nations long held by Mazzinians across national boundaries.[124] Croce's suggestion that the analysis of the condition of Italy at the turn of the century by Bolton King and Okey could help Italians to find their identity seems today as meaningful as ever.[125] Reclaiming the role that Victorian radicals played in understanding, interpreting, disseminating and making their own the message of transnational civil society and democracy elicited from Mazzini's readings is important today for British and Italian historians alike.

---

[121] F. Cammarano, *Storia dell'Italia liberale*, Bari 2011.

[122] The term post-Victorian is borrowed from P. Mandler and S. Pedersen (eds), *After the Victorians: private conscience and public duty in modern Britain*, London 2005.

[123] For a commentary on Carlo Rosselli's use of the 'popular Risorgimento' in fascist Italy see M. Isnenghi, 'Il mito di Garibaldi', in M. Ridolfi (ed.), *Giuseppe Garibaldi: il radicalismo democratico e il mondo del lavoro*, Rome 2008, 159–61.

[124] There is a long historiography on the uses and misuses of Mazzini. For an overview see R. Balzani, 'Il problema Mazzini', *Ricerche di storia politica* ii (2005), 159–82. See also the more recent S. Levis Sullam, *L'apostolo a brandelli: l'eredità di Mazzini tra Risorgimento e fascismo*, Bari 2010, and the review by R. Sarti, 'L'apostolo a brandelli: l'eredità di Mazzini tra Risorgimento e fascismo', *JMIS* xvi/4 (2011), 555–7. For a recent response to this historiographical debate see the introduction by G. Limiti and M. Di Napoli in U. della Seta, *Giuseppe Mazzini pensatore: le idee madri*, Rome 1910 (2011). For a reflection on the 'global' misuses of Mazzini see the introduction to Bayly and Biagini, *Mazzini*.

[125] B. Croce, 'Avvertenza', in Bolton King and Okey, *L'Italia d'oggi*, p. vi.

PART I

VICTORIAN RADICALS AND THE 'MAKING OF ITALY'
1837–1860

1

Mazzini amongst Chartists and Early Co-operators, 1837–1848

'The organisation of the working classes is making gigantic leaps: especially in the North of England where men are recruited in their scores.'[1]

In approaching the origins of the long connection between Victorian radicals and Risorgimento democrats this book draws upon the ideological and political debates which took shape in provincial, industrial England as Mazzini's doctrine was being refined and disseminated in his country of exile. In general historians analysing the circulation of ideas which helped to define the concept of European democracy have focused on the role played by continental *émigrés* concentrated in mid-Victorian London. It was here that the People's International League, the first English association which showed an interest in foreign affairs, was established in 1847, at Mazzini's suggestion.[2] Studies on the London exiles include works by Iowerth Prothero, Maurizio Isabella and Salvo Mastellone; the latter, in particular, focused upon the London reception of Mazzini's 'Thoughts upon democracy', published in John Sanders's *People's Journal* between August 1846 and June 1847.[3] Studies on the establishment of early Chartist internationalism similarly concentrated on London, deemed to be until 1848 the exclusive hub for the propagation of European ideas.[4] By analysing provincial sources, the 'exceptionality' of the capital implicit in the London-centred approach is here put into question.

---

[1] 'L'organisation des classes ouvrières fait des pas gigantesques; le nord de l'Angleterre surtout est enrôlé presqu'en masse': G. Mazzini to L. Mandrot, 20 Feb. 1839, *SEI* xv. 377–82 at p. 381.

[2] In April 1847, at Mazzini's suggestion, the People's International League had been formed in London 'to enlighten the British Public as to the political conditions and relations of foreign countries' and 'disseminate the principles of national freedom and progress': 'Address of the Council of The People's International League', London 1847, CP, TWAS, A8. Amongst its trustees were W. H. Ashurst, P. A. Taylor and J. Toynbee, loyal Mazzinians throughout their lives.

[3] I. Prothero, 'Chartists and political refugees', in Freitag *Exiles*, 209–33; Isabella, 'Italian exiles', 5–87, and *Risorgimento in exile*; Mastellone, *Mazzini scrittore*, 131–9.

[4] H. Weisser, 'Chartist internationalism: 1845–1848', *HJ* xiv/1 (1971), 49–66 at p. 64. Weisser indicates in a footnote that the *Labourer* and the *Northern Liberator* had internationalist interests.

Fig. 1. George Jacob Holyoake (1817–1906). (George Jacob
Holyoake Archive, Bishopsgate Foundation and Institute
13/1).

This chapter focuses on three areas: firstly, the Italian exile's gaze on the
political and social developments of northern industrial England; secondly,
the osmotic exchanges between centre and periphery which shaped the
development of the adult education movement (including the founding of
Mazzini's London Free School); thirdly, the early representation of Mazzini's
thought in the industrial radical provinces, especially the North-East, Yorkshire, Lancashire and the Midlands, where the dissemination of Mazzinian
ideas was closely associated with the Chartist movement and early experiments in co-operation.[5] The secularist George Jacob Holyoake emerges from

5   J. Allen, *Joseph Cowen and popular Tyneside radicalism, 1829–1900*, Monmouth 2007,

this early stage of the narrative as a central figure in the propagation of Mazzini's ideas amongst an English working-class readership (*see* Figure 1).

Historians have previously underlined the need to recognise a dual narrative within Chartism, one in London, the other in the industrial provinces. The importance of focusing on the 'local' peculiarities of provincial Chartism, first highlighted by Asa Briggs, was nuanced by Miles Taylor's suggestion that a national history of Chartism could only be constructed by taking into account the interconnections and 'dynamic complexities' linking together local histories of Chartism.[6] Clearly, the radical developments in provincial England demanded scrutiny. Detlev Mares called for a 'transcending [of] the metropolis' in order to identify the interrelations within local popular politics and to chart a nationwide geography of radicalism.[7] Indeed, Malcolm Chase, in his book on Chartism, drew together the local and the national, arguing that in order 'to understand why The People's Charter captured the popular imagination, we have to look elsewhere than London'.[8] Similar arguments have also been made for the dissemination of republicanism beyond the metropolis.[9] It is hard to grasp how Mazzini's radical vision for a united Italy could capture and firmly harness the popular imagination of Victorians without taking into account the familiarity with Mazzini's ideas of co-operators and adult learners concentrated in provincial England.[10]

Mazzini's early gaze on industrial England, 1837–44

Mazzini's arrival in London in 1837, the year of Queen Victoria's accession to the throne, was a new beginning for him. He had long left behind his early, uneasy association with secret societies, from which he had retained, however, the teachings of Carlo Bianco of St Jorioz (1795–1843), who preached guerrilla tactics for the peoples' warfare.[11] Hounded as a conspirator, Mazzini had at first sought refuge in France, where the revolution of

13; E. F. Biagini and A. J. Reid (eds), *Currents of radicalism: popular radicalism, organised labour and party politics in Britain, 1850–1914*, Cambridge 1991.

6   For the debate see M. Taylor, 'Rethinking the Chartists: searching for synthesis in the historiography of Chartism', *HJ* xxxix/2 (1996), 479–95.

7   D. Mares, 'Transcending the metropolis: London and provincial popular radicalism, c. 1860–75', in M. Cragoe and A. Taylor (eds), *London politics, 1760–1914*, London 2005, 121.

8   M. Chase, *Chartism: a new history*, Manchester–New York 2007, 11.

9   Idem, 'Republicanism: movement or moment?', in D. Nash and A. Taylor, *Republicanism in Victorian society*, Stroud 2000, 35–50 at p. 36.

10   While individual cases have been noted by Biagini, as in the case of Chester Armstrong, the provincial dimension of Mazzinian radicalism has not been explored.

11   For the intellectual legacy of 'secret societies' in Mazzini's thought see M. Isabella, 'Mazzini's internationalism in context', in Bayly and Biagini, *Mazzini*, 37–58.

July 1830 had crowned the supposedly liberal Louis Philippe. By mid-1831, however, French republicans and Italian exiles, hoping to spearhead an invasion of Savoy and trigger a revolutionary war in Italy, had been dealt a severe blow by the unmasking of their insurrectionary expedition, which resulted in hundreds of arrests. After these events Mazzini had penned a virulent attack on Louis Philippe, accusing him of duplicity and permanently distancing himself from any future support for a liberal monarch.[12]

In 1831, having also lost faith in the organisation of secret societies – elitist 'brotherhoods' which could not reach the 'people' – Mazzini drew up the programme for a new political organisation, 'Young Italy' ('Giovine Italia'), in which each member would recognise himself and the 'association' as motors of a national revolution.[13] The work of 'Young Italy' was 'not one of a sect, but one of apostolate'.[14] The language of 'apostolate', with its religious connotations, rooted Mazzini's revolutionary project within the deeply-seated Italian religious tradition. In his use of language Mazzini borrowed liberally from religious texts, aware of the centrality of the 'religious question' to national 'resurgence'.[15] Yet, rejecting interpretations which based Italy's traditions on Catholicism, Mazzini embraced Christianity as a whole, without the divisions between Catholics and Protestants, which fragmented the universal roots of what he saw as a religion of humanity.[16] Moreover, he dismissed the authority of the pope and the clergy as intermediaries between the 'People' and 'God'. His design was, in Roberto Balzani's words, both 'global' and 'ecumenical'.[17] As Eugenio Biagini has highlighted, amongst 'Young Italy's' precursors, Mazzini included Christ, Luther and the English Puritans (as well as Socrates) – all those who had understood their times and unveiled the truth through revelation or reform.[18]

Mazzini's 'Giovine Italia' soon gathered members, numbering, by 1833, between 50,000 and 60,000 men and women and becoming, in Balzani's

[12] For a detailed study of the events see Sarti, *Mazzini*, 47–94.

[13] See G. Mazzini, 'Istruzione generale per gli affratellati nella Giovine Italia' (1831), *SEI* ii. 45–56.

[14] Idem, 'Giovine Italia' (1840), *SEI* xxii. 407–9 at p. 409.

[15] On the relationship between religion and the Risorgimento see Banti, *La nazione del Risorgimento*; an arguable analysis of Mazzini's religious lexicon is in S. Levis Sullam, '"Dio e il popolo": la rivoluzione religiosa di Giuseppe Mazzini', in Banti and Ginsborg, *Storia d'Italia*, 401–22. An important critique of similar positions is in Balzani, 'Il problema Mazzini', 173–6.

[16] For a discussion of the 'universal', religion and 'humanity' in Mazzini see R. Balzani and A. Varni, 'L'influenza della tradizione cristiana nella formazione del pensiero di Giuseppe Mazzini', *Annali di storia dell'esegesi* i (1992), 191–200.

[17] Balzani, 'Il problema Mazzini', 173.

[18] Mazzini, 'Les Patriotes et le clergé' (1835), *SEI* vi. 162–208, and 'I collaboratori della Giovine Italia ai loro concittadini' (1832), *SEI* iii. 27–74 at p. 55. See also Biagini, 'Mazzini and anticlericalism', 144.

words, the only 'agency of nationalization' in the peninsula.[19] Discontent in Italy had spread after more uprisings in the papal legacies (in Romagna) had been repressed. Between 1832 and 1833 Mazzini also attempted to instigate a revolution in Liguria and Piedmont. The conspiracy was unveiled and scores of 'Young Italy' bourgeois patriots were arrested and executed. Undeterred, in 1834, Mazzini organised a new expedition to Savoy which would end in defeat and recriminations. Known by continental governments as the main organiser, Mazzini became increasingly unwelcome even in republican Switzerland: he had gained a reputation for being – in Metternich's view – the most dangerous man in Europe.[20] Following the pressures exercised by France, where it was believed that he was plotting against Louis Philippe's life, Mazzini began to contemplate repairing to England.

He reached London in the company of other Italians – famously the Ruffini brothers – yet personal tensions and political differences would lead the exiles in opposite directions: the brothers both moved to Scotland, distancing themselves from their friend in more ways than one. Mazzini's long-term condition as an exile would turn him into a 'hybrid', often isolated from and in competition with other Italian democrats, who resented a leadership from afar.[21] As Roland Sarti has affirmed, 'in exile he lost touch with the changing realities of his country, which in his mind existed frozen in 1830'.[22] Yet, he would be admired and, indeed, sometimes worshipped, by young Victorian radicals who became familiar with his doctrine.[23]

Whilst in London, Mazzini would plough his own furrow through the length and breadth of Britain, aiming to reach the British public with a new message from Italy and distancing himself from the circle of Italian political exiles already settled in England. Mazzini's own understanding of British society developed in the early years, between his time as a relatively obscure exile and his sudden leap to fame, due to the scandalous *dénouement* in 1844 of secret spying on his private correspondence by the British government. London was, for Mazzini, a window from which he could observe the impact of industrialisation on society, reflecting and relating his thoughts to the outside world through his early correspondence with *Le Monde* in Paris and *La Helvetie* in Switzerland. Here Mazzini's early criticisms were a measure of his still embryonic grasp of the British polity and of the powers which public pressure, meetings, petitions and the press, could exercise within British society.[24]

---

[19] This estimate is given in Sarti, *Mazzini*, 64, and Balzani, 'Il problema Mazzini', 171.

[20] Sarti, *Mazzini*, 63.

[21] Duggan, 'Giuseppe Mazzini', 187.

[22] Sarti, *Mazzini*, 49.

[23] Ibid. 105–15; Mack Smith, *Mazzini*, 89–96.

[24] On Mazzini and Chartism see W. Roberts, *Prophet in exile: Joseph Mazzini in England, 1837–68*, New York 1989, 49–76, and his 'Mazzini's thought in the development of

Mazzini soon came to engage with the political, social and philosophical debates which had found expression in the writings of Victorian radical thinkers. He disliked utilitarianism and had strong reservations regarding Britain's free-trade model. What he offered to his hosts, as Sarti has argued, was a rejection of the utilitarian model and a new, passionate faith – something which would inspire the languishing spirits of Victorian republicans.[25] His thought would be profoundly shaped by the reciprocal influences of his ideas and John Stuart Mill's political vision of society, elaborating on the concepts previously expressed by Coleridge, who placed education at the centre of social organisation within English political thought. Both Mill and Mazzini, who met in 1837, linked the idea of education and nationality to progress; they found in association and co-operation the answer to the social conflicts emerging from class struggle, competition and capitalism, all the while rejecting as utopian the socialist solutions proposed by Robert Owen.[26] Mazzini's desire to engage with the debate on co-operation in England was matched by his frustration at being unable, as a foreigner, to delve deep into the English workers' associations and give them a direction which would set them apart from materialism and socialism.[27]

Mazzini's introduction to Thomas Carlyle also gave him an early sounding board. Mazzini found a critical affinity with Carlyle in his condemnation of the materialistic Benthamite utilitarianism which he disliked in British radicalism and he valued the opportunity to exchange thoughts with an indigenous, respected member of the liberal establishment concerned about the 'ominous' 'condition of England': since the inception of the industrial revolution the rich 'English Nation' had been starving beyond the remit of the capital.[28] Carlyle's concern for the riots in provincial England and his likening of the insurrection of the Manchester operatives, in August 1842, to the famous massacre of Peterloo in the same city in 1819, was in line with Mazzini's own concerns regarding England's social problems. However, Mazzini, like Carlyle and Mill, regarded Chartism and its leanings towards 'physical force' with suspicion, and preferred to ascribe social unrest to the inadequate education which the ruling classes were responsible for imparting to the lower classes.[29]

A sensitive observer of England's social inequalities and of the ensuing

British culture, politics and society', in Limiti, *Il mazzinianesimo nel mondo*, i. 3–75 at p. 42.

[25] N. Mayper and R. Sarti (eds), '*Dear Kate: lettere inedite di Giuseppe Mazzini a Katherine Hill, Angelo Bezzi e altri italiani a Londra (1841–71)*, Soveria Mannelli 2011, 20.

[26] Pichetto, 'John Stuart Mill', 1–28.

[27] Mazzini to Mandrot, 20 Feb. 1839, *SEI* xv. 377–82 at p. 381.

[28] T. Carlyle, *Past and Present* (1843), Berkeley–Los Angeles–London 2005, 5. Mazzini's critique of Bentham's position was clarified in his 'Thoughts upon democracy, no. IV', *People's Journal* lii, 26 Dec. 1846, 361.

[29] Carlyle, *Past and Present*, 19; Pichetto, 'John Stuart Mill', 17.

political debates, Mazzini had become aware of the important role played by the provinces as early as 1838, when he had followed the circulation of the National Petition. In an early letter from England to his close collaborator, Luigi Amedeo Melegari, Mazzini reported a meeting in Birmingham which had been led by 'a big industrialist, (Thomas) Attwood', who had first referred to the 'industrious classes' as including 'productive capital' and 'productive labour'.[30] The effect of the National Petition, signed by 1,200,000 'commons of England', which included the 'working classes' and the 'middle classes', determined to obtain liberty and justice after twenty-two years of repeated petitions, had been felt in the Houses of Parliament. Birmingham, insisted Attwood, was not only expressing the demands of its citizens: 'the men of Birmingham were England'.[31] While provincial politicians came to London to fight the cause of the 'people', newspapers reported on episodes of unrest in the provinces. Again, in 1839, Mazzini's attention was drawn to Birmingham, when he recounted the police attack on a Chartist gathering, notoriously known as the Bull Ring Riots.[32]

The adult education movement and Mazzini's London Free School

During that same year the self-doubt, which had held Mazzini in the grip of inaction since the failure of his Savoy expedition, gave way to a renewed desire to reorganise his political activities from England.[33] Despite Mazzini's early sensitivity to the voices of discontent which were coming from the regions, he decided to channel his energies within the capital. He saw his exile as an outpost, a platform from which he could organise an Italian uprising, educating a second generation of 'Young Italy' recruits, not demoralised by earlier failures. The restored 'Young Italy' movement would be galvanised by the injection of new men, who were to be found amongst Italian workers in London.

---

[30] Mazzini to L. A. Melegari, 24 Aug. 1838, *SEI* xv. 158; C. Flick, *The Birmingham Political Union and the movements for reform in Britain, 1830–39*, Hamden, CN 1978; N. LoPatin-Lummis, *Political unions, popular politics and the Great Reform Act of 1832*, New York 1999; C. Behagg, 'An alliance with the middle class: the Birmingham Political Union and early Chartism', in J. Epstein and D. Thompson (eds), *The Chartist experience: studies in working-class radicalism and culture, 1830–60*, London 1982, 59–86. On Thomas Attwood see C. Behagg, 'Attwood, Thomas (1783–1856)', *ODNB*.

[31] http://hansard.millbanksystems.com/commons/1839/jul/12/the-national-petition, accessed 17 May. 2013.

[32] Roberts, 'Mazzini's thought', 40–1, and *Prophet in exile*, 51. On the Bull Ring riots see also Behagg, 'An alliance', 80–1.

[33] The 'tempest of doubt' engulfed Mazzini from the end of 1836. On these three years see G. O. Griffith, *Mazzini: prophet of modern Europe*, London 1932, 109–17, and Bolton King, *The life of Mazzini*, London 1903, 51–60.

The 'peculiarity' of this community, which set its members apart from other *emigrés*, was that they lived in England, where the spread of 'associations' and educational institutions were beginning to shape society. In 1824 the repeal of the Combination Act, forbidding the formation of societies for the purpose of political reform, had reduced restrictions on establishing associations. Laws which excluded Catholics from political activities had also been amended. As Mastellone noted, the publication of an English translation of Alexis de Tocqueville's *Democratie en Amerique*, in 1835, had highlighted that the link between constitutional measures and the development of associations was central to the rise of democracy. The founding of the London Working Men's Association in 1836 was a clear signal of these developments: its desire to extend the associational practice to the numerous foreign workers exiled in London resulted, according to William Lovett, in the first international address to workers.[34]

If associationism was one pillar of workers' emancipation, another was education. Italian migrants had witnessed the educational impetus which had swept through Britain since the establishment of mechanics' institutes, the founding of Henry Brougham's Society for the Diffusion of Useful Knowledge, and the spread of Samuel Brown's itinerant libraries. George Birkbeck had first introduced educational classes for 'mechanics' (artisans) in 1799 in Glasgow, then moving to establish similar courses in Birmingham between 1804 and 1805, in Liverpool and in Hull.[35] The London Mechanics' Institute, founded in 1823, had established itself as a centre for learning, and other provincial establishments – in Manchester (1824) and Cheltenham (1834) – had since shown the value of such institutions as deliverers of knowledge, predominantly to skilled workers. While politics was officially excluded from the educational aims of the institutes, the reading rooms that they provided, with an array of newspapers – including radical ones – were the best channels for disseminating ideas amongst the lower middle classes and skilled workers.[36] In some particularly enlightened cases, as in the Winlaton Literary, Scientific and Mechanical Institute established in Tyneside by Joseph Cowen Jr, the mechanics' institutes also succeeded in enticing through their doors unskilled workers and, indeed, women. However, these were definitely a minority.[37]

[34] M. Bianco, 'La democrazia di William Lovett', *Il pensiero mazziniano* lxvii/3 (2012) 9–18.

[35] The term 'artisan' (or 'mechanic'). as defined in E. P. Thompson, separated skilled workers from factory workers: *Making of the English working class*, 259.

[36] Altick, *English common reader*, 189–92; Tylecote, *Mechanics' institutes*, 271–2. See also E. Royle, 'Mechanics' institutes and the working classes, 1840–60', *HJ* xiv/2 (1971), 305–21; J. Bord, *Science and Whig manners: science and political style in Britain, ca. 1790–1850*, Basingstoke 2009; and R. Ashton, *Victorian Bloomsbury*, New Haven 2012, ch. ii.

[37] Allen, *Joseph Cowen*, 26, 54. On the struggle to democratise mechanics' institute and open classes to women see B. Taylor, *Eve and the New Jerusalem*, London 1983, 232–7.

In March 1840 a delegation of Italian workers approached Mazzini in the hope that, with his help, they too could address the 'national education of their class'. Mazzini recognised in them a deep desire for knowledge.[38] The yearning of the Italian immigrants for self-improvement, and that of the Genoese exile to educate them, was a reflection of the impact that Mill's philosophical thought and, more generally, the example of the English adult education movement had had on the political exile and on the Italian community at large. As Mazzini wrote in 1840, Italian workers living abroad were shamefully aware of the gap in the moral, rather than material conditions of Italian workmen and foreign workers: abroad 'the worker reads, attends classes, has books and papers written especially for him, develops gradually, despite the very little time after work, his intellectual and moral faculties'.[39]

Concentrating upon the needs of poor Italian migrants, Mazzini founded, in November 1840, the *Unione degli Operai Italiani* as a section of 'Young Italy'.[40] The Union would introduce Italian workers in London to the idea of 'association' according to the principles of true republican brotherhood, an important milestone in the history of the Italian working classes.[41] Confronted for the first time with the social problem of workers, and determined to 'educate' the 'people', Mazzini established, in 1841, the Free Italian School in London, which, like the majority of the mechanics' institutes, attracted not so much the unskilled workers or the street organ-grinders, but the artisans, the same type of skilled workers that was embracing self-improvement in many corners of England.[42]

Like the mechanics' institutes, Mazzini's Free Italian School relied heavily on voluntarism for its administration, benefiting also from the financial and moral support of sympathisers, such as John Stuart Mill, the Carlyles, William Shaen, Harriet Martineau, the Ashurst sisters and the society hostess Arethusa Milner Gibson, wife of the radical MP, Thomas Milner Gibson.[43] Additional supporters were George Toynbee and his brother Joseph, whose son, Arnold Toynbee, a 'meteor of the late Victorian reform movement',

---

38 Mazzini to M. Drago, 8, 13 Apr. 1840, *SEI* xix. 57, 66.

39 G. Mazzini, 'Agli italiani, e specialmente agli operai italiani' (1840), *SEI* xxv. 3–20 at pp. 3, 7.

40 Idem, 'Agli operai italiani: del dovere di associarsi nazionalmente', *SEI* xxv. 53–7.

41 F. Della Peruta (ed.), *Scrittori politici dell'ottocento: Giuseppe Mazzini e i democratici*, i, Milan–Naples 1969, 230.

42 E. Morelli, 'L'azione di Mazzini in Inghilterra per l'Italia', *Il Risorgimento*, special issue (1973), 25–32 at p. 27; M. Finelli, *Il 'prezioso elemento': Giuseppe Mazzini e gli emigrati italiani nell'esperienza della scuola italiana di Londra*, Verucchio 1999, 93.

43 Tylecote, *Mechanics' institutes*, 280–5. E. F. Richards, *Mazzini's letters to an English family, 1844–54*, London–New York 1920, 54; Morelli, *Mazzini in Inghilterra*, 52–3.

would later become the inspiration for the founding of the East London workers' educational institute, Toynbee Hall.[44]

Mazzini recognised the power of the press which he invested with 'immense responsibility' and mission. He had arrived in England at an opportune moment, a turning point for the editors of radical periodicals who, between 1830 and 1836, had waged a campaign against the 'taxes on knowledge'. The exile's view was that the press alone was the 'interpreter between the people and power': it could either regulate or inspire.[45] With the help of one of the protagonists of the 'war of the unstamped', the Chartist John Cleave, also a leading propagandist for the British Association for the Promotion of Co-operative Knowledge, Mazzini was able to print and distribute a new Italian paper in London.[46] The *Apostolato Popolare* (published between November 1840 and September 1843), according to Emilia Morelli 'one of the best Mazzinian papers', modelled on the English Chartist press, became a vehicle of political education for Italian workers.[47] Mazzini tirelessly promoted it, supplying copies to his British friends, who also helped to fund it.[48]

The early fame of Mazzini in the radical Tyneside press

Mazzini's resolve, in 1839, to rekindle the revolutionary impetus of 'Young Italy' and his commitment to alerting the British public to Italy's struggle for freedom from foreign rule ran in tandem.[49] In the context of the English radical press, Mazzini found a keen promoter in the *Northern Liberator*.[50] Tyneside radicalism had gained in its founding editor, Augustus Beaumont, an *avant-garde* interpreter of northern commitment to republican continental causes, a political activist who had not hesitated to accuse the London Working

---

[44] Arnold Toynbee died at the age of thirty-one: J. O. Baylen and J. B. Brown, 'Arnold Toynbee (1852–83)', *DMBR* iii. 815–17; *Il Secolo*, 21 Aug. 1902.

[45] G. Mazzini, 'De la mission de la presse périodique' (1836), *SEI* vii. 237–65 at p. 237.

[46] Mazzini to M. Mazzini, 5 Nov. 1840, *SEI* xix. 330; E. Royle and J. Walvin, *English radicals and reformers, 1760–1848*, Lexington 1982, 138.

[47] E. Morelli, *G. Mazzini, quasi una biografia*, Rome 1984, 14.

[48] In addition to *L'Apostolato Popolare* there were two more publications connected with Mazzini's school: *Il Pellegrino* (June 1842–June 1843), and *L'Educatore* (Aug. 1843–Aug.1844): A. Del Cornò, 'Un ritrovato giornale mazziniano: "Il Pellegrino"', in *Le fusa del gatto: libri, librai e molto altro*, Siena 2013.

[49] Between May and September 1839 Mazzini published four letters on the condition of Italy and its future in the *Monthly Chronicle*.

[50] See J. Allen, 'Northern Liberator', *DNCJ*, 458–9. See also Joan Hugman, '"A small drop of ink": Tyneside Chartism and *The Northern Liberator*', in O. Ashton, R. Fyson and S. Roberts, *The Chartist legacy*, Monmouth 1999, 24–47 at p. 32.

Men's Association 'of being corrupt middle-class coadjutors'.[51] His successor
Robert Blakey, who bought the paper in 1838, had maintained an impressive
editorial team committed to being 'proactive' and ensuring that the paper
would be 'an agent of change rather than a mere chronicler of events'.[52]
Published between October 1837 and December 1840, the *Northern Liberator*
was from the outset 'the best selling journal on Tyneside', 'circulated extensively by agents in twenty towns, mostly in northern England but also in
London, Glasgow and Edinburgh'.[53]

On 16 November 1839 a long descriptive article about Mazzini appeared
in the paper, considerably earlier than any other writings published by his
Chartist admirers. The early date is remarkable, as Mazzini is considered to
have been 'comparatively unknown' in Britain until 1844.[54] Some of Mazzini's articles had been published previously in John Stuart Mill's *Westminster
Review*, describing him as the 'most eminent conspirator and revolutionist in
Europe', and other reviews, the *British Foreign Review* and *Tait's Magazine*, had
indeed followed suit by commissioning Mazzini to write articles. These were
mostly concerned with topics of Italian literature and culture[55] and included
an article written for *The London and Westminster Review* in October 1838 on
'Italian literature since 1830', where Mazzini hailed Dante as the precursor
of a national literary movement.[56] In the light of the still relative obscurity
of the exile amongst the non-intellectual readership, the publication of an
article on him in one of the 'liveliest' Chartist papers, known to outsell
established Tyneside papers, was a sign of the unique character of early radicalism in the North-East, validating the contention that internationalist
ideas had long featured on Tyneside. Once Joseph Cowen Jr had established
himself as a local newspaper magnate, Mazzini would become a household
name in the North-East.[57]

---

[51] On Augustus Beaumont see Prothero, 'Chartists and political refugees', 211–12, 215,
and A. R. Schoyen, *The Chartist challenge: a portrait of George Julian Harney*, London–
Melbourne–Toronto 1958, 25.

[52] For Robert Blakey's biography see R. Welford, *Men of mark 'twixt Tyne and Tweed'*,
London–Newcastle-upon-Tyne 1895.

[53] Allen, *Joseph Cowen*, 35; Hugman, 'A small drop of ink', 32.

[54] See Claeys, 'Mazzini', 227.

[55] See Mack Smith, *Mazzini*, 24. Mazzini ascribed to literature a political role: R. Sarti,
'Giuseppe Mazzini e la tradizione repubblicana', in M. Ridolfi (ed.), *Almanacco della
repubblica: storia d'Italia attraverso le tradizioni, le istituzioni e le simbologie repubblicane*,
Milan 2003, 56–67 at p. 58.

[56] On this see C. Riccardi, 'Sconfitte critiche del Risorgimento: il moto letterario in Italia
di Mazzini', in Q. Marini, G. Sertoli, S. Cedrino and L. Cavaglieri, *L'officina letteraria e
culturale dell'età mazziniana, 1815–1870*, Novi Ligure 2013, 65–74.

[57] Allen, 'Northern Liberator', *DNCJ*, 458–9; Allen, *Joseph Cowen*, 35. On Joseph
Cowen see Allen, *Joseph Cowen*, and N. Todd, *The militant democracy: Joseph Cowen and
Victorian radicalism*, Whitley Bay 1991.

The article introduced Mazzini as a 'lawyer from Genoa', a political exile in Paris who had 'presided over a republican association known by the name of "Younger Italy"'. Details were not spared. The paper explained that 'He belonged to that fraction of the first French revolutionists, who in some sort worship the principles of that revolution, and would spare no sacrifice to realise his ideal salvation of humanity. Such is the intense enthusiasm of the men of that school. Mazzini is distinguished among most of the leaders by his character, intellectual faculties, and extraordinary activity.'[58] Extracts from 'Younger Europe' were quoted with references made to Mazzini's 'emphatic style'.[59] There was no hint of the aborted and failed insurrections, which in time would threaten Mazzini's leadership amongst his followers.[60] Tyneside readers were instead introduced to a system of thought and a style which was later to become familiar to them: 'One God, one Master; His law; one interpreter of the law: Humanity.'[61]

That such a level of familiarity with the political ideas of a continental republican exile would be afforded to Tyneside readers as early as 1839 is quite extraordinary. The article therefore brings into question Miles Taylor's assertion that 'despite his long residence and the public interest aroused in 1844, Mazzini was still something of an unknown figure in 1848–49'.[62] The evidence drawn from the *Northern Liberator* suggests the opposite, certainly in the North of England, where radicals, ten years before the establishment of the Roman Republic, praised and celebrated him. Moreover, the article signals that the vital interest of provincial radicals in foreign affairs was independent of cues from the capital. If anything, the influence of Scotland on northern radicals could be more tangible than that of London.

The 'post-office scandal': between Scottish Enlightenment and provincial radicalism

In line with Emilia Morelli's early assessment, historians agree that in June 1844 Mazzini's name 'suddenly came to the attention of England'.[63] This followed a petition presented to the House of Commons by Thomas Duncombe MP, complaining of a personal grievance suffered by William

---

[58] 'Intrigues of the refugees abroad', *Northern Liberator*, 16 Nov. 1839, 3.

[59] This was 'Young Europe', an international organisation which brought together members of different national societies with the aim of establishing republicanism across nations through insurrections: Karma Nabulsi, 'Patriotism and republicanism in the "Oath of allegiance" to Young Europe', *EJPT* v/1 (2006), 61–70.

[60] F. Della Peruta, *Mazzini e i rivoluzionari italiani: il 'partito d'azione', 1830–45*, Milan 1974, 159–60, 227–8.

[61] 'Intrigues of the refugees abroad', *Northern Liberator*, 16 Nov. 1839.

[62] M. Taylor, *The decline of British radicalism, 1847–60*, Oxford 1995, 191.

[63] Morelli, *Mazzini in Inghilterra*, 43.

Linton, the Chartist wood engraver, poet and journalist, and Joseph Mazzini.[64] The complaint soon came to be known as the 'mail scandal' – which exposed the government as having violated the constitutional right to individual privacy by requesting that the Post Office spy on Mazzini's correspondence – an affair which was later debated at length in parliament.[65] Assertions of the national resonance of the scandal have not been corroborated by analysis of the actual regional spread of Mazzini's fame. In fact, more recently, Mastellone's detailed studies of the publicity given to the 'letter-opening affair' in the radical press have brought the focus of the investigation back to the capital, and to the London papers which were read by continental émigrés.[66]

Yet Mazzini's name appeared widely in the national and provincial press, and also found fertile ground in Scotland, where support for the Italian Risorgimento had been kindled by the presence of Agostino Ruffini. Arriving in Edinburgh in 1840, Ruffini had rallied a keen group of devotees – who came under the name of 'Ruffinians' – and support for Italy was thereafter destined to grow.[67] The news that the Home Office Secretary, Sir James Graham, had issued a warrant 'instructing the "inner office"' of the General Post Office to withhold, open and copy letters addressed to Mazzini in London had created a moral uproar which rested on the accusation that the government had acted unconstitutionally. The situation was aggravated by the allegation that the Austrians, on information supplied by the British government, had subsequently unmasked conspirators, executing the two Bandiera brothers in Cosenza.[68]

Ideas which germinated and grew in the Scottish intellectual milieu were absorbed by English students in Scotland, whose openness to enlightened ideas and desire to disseminate radical approaches in their home regions would successfully blur the boundary between Scottish and English supporters of the Italians. Indeed, it has been noted before that many of the most active English philo-Italians were educated at Edinburgh University, where the Scottish minister, the Revd John Ritchie, a Chartist, and 'fearless Radical

---

[64] For the petition see Hansard's parliamentary debates, 'Minutes Commons', 14 June 1844, http://hansard.millbanksystems.com/search/Mazzini?sort=date&year=1844, accessed 12 Jan. 2011.

[65] On the affair see Mastellone, Mazzini scrittore, 25–39; F. B. Smith, 'British Post office espionage 1844', HS xiv/54 (1970), 189–203; Hansard's parliamentary debates (1844), lxxv. 892–96, 164–1308; lxxvi. 74–87, 212–59, 294–314, 776–7, 1010–25, 1714–17.

[66] Mastellone, Il progetto politico di Mazzini, 207.

[67] J. Rothney, 'La Società degli amici d'Italia e la nuova riforma', RSR xlviii/1 (1961), 21–58 at p. 34.

[68] Mazzini actively contributed towards elevating the Bandiera brothers to the 'pantheon' of 'martyrs'. Amongst exiles, martyrs were object of patriotic cult. On the cult of the Bandieras see L. Riall, 'The politics of Italian romanticism: Mazzini and the making of a nationalist culture', in Bayly and Biagini, Mazzini, 167–86 at pp. 174–5, and her 'Martyr cults in nineteenth-century Italy', JMH lxxxii/2 (2010), 255–87.

platform speaker', was very influential.[69] Exposure to Scottish enlightened ideas may well also have had some bearing on the heterodox preacher George Dawson, 'one of the most colourful figures of mid Victorian Birmingham', and 'creator of the municipal doctrine', who spent a few months at Aberdeen University and then at Glasgow University before returning to Birmingham in 1844, where in the 1850s he would preach the cause of Italy.[70]

Amongst those studying at Edinburgh University at the time of the 'letter-opening affair' was Joseph Cowen Jr of Tyneside, chairman of the Eclectic Debating Society, where the scandal was discussed. This occasion was to prove a turning point in Cowen's life as it marked the beginning of a friend-ship which would impact later on the dissemination of republican ideals amongst Tyneside workers. The debate spurred Cowen to write to Mazzini, the beginning of a long correspondence. A year later, in 1845, the two men were to meet for the first time in London, 'at Mazzini's house', where Cowen agreed 'to distribute "Mazzinian literature"' in the provinces – literature, which, according to a manuscript left by his daughter, Jane Cowen, 'mysteri-ously appeared in the land, where' it was 'forbidden'.[71]

The Northern Star and the 'letter-opening affair'

While Joseph Cowen was being imbued with Scottish enlightened ideas, northern readers were kept abreast of radical views by the working-class editors Julian Harney and Joshua Hobson, whose paper, the Northern Star and Leeds General Advertiser, considered the 'pre-eminent newspaper of the Chartist movement', enjoyed vast circulation in the 1840s.[72] The widespread influence of the Northern Star, averaging a weekly circulation of 43,000 throughout the provinces, should not entirely obscure the fact that at its outset, in 1837, the paper 'almost entirely depended upon a circulation in the Yorkshire textile districts and adjacent areas of Cheshire and Lanca-shire', having its powerbase in the 'northern textile region' and being simply, in J. F. C. Harrison's words, a 'great Yorkshire Radical newspaper'.[73] The paper's 'early success' was undoubtedly dependent on the 'militant northern

---

[69] See Fyfe, 'Scotland and the Risorgimento', 79.

[70] E. P. Hennock, Fit and proper persons: ideal and reality in nineteenth-century urban government, London 1973, 62–3; I. Sellers, 'Dawson, George (1821–76)', ODNB, 554–6.

[71] Jane Cowen, 'Manuscript', TWAS, 16 (19) viii.

[72] G. Vargo and M. Chase, 'Northern Star', DNCJ, 459. With regard to the circulation of the paper Malcolm Chase mentions 'peak sales in the order of 50,000 (outselling even The Times)': 'Building identity, building circulation: engraved portraiture and the Northern Star', in J. Allen and O. R. Ashton, Papers for the people: a study of the Chartist press, London 2005, 25.

[73] Vargo and Chase, 'Northern Star', 459; Chase, 'Building identity', 31; J. F. C. Harrison, 'Chartism in Leeds', in A. Briggs, Chartist Studies, London–Basingstoke 1977, 74.

centres of the West Riding', yet its move to London at the end of 1844 reflected the editors' ambition to produce a national paper.[74]

In June, however, when the initial denunciations of the 'letter-opening affair' first came into the public domain due to two letters published in *The Times* – one of which was signed by Carlyle – the *Northern Star* was still based in Yorkshire, albeit with a national reputation as an established radical paper.[75] Mastellone's definition of the *Northern Star* as one of the 'London papers' may only therefore apply from the move in 1844.[76] Not only did the 'post-office scandal' occur when the circulation of the *Northern Star* was still heavily weighted in favour of its Yorkshire and Midlands readership, but even after the move the paper could hardly qualify as a 'London weekly'. In 1848 the distribution of the paper was organised through fifteen regional centres, which included 'Glasgow, Edinburgh, Newcastle, Leeds, Bradford, Huddersfield, Sheffield, Derby, Nottingham, Grantham, Staffordshire, Warwickshire, Loughborough and Manchester, with the rest of the UK (specified as Shropshire, Worcestershire, Gloucestershire, Somerset, Berkshire, Dorset, Devon and Cornwall) served from London'.[77]

On 22 June 1844 it was, therefore, the predominantly provincial radical northern readership of the *Northern Star* that was introduced to the government espionage affair and to the name of Mazzini. In reporting on the debate in the Commons, the paper explained how Sir James Graham 'had issued a warrant by which the letters of a Mr. Mazzini were detained at the post-office'.[78] 'Neither statute' nor 'dread of public opinion' had stood in the way of such a decision, which the *Northern Star* took to discredit the country and 'the honour of the English name'. With regard to Mazzini, the paper pointedly added that 'this individual being a foreigner, that circumstance constitutes a material aggravation of the offence committed'. The paper concluded:

> It has always been the boast of England that the friends of freedom, when driven from the other countries by the bloodhounds of despotism have ever found a refuge in England. Hence the exiles of all countries flock in crowds to our shores. If the espionage system introduced by Sir James Graham were to be sanctioned or winked at by Parliament, this would be so no more.[79]

The fact that the paper was not addressing the cosmopolitan readers of the capital, but provincial ones, renders this statement particularly powerful, as it conjugates at a very early date provincial pride, national honour and

---

[74] Vargo and Chase , 'Northern Star', 459.

[75] *The Times*, 15, 16 June 1844.

[76] Mastellone, *Mazzini scrittore*, 55–66.

[77] Chase, 'Building identity', 32, 52; Mastellone, *Mazzini scrittore*, 55.

[78] 'Post-office espionage: the English Fouche', *NS*, 22 June 1844.

[79] Ibid.

international sympathy. News of the 'Post-Office affair' was reported in numerous articles between June and September, prior, therefore, to the *Northern Star* headquarters being transferred to London. The debate in the Commons was reported at length, as were parts of the report of the Secret Committee charged to investigate the affair. The report of the enquiry was considered 'meagre'.[80] A *résumé* of the whole affair was published again by the *Northern Star* in September, and more publicity was given to Mazzini that same month, when it was announced that he was about to publish a pamphlet on the execution of the Bandiera brothers and their comrades.[81]

Holyoake, the *Movement* and the 'letter-opening affair'

While in 1844 the *Northern Star* was effectively still an important provincial paper, it was by no means the only northern radical paper to report the 'letter-opening affair' to regional readers. Indeed, as Miles Taylor underlined, the *Northern Star* ought to be relieved of the 'burden' of responsibility for all dissemination of radical ideas.[82] Lancashire, the Midlands and the North beyond were regions where radicalism was expressed also through consumption of the *Movement* (1843–6), a weekly journal which, according to a well-rehearsed practice of mutual endorsement amongst radical editors, had at its inauguration the blessing of the *Northern Star*.[83] In recommending the new publication Harney felt safe. He had first met one of the paper's editors, George Jacob Holyoake, in Birmingham in 1839.

This self-improved artisan, who so well reflected the characteristics of his town – seedbed of his intellectual growth, cradle of the Birmingham Political Union – had been educated, under the guidance of the Unitarian Daniel Wright, at the Birmingham Mechanics' Institute, where he soon became one of its teachers.[84] In 1838 Holyoake had joined the Owenite Association of All Classes of All Nations (1835), which had sixty branches throughout the country, attracting audiences interested in anticlerical lectures.[85] Establishing himself as a respected itinerant orator, in 1843 he had delivered a speech at the Mechanics' Institute in Cheltenham, a famously radical institution,[86] which caused him to be imprisoned on a common law charge of blasphemy: William Ashurst, who provided him with legal assistance, was unable to

---

[80] *NS*, 6 July; 17, 24 Aug. 1844.

[81] *NS*, 21, 28 Sept. 1844.

[82] Taylor, 'Rethinking the Chartists', 492.

[83] Finn, *After Chartism*, 115.

[84] G. J. Holyoake, *Sixty years of an agitator's life*, i, London 1893, 45–6.

[85] E. Royle, *The infidel tradition from Paine to Bradlaugh*, London 1976, 40.

[86] O. Ashton, 'The mechanics' institute and radical politics in Cheltenham Spa (1834–1840)', *Cheltenham Local History Society Journal* ii (1984), 25–8.

stop him being convicted. Holyoake's period of confinement was succeeded, however, by one of feverish political activity concerning free thought.[87] On his release from jail he joined the Owenite Maltus Questell Ryall, a London engraver and a member of the Lambeth branch of the Owenite Rational Society, in editing the new paper.[88]

Replacing the *Oracle of Reason*, the first periodical devoted explicitly to free thought and edited by the 'infidel' socialist Charles Southwell, the *Movement* was published under Bentham's motto 'Maximize morals, minimize religion'.[89] The new weekly gathered readers in Bristol, Leeds, Sheffield and Edinburgh, yet the majority was concentrated in Manchester, Salford, Mosley, Rochdale, Stockport and Oldham, in fact, as the editors put it, in 'every town in the North, unless we are wrongly informed'.[90] According to the editors, 'liberal agents' prepared to stock the *Movement* could be 'found in every place' and readers who had any 'difficulty in procuring' it would 'oblige ... by sending word'.[91]

In 1844 the *Movement* – later to become the *Reasoner* – took a position on the case of Mazzini's 'letter-opening affair'. To the delight of Mazzini, Mill's *Westminster Review* had published in September an article entitled 'Mazzini and the ethics of politicians' which violently attacked the actions of the government.[92] In December the *Westminster Review* allowed the article to be republished in the form of a pamphlet by James Watson under the title 'Letter-opening at the Post-Office', printed with an accompanying letter from Mazzini on the Bandiera Brothers. As Mazzini wrote both to his mother and to Harney, what really mattered to him was that the pamphlet should reach the British 'People' through a second cheap edition.[93] He was anxious that 'the silent indifference of the Whig and Tory press' would eclipse the relevance of the publication and 'after scrupulous research' became convinced that copies of the pamphlets might have been destroyed by the British government.[94] His fears were unfounded and the pamphlet had in fact a 'wide circulation in England'.[95]

Indeed, on 11 December 1844, an announcement appeared in the *Movement* recommending Watson's pamphlet to its predominantly northern read-

---

[87] Royle, *Victorian infidels* 80.

[88] *NS*, 30 Dec. 1843; Holyoake, *Sixty years*, i. 85. On M. Q. Ryall see Gurney, 'George Jacob Holyoake', 58.

[89] Royle, *Victorian infidels*, 69; *Movement*, 20 Dec. 1843, 2, 13.

[90] *Movement*, 20 Dec. 1843, 2, 13.

[91] Ibid, 13 June 1844, 33, 264.

[92] *WR* (Sept. 1844), 225–50.

[93] Mazzini to his mother, *SEI* xxvii 32; Mazzini to Harney, 31 July 1845, in F. G. Black and R. M. Black, *The Harney papers*, Assen 1969, 49–50.

[94] Mastellone, *Mazzini scrittore*, 34.

[95] Ibid. 34–5.

ers.[96] An editorial by Ryall followed which underlined how the British public was 'deeply indebted to Mazzini for the energetic and persevering course he had pursued in tracing out and making known to them a moral canker eating into the very vitals of the body politic' and opening 'the eyes of the people of England'. Although most of the article dealt with the arguments against the government, on constitutional and moral grounds, the latter part of it provided a commentary on foreign affairs and democracy abroad, a topic not ordinarily approached by the *Movement*.[97] The denunciation was followed by praise for the courage of the Italian patriots, and the article concluded with an exhortation:

> I am informed that a considerable number of copies still lie upon the publisher's shelves. How is this? If there were not one individual besides, interested in so great a theme, are there not Movement readers numerous enough to clear off an entire edition, without reckoning those of the *Northern Star, New Moral World Communist Chronicle* and *National Reformer* as well as the new candidate for the democratic favour, the *Plebian?*[98]

The *Movement* further appealed to its 'thousand subscribers' to clear the shelves of the remaining copies, as such 'well-timed, watchful attention to the public interests and advancement … should meet with corresponding encouragement' and, furthermore, the publisher who had taken on an '*uncertain in the production of profits*' deserved the readers' support.[99]

Mazzini amongst co-operators in Lancashire and Yorkshire

In 1844 'the failure of Owenism' had thrown 'masses of workers into a state of apathy'.[100] This was bitterly ironic, as in Robert Owen's 'grand plan' for the 'salvation of the world' that year had been expected to be a turning point. A model community, 'Harmony Hall', in provincial Hampshire, had opened under the sign 'C.M. 1844', indicating the Commencement of the Millennium. By the end of 1844, however, Owen's community at Queenswood was suffering its final agonising days, following the folding of earlier experiments – from Scotland, with New Lanark (1816) to Lancashire with Manea Fen (1839–41).[101] On visiting Queenswood, Holyoake's verdict on the 'last of the English communities' had been damning: Queenswood had been built by Owen and his colleagues in a 'panic of pride' on land which was 'flinty

---

96   *Movement*, 11 Dec. 1844, 53, 456.
97   Ibid. 18 Dec. 1844, 54, 461.
98   Ibid.
99   Italic in the original.
100   McCabe, *Life of Holyoake*, i. 108.
101   On Owenite communities see E. Royle, *Robert Owen and the commencement of the millennium: a study of the Harmony Community*, Manchester 1998.

and poor', 'miles away from the markets', and despite 'noble sacrifices on the part of hundreds of working men' for its success, 'nature had done little, and the directors less'.[102]

After the repeated failure of successive communitarian experiments, the Rochdale weavers, inspired by lectures on 'self-help', opened, in December 1844, a northern store, which would survive the many challenges ahead, becoming a beacon for national and international co-operators.[103] The year 1844 would be remembered not for the 'end of Owenism', but for the birth of co-operation, which would flourish particularly in the northern provinces.[104] As Holyoake noted, the 'ordinary', 'stolid and tame' provincial towns had a better chance of succeeding in co-operation than the capital, where too many 'attractions' provided endless distractions.[105] The new co-operative formula hinged on the values of 'respectability, self-help, thrift, improvement' and 'progress', conjugating idealism with 'practical knowledge'.[106] As G. D. H. Cole put it, 'The Pioneers had settled down to develop Co-operation not apart from the world as it was but in that world and subject to its limiting conditions. They had become realists, even if they had not shed their idealism.'[107]

Holyoake's part in facilitating the move of co-operators towards realism and in spreading the movement beyond its regional and national remit, was underlined by Holyoake's biographer, who wrote that 'His (Co-operative) work from 1844 to 1854 had great influence on the fortunes of the movement. Through him men like Mazzini and Saffi became interested in it, and took the idea with them into the new Italy of a later year.'[108] The role played by Aurelio Saffi amongst Italian workers' associations would become prominent in later years, after Mazzini's death. In the early days, however, Mazzini promptly manifested his interest and support for the co-operative societies of the North. After the political unification of Italy, Owen, the Rochdale Pioneers and indeed Holyoake would remain a source of inspiration for Mazzini.

The 'Leeds Pioneers', as Holyoake defined them, stood 'next to Rochdale as the foremost English Co-operative association'.[109] Leeds working men too had been introduced to the idea of 'self-help' by Samuel Smiles,

102 Holyoake, *Sixty years*, i. 203; McCabe, *Life of Holyoake*, i. 104.

103 McCabe, Life of Holyoake, i. 180.

104 Ibid. i. 88.

105 G. J. Holyoake, *Self-help by the people: the history of co-operation in Rochdale: the Society of Equitable Pioneers, 1844–57*, London 1867, 59.

106 P. Gurney, *Co-operative culture and the politics of consumption in England, 1870–1930*, Manchester 1996.

107 G. D. H. Cole, *A century of co-operation*, Manchester 1945, 89.

108 McCabe, *Life of Holyoake*, i. 198.

109 G. J. Holyoake, *The jubilee history of the Leeds Industrial Co-operative Limited from 1847 to 1897 traced year by year*, Manchester 1897.

who had delivered a momentous lecture there in the middle of the 1840s.[110] Following the example of the Lancashire men, the Yorkshire co-operators had set up the Leeds Society, with the inspiring name, the 'Redemption' Society. On 7 January 1847 a meeting was held in the Music Hall in Leeds: 'the audience assembled appeared to be about five hundred, a fair proportion of them females'.[111] Congratulatory letters were read out, including one from Linton and another from Mazzini, who, in sending a subscription, 'asked to be enrolled as a member' and offered to pay 3d. a week as a token of his sympathy.[112] The Leeds Redemption Society prided itself on being the first association of English working men to 'have the honour of carrying out for themselves the substantial portion of Owen, St. Simon, or Fourier'.[113]

Saint-Simon in particular was very influential in the early formulation of Mazzini's thought and may well have had a bearing on his decision to become a member.[114] The relationship between Mazzini's thought and Saint-Simonian doctrine is contested territory, and there is much disagreement amongst historians on the degree, timing and content of Saint-Simon's influence upon him.[115] Mazzini did not consider himself a Saint-Simonian, yet he did praise, in the *People's Journal*, the principle of association as a vehicle for social regeneration.[116] The Redemption Society responded to this ideal, which Mazzini was promoting amongst the exiled Italian workers. James Hole – a prominent Leeds socialist and Honorary Secretary of the Yorkshire Union of Mechanics' Institutes between 1848 and 1867 – responded to Mazzini's subscription by engaging in a controversial diatribe which was being played out in London, in the *People's Journal*.[117] Writing in the Society's organ, the *Herald of Co-operation, and Organ of the Redemption Society* Hole published a series of five articles entitled 'Mazzini and Communism'.

---

[110] A. Briggs, *Victorian people: a reassessment of persons and themes (1851–67)*, Harmondsworth 1965, 129.

[111] 'Soirée of the Leeds Redemption Society', *Howitt's Journal* (1847), i. 7.

[112] Ibid. Holyoake, *Jubilee history*, 3. See also 'The first soirée of the Leeds Redemption Society', *Herald of Redemption* (Feb. 1847), 11, and Brown, 'Mazzini ispira i cooperatori britannici', *BDM* (1956), 11–16.

[113] William Howitt, 'Letters to the working men of England', *People's Journal* xxv, 20 June 1846, 338–42 at p. 341.

[114] On the topic see R. Pozzi, 'Mazzini e il Sansimonismo', in Limiti, *Il mazzinianesimo nel mondo*, iv. 33–48.

[115] While there is consensus on the early influence of Saint-Simon on Mazzini's ideas, the view of his long-term sway, as advanced by Levis Sullam in '"Dio e popolo"', has been cogently challenged: Biagini, *Mazzini and anticlericalism*, 145, 149, and Pozzi, 'Mazzini e il sansimonismo'.

[116] Pozzi, 'Mazzini e il sansimonismo', 35 n. 4.

[117] G. Mazzini, ' Thoughts upon democracy in Europe, no. V', and 'Thoughts upon democracy in Europe, no. VI', *People's Journal* lviii, 6 Feb. 1847, 79–81; lxviii, 17 Apr. 1847, 219–22. For the debate in London see Mastellone, *Mazzini scrittore*, 139–46.

Hole's critique of Mazzini's position demonstrates how radical provinces responded promptly to the debate surrounding Mazzini's political manifesto: beyond the capital, Mazzini's ideas were being digested and debated in the heart of industrial Yorkshire as early as 1847. Hole proudly pointed to the special relationship that the Redemption Society had with the 'deservedly popular writer'. As the paper announced, 'From Mr. M having enrolled himself a member of the Redemption Society, ... we almost imagine, and yet dare scarcely hope, that there is no substantial difference between the plan of the Redemption Society and the views of Mr. Mazzini.'[118] The association of Mazzini with the Redemption Society was not in fact a unique relationship between him and a provincial co-operative society, as he subsequently wrote similar letters of support to the Oldham Equitable Society and to the Halifax Co-operative.[119] Indeed, in 1863 the Sunderland co-operative society would receive a congratulatory letter from Mazzini for having formed an education committee;[120] and later the Co-operative Congress also read out a letter of support from him.[121] Yet, the Redemption Society is likely to have been the first.

Hole's engagement with Mazzini's ideas on association no doubt gave the *Herald of Co-operation* readers plenty of opportunities for discussion. Hole highlighted what he saw as possible differences between Mazzini's thought and the Society's intentions:

He asserts that there *is* a difference between Communism and Association. If there be any, save that of degree – Association being limited Communism, and Communism more intense Association – we should like to see it pointed out, and also the kind and degree of Association of which our author *does* approve. Without this information, the letters on Democracy will do more harm than good, because the evils they attribute to *some* forms of Communism will, by a very common fallacy, become considered as applying to *all* forms of Association.[122]

James Hole's diatribe against Mazzini's ideas on 'democracy', 'communism' and 'association' reveals his frustration with the exile's attacks on materi-

---

[118] J. Hole, 'Mr. Mazzini and Communism, no. I', *Herald of Co-operation and Organ of the Redemption Society* 10 (Oct. 1847), 73–4.

[119] McCabe, *Life of Holyoake*, i. 185.

[120] P. A Darvill, 'The contribution of co-operative retail societies to welfare within the framework of the North East coast area', unpubl. M.Litt. diss. Durham 1954, 200 n. 1, quoted in Todd, *Militant democracy*, 108.

[121] According to Holyoake the letter, sent by the very ill Mazzini, had been read out at the Co-operative Congress in Halifax. However, as this congress took place in 1874, after Mazzini's death, it is more likely that the exile had sent the letter to one of the earlier Congresses, either in Bolton (1872) or in Birmingham (1871). See J. White Mario, 'Il Congresso delle cooperative a Milano', in I. Biagianti *La 'nuova Italia' nelle corrispondenze americane di Jessie White Mario*, Florence 1999, 166.

[122] Hole, 'Mr. Mazzini and Communism, no. I', 73.

alism, socialism and communism. The *People's Journal* had already received letters of protest about Mazzini's 'partially or entirely erroneous' views on Fourier. Interestingly, Goodwyn Barmby, a Suffolk Chartist and socialist who had supported the establishment of the 'People's International League', had written an article, *Defence of Communism*, arguing that English Communism, unlike the socialist systems of Saint-Simon, Fourier and Owen, was represented by the 'Communist Church', by the 'Co-operative League', and by the 'Leeds Redemption Society'. Barmby, who rejected materialism and had quoted Mazzini's *Foi et avenir* (1835) in his own writings, conjugated 'communism' with 'faith', believing that 'nations ... should rise again as a religious party' which would form 'the Catholicism of mankind – the universal association of the nations'.[123]

It is clear why Mazzini's 'assaults' on materialism, Benthamite self-interest and the dogma of 'rights' as opposed to the religion of 'duties', had created such a stir amongst radical readers. As doctrines were being formulated, the boundaries between socialism, communism and religion, as those between faith, secularism and atheism, were being negotiated in the context of the debates sparked by the publication of Mazzini's 'Thoughts'. The encounters of the London exile's doctrines with the ideas which were being reformulated by Yorkshire co-operators, following the disappoinments of Owenism, were part of the reflections on the new pathway that 'association' should take: reading, challenging, interrogating Mazzini's writings was part of what provincial co-operators did at this crucial crossroad.

Regardless of the religious association which the reference to 'Redemption' in the Society's name might evoke, Hole struggled with the loftiness of Mazzini's 'democratic idea', which he defined as 'a new name for practical Christianity'.[124] Hole was frustrated by what seemed to him a lack of indication as to how Mazzini would propose to achieve the 'divine society' and the 'heavenly country' to which he aspired; indeed, he lambasted, Mazzini should 'do something more than preach'.[125]

It is evident from Hole's co-operative anxiety and his desire for Mazzini to provide solutions to the practical realisation of the associational ideal, that the Rochdale store had not yet yielded the success which would reassure crestfallen Owenites, and provide them with a 'third way'. That Mazzini's ideas were disseminated, questioned and debated amongst northern co-operators at such an early stage is, however, siginificant. The space given to the political thought of a foreign exile in the *Herald of Co-operation* suggests that Mazzini was increasingly recognised in provincial England as an important contributor to the debate on democracy and co-operation. How

---

[123]   G. Barmby, *The Promethean, or Communitarian Apostle*, iv. 72, quoted in Mastellone, *Mazzini scrittore*, 141.

[124]   J. Hole, 'Mr. Mazzini and Communism, no. II', *Herald of Co-operation* 11 (Nov. 1847), 81–3.

[125]   Idem, 'Mr. Mazzini and Communism, no. I', 73.

Mazzini's doctrine differed from earlier formulations of co-operation would be clarified from 1850, when Mazzini famously accused Saint-Simonians and Communists of eliminating the concept of liberty within their formula of 'association'.[126] These issues would be discussed in much more detail in Linton's *English Republic* (1851–5), where Mazzini was quoted as affirming that 'Fourierists, St. Simonians, Communists' were 'all worshippers of utility' and had 'no other moral than that of interest.'[127]

Neverthess, the debate on Mazzini's 'thoughts' on communism which had taken place in the organ of the Leeds Redemption Society illustrates how the dissemination of Mazzini's ideas in the North helped to define his following amongst working-class provincial co-operators. Mazzini's critique of Benthamite utilitarianism was expressed in his attacks on materialism (which emerged more clearly in the 1850s) and atheism. The reactions of Northern co-operators were mixed: their main reference point in 1847 was still Owen's socialist communities, which had embraced Paineite atheism.

Yet, with the crisis of Owenism, things were about to change. Holyoake would provide co-operators with new leadership and vision, abandoning atheism for free thought: this was steeped in the religious conscience. Departing from his youthful atheist positions, too close to the materialism and utilitarianism of socialism, Holyoake founded the ill-defined space of 'secularism', which married free thought with 'duty'. In a revealing letter to Holyoake, Mazzini identified the common philosophical ground that he shared with secularists: 'We pursue the same end – progressive improvement, association, transformation of the corrupted medium in which we are now living, overthrow of all idolatries, shams, lies and conventionalities.' Yet, he argued, 'the *how* and *why*', differed as, while secularists, in 'spurning earth', also spurned heaven, heaven and earth were to him 'the two poles of the axis'. Mazzini's aim was to 'relink' heaven and earth. As he explained to Holyoake, 'You do not understand Immortality; I do not understand Death.' The common aims that Mazzini recognised, however, were important ones: 'All that we are now struggling, hoping, discussing, and fighting for, is a religious question.'[128] Mazzini sympathised with secularists, whom he regarded as honest democrats: their limits, in his view, were in their inability to marry reality with the ideal, earth and heaven.[129] Indeed, within the long connection of Victorian secularists with Mazzini's global vision, 'culture wars' would be seemingly silenced by the mutual recognition of the communality of aims.[130]

---

[126] G. Mazzini, 'From a revolutionary alliance to the United States of Europe' (1850), in Urbinati and Recchia, *Cosmopolitanism*, 132–5 at p. 133.

[127] W. Linton, 'Socialism and communism', *English Republic* (1851), 264–71 at p. 265.

[128] Mazzini to G. J. Holyoake, Apr. 1855, *SEI* liv. 186–93 at pp. 187, 192.

[129] Mazzini to Francesco Crispi, 25 May 1855, *SEI* liv. 216–17.

[130] The term 'culture wars' is drawn from C. Clark and W. Kaiser (eds), *Culture wars: secular-Catholic conflict in nineteenth-century Europe*, Cambridge 2003.

Moreover, in the years which followed the establishment of the Rochdale store atheism lost ground: co-operation was increasing associated with the religious frame of mind, attracting both Holyoake's secularist followers and Unitarians, who believed in the ethical teaching of Christianity, while denying the divinity of Christ.[131] Indeed, after 1848 a further strand of religious spirituality would be felt within the movement, with the involvement of the Christian Socialists, Frederic Maurice, John Ludlow and Edward Vansittart Neale, in the growth of co-operation. In this new context, where Paine's 'infidels' and Owen's atheists appeared to have lost their following, Mazzini's spiritual message of Christianity and humanity, although rooted in vehement hostility towards the papacy and clericalism, found fertile ground.

Mazzini's religion of humanity found a power base among provincial co-operators which would be long-lasting.[132] Based in Leeds, the *Herald of Co-operation* aimed to reach all classes. In its initial address to its readers the organ of the Redemption Society had stated its intention to appeal to a wide section of society:

> the Redemption Society knows of no party either in religion or politics. Its project is primarily economical. Men of all sects and all parties have, during its short existence joined it.... The legislator, the minister of religion, the philosopher, the rich and the poor, all can, all ought to support it.... The Redemption Society has now upwards of 600 contributors'.[133]

Beyond the wide range of subscribers, Yorkshire working-class 'common readers' were able to tap into current debates on co-operation by frequenting the very successful 'Leeds Mechanics' Institute and Literary Society', which would become in 1860, under Hole's vigilant eye, 'the largest and most successful in the kingdom'.[134] Here, as Hole asserted, 'Newspapers and Magazines' had 'succeeded; and for his three pence a week, the working man' not only could 'command, besides the advantages of a reading room well supplied, the use of a large library', but could also 'attend the best lectures, and see all the telegraphic dispatches as well as the wealthy man' could see them in his club.[135]

It is debatable whether as early as the 1840s 'the working man', as Hole put it, would have entered the Mechanics' Institute. In April 1842 Edward Baines, editor of the middle-class newspaper, the *Leeds Mercury*, wrote in his paper that there were not enough working men flocking to the Mechanics'

---

[131] Biagini first highlighted the important connection between Unitarians and Mazzini: *Liberty*, 47–50.

[132] For Mazzini's long legacy amongst co-operators see Sutcliffe, 'Mazzini's transnational legacy'.

[133] 'Address to our readers', *Herald of Redemption* (Jan. 1847), 1.

[134] On forms of middle-class sociability in Leeds see Morris, *Class*, 161–204.

[135] J. Hole, *'Light, more light!' On the present state of education*, London 1860, 55.

Institutes, which 'people like him had founded for people like them'.[136] Studies of mechanics' institutes have shown that it was mainly aspiring clerks, schoolteachers and the more educated shop assistants who attended the classes.[137] Yet the picture was possibly more nuanced than this: Leeds Mechanics' Institute had amongst its members artisans and co-operators; mechanics' institutes grouped in 1848 under the Northern Union of Mechanics' Association in Tyneside also boasted a crossover of member-ship spread between co-operative societies and mechanics' institutes.[138] These members' sympathies for Owenite and Chartist ideas would make them discerning readers of the *Northern Star*, the *Leeds Times*, the *People's Journal* and indeed the *Herald of Redemption*, available in the reading rooms. Hole's series of articles on 'Mazzini and Communism', published between November 1847 and April 1848 had every chance of being read, discussed and challenged by Yorkshire co-operators and adult learners frequenting the numerous educational institutions in Leeds.[139]

The circulation of ideas facilitated by the dissemination of radical news-papers was inevitably more marked in some regions than others and varied from one year to the next. In 1844, for example, Holyoake considered that in some rural areas 'there were no village reading rooms. Hetherington's *Poor Man's Guardian* had never been heard of in Stockbridge'.[140] Yet this situation was quickly evolving and individual cases differed. The newsroom of the Rochdale People's Institute, for instance, was deemed to be particu-larly attractive as early as 1846: the *Northern Star*, which critically reported upon Mazzini's 'Thoughts', was one of the papers read there.[141] Mazzini's ideas on democracy and his views on association could equally be pondered by reading co-operators of either working- or middle- class extraction.[142] Beyond the institutes and libraries, popular newspapers were also reaching common readers in coffee-houses, taverns, public houses, beer shops and clubs and, together with the habit in working-class families of reading the weekly newspaper aloud, could magnify the resonance of political ideas by reaching across generations to an ever-widening, working-class audience.

The opportunities for skilled workers to 'encounter' Mazzini were many. Mechanics' institutes proliferated in the late 1840s both in Lancashire

---

[136] Morris, *Class*,164. There is a vast literature on the 'social control' element of these institutions.
[137] Ibid. 167.
[138] Harrison, *Learning and living*, 148; Allen, *Joseph Cowen*, 58.
[139] Harrison, *Learning and living*, 148.
[140] Holyoake, *Sixty years*, i. 199.
[141] Tylecote, *Mechanics' institutes*, 272 n. 4.
[142] McCabe, *Life*, i. 144.

Table 1
Local educational institutions in Leeds, 1860

Year ending April 1860	Total for the sixteen local institutions	Leeds mechanics' institutes	Total
Members	3,247	1,548	4,705
Annual income	£ 1,564	£ 908	£ 2,472
Number of volumes in library	16,494	10,849	27,342
Annual issues	51,555	45,895	97,450
Periodicals	187	72	259
Newspapers	123	42	165
Lectures	93	28	121
Number of pupils in classes	1,140	149*	1,289

Source: Hole, '*Light, more light!*', 80–1.

* Exclusive of 133 in the School of Arts

and Yorkshire and by 1848 they were improving their organisation.[143] The classes taught varied: curiously, the Wakefield Mechanics' Institute set up Italian classes for its members to facilitate their appreciation of opera, an indication that for some aspiring learners at least associating with Italian culture could be read as a mark of 'respectability'.[144] In addition the mutual improvement clubs need to be taken into account: informal reading groups where radical politics was often discussed were so numerous that Richard Altick reckoned that 'there was hardly a village without one'.[145] Their spontaneous generation meant that they were often ephemeral.[146] Sadly, there is no statistical record of them. From 1846 the industrial North also benefited from another important phenomenon, the expansion of friendly societies devoted to the problem of national education. As P. H. J. H Gosden has shown, large and influential associations, such as the *Oddfellows* and the *Foresters*, which 'had far more members than' 'the co-operative societies', also supplied their reading rooms with London and provincial newspapers and periodicals.[147] Besides the mechanics' institutes and friendly societies,

[143] Tylecote, *The mechanics' institutes*, 67.
[144] Ibid. 273.
[145] Altick, *English common reader*, 205.
[146] Rose, *The intellectual life*, 65.
[147] P. H. J. H. Gosden, *The Friendly Societies in England, 1815–75*, Aldershot 1961, 236.

which proliferated around England, Yorkshire in particular experienced a rarely recorded mushrooming of institutions and associations for the diffusion of knowledge, which included literary societies, circulating libraries and smaller institutions. The borough of Leeds counted sixteen of these smaller institutions (*see* Table 1).

The figures confirm the view that, at least in Yorkshire, mechanics' institutes did not fold around 1850, but continued to thrive well into the second half of the century, when interest in the 'Italian question' reached its peak.[148] All associations of this kind were voluntary, and as such were particularly open to 'innovation, adaptation and experimentation'.[149] It was through these loose channels of sociability that Mazzini's ideas, published in an array of Chartist papers and co-operative societies' organs, would reach provincial towns across Yorkshire, the Midlands, Lancashire and beyond. Through the dissemination of his writings, Mazzini was emerging as a more complex figure than the 'Jacobin' friend of French revolutionaries, which was how the *Northern Liberator* had described him soon after he had arrived on British shores. Victorian radicals would become familiar with the his thoughts and style. The presence of Mazzini's works on the shelves of co-operative libraries around the country would indeed remain a feature recorded well into the 1890s.[150]

---

[148] J. Laurent, 'Science, society and politics in late nineteenth-century England: a further look at mechanics' institutes', *Social Studies of Science* xiv (1984), 585–619.

[149] Morris, *Class*, 168.

[150] Anon., *Two hundred and fifty good books for co-operative libraries*, Manchester 1894, 13.

2

'Joseph Mazzini': Learning and Living his Mission, 1849–51

'I shall henceforth place Ernest Jones, if not as the most talented man amongst the democrats of England, at least I shall put him in the first rank, for truly he deserves such a place: I will call him the English Mazzini.'[1]

The episode of the Roman Republic gained Mazzini some keen followers in the English provinces. Chartist and republican in background, these radicals were self-educated provincial workers, who embraced Mazzini's doctrine, trusting it with a passion. They expressed their feelings in the private sphere by revealing their innermost emotions in the trusted pages of a journal, or in the public sphere in the poetical compositions that they contributed to the Chartist press. Most patently they shared their emotions in mechanics' institutes, republican families, Chartist branches, in short, wherever the web of self-improvement welcomed debates on international questions.

The early support for Italy which could be found amongst provincial radicals, such as Linton, Thomas Cooper and W. E. Adams would become a deeply-rooted allegiance to Mazzini, able to empower radical followers to weather the signs of Mazzinian dissent when they manifested themselves amongst Italian republicans. Holyoake was an uncompromising Victorian Mazzinian at heart. Yet, as editor of the *Reasoner*, he erred towards cautious compromise, poised between cultivating affection for Mazzini among radical, working-class admirers and reassuring his wider readership, inclined to be suspicious of republican ambitions. In the years between 1849 and 1851 building bridges between opposing factions was one of Holyoake's concerns. In the light of the tensions which surfaced amongst Italian democrats following the fall of the Roman Republic his caution was justified: defections were in sight, and Mazzini's falling-out with French socialists would soon complicate the picture further. Yet, for some British radicals, the experience and memory of the Roman Republic had all the characteristics of a 'myth'.[2]

British reactions to the Roman Republic, in 1849, have lately been the focus of historiographical revisionism. For many years historians concurred that it was only in the aftermath of the bloody intervention of French

---

[1]   Adams journal, entry for 15 July 1850, AP, AIISH, 0211/1995.

[2]   Mastellone referred to a 'European myth' of the Roman Republic in 'Garibaldi e i "red republicans"', in A. M. L. Del Grosso (ed.), *Garibaldi nel pensiero politico europeo*, Florence 2010, 33–6 at p.34.

troops in Rome, which crushed the Republic, that public opinion in Britain became sensitive to the Italians' plight.[3] By extending the research beyond the remit of the conservative press, Mastellone was at the forefront of historiographical reinterpretations, demonstrating that the *Northern Star* had been supporting the constituent assembly of Rome from its outset (*Northern Star*, 24 February), well before its brutal repression by the French (3 July) and the tardy international condemnation of their intervention.[4] Mastellone unequivocally mapped radicals' celebration of Mazzini's leadership and their prompt reactions to the 'siege of Rome' within the capital.[5] In line with this recent historiographical direction, Giuseppe Monsagrati nuanced earlier arguments on the belated reactions of the British by showing how the republican foreign minister, Carlo Rusconi, reaching London in the spring of 1849, had been impressed by the Londoners' enthusiastic display of support for the new government in Rome.[6] Although this modified perspective has helped to redress earlier interpretations, searching beyond the protracted diffidence of *The Times*, Britain's 'peripheries' have not been analysed.

That prompt support for the Roman Republic would be found in the metropolis is not so remarkable: not only did the capital provide the hub for the People's International League, but Mazzini could also count on another powerful base of middle-class supporters, his Nonconformist London friends.[7] This group of 'faithful Mazzinians' gathered at the Unitarian, radical Whittington Club (established in 1846), which offered London clerks recreation, a reading room and a library.[8] Here Mazzini, talking about the 'Italian question', had 'made converts', drawing parallels between Cromwell's fight for England's liberty and the need for 'physical force' in Italy's quest for freedom.[9] Revealingly, it was not only Chartist papers, like the *Northern Star*, which were prompt in welcoming the Roman Republic but also the

[3]   Laven, 'Mazzini', 268; G. Monsagrati, 'Alle prese con la democrazia: Gran Bretagna e USA di fronte alla Repubblica Romana', *RSR* lxxxvi (1999), 279–306.

[4]   Mastellone, *Mazzini, scrittore*, ch. xvi; Mack Smith, *Mazzini*, 74–5.

[5]   Mastellone, *Mazzini, scrittore*, 196–7.

[6]   C. Rusconi, *La repubblica romana del 1849*, Rome 1879, 63–6, quoted in Giuseppe Monsagrati, 'Nella morsa delle potenze: la politica estera della repubblica romana', in C. Cipolla (ed.), *Il sogno di Garibaldi*, Milan 2013, 79–90. Indeed, on 19 May 1849, the *Illustrated London News* had dedicated an encomiastic article to the 'roman triumvir', including a portrait of Mazzini.

[7]   Biagini, 'Mazzini and anticlericalism', 149.

[8]   The definition is in Morelli, *Mazzini in Inghilterra*, 96. In *Romance of Italy*, ch. iii, O'Connor referred to this group of supporters as being attracted to the 'romance of liberal politics'.

[9]   Jessie White Mario, *The birth of modern Italy*, London 1909, 140–1. For the myth of Cromwell amongst Victorian radicals see ch. 4 below, and also Biagini, *Liberty*, 47–50, and B. Worden, 'The Victorians and Cromwell', in Collini, Whatmore and Young, *History, religion and culture*, 112–35, and *Roundhead reputations: the English civil wars and passions of posterity*, London 2001, 215–95.

London-based *Nonconformist*, organ of middle-class Liberal Dissenters. As early as 21 February that paper celebrated the end of 'priestley hierarchy'.[10] Following the siege of Rome, Jerrold Durrell, the radical founder of the Whittington Club, proposed a subscription for a 'Mazzini medal' to mark British support for the Roman Republic.[11]

The combined action of middle-class dissenting Liberal Londoners and the Chartist network of the London-based People's International League therefore granted Mazzini and the Roman Republic a metropolitan platform of support from the start. Yet how did the news of the Roman Republic percolate and echo in the radical circles outside the metropolis? Surveying reports appearing in a handful of provincial Chartist papers, this chapter shows how sensitive editors ensured that the news from Rome reached the radical readership of the peripheries, spreading early awareness of Italy's plight in provincial reading rooms frequented by self-improving artisans. Since the Roman Republic represented an important turning point in the way in which British Protestants looked towards the Italian Risorgimento, this chapter analyses which papers informed radical provincial readers; who were the working men who read the papers; and where these 'common readers', ignited by passion and faith in Mazzini's 'mission', discussed the exile's vision for 'humanity'.[12]

Underscoring the timely provincial dissemination of reports on the Roman Republic is critical, as the new perspective gained brings into question the hitherto undisputed view that the Society of Friends of Italy (SFI), established in 1851, in propagating news on Italian freedom constituted an *avant-garde* which penetrated virgin territories in provincial England.[13] Indeed, while it is true that the SFI was an outpost for Italian propaganda in the regions, aimed at drawing financial subscriptions from the well-to-do bourgeoisie, it was not the cause which was new to the provinces, but the language of moderation and liberty in which Italy's plight was now cloaked.

In Rome

Salvo Mastellone's analysis of the coverage of the Roman Republic by the *Northern Star* went a long way towards correcting the view, underlined by

[10] *The Nonconformist*, 21 Feb. 1849, 143, quoted in Biagini, 'Mazzini and anticlericalism', 152. The Roman Republic was declared on 9 February.

[11] Jerrold Durrell's letter was reproduced in the *Northern Star* (11 Aug. 1849) and provincial papers (*Leicestershire Mercury*, 4 Aug. 1849).

[12] For Victorians' understanding of the meaning of 'humanity' in relation to 'patriotism' see G. Varouxakis, '"Patriotism", "cosmopolitanism" and "humanity" in Victorian political thought', *EJPT* v/1 (2006), 100–18.

[13] Morelli, *L'Inghilterra di Mazzini*, 115; Rothney, 'La società degli amici', 22; O'Connor, *Romance of Italy*, 78; Finn, *After Chartism*, 166.

Finn, that due to Fergus O'Connor's aversion, only a few columns of the paper were devoted to foreign affairs.[14] The timing of the proclamation of the Roman Republic, on 9 February 1849, came as Chartism was at its lowest ebb, having entered a phase of rapid decline following what was referred to by contemporaries as the 'fiasco' of the Kennington Common demonstration in April 1848.[15]

Indeed, that same month Pius IX had changed the course of Italy's Risorgimento by declaring in his famous 'allocution' that, despite the popular national enthusiasm which had grown throughout the peninsula and which he had helped to generate, he could not declare war against Catholic Austria, and, therefore, Catholics should oppose militant nationalism. It was then that the 'neo-Guelph moment', which had fed the recent national hope that Italy's regeneration would be realised under the guidance of a liberal pope, evaporated.[16] Even Manchester workers, attending the local mechanics' institute, had learned at a lecture that the present pope was 'deservedly popular', 'being the most enlightened and liberal' that Rome had seen for centuries.[17] Yet, overnight, the Catholic Church became associated with the anti-Risorgimento – and the Italian Risorgimento turned anti-Catholic.[18]

Weeks of rioting in Rome eventually culminated in Pius IX's flight to Gaeta in November 1848.[19] On his arrival in Rome Mazzini's first aim was to restore calm, sweeping away any sense of hostility between patriotism and religion: quoting Cromwell, he asked Romans to put their trust in God and keep their powder dry.[20] The formation of a republican government headed by the triumvirs Mazzini, Saffi and Carlo Armellini followed in March 1849. In July 1849 a constitution was penned for the citizens of the Republic, declaring that sovereignty was by eternal right vested in the people, whose civil and political rights were affirmed. On confessional issues the constitu-

---

14 Mastellone, *Mazzini scrittore*, 193–204; Finn, *After Chartism*, 108.

15 H. Cunningham, *The challenge of democracy: Britain, 1832–1918*, Harlow 2001, 49; Chase, *Chartism*, 300–3; H. G. Weisser, *April 10: challenge and response in England in 1848*, Lanham–London 1983; D. Thompson, *The Chartists: popular politics in the industrial revolution*, New York 1984, 332–5.

16 The inspiration for the movement, which sought to offer an alternative to the democrats' idea of unity, was drawn from V. Gioberti's *Primacy of the Italians*, published in 1843.

17 'Mr Buckingham's lectures on Italy', *Manchester Time and Gazette*, 14 Mar. 1848.

18 See Borutta, 'Anti-Catholicism', 191–213.

19 For a summary of the events which led to the Roman Republic see G. Monsagrati, 'La repubblica romana del 1849', in Ridolfi, *Almanacco della repubblica*, 84–96. For more detailed articles see *La repubblica romana nel movimento europeo tra il 1848 e il 1849*, RSR, special issue, lxxxvi (1999), and G. Natalini, *Storia della repubblica romana del quarantanove*, Rome 2000.

20 Mack Smith, *Mazzini*, 65.

tion stated that religious belief would not affect civil and political rights.[21] As Giorgio Spini underlined, the experience of the Roman Republic represented a defining turning point in the relationship between the Italian Risorgimento and the Protestant world.[22] Conservative Protestants started to look at Italy's political, moral and religious resurgence with new interest.[23]

The five months devoted to republic-building in Rome were marred, however, by the repeated attacks of Louis Napoleon's troops, sent in response to the pope's appeal for help to Catholic Europe. Republicans across the world were baffled by the change of policy in Paris, where Ledru Rollin, until recently leader of the 'red' republic, had been silenced by Louis Napoleon; equally, republicans were inspired by the brave defence of the city. Mazzini had emerged as the true leader of the short-lived republic, yet reports from Rome had also introduced most British readers to the name of Garibaldi.[24] Indeed at this stage in Britain Garibaldi and Mazzini were regarded as two Italian revolutionary allies working towards a common end.[25] As the French advanced in their military offensive, provincial Chartist readers received the news from Rome with bated breath.

Chartist poets of the Roman Republic

British travellers in Rome, meanwhile, found the Roman siege a nuisance. Edward Lear was positively annoyed by the events which disrupted his *grand tour*, leading him to abandon Rome in haste. Arthur Hugh Clough, a Fellow of Oriel, who remained in the Eternal City, wrote an epistolary novel in five cantos, describing the siege through the eyes of a supercilious traveller, alternating – in his display of *sang froid* – cynical detachment and affected indifference. Although the verses in Clough's *Amours de voyage* immortalised a tourist in besieged Rome, the tone chosen to describe the dramatic events was understatement. This was not the language of Chartist poets.[26] They were far from the action; they could not afford continental travel; they could only 'imagine' the Roman Republic, which Mazzini's 'people' were

---

[21] E. Biagini, 'Citizenship and religion in the Italian constitutions, 1796–1849', *History of European Ideas* xxxvii/2 (2011), 211–17

[22] Spini, *Risorgimento e protestanti*, 225.

[23] Idem, 'Mazzini e la dimensione religiosa', 257. For the admiration of conservatives for Mazzini's administrative and diplomatic skills see Mack Smith, *Mazzini*, 67, and Recchia and Urbinati, *Cosmopolitanism*, 5.

[24] *NS* (Jan.–Sept. 1849).

[25] *The Times* (20 Oct. 1849) referred to 'Mazzini, Garibaldi and their band'.

[26] On Clough's poem see R. D'Agnillo, '"Now in happier air": Arthur Hugh Clough's "Amours de voyage" and Italian republicanism', in Vescovi, Villa and Vita, *The Victorians and Italy*, 99–112.

Fig. 2. 'The French cock and the Roman eagle', *Punch* xvi (Jan. – June 1849), 263.

defending, combining 'moral force' and 'physical force'. At home, provincial Chartists read about it, and they wrote about it – with a passion.

Provincial Chartist readers were kept abreast of the events in Rome by the *Northern Star* and by other popular papers, locally distributed, which variously professed their sympathies towards the republican cause. These included the radical *Punch* (established in 1841), heavily consumed in Leeds and the Yorkshire towns, the northern-circulating *Cooper's Journal* (1850), Linton's *English Republic* (1851–5), first published in Leeds, and Holyoake's *Reasoner* (1846–60), known to be one of the most popular free-thinking papers sold in Manchester.[27]

Punch was particularly timely in its outright condemnation of the French, albeit expressing this in the most light-hearted play on words.[28] In an 'Ode

[27] The figures are given by Abel Heywood, 'a Manchester bookseller, publisher and wholesale newsagent' quoted in Altick, *The English common reader*, 351.

[28] The Leeds editor Samuel Smiles estimated that in 1846 Punch was the most popular periodical. Between 1842 and 1851 it was at its most radical thanks to the then editor Jack Lemon: R. D. Altick, *Punch: the lively youth of a British institution, 1841–1845*, Columbus [1997]. Circulation reached 6,000 copies in the early years: Brian Maidment, 'Punch', *DNCJ*, 517–19.

to Louis Napoleon – French and Roman Republicans' the paper scorned the way in which the French defended their own 'République' while quashing the Roman one, and condemned British non-intervention in verse, affirming that: 'But Alas! We can't crow over the pope's overthrow/ And be joyful for Rome's revolution;/ For in place of his throne,/We should then have to own/ A republic – abhorr'd institution!'[29] Further bitter humour was steered towards France in illustrations depicting the Gallic cock set against a proud and chained Roman eagle (*see* Figure 2).[30]

The Roman Republic also provided inspiration for a flurry of politically radical poems dedicated to Mazzini. These were an unconventional expression of the 'poetry of the Risorgimento': they were a manifesto of Victorian Mazzinians' admiration for the 'calm courage' of the 'Triumvir' (Mazzini), their condemnation of the 'brutish force' of the 'fierce' invader' and their celebration of new and ancient 'heroes' and 'martyrs'. In *Punch*, the words, 'Bravo Mazzini!', gave rhythm to the flow of the verses, evoking the glories of ancient Rome:

> BRAVO, MAZZINI!
>
> Through brutish force the game has won,
> Triumvir, thou hast nobly done;
> Calm courage in a rightful cause
> Gains thee a loftier world's applause;
> And Rome's old heroes from their spheres
> Shout, chiming in with British cheers
>   BRAVO, Mazzini!
>
> He who, as now, in time of youre,
> Tyrannic rule when to restore
> In Rome a fierce invader sought,
> Accounted pain and death as nought,
> His hand unshrinking in the flames;
> He, Mutius SCAEVOLA, exclaims,
>   BRAVO, Mazzini!
>
> He who the fearful gulf defied,
> Which, in the Forum, yawning wide,
> Gaped for a victim to appease
> The ire of wrathful deities,
> A self-devoted sacrifice;
> Behold, the dauntless CURTIUS cries,
>   BRAVO, Mazzini!
>
> And they, the grandsire, sire and son,
> Who each their country's safety won,

---

[29] 'French and Roman Republicans', and 'The True Blues Dilemma', *Punch* xvi (Jan.–Jun. 1849), 214, 259.

[30] 'The French cock and the Roman eagle', ibid. 263.

By meeting voluntary death:
They too, with one united breath,
The plaudits of their brethren swell:
The DECII cry aloud as well
    BRAVO Mazzini!

The martyr to his plighted word,
He who a thousand deaths preferred,
Braving unmoved the direst doom,
To tampering with the weal of Rome;
REGULUS also joins the call
  – While Punch cries ditto to them all –
    BRAVO, MAZZINI![31]

'British cheers' and the world's applause for Mazzini were joined by a chorus of approval from the Roman past, Rome's former republican glory with its ancient 'heroes', whose unforgotten deeds were a beacon for those dreaming of the republic today.

Other provincial radical papers too rose up for Mazzini. In January 1850 Thomas Cooper, one of the founding members of the International League, set out to publish a paper 'devoted to the instruction and elevation of ... the veritable working men of England'. A shoemaker by trade and self-educated Leicester Chartist, Cooper aimed to succeed where he felt that the mechanics' institutes had failed – in addressing unskilled workers.[32] Despite operating for many years in London, Cooper had retained strong links with his provincial audience. Through the pages of his newly founded *Cooper's Journal*, he strove to reach out to workers in every corner of the land, by cultivating his contacts with country agents. Indeed, in his new capacity as editor, he expressly embarked upon a tour in order to renew acquaintances and establish fresh contacts with the provincial vendors: his itinerary included spending some days in Newcastle-upon-Tyne, Alnwick, Carlisle, Stockton-on-Tees, Middlesbrough, York, Leeds, Bradford, Keighley, Wakefield, Huddersfield, Doncaster and Sheffield. On top of a circulation of between 5,000 and 9,000 copies per week, Cooper also produced 50,000 additional bills of which 40,000 were sent to agents, 'mainly in the North'. Amongst the paper's regular readers were factory operatives from Manchester, power-loom weavers from Ashton-under-Lyme, young apprentices from Leicester, workers from the potteries of Staffordshire and others

---

[31] 'Bravo Mazzini', ibid. xvii (July–Dec.) 1849, 35.

[32] S. Roberts, *The Chartist prisoners: the radical lives of Thomas Cooper (1805–92) and Arthur O'Neill (1819–96)*, Oxford 2008, and 'The later career of Thomas Cooper (c. 1845–55)', *Leicester Archaeological and Historical Society Transactions* lxiv (1990), 62–72. On Thomas Cooper see also his autobiography, *Life of Thomas Cooper*, London 1872. On the long tradition of leading radical shoemakers see Chase, *Chartism*, 24, and E. Hobsbawm and J. W. Scott, 'Political shoemakers', in E. Hobsbawm, *Worlds of labour: further studies in the history of labour*, London 1984, 103–30, and *Cooper's Journal* i/1, 5 Jan. 1850.

defining themselves simply as 'radical' and 'young' labourers. Some of these, sending their poetical compositions to the paper, had the pleasure of seeing them published. The topics which fired them up were various, and include political themes. [33]

In supporting internationalism, *Cooper's Journal* was instrumental in the promotion of Mazzinian literature, galvanising enthusiasm for the exile's cause. In March 1850, while reviewing Mazzini's *French intervention in Rome: a letter to Messrs De Tocqueville and De Falloux*, Cooper noted that 'Every earnest working man should read it. One feels as if undergoing an electric shock while perusing it. It is seldom that any Age receives such a lesson of eloquent truth from its GREATEST MAN [sic] of action.' As working-class readers became familiar with the principled integrity of continental revolutionaries, emotions were stirred and poems – to both Mazzini and Kossuth – poured in from provincial workers and were published.[34]

In 1850 William Whitmore, a house painter from Leicester, published a poem 'To Kossuth and Mazzini'.[35] Leicester had become a Chartist stronghold as a result of Cooper's ultra-radical activities in his home town. Whitmore was a local working-class poet and Chartist, who would later come to the attention of the Christian Socialist Tom Hughes, one of the founders of the London Working Men's College. Thanks to Hughes, Whitmore would eventually publish his poems with Macmillans.[36]

In 'To Mazzini and Kossuth', Whitmore's attacks on the 'corruptions' of 'throned powers' (the papacy and the empire) were paired with the celebration of liberty and Italy's past heroes: Cola di Rienzo ('Rienzi'), the medieval tavern-keeper, turned popular leader, who had tried to restore the greatness of republican ancient Rome, and the Polish Tadeusz Kosciuszko, who had led the uprising against imperial Russia in 1794:[37]

> 'Twas the old story! Liberty uprose
> And gloriously her world-wide march begun –
> But to be crushed again by banded foes.
> Yet though now baffled, seemingly undone,
> Ye have, transcendant heroes, our age won
> From tame degeneracy; your life deeds give
> Assurance that the hopes of ages gone, –
> Rienzi's Kosciuszko's souls, – yet alive;

[33] *Cooper's Journal* i/9, 2 Mar. 1850, 150; i/11, 16 Mar. 1850, 166; i/16, 20 Apr. 1850, 246; i/20, 18 May 1850, 310; i/22, 1 June 1850, 342; i/30, 26 Oct. 1850, 471.

[34] Ibid. i/9, 2 Mar. 1850, 140. Claeys indicated Mazzini and Kossuth as 'two immensely popular European republicans' in those years: 'Mazzini', 225–61 at p. 226.

[35] B. Harrison, 'Chartism in Leicester', in Briggs, *Chartist studies*, 145; *Cooper's Journal* i/4, 26 Jan. 1850, 56.

[36] J. F. C. Harrison, *A history of the Working Men's College*, London 1954, 51–2.

[37] Kosciuzko's name had been popularised by Thomas Paine's follower, John Thelwall, a democratic agitator and poet who was arrested for sedition in 1794.

And with them are your names, though now maligned,
In man's deep heart of hearts, Fame's noblest temple, shrined!
Ay, and your cause its failure shall retrieve!
Kossuth, droop not, the Magyar's strength matures:
Mazzini, to thy life's idea still cleave!
Triumph for Right the coming time assures;
The patriot flame, ye kindled, yet endures;
And though a while it smoulder, soon elate, –
Consuming all Time's rubbish, pomps, throned powers,
Corruptions, – 'twill the nations renovate.
The phoenix, Freedom, aye will spring replete
With fresh life-vigour from the ashes of defeat![38]

Whitmore's example was soon emulated by two more sonnets, respectively
'To Mazzini' and 'To Kossuth', both sent in by a Birmingham worker and
poet. The one dedicated 'To Mazzini' reads:

The noble Gracchi to the People's cause,
Devoted heart, and thought, and speech, and life,
Undaunted, though opposed in deadly strife,
By all whose power lay in the ancient laws,
They fell; but others from their ashes rose,
Whose spirits roused by Freedom's holy cry,
Resolved to bravely win, or bravely die.
Again these fell, o'erwhelmed by mighty foes;
Then, doubters deemed no more again for Rome
Would daring Tribunes rise. But this our time
Hath seen thee – noblest, purest, most sublime,
That ever told to earth the tyrant's doom;
And proudly to Rienzi's age-stamped fame,
We join, with hopeful hearts, Mazzini's name![39]

The Birmingham poet was John Alfred Langford, Holyoake's friend, who,
while working as an apprentice chair-maker, had been a student at the local
mechanics' institute. Langford was a member of a people's library and in
1846 had been made honorary secretary of the Birmingham Co-operative
Society, becoming a regular contributor to *Howitt's Journal*. He wrote political pamphlets, as well as poetry, and from 1848 he attended the Church
of the Saviour, established by the charismatic, Mazzinian preacher, George
Dawson. Within the adult courses set up by Dawson, Langford taught evening
classes. Langford was devoted both to self-improvement and to the education of the people. He supported many causes, including the liberty of Italy.
The reference that the poem made to the Gracchi brothers, who had tried
to introduce social reform in ancient Rome, and to Cola di Rienzo, hailed

---

[38] *Cooper's Journal* i/4, 26 Jan. 1850, 56.
[39] Ibid. i/13, 30 Mar.1850, 198.

as a precursor of the Risorgimento, demonstrated Langford's familiarity with Italy's glorious, yet tormented, past.

Victorian representations of Italy's past were influenced by a number of sources: Edward Gibbon's *History of the decline and fall of the Roman Empire*, published in 1776; Lady Morgan's *Italy*, published in 1821; and, most significantly, Sismonde De Sismondi's *Histoire des républiques italiennes du moyen âge*, translated in 1832. These texts contributed towards constructing an image of the traits of the Italian 'character' in relation to their lost 'civic virtue'. Indeed, Sismondi, a Swiss intellectual from Geneva, went so far as to claim that it was in the Italian medieval republics that the seeds of public virtue had been first displayed, subsequently spreading to the rest of Europe.

Linking the ancient freedom of the Italian medieval republics and 'liberty', Sismondi, during his stay in London, actively endeavoured to influence British liberals to favour the Italian cause.[40] He was particularly keen to draw a parallel between England and the Italian medieval communes, where cultural vitality and prosperity were shown to have been directly proportionate to the degree of freedom and self-government secured.[41] Sismondi, like other European progressive intellectuals, also stressed that Catholicism had impaired Italy's economic and cultural development. Mazzini used similar arguments to convince his British audience: he had read the first edition of the *Histoire des républiques italiennes du moyen âge*, published anonymously in 1817, and had drawn and reshaped Sismondi's ideas within his own vision of the history of Italy.[42]

Sismondi's influence on figures like Thomas Carlyle and John Ruskin, whose names were well known to Victorian common readers, led Adrian Lyttelton to suggest a survey of the dissemination of Sismondi's masterpiece in free libraries and working men's colleges. It is known that the close links between Byron and Sismondi enabled the latter's ideas on freedom to reach Chartist circles – and indeed Lyttelton has shown how an 'educated and romantic' Chartist, such as the poet and agitator Ernest Jones, commonly referred to the popular uprisings of the Italian medieval communes.[43]

The poetical references to 'Rienzi', offered by two self-improving workers, suggest that the knowledge of Italy displayed by someone like Jones was also part of the culture of aspirational, working-class, middle-rank radical activists: provincial self-improvers read, understood and celebrated the connec-

---

[40] For the influence exercised by Sismondi on the Holland House circle see A. Lyttelton, 'Sismondi, the republic and liberty: between Italy and England, the city and the nation', *JMIS* xvii/2 (2012), 168–82.

[41] On this see Isabella, *Risorgimento in exile*, 113, and A. Lyttelton 'Sismondi, il mondo britannico e l'Italia del Risorgimento tra passato e presente', in L. Pagliai and F. Sofia (eds), *Sismondi e la nuova Italia*, Florence 2011, 145–80.

[42] A. Nicosia, 'Sismondi e Mazzini', in Mastellone, *Mazzini e gli scrittori politici*, ii. 291–8 at p. 292; M. Ridolfi, 'Visions of republicanism', *JMIS* xiii/4 (2008), 468–79 at pp. 469–70.

[43] Lyttelton 'Sismondi, il mondo britannico', 178.

tion between Italy's medieval republicanism and the Victorian concept of 'liberty' in the radical, working-class press. Whether these amateur, provincial poets had actually read Sismondi is a question that cannot be answered here. However, these poems demonstrate how the links between internationalism and patriotism, which the experience of the 'Roman triumvir' brought to the fore, could stir working men of provincial background.[44] Although the poetical value of the compositions of these self-educated working men was negligible, the poems are remarkable. As J. F. C. Harrison has commented with regards to Chartist poetry in general, 'the wonder was not that it was indifferently done, but that it was done at all'.[45] The poems dedicated to the Roman Republic show how, in 1849, Mazzini's vision for republican Italy was embedded in popular reading and writing practices in provincial England. Langford's credentials as an Italian supporter, displayed in *Cooper's Journal*, would warrant him in 1851 the position of honorary secretary of the Birmingham branch of the Society of Friends of Italy.

Echoing Mazzini's mission in provincial England

Another important radical paper, which was published between 1851 and 1855, was Linton's *English Republic*.[46] First issued in Yorkshire, it attempted 'to adapt Chartism to new needs and conditions', closely monitoring the progress of republican associations in the provinces, and, indeed, 'chronicling their establishment in Bethnal Green, Cambridge and Cheltenham as well as Newcastle, Stockton and Sunderland'.[47] As Mastellone has claimed, the *English Republic* was in fact a 'Mazzinian paper'.[48] Victorian republicans were able to read Mazzini's writings in abundance, including early extracts from the *Duties of man*, and his teachings addressed to Italian operatives in the *Apostolato Popolare*. Such principles were, according to Linton, 'not less applicable in 1851, to our English workmen'.[49]

While Linton's paper was first published well after the pope's authority in Rome had been restored, it still strove to stoke the transnational flames of republicanism, keenly reporting on any signs of republican dissent still rumbling away in the Papal States. Common readers were made aware of the more covert aspects of Mazzini's political strategy and clandestine activities aimed at re-establishing the republic in Rome. The paper opened with an

---

44 For the impact of the two revolutionaries on British radicals see Claeys, 'Mazzini'.

45 Harrison, 'Chartism in Leicester', 146.

46 Mastellone, *Mazzini e Linton*, 89–164. See also J. Allen, 'English Republic', *DNCJ*, 204.

47 Harrison, 'Chartism in Leeds', 96; J. Allen, '"Resurrecting Jerusalem": the late Chartist press in the north-east of England, 1852–9', in Allen and Ashton, *Papers for the people*, 168–89 at p. 172.

48 Mastellone, *Mazzini e Linton*, 89–164.

49 W. Linton, *English Republic*, London 1851–4, 195.

article on Mazzini's 'invisible government', described as 'an extensive and complete organisation pervading Italy, but more developed in Lombardy and Romagna, having for its object Italian unity and independence, and possessing its funds, revenues, arms, soldiers, agents and police'.[50] The *English Republic* was well informed as it was indeed the Papal States (in Romagna) and Lombardy which provided the most fertile ground for the clandestine organisation.[51]

Despite such networks, Linton's representation of Mazzini's following in Italy was rather optimistic, as the fall of the Roman Republic had led to far more division than unity. Italian democrats were gradually defecting. Indeed, the 1848–9 revolutions marked the beginnings of Italy's republican diversity: there were republicans who leaned towards monarchical Piedmont, like Antonio Mordini; republicans with socialistic sympathies, like Giuseppe Ferrari and Carlo Pisacane; republicans in favour of a federal solution, like Carlo Cattaneo and Alberto Mario; and republicans who occasionally fell out with Mazzini, like Filippo De Boni.[52] In the latter group was also Giuseppe Garibaldi. In the aftermath of the 1848–9 defeats many followers would become 'convinced' that their 'democratic and republican beliefs' ought to be 'sacrificed' for the sake of independence and unity. Mazzini's leadership increasingly became contested.[53] Such early divisions, which would become more defined as events unrolled, largely escaped British eyes.

In parallel with the *English Republic*, *Cooper's Journal* and the *Northern Star*, Holyoake's *Reasoner* worked tirelessly to secure support for the Italian cause.[54] First published in London in 1846, the paper had every intention of reaching readers beyond the capital, as the first issue expressed concern about ways to reach 'country subscribers'.[55] Indeed, by 1849 Holyoake was looking for 'an active friend in each town who will identify and deliver one copy weekly to vendors in different towns which will be able to assist the circulation of the *Reasoner*'. According to Royle, at its highest, the paper's circulation reached 5,000.[56]

Aware of the need to defend the Roman Republic against the attacks of 'prejudiced travellers', Holyoake did not rest: in June 1849 he organised through the pages of the *Reasoner* a £1 subscription for 'the families of the brave defenders of the republic'.[57] While meetings in support of this cause

---

[50] Ibid. 287–88.

[51] Mack Smith, *Mazzini*, 79–82.

[52] Recent works on Italian democrats include G. Angelini, *Il Risorgimento democratico: tra unità e federazione*, Milan 2011, and F. Sabetti, *Civilization and self-government: the political thought of Carlo Cattaneo*, Lanham 2010.

[53] P. Ginsborg, *Daniele Manin and the Venetian revolution of 1848–49*, Cambridge 1979, 376.

[54] M. W. Turner and L. Brake, 'The Reasoner', *DNCJ*, 532.

[55] *Reasoner* i/14–15, 3 June 1846.

[56] Ibid. viii/125–6, 22 Aug. 1849; Royle, *Victorian infidels*, 206.

[57] *Reasoner* clviii/360, 6 June 1849; clix/383, 13 June 1849.

took place 'in various parts of the metropolis', as early as June 1849 Holyoake felt the need to appeal to the rest of England, exhorting his readers: 'Could not the same thing be done in the provinces?'[58] Soon the propaganda initiated by his paper found fertile ground amongst provincial readers. On 15 July 1849, only a couple of days after Mazzini left Rome, the Roman Fund received from Mr George Sunter Jr, of Middlesbrough, a contribution of 10s. 'subscribed by a few 'common people' at a picnic party at Eston Nab', 'with their earnest prayers for the total and eternal overthrow of *kingcraft* and *priestcraft*'.[59] The language employed was resonant of Thomas Paine's rhetoric against both royalty and the clergy: while in Middlesborough the secularist tradition was weak, Holyoake could draw on the wide reach of anti-papal feelings.[60] As Royle has indicated, the anti-Catholic argument always 'paid off', boosting sales and also helping the cause of free-thought.[61]

While 'traditional' forms of anti-Catholicism had declined in the early nineteenth century Protestant mobilisation of popular anti-Catholicism increased across Britain between the 1840s and 1850s, reaching its peak in 1850 as the reestablishment of the official Roman Catholic hierarchy in England and Henry Newman's conversion to Catholicism heightened anxieties.[62] It is not surprising therefore that the *Reasoner*'s 'friends in the provinces' chose to tap into anti-Catholic sentiments in order to swell the numbers of contributors.[63] Beyond Mazzini's Unitarian London friends, the fight against 'papal tyranny' could extend support for the Roman Republic across regions, classes and political convictions in Britain.

W. E. Adams: a Mazzinian artisan in Cheltenham

Far from the industrial North, in the genteel town of Cheltenham Spa, the anxieties of some members of the Church of England to safeguard their flock from external encroachments were patently displayed. The energetic evangelical, the Revd Francis Close, who opposed Catholicism, Nonconformity, radicalism, Owenism and temperance with inquisitional zeal, contributed towards polarising political positions in this provincial town: Cheltenham became a centre of radical resistance and a Chartist stronghold.[64] It was within Cheltenham's lively artisan culture that W. E. Adams, born in 1832,

---

58 Ibid. clix/383, 13 June 1849.

59 Ibid. vii/112, 15 Aug. 1849.

60 In Middlesborough Holyoake could count also on the support of the local Chartist printer and postmaster, J. Jordison: Chase, 'Republicanism, 36.

61 Royle, Victorian infidels, 216.

62 Wolffe, *Protestant crusade*, 145–97.

63 *Reasoner* xv/240, 10 Oct. 1849.

64 O. Ashton, *W. E. Adams: Chartist, radical and journalist (1832–1906)*, Whitley Bay 1991, and 'The Mechanics' institute', 25–8.

was formed, a provincial self-educated compositor of Wesleyan background. His intellectual and political development was shaped by the counter-culture of local Chartism. Adams joined the local Chartist branch when he was only fifteen, and while an apprentice printer began his journey of self-improvement.

In 1847 the arrival of the Revd Richard Solly, a Unitarian minister, was an important stepping stone for Adams, who frequented his progressive Working Men's Institute. While Solly's autobiography helped to construct a picture of a conciliatory individual, he has recently been described as an 'earnest radical'.[65] His activities and closeness to the Cheltenham Chartists confirm this. In Cheltenham Solly opened three reading rooms and set up a lending library, where weekly lectures and debates were held. By 1851 his Working Men's Institute counted 651 members and the library held two hundred books. In addition to Solly's progressive initiatives the Cheltenham General Literary Union ran the chapel school-room, supplied with newspapers, including radical ones.[66] It was thanks to access to a variety of local reading rooms that Adams was introduced to Mazzinian literature. He was also able to listen to George Dawson, the charismatic Mazzinian preacher from Birmingham.

It was in educational institutes that Adams's republicanism and internationalism were shaped. On 9 April 1848, while still only sixteen years of age, he started a journal in which he described over many years his enthusiasm for the political events unrolling both in England and on the continent – in Paris, in Hungary, in Poland, in America and in Italy.[67] Beginning the journal on the eve of the Kennington demonstration, Adams displayed the millenarian anticipation which permeated Owenite Chartists and popular Nonconformists in the first half of the nineteenth century.[68] In the aftermath of the Chartist *débâcle* young Adams's millenarian convictions would transfer to Italy. Mazzini's vision of the imminent coming of a new era which he called the 'Third Rome' resonated powerfully with the young Cheltenham Chartist.

In his journal Adams passionately expressed his views on continental revolutionaries: he agreed with Thomas Cooper that Mazzini was the greatest

[65] O. R. Ashton and P. A. Pickering, *Friends of the people: uneasy radicals in the age of the Chartists*, London 2002, 29–53. For the interpretation of the Revd Richard Solly as an agent of 'social control' see R. N. Price, 'The Working Men's Club movement and Victorian social reform ideology', VS xv/2 (1971), 117–47.

[66] Adams journal, entry for 14 July 1850, AP, 0211/1995/0299. See M. Demoor, 'Athaeneum'; J. Mussell, 'Leader'; and A. Humpherys, 'People's Paper', *DNCJ*, 26–8, 351, 489–91. All of these papers published articles on Mazzini.

[67] Ashton's Gramscian perspective led him to downplay the power which Mazzini's religious afflatus had on Adams. Consultation of Adams's journal nuances such perspective.

[68] On millennial republicanism and puritan radicalism see G. Claeys, *Citizens and saints: politics and anti-politics in early British socialism*, Cambridge 1989, 30–6, and Biagini, *Liberty*, 36.

man of the times.[69] Adams, who had read in *Reynolds's Newspaper* the 'stirring, eloquent, beautiful addresses' by Mazzini and Ledru Rollin, referred to these men as 'illustrious'.[70] He was deeply stirred by Mazzini's religious vision of the world, noting in his journal on 15 July 1849 that 'Mazzini proclaims to the world that the catch word of the Religion of the Future is this – "God is God; and Humanity is his Prophet"'. He continued:

> The spirit of Mazzini, the idol of the people, the <u>Devil</u> [*sic*] of tyrants and despots … is found wherever good is to be done, wherever Freedom is the motive action of a great, glorious, though bloody conflict. He wishes to realize those dreams which for some time (too much) are doomed I fear to disappointment. The Fraternity of Nations, Brotherly Love – these are the principles he wishes to see triumphant! … May his prayers be granted immediately by that Great good God, the giver of all Good, the friend of the human race … These are my earnest wishes.[71]

As Owen Ashton eloquently put it, 'in the evolution of Adams's radical political thought if Tom Paine's works had acted as a first stimulus, then Mazzini's doctrines represented a vitally important watershed'.[72] However, as his journal entry indicates, along with Paine's ideals, Adams had also shed his atheist perspective, wholly embracing Mazzini's universal Christianity.

While the Roman Republic was in the throes of its battle for survival, Reynolds's newspapers, readily accessible in local mechanics' institutes, kept working-class readers abreast of developments.[73] Soon after the fall of the republic, *Reynolds's Political Instructor*, Adams's 'firm favourite' paper, featured a portrait of Mazzini on its front page (*see* Figure 3.).[74]

Adams strove to procure for himself all the radical papers, including Harney's *Red Republican* – which published Linton's translation of Mazzini's important manifesto, 'Royalty and republicanism in Italy': this was indeed, according to Emilia Morelli, the first time that Mazzini had openly professed his republican creed to his British readership.[75] It is no wonder that Adams, who owed his introduction to republicanism and Mazzini to Linton, craved

---

69 Adams journal', entry for 14 July 1850, AP, 0211/1995/0299.

70 Reynolds named his sons Kossuth, Mazzini and Ledru Rollin: M. Shirley, 'Reynolds's Weekly Newspaper', *DNCJ*, 540. On *Reynolds's Newspaper* see also A. Humpherys and L. James (eds), *G. W. W. Reynolds: nineteenth-century fiction, politics and the press*, Aldershot 2008, and Adams journal, entry for 14 July 1850, AP , 0211/1995.

71 Adams journal, entry for 15 July 1850, AP, 0211/1995.

72 Ashton, *W. E. Adams*, 50.

73 Adams, *Memoirs*, i 235.

74 R. McWilliam, 'Reynolds's Political Instructor', *DNCJ*, 54. See also Ashton, *W. E. Adams*, 35.

75 Morelli, *Mazzini in Inghilterra*, 104.

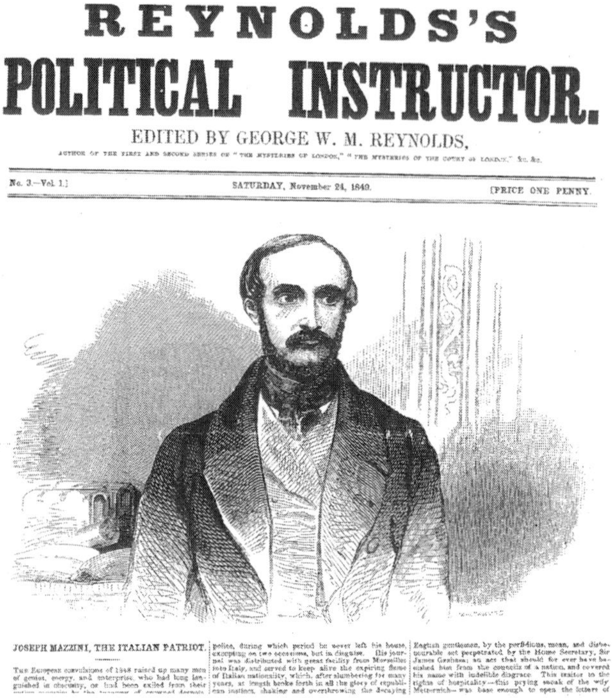

REYNOLDS'S

POLITICAL INSTRUCTOR.

EDITED BY GEORGE W. M. REYNOLDS,

AUTHOR OF THE FIRST AND SECOND SERIES OF "THE MYSTERIES OF LONDON," "THE MYSTERIES OF THE COURT OF LONDON," &c. &c.

No. 3.—Vol. 1.] SATURDAY, November 24, 1849. [PRICE ONE PENNY.

JOSEPH MAZZINI, THE ITALIAN PATRIOT.

The European convulsions of 1848 raised up many men of genius, energy, and enterprise, who had long languished in obscurity, or had been exiled from their ... police, during which period he never left his house, excepting on two occasions, but in disguise. His journal was distributed with great facility from Marseilles into Italy, and served to keep alive the expiring flame of Italian nationality, which, after slumbering for many years, at length broke forth in all the glory of republican instincts, shaking and overthrowing the decaying ... English gentlemen, by the perfidious, mean, and dishonourable act perpetrated by the Home Secretary, Sir James Graham; an act that should for ever have banished him from the councils of a nation, and covered his name with indelible disgrace. This traitor to the rights of hospitality—this prying sneak of the wily Metternich—was base enough to open the letters of

Fig. 3. 'Joseph Mazzini, The Italian patriot', *Reynolds's Political Instructor*, 24 Nov. 1849.

reading it. On 27 March 1851, at the age of eighteen, he founded the Cheltenham Republican Association.[76]

In July 1850 the news that the Chartist orator, Ernest Jones had been released from prison was met with popular acclaim in Halifax. Adams was profoundly struck by Jones's eloquent speeches. Comparing Jones to Mazzini, Adams noted in his journal that he wished 'that the Italian Mazzini and the English Mazzini' might 'both live long to pace the ranks of democracy'.[77] Recording Jones's release gave Adams the opportunity to reflect on Mazzini's recent writings on republicanism:

> now I am talking about this great man, I may as well say that I have just been reading a portion of his celebrated work on Republicanism in Italy. It is, if I am capable of judging its merits one of the most celebrated works in Democracy that has been published this year, so far as I have seen or read: it is a fit companion to his previous work 'The pope in the nineteenth century'.[78]

[76] Adams, *Memoirs*, i. 152, and Adams journal, entry for 23 Mar. 1851, AP, 0211/1995.

[77] Adams journal, entry for 15 July 1850, AP, 0211/1995.

[78] Ibid.

That Adams knew and admired Mazzini's pamphlets, including 'The pope in the nineteenth century' is revealing. The latter had been published in December 1850, with a preface by Mazzini which introduced his thoughts on the religious question, within which, in his mind, 'all great questions agitating the world were resolved'.[79] The commentary was provocatively coloured by the failure of the British to intervene in favour of the Roman Republic. This topic had already been explored by Mazzini when, on 6 August 1849, he had published an article in the *International Magazine* addressed to the British liberal progressive audience: here he had stated that England had understood nothing of what 'was sublime and prophetic in this cry of emancipation, in this protestation in favor of human liberty ... in the face of the Vatican'.[80] His argument, reiterated in 1850, was rendered more forceful by the recent fears which had engulfed British Protestants 'on account of the attempted encroachments of Catholicism': 'Think you that the Pope would have sent his Catholic hierarchy from Gaeta (if the people's banner were still floating at Rome)?'[81] The pamphlet suggested that the liberation of Italy from the papacy and of the Italians from superstition was pivotal for ridding the rest of the world of Catholicism. 'Young Italy', and the Roman Republic, continued Mazzini, had risen against two things: superstition, which deprived people of education and 'all consciousness of the true life of citizens', and its opposite, materialism, which had only rights and enjoyment, not duty, at its heart. Only by emancipating itself from superstition and materialism could Italy become a nation. Yet Britain had not rendered testimony to the unity of the human race.

Mazzini went even further in the preface, pointing to the 'moderate' party, which had crossed the democrats' path: 'this party has no *belief* [sic], it has only opinions, it accommodates everything in turn ..., it seeks material strength, it has called itself opportunist'. Mazzini commented: 'Strange, that this is the party which in England, in this ancient land of Liberty and of good sense, finds favour; whilst the popular party ... is received coldly.'[82]

Due to the circulation of Mazzini's pamphlets in radical circles throughout Britain, there was real potential for these powerful ideas to penetrate the Nonconformist conscience of common readers. Mazzini appealed to the readers' sense of the 'sacredness' of 'liberty', to their sensitivity to the equation between religious and political belief, duty to one's conscience and duty

---

[79] The pamphlet had been praised by George Sand in a preface to the French edition of 'Republic and Royalty'. The second issue of the *Red Republican* (29 June) had published translated extracts from the 'Republic and Royalty' writing, including Sand's preface.

[80] G. Mazzini, 'Concerning the fall of the Roman Republic (1849)', in Recchia and Urbinati, *Cosmopolitanism*, 208–12 at p. 211.

[81] Mazzini also condemned the lack of Britain's intervention in the *Northern Star* on 8 Sept. 1849 (reported in Mastellone, *Mazzini scrittore*, 197–201). However this new pamphlet was more powerful, as it was written *after* the 'Papal aggression'.

[82] G. Mazzini, *The pope and the nineteenth century*, London 1850.

to liberty and humanity. Mazzini's language was carefully crafted, as he did not pander to the missionary aspirations of some Protestants, Evangelicals in particular. Indeed he wrote:

> We have sometimes been asked, if once emancipated, we should proclaim ourselves Protestants. It is not for individuals to reply. The country free to interrogate itself, will follow the inspiration that God will send it.... But this, with my hand upon my heart, I can answer to them. Catholicism is dead. Religion is eternal. It will be the soul; the thought of the new world.[83]

As for many self-educated workers, reading for Adams was part of a shared experience. Mazzini's views were aired and discussed at the evening gatherings of the Cheltenham Chartists, held at the Working Men's Institute. The scheduled lectures of the Cheltenham Republican Association included Thomas Cooper's 'Republican Rome and papal Rome': no doubt Mazzini's perspective was closely scrutinised.[84] Adams shared his ideas at the weekly meetings of his republican 'family' in Cheltenham, read the papers aloud whenever chairing a Chartist meeting, initiated discussions advocating the rights of women, attended debates on land reform, condemned British imperialism and the claims of 'civilisation' and also discussed Mazzini's doctrines with friends. Cole and James Glover, a handyman and gardener, would join him after work on late evening walks in Cheltenham park, where the merits of 'Republicanism and Christianity', 'as expounded in the *Duties of Man*' were the cause of heated discussions and the merits of the Italian Petition were debated.[85] Adams however did not limit his activities to reading and discussing Mazzini. Determined to propagate the Italian exile's ideals amongst other workers he wrote essays on topical 'Mazzinian' subjects such as 'faith', 'heroism', 'future' and 'mission': his clear intention was to educate fellow workers frequenting Solly's Working Men's Institute.[86]

On 21 March 1851 the delivery of Adams's essay, 'Man's mission' 'was intended more as a lesson to those who heard it than as an attempt to display the capabilities of an individual' and, as such, it was 'read to the members of the Essay Class of the Working Men's Institute'.[87] Having equated Mazzini

---

[83] Ibid. reproduced in Mastellone, *Mazzini scrittore*, 197–201.

[84] See also Ashton, *W. E. Adams*, 32, and Adams journal, entry for 23 Mar. 1851, AP, 0211/1995.

[85] Linton named as 'families' the local groups of republicans who met, 'certainly not less often than once a week', to discuss each member's weekly progress in proselytising ideas: see W. Linton, 'Republican organisations', *English Republic* (1851), 58. Adams journal, entries for 5 Nov. 1853, AP , 0211/1995/0217; 18, 25 Nov. 1853, 0211/1995/0220; 15 July 1853, AP, 0211/1995.

[86] W. E. Adams, 'Man's mission', 21 Mar. 1851, AP, 0211/1995/0603. Other essays included 'The Future', 'Heroism' and 'Faith', AP, 0211/1995/0618; 0211/1995/0666; 0211/1995/0647.

[87] Adams, 'Man's mission', 21 Mar. 1851, AP, 0211/1995/0603.

with Socrates, Plato, Hegel, Rousseau, Robespierre and Franklin, Adams expounded on his doctrine and on the necessity of uniting happiness with duty. His undoubtedly heavy tone was probably not the most inspiring medium to communicate Mazzini's vision, as Adams admitted that the effects of the reading had not been 'as complete as was desired'. 'However', concluded an optimistic Adams, 'I have done my best', adding: 'I thought my success was not as great as I could wish: my motto shall be "Nil desperandum"'. Despair, indeed, Adams would not. In subsequent years he would embrace new opportunities to propagate Mazzinian republican ideals. In a letter written to Linton on the first anniversary of the *English Republic*, Adams, 'considering that Thought and Action are inseparable', had vouched his determination 'to battle on and bravely for the accomplishment of that grand reality – the English Republic'.[88] Indeed, he would do so in the years to come: when working as a provincial journalist and editor he would tirelessly promote not only the future coming of an English Republic, but also the establishment of Mazzini's republican Italy.

The Society of Friends of Italy and the *Reasoner*

The defeat of the Roman Republic had also increased Mazzini's popularity in Britain amongst more conservative observers. The threat of republicanism averted, the cause of Italy – fuelled by both anti-French sentiment and fear of the reestablishment of an official Roman Catholic hierarchy in England – became more widely acceptable in Britain, acquiring broader public support through the fundraising effort of the Italian Refugees Fund and, eventually, through the establishment of the Society of Friends of Italy on 15 May 1851.[89]

In December 1851 Louis Napoleon's *coup d'état* further convinced Mazzini that any democratic initiative in Europe could only come from Britain. In a violent attack he accused French socialists of having allowed the degeneration of democracy by mistakenly directing their accusations at the power of the bourgeoisie. The socialist exiles responded with a damning reply published, to Mazzini's regret, in the progressive *Leader*, established in 1850 by Thornton Leigh Hunt and George Henry Lewes.[90] While the *Leader* gave space to the French, allowing 'Blanc unlimited use of its columns to defend French republicanism from Mazzini's outbursts', Linton's *English Republic*

---

[88] W. E. Adams to W. Linton (1852?), FL AGF.

[89] Monsagrati, 'Alle prese'; Morelli, *L'Inghilterra di Mazzini*, 112–15; Rothney, 'La società degli amici', 22; The Italian Refugees Fund was founded in London in August 1849 by friends of Mazzini and former members of the People's International League.

[90] On this dispute see Claeys, 'Mazzini', 234–6. On the *Leader* see Holyoake, *Sixty years*, 235–42.

supported him, and the Mazzinians' religious republicanism.[91] Inevitably, the diatribe between the papers was counterproductive, not only because it created a split between English papers that until then had been unanimously 'sympathetic' to the Italian exile, but also because it generated what Miles Taylor has defined as 'a confusion of loyalties for some of Mazzini's English friends'.[92]

In this context the founding of the Society of Friends of Italy may be seen as another initiative which adversely affected the unity of purpose of Mazzini's followers in Britain. Due to its ambition to reach the widest possible British public, the SFI avoided radical tones. Considered the key to promoting in the provinces the plight of Italian independence, the main weakness of the Society of Friends of Italy was the very loose association of its members, whose differences 'in class and interests', beyond their support for Italy's freedom, were, according to John Rothney, a 'fatal hindrance' to the Mazzinian cause.[93] Indeed, many liberal supporters of the Italian cause were likely to back the party of 'moderates' which Mazzini had vehemently condemned. Mack Smith has shown how the Society of Friends of Italy 'had no political affiliation' and its 'eight hundred members ... represented widely different opinions: Protestant clergy alongside secularists, monarchists together with lifelong republicans'.[94] Detailing the picture further, Finn accurately described the diverse political, religious and social composition of the Friends: significantly, while there were some republican Mazzinians who endorsed the Society of Friends of Italy, such as Adams, Holyoake and Linton, 'Chartists largely avoided the Society'.[95] Mazzini's Unitarian friend, Peter A. Taylor, who was the treasurer, by linking political convictions with anti-Catholic religious feelings, could draw on the heightened public anxieties which had followed the so-called 'papal aggression' in 1850. This helped to widen the pool of supporters of the Society: as Danilo Raponi has highlighted, anti-Catholicism was strong amongst liberals.[96] The diversity of the Society of Friends of Italy was its main distinguishing feature: at the same time it was a fundamental weakness and a function of enlarged British support for the political unification of Italy.

The establishment of the Society of Friends of Italy prompted Holyoake to broaden the message which the *Reasoner* conveyed to its readers. Responding to the need for fundraising expressly voiced by Mazzini in the summer of 1852, the *Reasoner* published an appeal for a 'One Thousand

---

[91] *Leader*, 21 Feb.–27 Mar. 1852; Taylor, *Decline*, 211; Mastellone, *Mazzini scrittore*, 288–89.

[92] Taylor, *Decline*, 211.

[93] Rothney, *La società degli amici*, 30.

[94] Mack Smith, *Mazzini*, 95.

[95] Finn, *After Chartism*, 166.

[96] Raponi, 'Gran Bretagna', 144.

Shilling Subscription for European Freedom'.[97] Initially this was aimed at working men: by tradition 1s. subscriptions, which depended on the appeal and charisma of the men who championed individual causes, had demonstrated the good will of England's workers (*see* Figure 4).

In this case the success of the subscription was, according to Holyoake's recollections, entirely due to 'the influence of Mazzini's great name. Workmen in mill and mine gave because he wished it'.[98] A tangible reward for the subscribers reflected the 'cult-image' which was taking root in provincial working-class households: an engraved card had been 'issued at a shilling each on behalf of funds for European freedom, signed by Mazzini for Italy, Kossuth for Hungary, and Worcell for Poland'. According to Holyoake, writing in 1905, such an engraved card could be found 'still hanging in a little frame in many a weaver's and miner's house in the North of England'.[99] Indeed, the language employed by the *Reasoner* in the early stages of the subscription was suggestive of a working-class tribute to international brotherhood: 'It is the gift of the people to the brave', it stated, 'of British workmen to their brethren abroad.'[100]

Within a few weeks, however, the growing popularity of the Italian cause had greatly diluted the political significance of the subscription. Revealingly, in publishing the names of the subscribers, the *Reasoner* pointedly clarified that 'we are requested to state that the majority of these subscribers, in 1852, have no sympathy with the views of the *Reasoner* but cheerfully aid its object' – an indication of the paper's awareness that its republican ambitions for Italy would not be underwritten by the growing numbers of signatures pleasingly swelling the subscription list.[101] In targeting the 'friends of popular progress in all classes in this country' the 'Shilling Subscription in aid of European Freedom' employed the language of liberalism, not the rhetoric of internationalist brotherhood.[102] As the list of members of the SFI showed, the supporters of Italy were a large community, made up of people of different political inclinations: the SFI, according to Mazzini's recommendations, was also to be backed by a 'Ladies Committee'.[103]

This was evidently a sign of Mazzini's desire to reach women beyond a select circle – that of the radical Ashurst sisters and the metropolitan bazaar organisers gravitating around his Free School. In 1852 the commitment of women to the Italian cause was still limited. Significantly, a powerful article in the *Reasoner*, signed by Sophia Dobson Collet under the pseudonym

---

[97] *Reasoner* xiii/55, 7 July 1852.
[98] G. J. Holyoake, *Bygones worth remembering*, i, London 1905, 211.
[99] Ibid. i. 209.
[100] *Reasoner* xiii/55–7, 7 July 1852.
[101] Ibid. xiii/135.
[102] 'The shilling subscription in aid of European freedom': CP, TWAS, A176.
[103] Mazzini to Emilie Hawkes, 12 May 1851, *SEI* xlv. 258–61 at p. 260.

Fig. 4. 'One thousand shilling subscription for European freedom'. (George Jacob Holyoake Archive, 3/3).

Panthea, appealed to the 'women of England' with vehemence. Calling for sympathy for Italian women, the piece aptly introduced the idea of international 'sisterhood', which paralleled the familiar term of 'brotherhood', closely connecting it with the idea of political freedom.[104] As Alberto Banti has demonstrated, gendered 'parental relation' was central to the Risor-

---

[104] *Reasoner* xiv/215, 15 Sept. 1852.

gimento experience.[105] Panthea lamented that there were not more than twelve women's names among the 500 signatures so far collected by the *Reasoner*'s Shilling Subscription and that only one in nine members of the SFI was female. The gendered propaganda employed the language of internationalism, with 'feminist' overtones.[106]

The analysis in Panthea's article of the effects of despotic policies on the lives of individual households brought together the public and the private sphere in a way which made the condition of Italian women, wives and mothers directly relevant to British women and their concepts of freedom. As the article explained, one of the peculiar effects of despotism was that the wife became 'a meek slave', whose children 'must not ask questions'. 'The home', Panthea argued, 'which should be the nursing place of all highest aspirations and nursing purposes, becomes stagnant and ... loses with its true aims, its holy purity.' Italian women, in other words, were stifled in their moral mission as 'angels of the hearth', a role which Mazzini ascribed to mothers, entrusted with the education of the nation. The denunciation then turned to heartfelt appeal:

> Let it not be said of us, let it not be written in our consciences that at this solemn time (of Liberty against Barbarism) the women of England were so blinded by frivolity and ignorance as not to throw their hearts into the scale of Freedom, or sympathise in the woes of their down-trodden sisters![107]

Amongst the worthy examples of Italian women Mazzini's mother, Maria Drago Mazzini, whose recent death had profoundly shaken her exiled and devoted son, was quoted.[108] Her death on 9 August 1852 had spurred his English friends to rally around the mourning exile, who had not seen his mother since 1848: from then on their role in his life would be much enhanced.[109]

Panthea's article stressed how exile had forced Italian families to languish in 'despotically-enforced separations', underlining thus the romantic tension between public duty and family affections, a trope dear to a number of Risorgimento texts.[110] The author showed sensitivity to the families torn apart, to maternal courage and to patriotic female bravery which defined the Risorgi-

---

105 See the 'Indirizzo delle donne lombarde alle donne degli Stati Sardi', quoted in A. M. Banti, *La nazione del risorgimento*, Turin 2006, 154.

106 'A woman's plea for Italian liberty', *Reasoner* xiv/215, 15 Sept. 1852.

107 Ibid.

108 On Mazzini's mother see Marina D'Amelia, *La mamma*, Bologna 2005, 54–9.

109 Mack Smith, *Mazzini*, 93.

110 Pictorial representations of these emotions are evident in many of Francesco Hayez's paintings, for example *Pietro Rossi*. For an analysis of these texts in the Risorgimento see A. Lyttelton, 'Creating a national past: history, myth and image in the Risorgimento', in A. R. Ascoli and K. von Hennenberg (eds), *Making and remaking Italy: the cultivation of national identity around the Risorgimento*, Oxford–New York 2001, 27–73.

mento.[111] Panthea sent a double message to the 'Women of England': on the one side there was the traditional view that 'the tenderest homes strengthen the heart for the sternest martyrdoms'. On the other there was a more subtle subtext: Panthea declared that 'while the nunnery and the harem alternate under the reign of despotic "order" – pure homes alone give birth to heroes and set nations free'. 'Women of England' were therefore an integral part of the fight for Puritan, Christian values, against papism and against the Orient: their loyalty to their own country and the values of 'liberty' that Britain stood for would be measured in their engagement to defend their 'sisters' in Italy against despotism and tyranny. Within 'sisterhood' too, therefore, national and transnational sentiments were closely entwined and cosmopolitan patriotism was invoked. Yet, the appeal to women all over England went hand in hand with a masking of the republican project which Mazzini and Victorian radicals still harboured.

The Roman Republic had been a watershed. The dashed hopes of moderate Catholics for a regenerated Italy under a liberal pope projected the national struggle for liberty into a new phase: in the eyes of some British observers the moral and spiritual resurgence of Italy could be linked to a specifically Protestant Risorgimento. Harnessing the revived anticlericalism and anti-popery of the 1850s appeared imperative to Mazzini and his English friends. Mazzini's need to finance his planned insurrections necessitated funds, not simply moral support, from his country of exile. The depoliticised message of the SFI capitalised on growing sympathy for Italy's cause, facilitated further by the publication in 1851 of Gladstone's letters to Lord Aberdeen, which exposed the horrors of the Neapolitan government's prison system.

Despite the growing sympathies of British liberals Mazzini was keen to reassure his republican English friends of his unaltered position. As he had clarified in a letter to Emilie Ashurst Hawkes, in 1848, 'I remain the republican Joseph you know.'[112] It was indeed this 'Joseph' who inspired those English radicals who celebrated him in the late Chartist press and in the republican associations dispersed around the provinces. Crestfallen Chartists and provincial radicals, demoralised by the 'fiasco' of the Kennington demonstration and frustrated by the lack of reform in Britain, mythologised the Roman Republic, which they celebrated in their writings and poetry. English republicans who had briefly seen Mazzini steer Romans towards affirming their civil rights and religious freedom found strength in the millenarian projection of Mazzini's Third Rome: the republic had been defeated, but, like the phoenix, it would soon emerge from the ashes.

---

[111] See M. Bonsanti, 'Amore familiare, amore romantico e amor di patria', in Banti and Ginsborg, *Storia d'Italia*, 127–52.

[112] Mazzini to Hawkes, 30 May 1848, *SEI* xxxv. 189–96 at p. 189.

Responding to the appeals of the late Chartist press, provincial working-class readers expressed their sympathy by consuming the Mazzinian literature found in reading rooms, taking part in debates within republican associations, attending lectures on the Roman Republic at local educational institutes, sending monetary contributions to the Shilling Subscription and, sometimes, writing topically inspired poems. Radical provincial support was therefore not totally 'emasculated', as Laven has affirmed: a minority of radical English Mazzinians, who, beyond the SFI's activities, fed on the news on Italy supplied by the late Chartist press remained. They would prove to be most resilient to the challenges to Mazzini's leadership that lay ahead.[113]

[113] Laven, 'Mazzini', 274.

3

Victorian Mazzinians and Italian Democrats
Defections and Loyalties, 1850–1860

'We do not upbraid Mazzini for having escaped, while his colleagues have perished. He has shewn courage before this. To die for a cause is one of the least things that a single and childless man can do for it. To live and suffer for it is much greater and much braver.'[1]

Historians have stressed that from the mid-1850s Mazzini's influence on his followers was greatly diminished. Contemporary sources and even early hagiographic histories show how the repercussions of the abortive Milanese insurrection of 1853 followed, in 1857, by the double failure of the Genoese uprising and Pisacane's Southern expedition – equally disastrous in their outcomes – had profoundly damaged Mazzini's reputation.[2] More recent historiography has reiterated such interpretations, in both their Italian and British respects.

Salvo Mastellone has underlined how the failed insurrection in Milan kick-started a virulent campaign against Mazzini in *The Times*, which was echoed by other papers.[3] John Rothney stressed how some SFI members became critical of Mazzini's anti-Piedmontese stance.[4] David Laven underlined how the news of Pisacane's death had 'appalled many British sympathisers with the Italian cause', while Maura O'Connor stressed how by the end of the 1850s men and women in Britain had jumped 'on Garibaldi's bandwagon' – leaving 'a handful of enthusiasts' to fight Mazzini's corner.[5]

Small, yet vocal, the minority of Victorian Mazzinians whose belief in republican Italy did not waver has not been given the attention that it deserves; nor has its power to disseminate pro-Mazzinian views through a range of radical papers and pamphlets which reached working-class readers. Rather, episodes of loyalty by Victorian radicals have escaped historiographical scrutiny. While Mack Smith suggestively asserted that in November 1854, on returning to England after the failed insurrection in Milan, Mazzini 'felt better understood' and 'much safer' than at home, he did not explain

---

1   *People's Paper*, 18 July 1857.
2   F. Orsini, *Memoirs and adventures*, London 1857, 189; White Mario, *Birth*, 242–3; King, *Life of Mazzini*, 169–170.
3   Mastellone, *Mazzini scrittore*, 295.
4   Rothney, 'La Società degli amici', 21–58.
5   Laven, 'Mazzini', 276; O'Connor, *Romance of Italy*, 91.

why the exile felt more at ease and who and where those loyal radicals were who openly supported him.[6] This chapter aims to identify Mazzini's British-based loyalists during this testing decade, when so many detractors surfaced on both sides of the Channel. Indeed, a small minority of these were also British radicals, such as David Urquhart's followers. Yet this was mainly a repercussion of the 'currents of radicalism' which in the mid-fifties thwarted British radicalism from within.[7] More importantly, this chapter addresses a point made by Emilia Morelli many years ago when analysing the events of 1856–7: 'too often historical reconstructions of British attitudes towards the Italian unification underestimate the inroads made by Mazzini's activities'.[8] These 'inroads' will be the focus.

Championing foreign causes was an important factor in 1850s radicalism, and papers published during this decade reflect this. Upholding Mazzini's cause could become a vehicle for keeping alive the language of democracy, insurrection and republicanism which the failure of Chartism and the distraction of the Crimean War risked making redundant. Although the average circulation of radical papers could not keep up with that of mainstream papers, largely shaping middle-class public opinion in Britain, the platforms for the dissemination of radical literature increased beyond the traditional mechanics' institutes. In 1850 the channels for accessing Harney's *Red Republican* were still limited, especially in provincial England. In that year, however, the Free Libraries Act crucially reshaped the landscape of opportunities for public reading, not only in London, but particularly in the provinces, where Victorian civic culture, local pride and the ethic of self-improvement were strong. In September 1852 the first Free Public Library opened in Manchester. It was frequented by working-class readers such as W. E. Adams, who lived there in those years. The library stocked Holyoake's paper, the *Reasoner*. The other reading room that Adams frequented in his home town was the Cheltenham General Literary Union, based at the Bay's Hill Chapel school-room. Although this was clearly a minor local institution, established for the 'Moral and Intellectual Improvement' of its members, the array of papers that it stocked provides an insight into the dailies and periodicals available to provincial workers in the mid-fifties. Besides *The Times*, common readers had the chance to read the *Daily News*, the *Leader*, the *People's Paper* and the *Athenaeum*, all of which boasted radical credentials. The Free Libraries Act was the catalyst for a flurry of educational activities: in Birmingham the charismatic preacher, George Dawson, campaigned for the establishment of a Free Library throughout the 1850s, encouraging

---

6   Mack Smith, *Mazzini*, 111.

7   Briggs, *Chartist studies*, 19. This term is borrowed from Biagini and Reid, *Currents of radicalism*.

8   Morelli, *L'Inghilterra di Mazzini*, 160–1.

people 'to go to the libraries and use them'.[9] As Asa Briggs highlighted when describing the high-Victorian era, 'clear thinking was preferred to impulse or prejudice and the battle of ideas to the dictatorship of slogans'.[10] What *The Times* affirmed was not universally accepted without criticism, indeed it was often challenged: radical papers, including the *Westminster Review*, distributed in radical circles in London and Oxford, devoted entire columns to highlighting the perspective of Italian republicans and publishing favourable accounts of Mazzini's actions.

Significantly, on the occasion of the failed Milanese insurrection, which inaugurated a period of condemnation and defection, the *Leader* unequivocally sided with Mazzini and Saffi, dismissing as 'ungenerous nonsense' the accusations of cowardice made against the two ringleaders:

> How shall this be said of Mazzini, who, without even a disguise, confronts the scrutiny of legions of spies; or of Aurelio Saffi, his brother in the Triumvirate, who, at the peril of his life, has bravely traversed the whole of *Central Italy* to convey the orders of Mazzini, and to arrest the hopeless flows of patriot blood?[11]

Words of support from Victorian radicals were a balm for Mazzini. In Italy ranks were closing; Mazzini's claims to a moral victory and the Christian 'sacrifice' of the 'martyrs' of the religion of the nation fell on deaf ears amongst members of the Milanese liberal establishment who had earlier supported him in his insurrectional plans.[12] The mood turned against the 'headquarters from abroad' imposing ideas or determining 'the time and manner of insurrection'.[13] The *Leader*, however, reproduced a lengthy letter from Saffi – 'the noble-hearted brother triumvir of Mazzini'– in which the loyal exile was able to explain his views on events in Milan, absolving Mazzini for his conduct. Radicals were sceptical of 'official' news regarding Mazzini: in April 1854 the news of Mazzini's arrest in Switzerland, reported by *The Times*, was met with suspicion by Linton, who told Adams that he had 'faith in Mazzini's destiny'.[14] As Mastellone has shown, Linton's *English Republic* became the mainstay of Mazzini's defence in the following months. Between July 1853 and September 1854 the paper published a letter of support from Polish democrats, which compared Mazzini to their national hero Kosciuzco, and a number of writings by Mazzini, in which he defended the need for the

[9] A. Ireland, *Recollections of George Dawson and his lectures in Manchester*, Manchester 1882, 22.

[10] Briggs, *Victorian people*, 9.

[11] *Leader*, 12 Mar. 1853, 247.

[12] On 'martyrs' see G. Mazzini, 'Faith and the future' (1835), in Bolton King, *Essays by Joseph Mazzini*, London 1894, 38–9, and Riall, 'Martyr cults'.

[13] Sarti, *Mazzini*, 162.

[14] Adams journal, entry for Sept. 1854, AP, 0211/1995/0902.

attempted insurrection in Milan and advocated a 'Party of Action'. During these same months Mazzini lobbied frantically with his friend, Peter Taylor, for the continued support of the SFI and exerted pressure for a parliamentary petition calling upon England to rise against despotism[15]

Saffi's support was also crucial. Following the establishment of the Party of Action, which replaced 'Young Italy' in 1853, Mazzini struggled to maintain his authority: alternative solutions were being flagged up by recently-arrived revolutionary exiles. Their presence in England was certainly a reason for concern.[16] Mazzini's primacy was beginning to be set against the growing popularity of Garibaldi, who was known to have become, during the defence of the Roman Republic, the 'man of the occasion'.[17] Felice Orsini, miraculously escaped from the Austrian dungeons in Mantua in 1856, was drawing crowds in the North of England as 'celebrity' exile, all the while refusing to rally to Mazzini's party. In addition, on the diplomatic front, following the participation of Piedmont in the Crimean War, the emergence of Cavour as a skilful negotiator for the peace settlements inaugurated an entirely new phase: the risk that the republican programme might fall victim to a pincer movement driven by the moderates took definitive shape. Despite all this, the unofficial, popular Risorgimento took strength from the transnational support for Mazzini offered by radical, Chartist, republican strongholds in various corners of Britain.

Saffi in Oxford: a loyal exile

The resilience of Mazzini's radical followers owed much to Saffi. Following the collapse of the Roman Republic, Saffi had in 1851 joined the group of Mazzinian exiles residing in London.[18] He had an easy introduction into English society. Due to his reputation as a Roman triumvir and his intimate friendship with Mazzini, he was soon able to meet Holyoake, Stansfeld, Leigh Hunt, the Ashursts and the Craufurds. Bearing letters of introduction from Carlyle, Benjamin Jowett and many others, he moved to Oxford in 1853, where for some years he taught Italian at the Taylorian Institute.[19]

Oxford was a particularly attractive environment for Saffi. The university gathered in those years a generation of young enthusiastic scholars and students who were galvanised by three political topics: the abolition of University Tests; the crimes of Napoleon III; and foreign affairs, especially

---

[15] Mastellone, *Mazzini scrittore*, 295–315.

[16] Laven, 'Mazzini', 274. There is no evidence of such feelings in Sarti, *Mazzini*, 168–9, 178–9.

[17] See *The Lady's Newspaper*, 19 May 1849, quoted in Riall, *Garibaldi*, 83.

[18] L. Gazzetta, *Contributo alla storia del mazzinianesimo femminile*, Milan 2003, 33; J.White Mario to A. Saffi, 22 Oct. 1856, FS, BCAB, ii/16/1, 15.

[19] See collection of letters at FS, BCAB, ix/87/3.

Italy. Individuals there included the radical Glaswegian John Nichol, a friend and 'ardent believer' in Mazzini, whom he had met in 1850; the idealist philosopher T. H. Green; the young poet Algernon C. Swinburne; and a small number of others who gathered around the philo-Italian 'Old Mortality' society.[20] In Oxford, Saffi was responsible not only for teaching Italian, but for introducing a number of graduates to Mazzinian ideas, including both the positivist, Frederic Harrison, who embraced republicanism, and James Bryce, who, having studied Italian with Saffi, would leave Oxford imbued with Mazzinian ideals.[21] Sympathetic Oxford academics included not only T. H. Green, who strongly influenced his students, but Arnold Toynbee and, later, Bolton King who was Benjamin Jowett's pupil at Balliol. These men too would contribute in different ways to promoting Mazzini's vision for Italy and for humanity amongst the wider British audience.[22] Undoubtedly, as Maurizio Isabella has indicated, of Mazzini's exiled friends Saffi 'did the most to uphold the Italian cause and Mazzini's ideas in Britain'. Moreover, Saffi would remain, in the age of liberal Italy, the living symbol of republican endeavour for both Italian democrats and Victorian radicals.[23]

Before leaving for Oxford in October 1853 Saffi contributed anonymously to the *Westminster Review* what was arguably his most important article written during his exile.[24] Edited by John Bowring (1792–1872), an early supporter of Mazzini's People's International League, the quarterly *Westminster Review* was also associated with John Stuart Mill: early contributors included Leigh Hunt and Harriet Martineau. From 1852 it was edited jointly by George Eliot (Marian Evans) and the radical Unitarian John Chapman, who was sympathetic to republican movements in Europe.[25] Published only months after the failure of the Milan insurrection, Saffi's article was concerned with 'Religion in Italy'. While its rhetoric – on papal despotism and the martyrdom of Italian patriots – would resonate widely amongst British Protestant readers, the message of the article was more than a plea for support. It is therefore worth examining in some detail.

What exactly did Saffi convey about Mazzini's vision to the readers of the radical *Westminster Review*? Saffi aimed to distil and disseminate the essence of Mazzini's 'civil religion' by elevating to the status of national heroes men who had championed the cause of free thought. This strategy was part of a widespread phenomenon in the nineteenth century, recently described by Robert Gerwarth as the 'politics of the past': the character of a nation's

---

[20] W. A. Knight, *Memoir of John Nichol*, Glasgow 1896, 140–1.

[21] F. Harrison, *Autobiographic memoirs*, i, London 1911, 55, 96; Finn, *After Chartism*, 199–200; Rudman, *Italian nationalism*, 236.

[22] 'Signor Saffi's proposed lecturing tour in Scotland', CP, TWAS, A492.

[23] Isabella, *Italian exiles*, 75; J. Nichol to J. Service, 20 Nov. 1881; Knight, *Memoir*, 218.

[24] 'Religion in Italy', WR, 1 Oct. 1853.

[25] F. Dillane, 'Chapman, John', DNCJ, 107.

people was styled and sanctified according to mythical moments within the lives of national heroes.[26] Mazzini recognised the power of religion as a popular element of national cohesion amongst the mass of Italians. He had felt it in Rome, in 1849, while witnessing the ecstatic crowd gathered opposite St Peter's, in the grand square designed by Bernini: he had then noted how religion was inevitably associated with 'the great beauty of form'.[27] In accord with Mazzini, Saffi's article aimed to harness the power of religion and Italy's artistic heritage within a popular national tradition which was rooted in the primacy of free thought and civic virtue: this shared national identity would provide the foundation for the 'Third Rome'.

Saffi surveyed the origins of anti-papal resistance in the context of a continuous Italian tradition of free thought: in the past Italy, 'the nation of Europe the most advanced in civilization', had also been 'the first to protest against the Catholic theology'. The examples were many: Arnaldo da Brescia (1090–1155), the radical priest who had initiated the 'protest of morality and freedom of conscience'; Cola di Rienzo (1313–54), 'the most extraordinary of the precursors of civic humanism', who had declared the authority of the Roman people over the pope;[28] Savonarola (1452–98), who had denounced corruption, called for a Christian renewal and prophesied civic glory; and Machiavelli (1469–1527), who had denounced the papacy's 'worldly tyranny'. After the Reformation in Europe had initiated and spread, free thought had continued to advance in Italy through philosophers and scientists like Giordano Bruno and Galileo and thinkers like Vico, whose metaphysical discoveries were linked to the birth of the philosophy of history.[29] There was a line of continuity from some of these men, condemned to death by the Inquisition, to the 'martyrs' of Young Italy.

Not only men of intellect, but the Italian people too had rebelled against the hideous papal yoke in its many forms. This was encapsulated in the odious weight of the dogma of infallibility: opposing the translation of the Bible 'in the vulgar tongue', it hampered individual enquiry, the search for truth and freedom of conscience, and ultimately encouraged superstition. Catholicism, according to Saffi, whose Italian references were mainly urban workers, and especially the papal Legacies, had therefore lost its following in Italy.

This did not signify, however, that Italy offered itself as a missionary field

---

[26] R. Gerwarth, 'Introduction: hero cults and the politics of the past: comparative European perspectives', EHQ xxxix/3 (2009), 381–7.

[27] N. Costa, Quel che vidi e quell che intesi, ed. G. Guerrazzi Milan 1985, 121, quoted in C. Duggan, 'Il culto dell'uno dal Risorgimento al fascism', in S. Soldani, L'Italia alla prova, Milan 2011, 41–64 at p. 42.

[28] The definition is from J. G. A. Pocock, The Machiavellian moment: Florentine political thought and the Atlantic republican tradition, Princeton 1975, 51.

[29] All these figures were well-known to English readers, with the exception of Vico, whose thought Thomas Arnold lamented was regrettably not familiar to the English.

for British Evangelicals, as some might have hoped. On questions of faith and religious reform, Saffi claimed that modern Italians needed to turn to their own past and traditions. Inspiration from one's own traditions was one of the building blocks of Mazzini's religion of the nation.[30] Amongst the 'glorious inspirations of their ancestors' Italians should turn, according to Saffi, to the initiators of Unitarianism, who, led by the Italian theologian Faustus Socinus, had left Italy for Poland, subsequently spreading their creed throughout Europe.[31] It was their view of the unity between heaven and earth that would touch Italians' hearts and minds, more prone to embrace a 'universal', 'philosophical' religion than the form and doctrine of the reformed Churches.[32] Through the exercise of individual duty, the nurturing of patriotic virtues and the progress of civic life, 'worked out in the sacred laws of the Republic, man could rise to God'.

This vision was what modern Italians could invoke as 'a truly *Civil Religion*'.[33] This was Mazzini's theism. Unlike Cavour, who, being more European than Italian, encouraged the missionary spirit of British Evangelicals, possibly welcoming their 'civilisational perspective', Saffi, with Mazzini, believed that the 'faculties', 'traditions', 'dynamic' and 'constructive forces' able to foster the harmony of a new civilised world needed to be drawn by Italians from within their own nation. Such patriotic perspective was evidently aimed at connecting civil religion with a form of 'national cult' which had republican roots. The national heroes chosen by Saffi were the promoters of the universal values of free thought, democracy and civil virtue. He therefore argued through the pages of the *Westminster Review* what has recently been well expressed by David G. Rowley, namely that 'the Italian character was made by ideas not by blood'.[34] Moreover, in a clear attempt at the 'aesthetisation of politics', Saffi claimed for the free thought tradition the masterpieces created by renaissance artists: their works of art had been inspired by the artists' desire to reach the 'Ideal' of perfection, which 'civil religion' stood for. This was the rhetoric which Saffi chose when addressing his British readership: it was a language which could speak, if not to the Italians, then to the many Unitarian radical followers who embraced Mazzini's vision and honoured the tradition of free enquiry, free thought, liberty of discussion and religious liberty. It was no coincidence that the Unitarian editor of the *Westminster Review* had agreed to disseminate this view.

---

[30] Mazzini, 'Faith and the future', 43. In making the connection between present and past national traditions Saffi was echoing Vincenzo Cuoco, who had highlighted that attempts to import ready-made models and institutions from foreign countries were destined to fail.

[31] This connection is highlighted in Spini, *Risorgimento e protestanti*, 287 n. 14.

[32] Saffi, 'The religion in Italy', WR, 337.

[33] Ibid. WR, 314–15.

[34] D. G. Rowley, 'Giuseppe Mazzini and the democratic logic of nationalism', *Nations and Nationalism* xviii/1 (2012), 39–56 at p. 46.

Following the publication of his article Saffi moved to Oxford.[35] Here, his unequivocal celebration of Mazzini's 'civil religion' would resonate amongst promoters of the Oxford reform movement, finding support further afield, amongst British freethinkers, positivists and secularists who adopted Mazzini's creed as their own. By building a reputation for personal integrity and producing numerous eloquent writings Saffi did not only fight Mazzini's corner: he secured his own transnational popularity.[36] Remarkably, even *The Times*, responding to one of Saffi's letters in 1856, acknowledged that the man possessed 'good sense'.

In 1857, under Mazzini's instruction, Saffi delivered a series of lectures on Italy. They were part of the fundraising effort which was coordinated by James Stansfeld, radical Halifax MP and Honorary Secretary of the Emancipation of Italy Fund Committee.[37] It was in the English and Scottish provinces that Saffi gained first-hand experience of the popularity that the Italian cause had acquired in the North. He had already experienced the warm informality of provincial supporters when visiting Manchester in 1855: in a letter to the Russian socialist, Alexander Herzen, Saffi remarked on the lack of 'English formality' of his host, the director of a college in Manchester.[38] In Scotland Saffi was also particularly struck by the warm welcome that he received.[39] Here he delivered lectures in Dalkeith, Dunferlabe, Kikaldy, Dundee and, finally, Hawick, which gave him a 'public ovation'. Genuine republican support was mixed with tamer liberal rhetoric. Yet for some, like Archibald Scott of Hawick, rebuilding the republic in Rome was the aim. Writing to Saffi on 29 April 1857 he stated that

> If the time should soon come again, and God grant it may, when the names of Saffi and Mazzini with the cry of God and the People shall again be heard in the streets of Rome, nothing should be left undone on our part to aid you in the Holy cause of Italy.[40]

Saffi could also draw on the substantial mobilisation of popular anti-Catholicism which had in Scotland one of its strongholds, reaching working men in deliberately-devised anti-popery evening classes.[41] Saffi's London and provincial lectures were peppered with the language of anti-Catholicism: in the texts of the lectures there are traces of antagonism to idolatry and to

---

[35] A. Saffi, *Ricordi e scritti (1849–57)*, iv, Florence 1899, 257.

[36] A. Milner Gibson to Saffi (c. 1857), FS, BCAB, ii/16/1, 35; White Mario to Saffi, ii/16/1, 16.

[37] On the *Fund* see O'Connor, *Romance of Italy*, 89–90.

[38]   Saffi to Herzen, 12 Nov. 1855, A. Herzen papers, AIISH, 32.

[39] Ibid; J. Fyfe (ed.), *Autobiography of John McAdam, 1806–83*, Edinburgh 1980.

[40] A. Scott to Saffi, Hawick, 29 Apr. 1857, FS, BCAB, ii/16/1, 29.

[41] Wolffe, *Protestant crusade*, 176–79.

God, between 'temporal power' and the 'progress of nationality', between arbitrary power and freedom of conscience.[42]

The tours were carefully prepared using a propaganda machinery which mellowed their republican tone. Yet Saffi retained the admiration of radical exiles like Karl Blind, who congratulated him in 1857, having just read an account of Saffi' speech in the *Morning Chronicle*, at the Literary and Scientific Institution of which he was a member.[43] The Scottish border was the focus of Cowen's carefully orchestrated campaign: in anticipation of Saffi's arrival, a profile of him had been printed in a handbill announcing the lectures. Saffi, the handbill explained, was a 'Professor at the Taylor Institute of the learned and time-honoured, but certainly not democratic, University of Oxford', where he was 'respected for his uncompromising national republican faith'. It was added, however, that Saffi was 'one of the few men' who gained 'the esteem and affection of all parties and opinions, without the sacrifice of a principle or the desertion of a cause'.[44]

Amongst Mazzini's loyal lecturers was also a young English enthusiast, Jessie White, who initially described herself as Stansfeld's 'humble Clark'.[45] She soon became one of the most sought-after lecturers: in 1857 and 1858 she repeatedly visited Newcastle-upon-Tyne, so great was the demand in the town. One of the lectures, shared with Saffi, was chaired by John Fyfe, whose position as mayor of Newcastle and as a political and municipal reformer, was sufficient to grant the event ceremonial status.[46] This was not unusual. In Leeds, in February 1857, Saffi's lecture had been presided over by Edward Baines, director and proprietor of the *Leeds Mercury*.[47] During the lecture tours Saffi and Jessie White consistently received long and prolonged applause. According to the report of the *Newcastle Chronicle*, published on 8 May 1857, Jessie White's 'powerful eloquence' had served to 'vindicate in our times and to all those who formerly doubted it, the character of the illustrious Mazzini'.[48]

Jessie White would further testify her commitment to the Italian cause by leaving for Italy as a foreign correspondent of the *Daily News* and the *New York Times*, where she would witness the Genoese insurrection, would be arrested and meet in prison her future husband, the Italian republican federalist Alberto Mario – a clear example of the interaction of love and

[42] Saffi's first lecture, London, 15 Jan. 1857, Saffi, *Ricordi*, iv. 390–406.

[43] K. Blind to Saffi, 27 Jan. 1857, FS, BCAB, ii/16/1, 23.

[44] Unknown correspondents, Hawick, 27 Apr. 1857, Saffi, *Ricordi*, iv. 441; Fyfe, 'Scotland and the Risorgimento', 110.

[45] Gazzetta, *Contributo*, 33; White Mario to Saffi, 22 Oct. 1856, FS, BCAB ii/16/1, 15.

[46] On John Fyfe see Welford, *Men of mark*, 226–35.

[47] Saffi to G. Craufurd Saffi, 27 Feb. 1857, FS, BCAB, ix/3, cited in in Bacchin, 'Il Risorgimento oltremanica', 183.

[48] 'Italy for the Italians! Lecture on Italian emancipation by Miss J. M. I. White', from the 'Newcastle Chronicle', 8 May 1857, CP, TWAS, A506.

politics.[49] The following year Jessie White – now known as Jessie White Mario – would travel to Newcastle again, with her husband in tow. Mario, who could not speak English, and had noticed laconically that Newcastle had the same latitude as Moscow, reluctantly agreed to the tour. Yet, he could not but be impressed by the 'respect, devotion and admiration' of the people of England once he got there.[50]

The loyalty of Tyneside republicans

Indeed, Tyneside was well known for its early support for the Italian cause. Three years before, in 1854, the arrival in Newcastle of Garibaldi, had confirmed the radical reputation of the North-East. The visit was a tribute to the esteem in which Joseph Cowen was held by European exiles. Garibaldi had just been to London, where he had clarified with Mazzini his position on Italy, privately exhorting him to abandon the republican solution in order to avoid sacrificing more victims for a revolution which, he felt, was not desired by the Italian masses.[51] On this occasion he also met the Polish exile, Stanislaus Worcell, who put him in touch with Cowen.[52]

As Garibaldi was welcomed as 'the Gallant Defender of the ETERNAL CITY' by a deputation of Friends of European Freedom and 'adopted as a Tyneside hero' by the local inhabitants, support for Mazzini remained unyielding. At this early stage Garibaldi's reservations concerning Mazzini's republican aims and insurrectional tactics were still kept under wraps. On the general's visit to Tyneside the language of brotherhood and republican solidarity celebrated both figures in unison, treading the then still popular line that Garibaldi was 'no more than a coadjutor of Mazzini'. The Newcastle delegation referred to Garibaldi as 'friend and worthy helpmate of Mazzini' while Julian Harney proposed the health of 'Joseph Mazzini, the illustrious compatriot of Garibaldi'.[53] Holyoake, reporting on Garibaldi's visit to Newcastle in the *Reasoner* referred to meeting him and Mazzini together, 'two of the most wonderful men in Europe at this time'.[54]

---

[49] On Alberto Mario see P. Bagatin, *Tra Risorgimento e nuova Italia: Alberto Mario un repubblicano federalista*, Florence 2000. On love and politics see Luisa Passerini, *Europe in love, love in Europe*, New York 1999.

[50] A. Mario to his father, in Bagatin, *Tra Risorgimento*, 449.

[51] G. Garibaldi to Mazzini, London, 26 Feb. 1854, in G. Garibaldi, *Epistolario*, Rome 1973–2002, iii. 62–4, letter 734.

[52] J. Cowen to Garibaldi, 8 Mar. 1854, ibid. iii. 66–7, letter 738.

[53] 'Broadsheet of a penny subscription', 4 Apr. 1854, CP, TWAS, A212; D. M. Jackson, '"Garibaldi and the pope!" Newcastle's Irish riot of 1866', *North East History* xxxiv (2001), 48–82; Mack Smith, *Mazzini*, 107; *NT* i (Jan.–July 1854), 175.

[54] 'General Garibaldi de Maggiore', *Reasoner* xvi/201, 19 Mar. 1854.

Cowen's close friendship with Mazzini ensured that Garibaldi's growing popularity in England would not be to the detriment of Mazzini's local fame. Garibaldi, who had taken a 'lively interest' in the Blaydon Mechanics' Institute, meeting 'several of its members', inevitably became an increasingly familiar figure amongst Tyneside workers, his biography and portrait appearing in the local radical paper, the *Northern Tribune*.[55] An admirer of Garibaldi, Cowen equally promoted the circulation of Mazzini's image. Not only did the *Northern Tribune* publish Gerald Massey's article on 'Mazzini and Italy' and a sensitive letter from Mazzini to Worcell advocating his condemnation of Britain's policy on the Eastern Question, but in 1856, responding to an appeal from Jessie White, Cowen raised contributions for the Emancipation of Italy Fund by selling to 'miners, potters, ropemakers, bakers, tailors, druggists, printers and stationers' twenty-three portraits of Mazzini, therefore helping to foster the personality cult of the exile amongst workers beyond the metropolis.[56]

Northern workers could capture further hints of Mazzini's charismatic *persona* in Ruffini's book, *Lorenzo Benoni: passages in the life of an Italian*, which was emphatically praised in a review appearing in 1854 in the *Northern Tribune*.[57] As the review described the context, the story began in 'republican Genoa, cursed with the rule of ruffian soldiers, infamous priests and scoundrel spies', recounting the adventures of Fantasio, the chief of the 'ardent band'. References to 'infamous priests' were intended to harness popular anti-Catholic sentiments; mention of Mazzini's home town drew attention to its 'republican' traditions; 'spies' and 'ruffians' were the weapon of the tyranny of empire. 'We see no good reason', clarified the reviewer, 'for withholding Fantasio's real designation. Who can mistake the portrait of Joseph Mazzini?' A long extract from the book – likened to masterpieces such as *Robinson Crusoe* – described Fantasio: his morals 'irreproachable', his conversation 'always chaste', 'well versed in history and in the literature not only of his own but of foreign countries', 'passionate lover of liberty under every shape' with 'an indefatigably active mind'. The book was recommended to readers from all walks of life:

> to railway and other travellers, to fireside readers and to readers who love the solitude of the forest shade, to ladies 'dying' for the last new novel and

---

[55] 'Public Address to General Garibaldi', 14 Sept. 1859, CP, TWAS, A649; 'Blaydon: public meeting to adopt an address to General Garibaldi', *Northern Daily Express*, newspaper cutting, CP, TWAS, A650; *NT* i (Jan.–July 1854), 150–7.

[56] G. Massey, 'Mazzini and Italy', and 'Mazzini on the Eastern Question', *NT* i (Jan.–July 1854), 402–5, 14–16; White Mario to Cowen, 'Subscription list for a portrait of Giuseppe Mazzini', 1856 (?), CP, TWAS, A484; D. F. Mackay, 'The influence of the Italian Risorgimento on British public opinion', unpubl. PhD diss. Oxford 1961, 242; 'Notes on portraits' subscription', CP, TWAS, A487.

[57] *NT* i/7 (July 1854), 234–9. On the book see M. Marazzi, *Il romanzo risorgimentale di Giovanni Ruffini*, Florence 1999, 163–5.

young artisans eager for 'light, more light', in relation to fair Italy's sufferings and aspirations, – in short, to every description of reader, we say, invest your half-crown in a purchase you will never regret. If labourers and apprentices have not yet half-crown to spare, let them club their six-pences and obtain a book which will impart to them truths they should know and pleasure that will afford them lasting satisfaction.[58]

Tyneside workers frequenting the Blaydon Mechanics' Institute would have had the opportunity to read the *Northern Tribune* review in the well-stocked reading room, possibly even accessing the book. Although a Free Library was slow to come to Newcastle, due to the monopoly exercised by members of the mechanics' institute movement in the region, Cowen's control of the Blaydon Institute, his friendship with Mazzini and the sympathetic review in his newspaper suggest that *Lorenzo Benoni* would have enjoyed a discreet circulation amongst Tyneside workers.

Cowen, who had set up with Holyoake, Harney and others the Republican Brotherhood in 1855, also cultivated links with Mazzinian democrats in Italy. In September 1856 the Genoese workers had sent, through Jessie White, an Address to the Working Men of England.[59] This had reached Holyoake with an accompanying letter from the worker Antonio Casareto – one of the Genoese Committee.[60] Casareto came from a well-known Genoese family of haulage contractors of Mazzinian and republican sympathies and was instrumental in organising the Genoese insurrection at the time of Pisacane's expedition to Sapri. Accused of the conspiracy and forced into exile he would accompany Mazzini to London in 1857, remaining with Saffi and Maurizio Quadrio amongst the handful of faithful Mazzinian democrats once Garibaldi had handed Italy to Victor Emmanuel in 1860. The tone of Casareto's letter to Holyoake, in 1856, responded to the ideals of 'civil religion', inspired by the motto 'God and the People'. It conjugated the language of Christian inspiration and civic virtue with that of the internationalist brotherhood. The letter was signed by eighty-two Italian men, mostly artisans, but many unskilled workers too: coalmen, carvers, painters, packers, builders, cabinet makers, joiners, dressmakers, wax workers, goldsmiths, porters, cleaners, shoemakers, compositors and hairdressers.[61] The working-class background of the signatories appealing to the English workers, and their link with a local association (*Consociazione Operaia Genovese*) set a precedent in transnational worker co-operation which would constitute a blueprint in years to come.

---

[58] *NT* i/7 (July 1854), 235.

[59] 'Printed circular from the working men of Genoa on the Emancipation of Italy Fund', CP, TWAS, A469.

[60] See A. G. Remedi, 'Antonio Casareto', *DBDI*. The other members of the committee were Giacomo Medici, Agostino Gnecco, Angelo Mangini and Antonio Mosto.

[61] A. Casareto to Holyoake, Genoa, 11 Sept. 1856, HP, HHM, 863.

The Newcastle workers promptly responded to the working men of Genoa.[62] Despite the 'unpropitious' weather – with 'rain positively coming down in torrents' – over 6.000 men assembled at a public meeting in the town, where they received the resolution 'with great unanimity and enthusiasm'.[63] Cowen, who chaired the meeting, communicated the resolution to the Secretary of the growing Genoese Workmens Association, Felice Casaccia, a democrat fisherman, who would emerge as one of the ringleaders of Mazzini's Genoese insurrectional organisation in 1857.[64] As working-class Mazzinians, Casaccia and Casareto shared many traits with their English counterparts who embraced social progress while condemning class conflict. Although democrat leaders in Italy were often of bourgeois origin, the traces of transnational exchanges between urban unskilled workers show that, on occasions, democrats like the Genoese working men were able to spearhead some political initiatives across national boundaries.

Cowen was proud of the contacts made, and indeed was clearly disappointed not to have received from Garibaldi an acknowledgement of the workers' donation. This was a sign that, at this point, Cowen did not realise that the political activities masterminded by Mazzini were not necessarily orchestrated in agreement with Garibaldi.[65] The news of Cowen's efforts to assist the Italian workers was nevertheless spread by another association, the Newcastle Foreign Affairs Committee. The reported 'sympathies of the artisans of Newcastle' were welcomed by other Italian exiles, such as the democrat Luigi Pianciani, the Mazzinian editor of the paper, *L'Homme*, who had settled in Jersey.[66] Here Pianciani would have become acquainted with radical Tyneside internationalism through Harney's paper, the *Jersey Inde-*

---

[62] 'Address of the English working men of Newcastle on Tyne to the Italian men of Genoa', 29 Sept. 1856, CP, TWAS, A479. On the Mazzinian movement in Genoa see B. Montale, *La confederazione operaia genovese e il movimento mazziniano in Genova dal 1864 al 1892*, Pisa 1960.

[63] 'Emancipation of Italy: public meeting', *Northern Daily Express*, 14 Oct. 1856, press cutting, CP, TWAS, A 481; 'The subscription for Italy', *The Leader*, vii. 939, 4 Oct. 1856.

[64] On 14 May 1862 Mazzini 'proudly wrote to inform Palmerston that his Genoese Working Men's Association had nearly five thousand members': Mazzini to Palmerston, 14 May 1862, Palmerston archives, Broadlands, quoted in Mack Smith, *Mazzini*, 198 n. 46. See also G. Monsagrati, 'Casaccia Felice', *DBDI*, 39–41, and Cowen to F. Casaccia, 3 Oct. 1856, CP, TWAS, A479.

[65] In fact, the money received would be channelled to fund the 1857 Genoese insurrection: Mack Smith, *Mazzini*, 119.

[66] The Newcastle Foreign Affairs Committee was instituted on 16 November 1854 'to watch the progress of the War, counteract the evils of Secret Diplomacy' and 'diffuse information on the relations of Great Britain with other States': 'Minute Book of the Newcastle-on-Tyne Foreign Affairs Committee', CP, TWAS, A247; L. Pianciani to Cowen, 22 Nov. 1855, CP, A423. On Luigi Pianciani's exile in England see Isabella, 'Italian exiles', 76. On the Italian democrats exiled in Jersey see F. Bertini, *La democrazia europea e il laboratorio risorgimentale italiano, 1848–60*, Florence 2007, 85–96.

pendent, which had benefited from the financial help received from Cowen and from the recently established Newcastle Foreign Affairs Committee.[67]

Birmingham: a test-bed for Mazzinian allegiance

Following the groundswell of interest in the mid-1850s, provincial radicals had established Foreign Affairs Committees aimed at surveying Palmerston's foreign policy by studying the Blue Books. In Newcastle, the Foreign Affairs Committee, with more than half its members former Chartists, was energetically steered by Cowen.[68] In 1855 a meeting of Foreign Affairs Committees was convened in Birmingham.

Mid-fifties British radicalism was increasingly thwarted by a variety of 'currents' within it.[69] Birmingham was no exception. Indeed, Thomas Attwood's Birmingham Political Union, known since the 1830s as 'the most influential Radical organisation in the country', had been laced from the outset with conservative principles.[70] These tendencies became evident when the Crimean War broke out. While the British cabinet's aims and strategy remained for a while unclear, the anti-Russian character of the enterprise was a constant motif which had the power to rally conservatives and radicals alike. The press acted for the first time as a potent force shaping public opinion. Palmerston was able to harness this. As Orlando Figes powerfully put it, 'his foreign policy captured the imagination of the British public as the embodiment of their own national character and popular ideals'.[71] Protecting Turkey against the tyranny of Russia came to be equated with standing up for 'British principles' – defending liberty, civilisation and trade – so that when David Urquhart, a radical Turcophile, rallied support for the war in the name of Russophobia, several thousands of radicals were quick to join him.

This was not entirely surprising. Since Napoleon III's seizure of power in 1851, some Victorian radicals had become alarmed. Fears of a potential threat of invasion by continental imperial governments – whether French or Russian – induced radicals to become more vigilant, more wary of foreigners, leading them to conjugate the language of patriotism with that of xenophobia.[72] The outbreak of the Crimean War therefore impacted on the discourses

---

[67] *Harney papers*, p. xii.

[68] Allen, *Joseph Cowen*, 38, and appendix ii.

[69] Briggs, *Chartist studies*, 19.

[70] M. Taylor, 'The old radicalism and the new: David Urquhart and the politics of opposition', in Biagini and Reid, *Currents of radicalism*, 23–44.

[71] O. Figes, *Crimea: the last crusade*, London 2010, 148.

[72] Taylor, *The decline of British radicalism*, 212–19; B. Porter, '"Bureau and barrack": early Victorian attitudes towards the continent', VS xxvii/4 (1984), 407–33 at p. 430; H. Cunningham, 'The language of patriotism', *History Workshop* xii/1 (1981), 8–33.

of a section of radicals and, ultimately, affected the course of Italy's unifica-tion. Initially, and crucially, patriotic concerns seemed to diminish interest in Italy; latterly, with the end of the war, peace negotiations with the Pied-montese government saw the 'Italian question' transferred to the diplomatic table, where monarchical Cavour, rather than republican Mazzini, came to orchestrate more subtly the British government's attitude towards Italian unification.

That the 'Eastern question' might provide an unnecessary distraction from the task at hand was something that Mazzini detected early on. In August 1855 he published *Two letters to the people of England on the war* spelling out his rejection of the intervention in the Crimea, by appealing to the 'brave' working men of England, whose 'blood' and 'money' would be 'lavished in an enterprise doomed to prove a failure by an immoral presiding policy'.[73] He was, indeed, correct, as British troopers in what Figes defined as the 'phoney war' would be drawn from the poorest class of society.[74] However, Mazzi-ni's anti-war stance would have a serious backlash: it triggered a campaign against him waged by the conservative press, a temporary folding of the Friends of Italy and the brief distancing of the radical MP James Stansfeld.[75]

In Birmingham, where Mazzini had built a respectable following, the question would cause an additional *fracas* and, indeed, a split between radi-cals. Here Mazzini had his most loyal supporter in George Dawson, who 'ably and constantly advocated the claims of Italy', and was known to have been placed in the 'black book' by the Austrians as a friend of Mazzini. Dawson was considered the first public man in Birmingham who understood foreign politics and could arouse a local interest in the European revolutions.[76] He had initially struggled to find a platform for expressing his progressive ideas, eventually settling as preacher in the Church of the Saviour, the 'chapel of the doubters' where he delivered his unorthodox sermons, becoming, according to the Christian Socialist Charles Kingsley, 'the greatest talker in England'.[77] He regularly included lectures on Italy.[78] Patently, his radical views raised a few eyebrows in the town, as republicanism was not openly embraced by many: 'I read the *E. Republic* regularly', Dawson wrote to Linton, 'whether anyone else does here I cannot say.'[79] Yet, from his pulpit Dawson was able to recruit some keen followers, such as John Alfred Langford, the apprentice and Chartist poet of *Cooper's Journal*, who had come to embrace Italy's cause.

[73] G. Mazzini, *Two letters to the people of England on the war*, London 1855, TWAS, CP, A361.

[74] Sarti, *Mazzini*, 171.

[75] Figes, *Crimea*, 165–200.

[76] Ireland, *Recollections*, 21, and Sellers, 'Dawson George', 554–6.

[77] Hennock, *Fit and proper persons*, 68.

[78] See the advertised lecture, G. Dawson, 'Italian affairs and the duty of England therein', Music Hall, Birmingham, *Midlands Counties and General Advertiser*, 8 Nov. 1860.

[79] G. Dawson to Linton, 2 July [1854?], FL, AGF 1, 30/5.

It was at one of the conferences which Dawson and Langford organised for the benefit of the Foreign Affairs Committees that a controversy on Mazzini's integrity ensued. Urquhart claimed not only that European republicanism aimed at destabilising the continent but, indeed, that Mazzini was a Russian spy.[80] While the accusations did not find many followers, apart from in Sheffield, where the *Free Press* newspaper gave voice to xenophobic concerns, the claims were incendiary enough to cause a split amongst Birmingham radicals and between different Foreign Affairs Committees. Unsurprisingly, the Newcastle delegates, in unison with Dawson and Langford, took Mazzini's side. Urquhart's unfounded claims nevertheless unleashed a wave of antipathy for Mazzini, which found fertile ground in the fear expressed in the pages of the *Sheffield Free Press* that Mazzini and Kossuth were 'at present the only persons who [had] any hold on the confidence of the English people'.[81] Beyond the discontent that was gathering pace in the Italian democrats' camp, where Cavour was beginning to make inroads, Mazzini's anti-Crimean stance had managed to elicit more suspicions amongst some British radicals than the arguments regularly peddled by the conservative press.

Provincial Mazzinians, failed insurrections and the *People's Paper*

Tyneside loyalty to Mazzini was destined to last many more years. Cowen's *Northern Tribune*, 'which had a strong regional focus', was followed in 1858/59 by the *Newcastle Daily Chronicle*, 'an "almost unique" Mazzinian paper', and thereafter by the *Newcastle Weekly Chronicle*. Both these papers, owned by Cowen, were 'exceedingly successful and influential', to be considered 'in the category of the best 'provincial' papers'.[82] Not only were they regarded as the best vehicles to give the people a radical education, but, in line with Mazzinian principles, they actively promoted the view, highlighted by Joan Allen, that 'mechanics' institutes, trade unions and co-op stores were the appropriate associations for those who espoused radical beliefs'.[83]

---

[80] M. Taylor, 'Urquhart, David (1805–77)', ODNB, 945–8. On Russophobic foreign policy see J. H. Gleason, *The genesis of Russophobia in Great Britain: a study of the interaction of public opinion*, Cambridge 1950; R. Shannon, 'David Urquhart and the Foreign Affairs Committees', in P. Hollis (ed.), *Pressure from without in early Victorian England*, London 1974, 239–61; and Taylor, 'The old radicalism', 23–44.

[81] David Urquhart's claims found some fertile ground in Birmingham (with Charles Attwood), in Sheffield, ('Mazzini and Russia', *Sheffield Free Press*, 29 Sept. 1855) and even in Newcastle where there were some members of the Newcastle Foreign Affairs Committee who in 1859, still harbouring suspicions against Mazzini, wrote to Garibaldi to be reassured: *Newcastle Daily Journal*, 5 Apr. 1861; *Sheffield Free Press*, 13 Oct. 1855, TWAS, CP, A366.

[82] Mackay, 'Influence', 197; Biagini, *Liberty*, 24; O. Ashton, 'Newcastle Weekly Chronicle', *DNCJ*, 447.

[83] Allen, *Joseph Cowen*, 113.

In 1857 the news of the failure of the Genoese expedition, financed through British fundraising efforts, far from deterring Cowen from supporting Mazzini, gave him a fresh opportunity to reiterate his allegiance. His loyalty at a time of widespread defections in Italy was as remarkable as that of Mazzini's loyal friend Maurizio Quadrio, who at this time remained in Genoa to edit *l'Italia del Popolo*, the only voice in defence of Mazzini's failed enterprise.[84] Similarly Cowen, with the help of Emilie Ashurst Hawkes (who resided at his home, Stella House, for weeks working as translator) provided a voice of support in England by ensuring that Mazzini's pamphlet, *The late Genoese insurrection defended*, was printed from his own small printing press.[85] The pamphlet contained 'long and difficult' 'articles written by Mazzini on the late movement in Genoa' and a preface, in the form of a letter from Mazzini to Cowen.[86] Both Cowen and Emilie Ashurst Hawkes were resolved 'to make an effort to get some respectable publishers to publish them': perhaps unsurprisingly, the articles would be published by Holyoake. The pamphlet was intended both to counter the accusations of Mazzini's enemies and to put forward the republicans' plan for Italy. Cowen posted to London, to the provincial press and to liberal supporters of the Italian cause 800 copies of the pamphlet – in the dim hope that a few might sell. Even sympathetic northern liberal editors, such as Samuel Smiles, a contributor to the *Leeds Times* and an ardent supporter of the public libraries' movement, were beginning to air their reservations on Mazzini's tactics.[87] As the *Leeds Times* commented:

> The recent attempt to stir up insurrection in Sardinia[88] has had the effect of alienating from Mazzini many of his best friends and supporters – men whom hardly any other course of action could have driven from his side. From our own part we do not accuse Mazzini of treachery; but we cannot so readily acquit him of that impracticability of character which leads men to attempt great enterprises with totally inadequate means, and thus brings defeat and disgrace upon the very interests they had themselves most at heart.[89]

The failed Genoese insurrection had given Mazzini's detractors plenty of ammunition, as shown by the comments made by conservative, moderate

---

[84] S. Pelosi, *Della vita di Maurizio Quadrio*, ii, Sondrio 1921, 58.

[85] G.. Mazzini, *The late Genoese insurrection defended*, London 1858, p. iv, TWAS, CP, A627; Jane Cowen, 'Notes', CP, E436.

[86] Hawkes to Holyoake, 12 Nov. 1857, FH, MRM, 4; Mazzini, *The late Genoese insurrection*.

[87] Hawkes to Holyoake, 12 Nov. 1857, FH, MRM, 4; Cowen to Holyoake, 14 Mar. 1858, HP, HHM, MM/96636/2.

[88] The reference is to Genoa.

[89] *Leeds Times*, 27 Mar. 1858.

and liberal observers.[90] It was left to loyal Mazzinians, such as Peter Taylor in London, Cowen in the North-East and John McAdam in Glasgow, to counter the accusations as licensed falsehood.[91]

The map of Mazzinian support however had further platforms. Harney and Linton had prepared the ground. Harney had given visibility to Mazzini's 'Royalty and republicanism in Italy' writing, by publishing it in the pages of his *Red Republican* (1850), while Linton, assisted by Eliza Lynn, had translated and published an early version of the 'Duties of man' in the *English Republic* (1851).[92] While all these papers had folded by the mid-fifties – including the *Northern Star* – Ernest Jones's *People's Paper* (1852–8) would ensure that Mazzini's flame was kept burning.[93] This paper was intended as the vehicle for the re-organisation of Chartism, and as such it divided its news and reports equally between the 'metropolis' and the 'provinces'. The latter were overwhelmingly represented by the radical industrial regions: as the first issue indicated, subscriptions had been paid in Halifax, Howbridge, Stockport, Staleybridge, Rotherham, Brighton, Burnham, Coventry, Newcastle, Worcester, Manchester, Rochdale and Leicester – soon joined by Cheltenham.[94]

If the *People's Paper* was known as a Chartist organ with local and national interests, it also took pride in reporting international news: 'he who subscribes to this Paper subscribes to Democracy', wrote Jones, anticipating that, on foreign news also, the paper possessed 'peculiar advantages' due to its 'intimate intercourse with many of the leaders of foreign democracy'.[95] The first opportunity to display such connections arose in February 1853: at a time when distribution of the *People's Paper* amongst Chartists was fuelled by its reports on the National Charter Association, the news of the Milan insurrection broke out. The *People's Paper* claimed that the 'insurrectionary progress' was monitored through the '*direct correspondence* [sic]' and 'the kindness of some of the leaders there', affording the readers a unique insight which 'the class organs' of Britain could not offer.[96] Like the *Leader*, the *People's Paper* challenged the accusation that Mazzini had recklessly sent the insurgents to their deaths, while he remained in hiding: 'perhaps if Mazzini and Saffi had come down from their refuge in Bellinzona, confidence could

90 For the resonance of the publication nationwide see the many cuttings collected in CP, A574–A586.

91 'Mazzini vindicated by a sketch of his eventful life, and the struggle for Italian liberty' (1857). The attribution of the latter to John McAdam is suggested by Mackay, 'Influence', 366.

92 See Mastellone, *Mazzini scrittore*, 223–94,

93 On the *People's Paper* see Taylor, *Ernest Jones*, 172–85, and A. Humpherys, 'People's Paper', *DNCJ*, 489–51.

94 *People's Paper*, 8 May 1852; 12 Feb. 1853.

95 Ibid. 8 May 1852.

96 Ibid.

have been given to the proletarians and sympathy awakened in the liberal portion of the middle classes. ... But revolutions are never made to order'.[97]

The slightly fatalistic tone assumed in reporting on the Milanese insurrection became an unequivocal apology in 1857, when the failure of the Genoa insurrection – coupled with the slaughter in Sapri of the revolutionaries led by Mazzini's coadjutor, Carlo Pisacane – brought even greater disgrace to the name of the Italian exile.[98] Jones, however, considered the 'abortive conspiracies' as 'the inevitable precursors of the real movement'.[99] Indeed, Jones's understanding of the need for abortive insurrections as precursors of future success anticipated some of the most recent attempts to reappraise Mazzini's role in the Risorgimento. As Lucy Riall has suggested, these failed insurrections became 'part of a process whereby Mazzini sought to invent and communicate a new political culture in Italy', able to 'shape the political consciousness of a generation'.[100] Jones also attempted to find an explanation for the failure of Pisacane's expedition in the peculiar social conditions of the South. In his view the absence of an uprising among the peasants was evidence that Southern Italy lacked the conditions for a revolution as the peasants had 'full stomachs': in Italy – this was Jones's verdict – despotism weighed not on the masses but on the middle class and aristocracy. Mazzini was absolved of all blame.[101]

If Mazzini was still portrayed as a guiltless martyr for the cause, others were glorified: 'An English girl has set the example to all would-be Democrats', thundered Jones, describing Jessie White, incarcerated in Genoa: 'She reflects more honour on England than a thousand Wellingtons, a thousand Pitts.'[102] The ultimate heroes, however, were Pisacane and his followers. As Jones emphatically announced, 'Marshalled by their leader – remember his name, Chartists and Republicans of England – led by/P I S A C A N E/ (let the name live in every honest heart) they awaited the deadly onset.' Somehow appropriating the Italian martyr for the Chartist movement, Jones concluded: 'Chartists! Democrats! Be proud! ... The same month has seen the death of Pisacane and Beranger – our warrior and our bard – let aristocracy and royalty produce two men to equal them – democracy shall yet see many more!'[103] The category of martyrdom of nineteenth-century Italian patriots, described by Lucy Riall for its 'essential elasticity', was not only applied to different discourses within the Risorgimento context, but, thanks

---

[97] Ibid. 19 Feb. 1853.

[98] Pisacane, who had spent a period of exile in London, was known in radical circles and had met Holyoake: L. Russi, 'L'Inghilterra di Pisacane', in Mastellone, *Mazzini e gli scrittori*, ii. 313–30.

[99] On Pisacane see Della Peruta, *Scrittori politici*, 1055–253.

[100] Riall, *Risorgimento*, 137.

[101] *People's Paper*, 18 July 1857.

[102] Ibid.

[103] Ibid. 25 July 1857. Pierre-Jean Béranger was an anti-establishment French poet.

to Jones, it crossed the boundaries of nation.[104] In line with the practice of idealising European democratic martyrs which followed the demise of Chartism, Pisacane, now dead, was glorified.[105] But Mazzini, still alive, could still count on the support of former Chartists.

English republicans and Italian democrats: different perspectives

Another provincial radical whose support remained unwavering was W. E. Adams. Since the *English Republic* experiment in Brantwood had folded in 1855, Linton and Adams had gone their separate ways. Yet, both remained convinced republicans and strenuous supporters of Mazzini during the critical junctures of the mid-fifties. Linton described the 1853 Milanese insurrection as 'carefully organised', overthrown by a 'mistake' which had caused the hanging of thirteen Milanese workmen: 'Mazzini's promptitude', however, was believed to have 'saved the mass of those implicated'. The failure of the 1857 insurrection was also seen to have been 'misrepresented by the Moderates', who had 'renewed their old exclamations of the unhappy importunity' of Mazzini's 'Republicanism, and the fatal character of his influence with the people.' Evidently Linton stood by Mazzini, endorsing the explanation which appeared in *The Genoese insurrection defended*.[106]

Adams too, who had settled in Manchester in the mid-1850s, consistently granted the Italian exile and his republican solution his unreserved support. As he continued his journey of self-improvement by frequenting the Working Men's College in Manchester (established in 1858), Adams took every chance that presented itself to 'pester' the editors of local papers, the *Examiner*, the *Guardian* and the *Courier*, with letters in defence of Mazzini or in explanation of his revolutionary enterprises.[107] In this way the 'tramping' experience of artisans – 'major conduits of information' – could facilitate the circulation of ideas on Mazzini, migrating from the mechanics' institute of one province to the educational institute of another and bringing discussion and debate into reading rooms by raising controversial questions from the pages of radical papers there distributed.[108] Just as the itinerant orator, Holman Hunt, had been instrumental in circulating Chartist ideas beyond the local through the public platform, so Adams helped to disseminate amongst adult learners and common readers Mazzini's vision of a republican

---

[104] Riall, 'Martyr cults', 255–87.

[105] Biagini, 'The politics of Italianism', 102.

[106] W. Linton, *European republicans: recollections of Mazzini and his friends*, London 1892, 133–4.

[107] Adams, *Memoirs*, ii. 392.

[108] P. Hudson, *The industrial revolution*, London 2004, 110; E. Hobsbawm, 'The tramping artisan', *Economic History Review* iii (1951), 299–320.

Italy by raising awareness of his writings in letters to the papers and in the discussions of his enterprises in working men's 'smoking rooms'.[109]

Adams's leaning towards extreme solutions found expression in 1858 in the publication of his pamphlet, *Tyrannicide: is it justifiable?* – following Orsini's attempt on Napoleon III's life. If, as Laven has suggested, Orsini's crime had caused 'widespread revulsion' among the British public, this certainly did not apply to Adams and his London publisher, Edward True-love.[110] In their headstrong determination to justify the ultimate crime, even when this was not backed by Mazzini, these men revealed how Victorian radicals who supported insurrectional methods against all odds, could even outdo Mazzini in their extremism.[111]

Indeed, since his arrival as an exile, Orsini had captured the political imagination of English republicans: Holyoake had been implicated in testing the bombs; Cowen had 'never had' Orsini 'out of his thoughts' from the day of his arrest to his execution.[112] Introduced to him by Mazzini, Cowen had welcomed the new exile into his home in 1856. Orsini was 'engaged in a lecturing tour in the district', relating his adventurous escape from the Austrian dungeons: his fortuitous escape from Mantua had captured the popular imagination of the British audience.[113] Yet Orsini was reluctant to channel funds towards Mazzini's enterprises: he had lost interest in Mazzini and when pressed to raise funds for the Genoese insurrection, refused to cooperate, drawing down on himself an accusing letter from Mazzini and venomous attacks from loyal Mazzinians.[114] Despite their disapproval, Orsini was received with great enthusiasm throughout provincial England. Recalling his lecture tours, which had taken him from Brighton to Tyneside, he had generous words for the working men of the North-East who had been 'a

[109] Taylor, 'Rethinking the Chartists', 492; H. Southall, 'Mobility, the artisan community and popular politics in early 19th century England', in G. Kearns and C. W. J. Withers (eds), *Urbanising Britain: essays on class and community in the nineteenth century*, Cambridge 1991, 103–53.

[110] Laven, 'Mazzini', 276. The 'Orsini affair' exposed the government to accusations of welcoming dangerous continental conspirators. The diplomatic tensions between France and Britain which ensued led to the establishment of the Volunteer Force in Britain. Palmerston's first attempts to pass a Conspiracy Bill to appease the French brought down his government: B. Porter, *The refugee question in mid-Victorian Britain*, Cambridge 1979, 170–99; Finn, *After Chartism*, 180–7.

[111] Sarti, *Mazzini*, 178–9.

[112] Holyoake's involvement in the commissioning and manufacturing of Orsini's bombs is discussed in M. Packe, *The bombs of Orsini*, London 1957. See Cowen to Holyoake, 14 Mar. 1858, HP, MHH, MM/96636/2.

[113] Cowen to Garibaldi, 22 Oct. 1856, FC, MRM 338/666.

[114] Sarti, *Mazzini*, 178; Mazzini to Orsini, 14 Oct. 1856, quoted in Packe, *Bombs of Orsini*, 223. See also p. 224.

good school' for him.[115] Orsini, like Kossuth, had been invited to become an honorary member of the Blaydon and Stella Mechanics' Institute.[116]

If Orsini had appreciated the warm support that he had found in Tyneside, he could also count on other radical friends in the provinces. In Birmingham he found an attentive and responsive audience and in Bath he benefited from the warm hospitality of the poet Savage Landor.[117] Two other provinces were home to Orsini's closest friends: Liverpool, which was associated with the radical Peter Stuart, and Glastonbury, which was home to Durrell Hodge.

Peter Stuart, of Italian descent, was a cooper, who, after attending evening classes, had become interested in phrenology and later homeopathy, a discipline which he came to practise.[118] Stuart had first come to public attention when rallying to help the Polish-Hungarian refugees who arrived in Liverpool in 1851.[119] In later years, having become a friend and correspondent of Mazzini, he directly supported the Italian cause by collecting the Liverpool subscriptions for the Emancipation of Italy Fund. Durrell Hodge was a young enthusiast from a well-to-do Glastonbury family 'of respectable connections and in easy circumstances', who also dreamt of a republican Italy.[120]

Despite his allegiance to republicanism, Hodge was, according to Orsini, thoroughly 'antimazzinian' ('antimazziniano per eccellenza').[121] Exasperated by the power struggle between Mazzini and his defecting followers, not least, the Venetian democrat, Daniele Manin, Hodge had decided in 1857 to set up his own party of 'true republicans' who would operate from inside Italy with funds raised in London by Orsini. Hodge and Orsini intended to finance *La Ragione* (1854), a philosophical, religious, political and social weekly edited by Ausonio Franchi in Turin, which had attracted the sympathies of Italian republicans estranged from Mazzini and which directly competed with Mazzini's Genoese paper, *Italia del Popolo*. A defrocked priest, Franchi had published anti-Catholic tracts which found in Britain a receptive audience. Saffi had contributed to Franchi's following by writing for the *Westminster Review* in 1853 an explanation of the ex-priest's position within the anti-Catholic stream of the democratic movement.[122] In Saffi's

115 Orsini, Memoirs, 187.

116 Jane Cowen, 'Notes', CP, TWAS, E436; 'Meeting in Blaydon mechanics' institute', 14 Sept. 1859, CP, A648.

117 L. Marchetti and E. Larsimont Pergamen (eds), *Felice Orsini: memorie politiche*, i, Milan 1962, quoted in Isabella, 'Italian exiles', 76, 188. See also A. M. Ghisalberti (ed.), *Lettere di Felice Orsini*, Rome 1936, 211, 216.

118 L. Finigan, *The life of Peter Stuart the Ditton doctor*, London 1920.

119 J. Belchem, 'Britishness, asylum-seekers and the northern working class: 1851', *Northern History* xxxix (2002), 59–74 at p. 66.

120 'Mr. Hodge at Genoa', *Lloyds Newspaper*, 12 Mar. 1858.

121 Orsini to Garibaldi, 26 Nov. 1857, *Lettere di Orsini*,, 249.

122 On Ausonio Franchi's influence in England see Bertini, *La democrazia europea*, 85–6, and Lovett, *The democratic movement*, 15.

view, Franchi represented Italian thought enfranchised from papal theology. Franchi's democratic and social ideology rested on the belief that Italy was stunted in its renewal by the power that the Catholic Church exercised in the country, a theory which found followers both amongst Italian patriots in exile, like Orsini, and within the circles of British supporters, like Hodge.

Hodge and Orsini orchestrated a plan in support of Franchi's vision which would never be translated into action. According to a letter from Orsini to Franchi, English friends willing to finance the project had backed out since Mazzini was not involved.[123] The alliance between Hodge and Orsini – while abortive in its outcome – is however revealing: it signals that republican purists, even English ones, were not easily prepared to compromise, and recoiled at the suggestion of temporarily placing Italy's unity before republican ambitions.[124] Hodge's extremist views would emerge when he was found to have been closely associated with Orsini's attempt on Napoleon III's life, risking extradition from Italy to France 'on suspicion of having had a guilty knowledge'.[125] His close brush with the law would temper the outward manifestations of his republicanism. In 1859 the London Committee which had organised, with Gladstone's approval, the reception of the Neapolitan exiles at Paddington Station was 'naturally fearful of republican speech-making, for which they would appear responsible' and which 'might produce diplomatic complications abroad'.[126] Yet Hodge was reported to have spoken 'judiciously.'[127]

Mazzini had been particularly weakened by Daniele Manin's defection from the ranks of his republican followers and by his burgeoning plan, orchestrated with Cavour, for an 'Italian National Society' aimed at uniting Italy under Victor Emanuel.[128] In May 1856 the dispute between Mazzini

---

[123] Orsini to A. Franchi, 26 Sept. 1857, in F. Orsini and C. Bonavino, *Memorie politiche, con un'appendice per Ausonio Franchi*, Lugano 1860, 378–9.

[124] Following Daniele Manin's distancing himself from his republican goal, Mazzini proposed temporarily uniting behind a 'neutral flag', aiming at national unity without excluding a monarchical solution.

[125] The British government was reluctant to allow Hodge's extradition and finally succeeded in pre-empting it. James Hudson was instrumental in guaranteeing Hodge the British government's protection. See J. Hudson to C. Cavour, Turin, 1, 2, 19 Mar. 1858, Lettere Ministri Esteri, Gran Bretagna, Archivio di Stato, Turin, GB 10. On Hudson see N. E. Carter, 'Hudson, Sir James (1810–85)', *ODNB*, and his 'Hudson, Malmesbury and Cavour'.

[126] Anon, 'The Neapolitan exiles', *Reasoner* xxiv/107, 3 Apr. 1859. On the involvement of Gladstone with the transfer of the Neapolitan prisoners see D. V. Reidy, 'Panizzi, Gladstone, Garibaldi and the Neapolitan prisoners', *Electronic British Library Journal*, (2005), 1–15, http://www.bl.uk/eblj/2005articles/article6.html, accessed 6 Aug. 2010.

[127] Anon, 'The Neapolitan exiles', 107.

[128] Raymond Grew has argued that with the establishment of the Italian National Society 'the era of Mazzini was really over': *A sterner plan for Italian unity*, London 1963, p. x.

and Manin was played out publicly in Britain: in a letter to *The Times*, also reported in other English papers, Manin condemned the Party of Action for its tactics, and called for the nation to separate itself 'solemnly, acutely and irrevocably from assassins'.[129] The episode is well-known and has been stressed in the historiography, which is summed up in Laven's assertion that Manin's letter 'helped to fuel British unease with the radical and revolutionary republicanism favoured by Italy's most famous resident exile'.[130]

Yet the support which radical Victorian papers gave to Mazzini, when challenged by Manin, deserves some scrutiny. The *Reasoner*, which was distributed across Britain's increasing number of Free Libraries, published a lengthy reply in three letters from Mazzini to Manin, which rebutted, point by point, any support lent to the Italian National Society, ending with a heartfelt appeal: 'Turn again to us, Manin'.[131] An equally important publication appeared in response to *The Times* article in the *Westminster Review* in January 1857. It was entitled 'State of parties in Italy since 1848'.[132] The detailed knowledge and the tone of the article would suggest that this was another anonymous contribution by Saffi: the timing, too, is significant, as in that month Saffi delivered his first lecture on Italy in London, referring to Mazzini as the 'great patriot' to whom Italy would be indebted.[133] The contributor to the *Westminster Review*, if not Saffi himself, was certainly very close to him. The article, which referred to the 'culpable inertia' of the British, quoted liberally from Mazzini's texts, particularly *Royalty and republicanism*, the pamphlet which Adams and Cooper both admired. There was no attempt to present a neutral perspective in describing Italy's parties: they were two, the Moderate Party, which 'had no sense of an Italian mission and attracted 'worshippers of expediency and opportunity, as opposed to principles and unity'; and the Party of Action, 'the sole hope of Italy', which 'preached the doctrine of the redemption of the nation by the nation'. The article also rebuffed 'superficial observers' who had moved accusations against Mazzini of inadequate tactics ('surprises', as they were referred to): the reference was clearly to Manin's article in the *Times*. The republican tradition of Italy's towns was pitched against Italy's monarchical history, equated with the downfall of her liberties, the onset of servitude and the dismemberment of the nation.

As it transpires from the documents, allegiance to Mazzini's programme mostly held firm in British radical circles, despite efforts by Manin and Cavour to steer British public opinion towards supporting the Italian cause

---

129 Manin letter, *The Times*, 28 May 1856.

130 Sarti, *Mazzini*, 172–3; Laven, 'Mazzini', 276.

131 Mazzini's response, published in the *Reasoner* (17 Aug. 1856) is in a 'revised edition' pamphlet, encompassing three open letters. See *Mazzini's letters to Daniel Manin*, London 1856, http://www.jstor.org/stable/60202125, accessed 21 May 2013. See also 'The "Reasoner" and the Manchester Free Library', *Reasoner*, 1854, 201.

132 'State of parties in Italy since 1848', *WR* (Jan. 1857), 98–133.

133 Saffi, *Ricordi*, iv. 406.

under the flag of the Piedmontese monarchy. Saffi no doubt contributed heavily towards continued republican support. It is no coincidence that Swinburne, an undergraduate member of the 'Old Mortality' society in Oxford, composed, in March 1857 – after Manin's accusations yet before Pisacane's expedition – a long poem entitled 'Ode to Mazzini'.[134] Despite Manin's call for a monarchical, diplomatic solution, the teachings drawn from Saffi, reaffirmed in the *Westminster Review*, combined with youthful enthusiasm for Italy's republican cause and personal closeness to Mazzini, were able to ignite the burning passion of this accomplished poet.[135]

The emotions which Mazzini still stirred amongst British radical supporters and the cohort of exiled democrats were quickly fading at home.[136] Indeed, Victorian radicals' readings of political conditions in Italy were potentially filtered by the perceptions of deluded exiled republicans, above all Mazzini. In Italy democrats accused Mazzini of 'formalism' – lacking a sense of political reality. In 1859 Antonio Mordini, a republican in principle, wrote to the exiled Nicola Fabrizi: 'Political exiles may well in England and in other parts of the world speculate with more or less abstraction about the current political questions, but the patriots who live in Italy must not, do not want and can't see but one solution and that is, the Austrian army against the Italian army of Piedmont.'[137]

Away from home, Mazzini struggled to keep up with the rapidly changing pace of political affairs.[138] His inability to feel the pulse of public opinion reflected a larger divide between Italian democrats: Italy's future was perceived differently by those residing at home and those residing abroad. As Alfonso Scirocco affirmed, 'patriots who lived outside the Italian environment still believed in the republican solution'.[139] In a letter written from London to Agostino Bertani in 1858, the Mazzinian Rosalino Pilo expressed his 'surprise and sorrow' that many 'good ones' in Italy had entrusted Cavour 'and his lot' (*compagnia bella*) with 'Italianness' (*italianità*). Pilo, it would appear, shared both Mazzini's views and his 'hybrid' condition of exile.[140] These Italian exiles were more likely to influence like-minded British followers than were their compatriots at home.[141] Consequently, the nuances of the divisions

[134] The dating of the poem is by Edmund Gosse: preface to A. C. Swinburne, *Ode to Mazzini, the saviour of society, liberty and loyalty*, London 1913.

[135] Rudman, *Italian nationalism*, 236.

[136] A. Mordini, 'Osservazioni sopra una nuova organizzazione in Italia presentate nel giugno 1852', in A. Galante Garrone, *I radicali in Italia, 1849–1925*, Milan 1978, 30–1.

[137] This is quoted in A. Scirocco, *I democratici italiani da Sapri a Porta Pia*, Naples 1969, 22.

[138] Galante Garrone, *I radicali*, 29.

[139] Scirocco, *I democratici italiani*, 22.

[140] On the concept of 'hybridity' see Duggan, 'Giuseppe Mazzini', 187.

[141] On the way in which the 'circulation of ideas' shaped the national consciousness of Italian exiles abroad see Isabella, *Risorgimento in exile*.

among Italian democrats largely escaped committed Victorian radicals, who remained keen that Mazzini's republican vision should be realised.

In the ensuing years, in a climate of growing disillusionment amongst Italian democrats and increasing moderate propaganda, the loyalty of Victorian radicals to Mazzini remained steadfast, if somewhat out of touch. This was underlined in 1859, at a public meeting held in the North-East, in Blaydon, where, in adopting a congratulatory 'Address to Garibaldi', the papers commented, in clear homage to Mazzini, that 'Young Blaydon' had shown its sympathy to 'Young Italy'.[142] It was September 1859. The outbreak of war against Austria had seen Victor Emanuel and Napoleon III dominate the scene, winning Lombardy for the Piedmontese; the Villafranca truce between the Austrian emperor and Napoleon III, in July, had left the future of central Italy uncertain. Yet one thing was beginning to be clear: thanks to the organisational network that stretched across the central states, skilfully orchestrated by the Italian National Society, the initiative for national unification was now firmly in the hands of the elitist moderates. In Tuscany a provisional government was formed, sidelining local republican, working-class leaders (*capipopolo*) like Giuseppe Dolfi.[143] As Roberto Romani has recently shown the 'moderate idiom' ('*concordia*' rather than 'liberty') would dominate the language of 1859.[144]

There was no doubt, however, where Tyneside workers' loyalties stood; they had emerged clearly in 1855, when the challenge to Mazzini from Birmingham radicals had been vehemently dismissed by the Newcastle Foreign Affairs Committee. If most Tyneside workers had remained steadfast, ignoring the accusations of Russian espionage and the blows dealt by Manin, this was due to their political education. Blaydon Mechanics' Institute, more than other similar institutes in the country, 'enjoyed a much larger share of popular support' than usual and was 'in reality as well as in name a "mechanics' institution"', where 'the working classes of the village', whose shillings had contributed to Italy's subscription by purchasing pictures of Mazzini, had 'an active and lively interest in its proceedings'.[145] Yet, in the rest of the country too, in the Manchester Free Library, in Birmingham's reading room chapel, in Cheltenham's Literary Society, in the many Leeds societies and co-operative associations which boasted an educational branch, the consumption of a variety of papers, including radical ones, would have

---

[142] 'Blaydon: public meeting to adopt an address to General Garibaldi', *Northern Daily Express*, newspaper cutting, CP, TWAS, A650, and 'Public address to General Garibaldi', 14 Sept. 1859, CP, A649.

[143] Grew, *A sterner plan*, and his earlier 'How success spoiled the Risorgimento', *JMH* xxxiv/3 (1962), 239–53.

[144] R. Romani, 'Political thought in action: the moderates in 1859', *JMIS* xv/5 (2012) 593–607.

[145] 'To the Editor of the "Times"', *Reasoner*, xxi/181, 7 Dec. 1856.

enabled self-improving working-men to read critically the 'official news' from Italy which was disseminated by *The Times*.

The unfaltering support for Mazzini's Party of Action at a time of crisis is evidence of the remarkable resilience of Victorian Mazzinians. While some radicals did embrace alternatives to Mazzini's vision, these were more likely to be found in Franchi's republican programme or in Orsini's desperate gesture of hatred towards Napoleon III than in Manin's compromise solution of the Italian National Society. Indeed the support given to Orsini's attempted tyrannicide by his provincial friends, Holyoake, Cowen, Hodge (as well as Thomas Allsop) and others, further demonstrates that, despite the 'emasculated' propaganda of the SFI, provincial radicalism was not easily tamed.

Indeed, Holyoake's *Reasoner* became suspicious of Garibaldi's sudden fame, writing in November 1859:

> What treachery can the 'Times' have in store to advise to Garibaldi, that it has taken to praising him? Suspicious are the laudations of Printing House Square. The celebrated guerrilla chief has suddenly become the foremost man in Europe. Well, he deserves the distinction.... But the sudden praise of the 'Times', accompanied by the most unjust disparagement of Garibaldi's illustrious friend, Mazzini, makes its intentions questionable.[146]

More surprises were in store for Holyoake, resolved to back a contingent of British Garibaldi volunteers. While a number of radical, republican, working-class volunteers had already set off, the British Legion would be co-ordinated by a London Committee Fund which Holyoake and Linton helped to set up. Linton designed the British Legion's flag.[147] Yet a banner as unifying symbol was no guarantee for communality of intents: republicans such as Holyoake, Hodge, Linton, Cowen, McAdam and the American De Rohan joined forces with moderate sympathisers with Garibaldi whose role within the Committee became increasingly dominant.[148]

Since Britain's official policy towards Italian unification had moved towards the tacit acceptance of the inevitable collapse of the old *régime* – with Palmerston, Russell and Gladstone meriting the appellative 'Italian triumvirate'[149] – the *Times* had increasingly displayed its support for Garibaldi – to

---

[146] 'Garibaldi and Mazzini', *Reasoner*, xxiv, 27 Nov. 1859, 181.

[147] Holyoake to Garibaldi, 21 Sept. 1860, FC, MRM, 441.

[148] On the British Legion see Sutcliffe, 'British red shirts', 202–18; 'L'amore per Garibaldi', 53–70; and 'Voluntari garibaldini inglesi: escursionisti in Sicilia: volontari inglesi a seguito di Garibaldi', in A. Garibaldi Jallet and A. Lazzarino Del Grosso (eds), *Garibaldi, orizzonti mediterranei*, La Maddalena 2009, 217–38.

[149] Trevelyan, 'Englishmen and Italians', 120.

the puzzled consternation of radical observers.[150] McAdam wrote to Garibaldi 'delicately' hinting that British friends 'expected his cooperation with Mazzini';[151] amongst increasingly faltering loyalties, McAdam desperately looked for reliable allies like Holyoake, whom he considered a 'true friend of Italy'.[152] Writing for the *Daily News* under the pseudonym Landor Praed, Holyoake also stressed that the organising Committee consisted 'of a few friends of Garibaldi only' but 'chiefly of attached friends of Mazzini'.[153] Yet, by the autumn of 1860, Holyoake's apprehension had mounted. In a letter to Richard Bagnall Reed, a radical chain-maker from County Durham who was Secretary of the Northern Reform Union (1857–62), Holyoake's associate, John McAdam, anxiously affirmed:[154] 'We are tenaciously holding on to the real Italian question here though our devotion to Mazzini creates jealousy among our magnates.... I trust G. [Garibaldi] will take care of Cavour – it is indeed painful to read as I have Mazzini's diary to Mrs Stansfeld of which she honoured me with a copy up to Aug. 24th.'[155]

The contribution made by the British Garibaldians was in many ways controversial, but what is worth highlighting are Holyoake's feelings of betrayal and disappointment following the outcome of Garibaldi's liberation of the South. Amongst the volunteers, Victorian Mazzinians had fought hard. As Holyoake recalled, 'The flag of the *Washington* would have been lost had it not been taken possession of by De Rohan. The last flag carried by the Mazzinians, which was shot through, would have been lost also had not Mr. J. D. Hodge sought for it before it was too late.'[156] As the ideals for which Victorian Mazzinians had gone out to fight appeared somewhat betrayed, Holyoake's frustration was vented in no uncertain terms in the *Daily News* on 17 December 1860:

> It is no secret to the world that Mazzini's influence supplied the men and Bertani's skill organised those expeditions which tracked with their blood the pathway which Garibaldi took to his miraculous victories. Italy and Victor Emmanuel owe as much to the genius and generosity of Mazzini as to the invincible sword of Garibaldi.... Indeed, I believe four-fifths of all the British Garibaldi funds have been collected and subscribed by personal friends of Mazzini, unhesitantly placed at the disposal of Garibaldi and every pound

---

[150] *Jersey Independent,* 4 Jan. 1860; 'Garibaldi', *Jersey Independent*, 6 June. 1860. On foreign policy in 1859–60 see Beales, *England and Italy.*

[151] J. McAdam to R. B. Reed, 1 Sept. 1860, TWAS, CP, C1519.

[152] McAdam to Holyoake, 28 May 1860, HP, HHM, 28, doc. 1220.

[153] 'Letter to the Editor', *Daily News*, 15 Oct. 1860.

[154] Ashton and Pickering, *Friends of the people*, 127–49.

[155] McAdam to Reed, 10 Sept. 1860, TWAS, CP, C1531.

[156] Holyoake, *Bygones*, i. 235. Both flags, symbols of hope for Italy's republic, would come into Holyoake's possession: according to his wishes, Holyoake's coffin was draped with them: Onnis, 'Battaglie democratiche', 918.

appropriated … to the establishment of an Italian Kingdom, and Italian unity, under the constitutional scepter of Victor Emanuel.[157]

The war had ended, yet Mazzini could not be satisfied with the monarchical outcome; nor were his Victorian friends, who could still be relied upon, as the new challenges of nation-building took priority in a unified liberal Italy.

[157]   L. Praed, 'Italian subscriptions and Sir Henry Ainslie Hoare', *Daily News*, 17 Dec. 1860.

PART II

VICTORIAN MAZZINIANS AND THE
'MAKING OF ITALIANS', 1861–1890

4

English Republicans, Liberal Italy and the Monarchical Turn, 1860–1872

'Signor Mazzini is to the thinking few just what General Garibaldi is to the unthinking many.'[1]

Dazzled by the dramatic sequence of military events in the 1860s, which were dominated by the charismatic figure of Garibaldi and by the 'Machiavellian' diplomacy of Cavour, historians have overwhelmingly interpreted British responses to Italian unification through the prism of public enthusiasm for the victorious, moderate, monarchical solution, totally obscuring the disappointment of the Victorian philo-Italian 'losers' who resented the political side-lining of Mazzini.[2] By modifying some of the underlying assumptions of 'official' interpretations, this chapter does two things: it highlights the reactions of Victorian republicans to the achievement of Italian unity under the aegis of a Piedmontese monarch and it focuses on the activities which they supported in liberal Italy.

While John A. Davis has provided a convincing interpretation of the part played by Trevelyan in posthumously inflating the collective memory of Garibaldi's popularity in Britain, it would be unfair to burden Trevelyan with the entire responsibility for the later whiggish reading of 'Britain's Risorgimento'.[3] In fact, as mid-Victorian Britain has been variously described in the historiography as an 'age of equipoise', a period of 'retrenchment and reform', and an era when the 'discourse of popular constitutionalism' prevailed over that of radicalism, it is not surprising that the disappointment of Victorian republicans with Italy's monarchical turn was given short shrift.[4]

---

[1] *The Athenaeum*, quoted in 'Joseph Mazzini', NR, 8 Oct. 1864.

[2] D. Mack Smith, *Cavour and Garibaldi, 1860*, Cambridge 1985. While foreign reactions to post-war Republican Italy, from 1945 to 2000, have attracted the interest of scholars (S. Woolf, *L'Italia repubblicana vista da fuori*, Bologna 2007) historians have until now not addressed how republicans abroad reacted to the failure of Mazzini's project for Italy in 1860.

[3] Davis, 'The many English lives of Giuseppe Garibaldi'.

[4] Idem, 'Garibaldi and England', 24; M. Hewitt, *An age of equipoise? Re-assessing mid-Victorian Britain*, Aldershot 2000; W. L. Burn, *The age of equipoise: a study of the mid-Victorian generation*, New York 1964; Biagini, *Liberty*; Taylor, *Decline of British radicalism*; J. Vernon, *Politics and the people: a study in English political culture, c. 1815–67*, Cambridge 1993.

Yet Duncan Bell has highlighted the need to balance 'the view of the mid-Victorian era as an age of equipoise' with the 'recognition of the existence of a widespread anxiety over Britain's place in the world'.[5]

Although the historiography of Gladstonian popular liberalism left little space for republican dissent, such imbalance has been partly redressed by recent studies by Frank Prochaska, David Nash and Antony Taylor.[6] Yet, in the context of British responses to the unification of Italy, republican reactions have found no voice. This may partly be due to the fact that, traditionally, historians have hesitated to consider republicans as representative of 'Englishness'; in fact, in Antony Taylor's words, republicans are more likely to be constructed according to their 'anti-Englishness', as the 'peculiarities of the English' have traditionally been linked to plebeian support for the monarchy.[7] In line with this view, Jonathan Parry has affirmed that, after the unification of Italy was secured under the Piedmontese monarchy, the consensus in Britain was that, with Cavour, the 'English of Italy' had won.[8]

Even more than Cavour, however, Garibaldi has been the main magnet for historians studying British reactions to Italy's unification. In the context of the 'politics of Italian enthusiasm' of the 1860s, many studies have concentrated on Garibaldi's triumphant visit to London, which, according to Derek Beales, 'helped Palmerston, his friends and colleagues, to preserve the social and political consensus of the "age of equipoise"'.[9] In any such description the part played by Mazzini is necessarily overshadowed – if not framed in his utter impotence, unable to steer Garibaldi's visit to the waiting

---

[5]   D. Bell, *Victorian visions of global order: empire and international relations in nineteenth-century political thought*, Cambridge 2007, 7.

[6]   For the historiography on liberalism in the age of Gladstone see Biagini, *Liberty*, 2; J. Vincent, *The formation of the British Liberal party, 1857–68*, London 1966; and H. G. C. Matthew, *Gladstone (1809–74)*, Oxford 1986. For an alternative perspective see N. J. Gossman, 'Republicanism in nineteenth-century England', *International Review of Social History* vii (1962), 553–74. For studies on republicanism see D. Nash and A. Taylor (eds), *Republicanism in Victorian society*, Stroud 2000; Prochaska, *The republic of Britain*; Taylor, *'Down with the crown'*, and 'Republicanism reappraised: anti-monarchism and the English radical tradition, 1850–72', in J. Vernon (ed.), *Re-reading the constitution*, Cambridge 1996, 154–78; J. Belchem, 'Republicanism, popular constitutionalism and the radical platform in early nineteenth-century England', *Social History* vi/1 (1981), 1–32; and E. Royle, *Radicals, secularists and republicans: popular freethought in Britain (1866–1915)*, Manchester 1980.

[7]   Taylor, *'Down with the crown'*, 14; Thompson, 'Peculiarities of the English'; P. Mandler, *The English national character: the history of an idea from Edmund Burke to Tony Blair*, London–New Haven 2006; Colls, *Identity*; R. Colls and P. Dodd (eds), *Englishness politics and culture (1880–1920)*, London 1986.

[8]   Parry, *The politics of patriotism*, 232, 242.

[9]   Beales, 'Garibaldi in England', 184–216; O'Connor, *Romance of Italy*, 149–85; Finn, *After Chartism*, 203–26; Davis, 'Garibaldi and England', 21–6; Funaro, 'Il viaggio di Garibaldi in Inghilterra', 129–57.

radical provinces.[10] This portrayal of Mazzini's isolation in 1864 sits comfortably in the context of Beales's interpretation of the exile as a 'lone figure in England' after 1859.[11] Biagini also underlined how Garibaldi 'best personified the reasons for the British love of the Risorgimento'.[12]

While Gregory Claeys highlighted the power of 'Italian republicanism in exile', his study concentrated on the 1850s. Nor was the opportunity to extend the investigation of Mazzini's popularity into the later years seized upon by Maura O'Connor who, while dedicating a chapter to the English Mazzinians, once again stopped short of investigating the 1860s.[13] Sarti too stressed how the British were satisfied with the constitutional monarchical solution, while Mack Smith did not explore the following that Mazzini retained amongst republicans.[14] Indeed, the lack of investigation into the perspectives of republicans has led historians to focus increasingly on Mazzini's notoriety as an agitator and his growing isolation after 1861.[15]

Yet British radicals did colour the political landscape of Gladstonian Britain, and their views on foreign affairs and empire were vociferously expressed.[16] Based on the idea that liberal societies afford space for critique, part II of this book teases out the voices of radical dissent which challenged the liberal assumption that the British constitutional monarchy should be the model for other nations. The aim of this chapter is to focus on the radicals' perspective on the newly-unified Italy: it shows how Victorian republicans, from the establishment of the Kingdom of Italy in 1861 to Mazzini's death in1872, supported the exile's continuing fight to re-establish in Italy the 'Ideal', which had briefly seen the light during the short-lived Roman Republic. Victorian republicanism, which had surged in the 1850s, experienced a significant revival in the early 1870s, when thousands of people attended meetings throughout the country: indeed, numbers of republicans are estimated to have doubled since the mid-nineteenth century. The significance that Victorian radicals continued to attach to Mazzini's name and role was a measure of how reluctant some of them were to accept Italy's monarchical turn. Indeed, Mazzini, with his relentless attachment to republicanism, was the personification of an uncompromising ideological integrity.

[10] See Ridley, *Garibaldi*, 547–64.

[11] Beales, *England and Italy*, 32. See also Barié, 'Il radicalismo inglese', 138; Laven, 'Mazzini'; Biagini, *Gladstone*, 79; Duggan, 'Giuseppe Mazzini', 193–4; Finn, *After Chartism*, 203–26, 274, 278, 285.

[12] Biagini, *Liberty*, 372, 374. See also Finn, *After Chartism*, 203–26.

[13] See Claeys, 'Mazzini', 225–61 at pp. 237, 244; O'Connor, 'Romance of Italy', 149–85.

[14] Mack Smith, *Mazzini*, 214; Sarti, *Mazzini*, 195.

[15] See A. McAllister, *John Bull's Italian snakes and ladders*, Newcastle-upon-Tyne 2007.

[16] See Bell, *Victorian visions*; Biagini, 'The politics of Italianism'; and Vargo, '"Outworks"'.

Voicing radicalism in the Gladstone era

The emergence of the Liberal Party in 1859 saw Palmerston and Russell bury their differences and form, with Gladstone, a 'triumvirate'; its cabinet would regard foreign policy as its main priority.[17] The aim was to lend support to the moderate party that emerged in Italy, which promised to curb the advances of the Italian democrats. Gladstone's sympathies for Italy were rooted in his sensitivity to the cry of moderate liberal aristocrats: his early references were Silvio Pellico's *My prisons*, which Gladstone had read in 1833, and the denunciations of the anti-republican historian Luigi Carlo Farini, whose work, *Lo stato romano dal 1815 al 1850*, he had translated. Gladstone was also familiar with the views of his friends, the Neapolitan James Lacaita and Antonio Panizzi, who arrived in England with the first wave of aristocratic exiles. Crucially, following pressure from Panizzi, Gladstone had visited the Neapolitan dungeons in 1850 and condemned the Bourbons' rule in his *Two letters to Earl Aberdeen*, which led to the eventual release of Count Poerio and a group of kindred compatriots in 1859.[18] During these years Gladstone's correspondence with members of Cavour's Piedmontese government had ensured that Mazzini's name was associated with insurrections dubbed as 'ridiculous' affairs. Unsurprisingly, by 1860, Gladstone's opinion of Mazzini had worsened. As he wrote to Lord Brougham, 'Still the name of Mazzini is to me of very ill savor and I am grieved to hear that he is or is likely to be on the ground. If Garibaldi does not ship him off, it will be a bad sign.'[19] Gladstone's vision for a unified Italy had clearly little in common with that of English republicans who loyally supported Mazzini and his project.[20]

Nevertheless, republicans were voicing their views vociferously. They had found new leadership in Charles Bradlaugh, a vigorous atheist who had side-lined Holyoake, choosing to move the headquarters of the *National Reformer* from Yorkshire to the capital in 1862. London was emerging, according to Edward Royle, as the 'principal scene of radical activity'.[21] The *National Reformer* became, according to Sari Altschuler 'for a time, the most important radical periodical in England'.[22] Provincial towns still made, however, a significant contribution to English radicalism: Leicester, whose radical traditions went back to Cooper's Chartist influence, reaffirmed its political

---

[17] Parry, *The politics of patriotism*, 227; Matsumoto, 'Palmerston and Italy', 79–96. On the 'triumvirate' see also G. M. Trevelyan, *British history in the nineteenth century, 1782–1901*, London 1922, 327.

[18] Biagini, *Gladstone*, 27; Isabella, 'Italian exiles', 59–87; Reidy, 'Panizzi'.

[19] Gladstone to Lord Brougham, 26 Sept. 1860, Gladstone papers, BL, MS 44531, fo. 51, quoted in Shannon, *Gladstone*, i. 426.

[20] Gladstone papers, MS 44386, fos 95–97–98, quoted in Shannon, *Gladstone* i. 323.

[21] E. Royle, *Radicals, secularists and republicans: popular freethought in Britain (1866–1915)*, Manchester 1980, 4.

[22] S. B. Altschuler, 'National Reformer (1860–91)', *DNCJ*, 439.

credentials by electing, in 1862, as its advanced Liberal MP, P. A. Taylor, Mazzini's Unitarian friend.[23]

Republican platforms providing endorsement and support for Mazzini's positions could be found in the South and in the North of England in the 1860s. P. A. Taylor regularly contributed to London papers, such as the *Morning Chronicle* and the *Examiner*, which he eventually purchased in 1872.[24] The republican W. E. Adams reached his audience from the pages of Cowen's *Newcastle Weekly Chronicle*, a paper widely read, with a circulation which went from 2,000 in 1864 to a claimed 45,000 by 1875.[25] In addition, Adams's articles could be read in the pages of Bradlaugh's *National Reformer*. Intended for a niche secular readership, The *National Reformer* nevertheless increased its circulation from an average of 3,000 in 1867 to double that number in 1872, when it became 'the standard bearer of pure republican argument'.[26]

Bradlaugh's paper was rarely found to be in agreement with mainstream papers. In the midst of the expedition to Sicily articles in the *National Reformer* balanced guarded expressions of admiration for Garibaldi's successes with profuse praise for Mazzini. The paper was suspicious of the sudden popularity that Garibaldi had acquired, not least with the conservative British press. 'Gratifying' as it might have seemed to witness all Britain – the House of Lords included – behind Garibaldi's enterprise, the *National Reformer* warned its readers that Garibaldi was 'the hero of the hour' not so much because he had a 'righteous cause' but because he had 'made it a successful one'. It was against 'this fatal hero-worship' that the English should be guarding themselves.[27] Throughout the campaign the paper was adamant that Mazzini's 'wonderful power and his no less wonderful success should be remembered in the midst of the successes in Sicily'.[28] Garibaldi was 'not the only hero engaged in the emancipation of Italy', but 'simply the centre of a brilliant group of kindred stars', including Sirtori, Medici, Nino Bixio and Saffi. It was to Mazzini, however, that Italy owed her redemption.[29] Such comments seemed to endeavour to mark the boundaries of the increasingly popular tide of opinion which would bestow on Garibaldi, rather than Mazzini, the undis-

---

[23] B. Lancaster, *Radicalism, co-operation and socialism: Leicester working-class politics, 1860–1906*, Leicester 1987, 76.

[24] L. Bersohn, 'The Examiner', *DNCJ*, 211.

[25] Ashton, 'Newcastle Weekly Chronicle', 446–7.

[26] Royle, *Radicals*, 7; Prochaska, *The republic of Britain*, 105.

[27] 'The Italian question', *NR*, 21 July 1860, 5.

[28] 'Danger in Sicily', *NR*, 16 June 1860, 4–5.

[29] Writing in September, only weeks after Nino Bixio's involvement in the brutal repression of the insurrection in Bronte, W. E. Adams, no doubt unaware of the event, included Bixio amongst the best of Mazzini's followers: 'Italy resurgent', *NR*, 15 Sept. 1860, 5–6.

puted title of 'father of the nation'.[30] Indeed, the poem dedicated to Mazzini by the Newcastle resident, Henry Gilpin, suggests that when Italy achieved unification, Victorian admirers were not exclusively linking her success with Garibaldi's triumph: as Gilpin declared, referring to Mazzini, 'But for thee/ A Garibaldi ne'er had taken arms, or found the hearts that throbbed for Italy' (see Appendix 1).[31]

It is important to take into account radicals' perspectives in the 1860s as it highlights the need for historians comparing the respective popularity of Mazzini and Garibaldi in Britain to give heed to both sides of the argument rather than feed the argument of 'polarised' constructions. Annemarie McAllister's appraisal of English representations of Garibaldi and Mazzini stressed that after Italy's unification 'the myth of Mazzini as a "notorious agitator" had become fixed'.[32] This contention was mainly based on Harriet Martineau's claim that Mazzini, in the aftermath of Italy's unification, ought to accept the monarchical outcome – a sign that not only conservatives and liberals, but also some radicals, had distanced themselves from the exile's republican dream.[33] However, as Harry Rudman perspicaciously put it, 'Harriet Martineau was merely expressing the feelings of the more influential English classes'.[34] Indeed, in January 1862, in response to Martineau's criticisms, the *National Reformer* argued that her 'false estimate' of Mazzini was due to a lack of understanding of the 'teacher'. Martineau's claim that Mazzini should have 'withdrawn into silence and invisibility' after unification were countered by W. E. Adams, who penned a defence in Bradlaugh's paper, insisting that Mazzini 'because he is Mazzini, will never be silent while Italy remains unredeemed'. The article closed with an admonition: 'that Republic for which he wrought is yet but a matter of the future'.[35]

Countering negative representations of Mazzini, the *National Reformer* relied for its sources on Italian papers of unequivocal republican credentials. The traffic of republican information across national boundaries was an important element in the transnational connections between Victorian radicals and Italian democrats in liberal Italy. Significantly, in 1862, the encomiastic description of Mazzini as a child, which pointedly mirrored the numerous accounts of Garibaldi's childhood and life circulating in Britain, was taken from Maurizio Quadrio's paper *L'Unità Italiana*, the Mazzinian

---

[30] R. Gerwath and L. Riall, 'Fathers of the nation? Bismarck, Garibaldi and the cult of memory in Germany and Italy', *EHQ* xxxix/3 (2009), 388–413.

[31] H. Gilpin, *Mazzini*, (1861?), FH, MRM, 18/28.

[32] McAllister, *Italian snakes and ladders*, 207.

[33] For the relationship between Mazzini and Harriet Martineau see G. Conti Odorisio, 'Giuseppe Mazzini ed Harriet Martineau: un'amicizia possibile', in Bocchi and Palazzolo, *Giuseppe Mazzini e John Stuart Mill*, 71–100.

[34] Rudman, *Italian nationalism and English letters*, 128.

[35] 'Harriet Martineau's false estimate of Mazzini', *NR*, 4 Jan. 1862.

organ in Milan which was the most openly republican in its views, even when compared with the Mazzinian *Popolo d'Italia*, edited in Naples.[36]

Victorian Mazzinians and the new Italy

In 1861, as the republican option appeared to be losing ground in Italy, Victorian Mazzinians gave voice to their frustrations through the publication of articles or vocal denunciations at public lectures. Criticism of Italy's monarchical solution was expressed in the *National Reformer*, the *Examiner* and the *Newcastle Weekly Chronicle*. Similar views were being aired in lecture theatres across the provinces and in the attempted publication of a controversial pamphlet a few years later.

Admittedly, a few radicals did abandon Mazzini's republican vision of Italy for 'the more practicable Cavour', as Thornton Hunt sheepishly confessed to Linton in 1860.[37] Yet many others held firm, and battled on, venting their frustration at the turn that events had taken with a mix of incredulity and desire to be vindicated in their beliefs. According to the *National Reformer*, Mr Mason Jones, having left for Italy a convinced supporter of Cavour – 'the man whose praises were in all the newspapers' – had returned to England a 'disciple' and 'champion' of Mazzini and was lecturing in London, Manchester and other parts of the country convinced that 'a simple narration in England of the principles and aims of the Republican party would change the opinions which thousands of Englishmen had regarding them'. Unsurprisingly, the article advised 'all readers' 'by all means' to attend the lectures.[38] They were held in a number of places in the provinces, such as Liverpool, Glasgow, Hull and Preston,[39] attracted large audiences, both men and women, and were described in the *Daily News* as eulogies of Mazzini.[40] Indeed, his detractors commented that Jones was under the influence of 'a disreputable party of English assembled in Naples, some of whom [were] deeply imbued with Mazzinian doctrines'.[41] Naples in 1860 did serve as a centre for members of the republican party: both Saffi and his wife, Giorgina Craufurd Saffi, were there. Mazzini intended to make Naples the headquarters of the republican movement and Saffi had been made co-director, with Filippo De Boni, of the new Mazzinian paper which was to be published there, *Il Popolo d'Italia*.

Returning from Naples, Mason Jones made a display of his republican

36 'The early days of Mazzini', *NR*, 22 Feb. 1862; Riall, *Garibaldi*, 253–67.

37 T. Hunt to W. Linton, 16 Mar. 1860, FL, AGF, 2, 72, 4.

38 'Mr Mason Jones's lectures on Garibaldi and Italy', *NR*, 15 Dec. 1860, 7.

39 *Liverpool Mercury*, 17, 18 Dec. 1860; *The Hull Packet and East Riding Times*, 21 Dec. 1860; *Preston Guardian*, 1 Dec.1860.

40 'Orations upon Italy and Garibaldi', *Daily News*, 7 Dec. 1860.

41 'The British Legion: Colonel Peard's reply to Mr. Mason Jones', *Leeds Mercury*, 11 Dec. 1860.

convictions. In mid-December 1860 the London paper the *Era*, when describing his lecture at the Free Trade Hall in Manchester, reported that 'The cheers and the plaudits during the evening' had been 'loud and frequent'. Yet the lecturer had openly condemned Cavour, whose name was said to be execrated from Palermo to Turin and especially in Milan; furthermore, equally damning remarks had been aimed at Victor Emmanuel. Conversely, the republican party headed by Mazzini was reported by Jones to be 'strong not only by its numbers and intelligence, but by its possession of a great idea' and attracting respected party members such as 'Crispi, Bertani, Saffi and Nicotera'.[42] Interestingly, the *Era* commented that, rather than 'Garibaldi and Italy', 'a better title to this second discourse would have been Mazzini, as the greater portion of it was descriptive of him and his party. Mr Jones spoke of him in terms of the highest praise, and also again brought up Cromwell as the greatest hero England ever saw'.[43]

The image of Cromwell, who had been calumniated since the Enlightenment as a traitor, had been gradually improving in the early nineteenth century thanks to the publication in 1825–8 of Thomas Macaulay's *History of England* and William Godwin's *History of the Commonwealth*. As Blair Worden has shown, in the 1840s Carlyle had definitively contributed to placing Cromwell within the pantheon of England's past heroes.[44] Mazzini, who knew Carlyle well, often drew parallels between the revolution that Italy needed and England's civil war: the continuity between England's past and Italy's projected future therefore became part of the language of Victorian radicals when referring to the 'Third Rome'. The link between Puritans and Mazzinianism has been highlighted by Biagini:[45] the same people who vindicated Cromwell as one of England's heroes often also admired Mazzini. Therefore the language which Mason Jones adopted in his lectures was familiar to his audience. George Dawson, a Mazzinian who gave lectures on Carlyle's vision of Cromwell, also lectured on Italy. Adams, whose veneration for Mazzini was evident in his articles published in the *Newcastle Weekly Chronicle* signed himself 'Ironside', in memory of the artisan members of Cromwell's 'new model army'. The other pseudonym that W. E. Adams adopted, as contributor to Bradlaugh's *National Reformer*, was 'Caractacus', a reference to the long British tradition of defiance towards power – military or spiritual – imposed from imperial Rome.

Mazzini's friends, to whom Mason Jones had referred in optimistic terms, were indeed struggling against the power exercised by the governmental authorities. During the convulsive first decade of Italy's unification Mazzin-

---

[42] 'Mr. Mason Jones and Garibaldi', *Daily News*, 13 Dec. 1860.

[43] Ibid.

[44] T. Carlyle, *On heroes, hero worship and the heroic in history*, London 1840; Worden, 'The Victorians and Cromwell', 114.

[45] Biagini, *Liberty*.

ians' febrile activities were closely monitored: censorship, policing and control meant that republican activities often went underground.[46] Victorian radicals supported them: Emilie Ashurst Venturi, who was now living in Italy, wrote to Holyoake that the police had been sending secret circulars instructing its agents to watch over her correspondence, as she was exposed as one of Mazzini's 'notorious friends'.[47] Victorian Mazzinians were aware of the national papers' misrepresentations of the activities of Italian republicans, construed as the actions of 'red' revolutionaries. Indeed, Sophia Churchill Craufurd, Saffi's mother-in-law, proposed to organise a network of interpreters to translate articles drawn from the Italian democratic papers, which would be published in the *Morning Star*, as well as in other British provincial radical papers.[48] Mazzini knew how politically sensitive this particular crossroads was, and hoped that much could still be done to reverse the course upon which Italy was set. Despite recent unification under a monarch, the nation had not yet secured important territorial gains – namely Rome and Venice – and the education of Italian workers could be crucial in returning the initiative to the 'people'.

Linking workers' associations across national boundaries

Mazzini encouraged democrats to promote the establishment of workers' associations, which he hoped would be organised nationally under the lead of Naples. 'Men', for Mazzini, were 'rational and social creatures *capable of intellectual progress only by means of association [sic].'*[49] By mid-1861 the progress of working men's societies in Italy seemed to be well under way. In Naples there were 1,200 members; in Leghorn, Romagna, Florence and Piedmont similar initiatives were sprouting up as popular papers, schools, circulating libraries and banks for the people were being established. Holyoake was kept informed and was expected to disseminate the news through the *Reasoner*.[50] Italian democrats were the first to encourage and involve English radicals in supporting them. In December 1861 De Boni – writing as co-editor of the *Popolo d'Italia* – contacted Holyoake on behalf of the Neapolitan Society of Working Men, enclosing a signed address to be presented to the Equitable

---

[46] J. Davis, *Conflict and control: law and order in nineteenth-century Italy*, London 1988. On the role played by the diplomatic service in keeping the government abreast of political developments in Italy see Wright, 'British representatives'.

[47] E. A. Venturi to Holyoake [end 1861), FH, MRM, 4/22.

[48] Gazzetta, *Contributo*, 31.

[49] Scirocco, *I democratici italiani*, 147; G. Mazzini, 'The duties of man', in Recchia and Urbinati, *Cosmopolitanism*, 89, 91.

[50] Mazzini to Holyoake, 17 May 1861, *SEI*, appendice, epistolario, vi. 166–70.

Pioneers of Rochdale which appealed to the 'British societies' to support Neapolitan workers in their pledge to unite Rome with the rest of Italy.[51]

The *Newcastle Weekly Chronicle* reported on the Italian workers' addresses to their 'fellow workmen' in England and Holyoake delivered a lecture in Manchester explaining their objectives.[52] He was accompanied by Charles Hadfield, a decorator educated at the Manchester Mechanics' Institute, who had turned journalist and was working for Cowen's *Newcastle Chronicle*.[53] Hadfield made a speech that was steeped in internationalist hopes: 'No sooner were the hands of a people unfettered than they were stretched abroad over land and seas to clasp the hands of neighbouring peoples.' Hadfield believed that now that Italy was emancipated from the foreign oppressor, political emancipation was within reach for Italian workers, who would indeed provide 'inspiration' to the working men of England:

> Politically the mass of English workmen exist on sufferance. English labour is the Lazarus of the constitution. Like the workmen of Italy, Englishmen will learn to owe to their trade organization the rights which will and must be conceded ... From the federation of labour founded by their Italian brethren, married as it is to the pure and lofty sentiment of patriotism, the workmen of England will gather inspiration.[54]

The link between patriotism, workers, franchise and transnational connections was exquisitely Mazzinian. The notion of 'humanity', by definition universal, was inherently 'transnational': education, work – through 'association' – and the franchise were considered by Mazzini 'the three main pillars of the Nation'; yet the mission was the 'moral unity of Europe'.[55] Inspired by such principles, Victorian Mazzinians continued to follow with keen interest the developments and progress of the Italians even after their country had been politically unified. English workers were familiar with Mazzini's *Duties of man*, published not only in the *English Republic* and in extracts in other radical dailies such as the *Examiner*, but 'constantly in print' from 1858 onwards and indeed 'widely circulated'.[56] Here was clearly stated:

---

[51] F. De Boni to Holyoake, Naples, 11 (?) Dec. 1861, HP, HHM, 1376; 'Italian address to the Equitable Pioneers of Rochdale', NR, 15 Feb. 1862. The address was signed by Francesco Rossi, president of the General Operative Society, and vice-presidents Giovanni Ciucci, Raffaele Cozzolins (?) and Gennaro Rovito; Tommaso Salerno; Raffaele Rosso; Michele Palumbo; Salvatore Ricci; Pasquale Amodio; Domenico Gatti; Gennaro Russo; Luigi de Santis; Salvatore Mozzo, presidents of the subdivisions; and secretaries Cesare Ferrari and Cesare Battaglia. See 'Italian and English workmen', NWC, 14 Dec. 1861.

[52] 'Italian and English workmen', NWC, 14 Dec. 1861.

[53] G. C. Boase, 'Hadfield, Charles (1821–84), ODNB.

[54] 'Italian and English workmen', NWC, 14 Dec. 1861

[55] Mazzini, 'The duties of man', 96.

[56] Idem, 'The duties of man', *English Republic* (1851), 195; 'Chapman and Hall', *Examiner*, 2 Apr. 1864; Duggan, 'Giuseppe Mazzini', 193.

The only lasting hope for you lies in the general amelioration, improvement and brotherhood of all the peoples of Europe, and through Europe of all Humanity. Therefore, my brothers, in the name of your duty and for the sake of your interest, never forget that your first duties are towards Humanity. Without fulfilling those latter duties, you cannot hope to fulfil those owed to family and country.[57]

Speaking at the Wakefield Mechanics' Institute, in October 1861, James Stansfeld had no doubt that local adult learners would reap great benefits from familiarising themselves with Italy's national struggle. When venturing beyond the narrow sphere of 'educational questions', there could be no subject 'more akin to the purposes' of the Institute than national movements, that equated to nothing but the 'partial evolution in time and space of that great problem of all problems – the problem of the education of humanity'.[58]

Radical papers kept British readers abreast of the progress of associations in Italy. In December 1861 The *Newcastle Weekly Chronicle* reported that 'large numbers of working men societies' had 'sprung up in Italy'. Holyoake continued to spread the good news. In 1862 he introduced the workers gathered at the Secular Institute in Rochdale to the progress of the Italian working men, hinting that the establishment of 'personal intercourse between them and the societies of England' would follow.[59] The *Rochdale Observer*, which reported on Holyoake's visit, also had words of praise for the progress which was underway in Italy.[60]

The link that the Rochdale workers established between the formation of workers' associations and the franchise was also a direct reflection of the discourses that had circulated in England since the establishment of the Northern Reform Union in 1858. As the hub of co-operation, Rochdale was, undoubtedly, in a privileged position for entertaining links with Mazzini's followers in Italy. While the Italian exile had contributed to the debate on 'association' in England, Holyoake and Mazzini's joint efforts had been at the forefront of the dissemination of the Rochdale co-operative model in Italy. In 1862 Holyoake sent the working men of Genoa a publication on the co-operative movement.[61] Although in the 1860s Italian co-operation was still in its early phases, the names of the Pioneers were, according to Nello Rosselli, steadily becoming 'famous in Italy and proverbial amongst

---

57 Mazzini, 'The duties of man', in Recchia and Urbinati, *Cosmopolitanism*, 91. Although these words were originally written for the Italian workers they were considered, by Linton in 1851, to be 'not less applicable' to English workers: *English Republic*, 195.

58 'Mr Stansfeld's Speech delivered at the annual soirée of the Wakefield Mechanics' Institute on 31 October 1861', in Cowen Tracts, Newcastle University, 31 7, 50–5.

59 *NR*, 4 Jan. 1862, 3.

60 Quoted ibid.

61 Mazzini to Holyoake, 19 Nov. 1860s (?), HP, HHM, MM96636/4, and 17 Dec. FH, MRM, 3/33, 4.

workers', and Rochdale was turning into a well-known place of pilgrimage for Italian co-operators.[62]

The co-operative work which was under way in Italy was well known to northern co-operators. In 1862 Jessie White Mario, who also promoted co-operation in Italy, had chosen to deliver new lectures on Italy in Preston, Oldham and Rochdale.[63] Encouraging news on the progress of Italian workers continued to percolate radical circles: the *Literary Examiner* informed its readers, in 1864, that 'prosperous industrial associations' had been formed throughout free Italy, and in each of them Mazzini's name was 'gratefully remembered'.[64] Yet the *National Reformer* was more vigilant, aware that amongst such popular associations there were signs that 'evil and intriguing' influences were, as ever, 'busily at work'.[65] This was a reference to how the progress of Italian workers could be hampered by competing ideologies.

Indeed, while Mazzini's initial battle with moderate elements for influence over the political direction of the workers' societies had been won, by the end of 1864 the influence in Italy of Marx and of Bakunin was increasingly being felt.[66] The London Italian Working Men's Society had been the first to join the International, 'holding out a promise that at no distant date the 100 Working Men's Societies in Italy would join the association in a body'.[67] Coming from the Italian workers in London, where Mazzini had first started his apostolic work towards the reform of society by organising the *Unione degli operai italiani*, this was a very serious blow.[68] From 1864 onwards the ripples of the First International would divide Italian workers.

---

[62] N. Rosselli, *Mazzini e Bakunin: dodici anni di movimento operaio in Italia, 1860–72*, Turin 1967, 123. Indeed, as early as 1867 the Rochdale Pioneers' store Visitors' Book displayed the name of Ugo Pisa, a banker, keen co-operator and one of the most influential, enlightened Milanese men connected with the democrats' paper *Il Secolo*. In 1869 the First International Congress of Co-operators, held in London, saw co-operative associations send three representatives – all Mazzinians: Cesare Cabella from Genoa, Giuseppe Dolfi from Florence and Francesco Viganò from Como. Other co-operative visits followed. Viganò, also collaborator of *Il Secolo*, attended the Newcastle-upon-Tyne Congress in 1880 and visited Rochdale: W. H. Brown, 'Mazzini ispira i cooperatori britannici', *Bollettino della Domus Mazziniana* (1956), 12 n. 3; *Newcastle upon Tyne Co-operative Congress Report* (1880), 42, in P. Gurney, 'A higher state of civilization and happiness', in F. V. Holthoon and M. V. d. Linden, *Internationalism in the Labour movement*, ii, Leiden 1988, 543–64 at p. 549.

[63] *NR*, 4 Jan. 1862, 3.

[64] *Literary Examiner*, 2 Apr. 1864, 4.

[65] 'Mazzini to the workmen of Naples', *NR*, 15 Mar. 1862.

[66] On the prevailing of the Mazzinian over the moderate line at the working men's congresses see G. Manacorda, *Il movimento operaio italiano attraverso i suoi congressi*, Rome 1953. On Bakunin's influence in Italy see Rosselli, *Mazzini e Bakunin*.

[67] In November 1864 a 'History of the International' was reported in all major English newspapers, including the *Newcastle Weekly Chronicle*.

[68] For a detailed account of Mazzini's reactions to the origins of the International see Rosselli, *Mazzini e Bakunin*, 129–39. Mazzini was initially under the impression that he

After Mazzini's victory over the moderates at the working men's societies' congress in Naples, which adopted the so-called 'Brotherhood Pact' ('*Atto di Fratellanza*'), the influence exercised by the First International would render powerless the newly-penned constitution of the Italian Workers' Societies.[69] Indeed, in Italy, the materialist discourse of 'class' and rights was threatening to overwhelm Mazzini's message on suffrage and duty. In Britain, conversely, the appeal of political enfranchisement to British workers as the only way to achieve 'political existence' would be fostered, from 1865 by the National Reform League, an organisational network which Italian societies were not yet able to replicate.[70]

London, April 1864: a counter-narrative

The year 1864 started ominously for Mazzini. He faced yet another accusation of conspiracy – this time against Napoleon III – since the Italian Pasquale Greco, arrested in Paris, was supposedly carrying a letter which implicated Mazzini in a plot.[71] The months that followed gave the British yet another opportunity to bring within the public arena the debate on Mazzini's character. Although the opportunity for reiterating old accusations of complicity in a plot to assassinate Victor Emmanuel was seized upon by Peter Hennessy in parliament, more measured views seemed to prevail.[72] Even Gladstone, as Chancellor of the Exchequer, in March 1864 stated that Mazzini was to be associated with 'perfect truth and integrity', and *The Times* conceded that the much disliked exile was nevertheless a 'man of perfect truthfulness'.[73]

Such weighty opinions counter views aimed at reducing English representations of Mazzini in this period to the negative opposite of Garibaldi. According to Annemarie McAllister 'the two men became locations for non-Englishness and Englishness in their identities as either the dark and duplicitous failure or the fair, brave, man'.[74] Although Garibaldi's popularity at this time is clearly not in doubt, radicals were well aware of the tendency

would be able to influence the direction of the First International: R. Hostetter, *The Italian socialist movement: origins (1861–82)*, New York–London–Toronto, 1958, 70–2.

[69] On the 'Brotherhood Pact' see B. Di Porto, *Storia del Patto di Fratellanza: movimento operaio e democrazia repubblicana, 1860–93*, Rome 1982.

[70] *NR*, 4 Jan. 1862, 3. On the *National Reform League* see Finn, *After Chartism*, 237–54.

[71] Mack Smith, *Mazzini*, 122, 165; Sarti, *Mazzini*, 178, 201.

[72] 'Mr Mazzini and the Greco conspiracy question', 14 Mar. 1864, *Hansard's Parliamentary Debates* clxxiii.1931–9, http://hansard.millbanksystems.com/commons/1864/mar/14/m-mazzini–and–the–greco–conspiracy, accessed 21 June 2013.

[73] http://hansard.millbanksystems.com/commons/1864/mar/17/mr–stansfeld–and–the–greco–conspiracy–1#S3V0174P0–18640317–HOC–136, accessed 21 June 2013; *The Times*, 15 Jan. 1860.

[74] McAllister, *Italian snakes and ladders*, 207.

of the press to manipulate it to the detriment of Mazzini, and were quick to alert their readers. On the eve of Garibaldi's visit to England, on 26 March 1864, the *Examiner* carefully reflected upon it, subtly hinting that it could become prey to political manipulations:

> Garibaldi's welcome will be spontaneous and universal. All we hope and wish is that no attempt may be made to pervert it to any passing or party purpose of the hour … [by] blackening the character of the man whom our expected guest has ever been the readiest to honour. We shall be no parties to the perpetration of this miserable fraud. The trick is too palpable not to be seen through.[75]

The day before Garibaldi's ship was to dock at Southampton, where enthusiastic crowds and keen journalists would congregate, the *Examiner* chose to publish long extracts from Mazzini's *The duties of man*.[76] The paper underlined that 'All true Englishmen love Fair Play. No longer then let Joseph Mazzini be judged from hearsay or report; but out of his own mouth let them judge and approve or condemn him.' By urging that Mazzini be judged from his own writings the *Examiner* was using the publication to enlighten readers, countering French accusations of Mazzini's involvement in the plot against Napoleon III. The timing of the article spoke volumes: only hours before Garibaldi was to set foot on the English shores, the paper seized the opportunity to underline how Mazzini, 'who of all foreign patriots is the one most English in tone and mind', had 'combated the errors of French revolutionists'. At a crucial time, when British crowds were about to come face to face with the 'English' Garibaldi, Mazzini's 'Englishness' too was being constructed in a radical paper.[77]

Arthur Munby's account of Garibaldi's visit to London is regarded with good reason as the most vivid description of the event: an occasion when popular enthusiasm was coupled with the display of an unusually orderly demeanour on the part of the crowd.[78] Numbers are estimated to have reached half a million.[79] The authorities' micromanagement of Garibaldi's visit was a triumph which upset Mazzini's plans to steer him towards the

---

75 'The visit of Garibaldi', *Examiner*, 26 Mar. 1864.

76 'The "duties of man" by Joseph Mazzini Chapman and Hall', *Examiner*, 2 Apr. 1864.

77 Raffaella Antoniucci has pointed out that Mazzini's 'English manner' was also celebrated in George Meredith's *Vittoria* (1867), a historical novel which ran in the *Fortnightly Review* and indeed dwelt upon the exile's magnetic personality: '"He had the English manner": Giuseppe Mazzini tra le pagine dei romanzieri vittoriani', in Q. Marini, G. Sertoli, S. Cedrino and L. Cavaglieri, *L'officina letteraria e culturale dell'età mazziniana, 1815–70*, Novi Ligure 2013, 113–28 at p. 123. Analysis of literary works written after 1860 confirms Mazzini's long-term appeal: Roberts, 'Mazzini's thought', 69–71.

78 D. Hudson, *Munby, man of two worlds: the life and diaries of Arthur J. Munby, 1828–1910*, London 1972, 186–7.

79 N. Blakiston, 'Garibaldi's visit to England in 1864', *Il Risorgimento* xvi (1964), 133–43.

radicals in the provinces. In fact, Mazzini had originally planned for the tour to start in the provinces. It was essential, according to William Ashurst, for Garibaldi to realise 'the importance of *coming out* as much as possible as a *pro-Mazzite*', and this would be less likely if the journey were to begin 'with the Londoners and the aristocrats'.[80] Mazzini's fury at Garibaldi on his sudden departure hinged on a double frustration: not only had the projected tour in the provinces, organised and much anticipated by Holyoake, P. A. Taylor, Cowen and McAdam, been deemed to be an important fundraising exercise towards the acquisition of Venice and Rome, but it had been expected to reinforce republican sentiments amongst English workers.[81] Garibaldi's early departure was a burning disappointment for northern radicals. The inability and impotence of Holyoake, Taylor and Cowen to entice Garibaldi to the more radical provinces had been the most spectacular demonstration of the triumph of the 'age of equipoise'.[82]

Despite the level-headed warnings that the *Examiner* had published on the eve of Garibaldi's visit, a considerable political commotion had ensued. It was not only Queen Victoria who drew a sigh of relief when Garibaldi finally left the country, but a shrewd Mazzinian such as T. H. Green was known to have been glad that he had gone, having disliked the mindless '*furore*' with which the English had marked the occasion.[83] The honours which had been bestowed on Garibaldi had somewhat embarrassed loyal supporters of Mazzini, English and Italian. The address to Mazzini by the Italian workers in London, which appeared in the *Unità Italiana* on 3 May 1864, was a revealingly long homage to the exile: the opening words of every other paragraph were either 'We have not forgotten' or 'We shall not forget'. As Saffi pointedly recalled in his writings, the address had been composed anonymously by Quadrio, in London with Mazzini at the time of Garibaldi's visit.[84]

In the autumn of the same year the *Athaeneum* critically reflected on the events of recent months, namely the implication that Mazzini and Stansfeld were involved in the Greco affair and Garibaldi's recent visit. According to the London paper, Mazzini, who had 'the misfortune of being a republican', was 'the best abused man in Europe', and just like an earlier great republican Englishman, John Milton, he would 'appear better in history than in life'. Having paid lip service to the common comparison made in radical literature

[80] TWA, CP, E436. See also Ridley, *Garibaldi*, 547.

[81] See Mazzini to G. Guerzoni, 18 Jan. 1864, *SEI* lxxvi. 308–10; lxxviii. 6, 29–31, 69–70, 72.

[82] This was first pointed out by Derek Beales in his 'Garibaldi in England', 216. See also J. Ridley, *Garibaldi*, London 2001, 559–64.

[83] 'Garibaldi, thank God! is gone', were the words written by Queen Victoria to the Crown Princess. See various sources quoted in Ridley, *Garibaldi*, 698 n. 55. See also R. L. Nettleship, *Memoir of Thomas Green Hill*, London 1906, 54.

[84] See Pelosi, *Della vita di Maurizio Quadrio*, ii. 147.

between the 'visible victory' of the 'man of action' and the obscured labours of the 'man of thought', the *Athenaeum* concluded that the significance of Garibaldi's visit to England was encapsulated in that 'proud moment' when the General had acknowledged his debt to his teacher.[85]

Republican rumblings

Mazzini hoped that the challenges of liberating Rome and Venice would provide republicans with the opportunity to regroup and reclaim the future direction of the nation for its 'people' rather than for the expansionist ambitions of the Piedmontese monarch. In Tuscany he could count on loyal republican artisans like Giuseppe Dolfi, who had joined the recently constituted Universal Republican Alliance. Mazzini's allies also counted on transnational republican support in Britain for liberating Rome and Venice. Jessie White Mario exhorted Cowen to 'get up a good meeting' in Newcastle to the 'death of Papacy cry' and not 'bother about flags' but to send anything that he could put together – by way of financial support – to Dolfi, of Borgo San Lorenzo, Florence.[86] Yet this was not a good time to set up an antipapal meeting in Newcastle: the year before the town had been the scene of 'Garibaldi riots' – at the hands of the local Irish Catholic community – and Cowen kept a low profile.[87]

Other Victorian Mazzinians, however, remained committed to lending their support to the final steps in the unification of Italy, showing signs of impatience with the unresolved 'Roman Question' and often wishing that they could influence the situation. In 1866 Saffi received a letter from a Mr M. Dunn who suggested forming a 'double Committee, an Italian and an English one' – to include a Council of War – which he proposed that Saffi should head.[88] Often well-informed about the preparations under way, Victorian working-class Mazzinians exchanged emotionally-charged correspondence on Italy and Rome.[89] However, as the veteran Mazzinian volunteer, De Rohan, wistfully acknowledged in a letter to Garibaldi, it was common knowledge by 1867 that 'foreign' volunteers were not welcome.[90]

---

[85] *Athenaeum*, quoted in 'Joseph Mazzini', *NR*, 8 Oct. 1864. Mazzini wrote two letters in Stansfeld's defence to *The Times* (15 Jan., 26 Mar. 1864).

[86] White Mario to Cowen, Arezzo, 23 Sept. 1867, TWA, CP, A882. On Dolfi see White Mario's biography, *Giuseppe Dolfi*, Florence 1883. See also M. Ralli, 'Dolfi, Giuseppe', *DBDI*, 451–62.

[87] Jackson, '"Garibaldi or the pope!"', 48–82; Allen, *Joseph Cowen*, 79–80; S. Gilley, 'The Garibaldi riots of 1862', *HJ* xvi/4 (1973), 697–732.

[88] M. Dunn to Saffi, 14 June 1866, FS, BCAB, ii/16/1, 55.

[89] J. Glover to W. E. Adams, 8 Oct.1867, Linton letters to W. E. Adams, 1855–92, Houghton Library, Harvard, MS Eng. 180.

[90] W. De Rohan to Garibaldi, Guernsey, 22 Aug. 1867, FC, MRM, 365/2599.

Victorian Mazzinians were nevertheless recruited for clandestine republican activities. Being English, they could more easily cross national boundaries carrying inflammatory republican material without patently raising the suspicions of the Italian authorities.[91] Yet, even with their help, conspiracies did not always go to plan. In 1866 republican activities were formalised into a military organisation, guided by a secret general committee. Giorgina Saffi was actively working to seek funds for it.[92] It was then that the young Englishman, David Nathan, while travelling between Switzerland and Italy with cases entrusted to him by Quadrio, was stopped at the frontier and found to be carrying documents, signed by Mazzini and embossed with the letterhead of the 'Universal Republican Alliance' – incriminating material which led to his imprisonment for three months.[93]

At this time Mazzini's work on behalf of the 'Universal Republican Alliance' was in full swing: a fundraising body promoted the Italian republic and worked on the purchase of arms. The organisation spread as far as the United States, with Linton entrusted by Mazzini with the role of ambassador and promoter. According to Roland Sarti and Giovanna Angelini, the 'Alliance' was one of the most significant initiatives in international politics which Mazzini undertook during that decade.[94] Yet it would soon falter.[95] In America Linton would pursue a solitary and unsuccessful battle which would give way to his increasing disaffection with Italy's cause.[96] Mazzini's view of this organisation was that Italy, not America, would be the epicentre of the worldwide republican network. Mazzini was indeed critical of the American model of republicanism, which he condemned for its *laissez-faire* social policies and for its racism.[97]

---

[91] Isastia, *Storia di una famiglia*, 46.

[92] Gazzetta, *Contributo*, 50.

[93] See S. Levi Nathan to H. Elliott, English ambassador to Florence, 10 Oct. 1866, and Elliott to Levi Nathan, 12 Oct. 1866, Fondo Nathan-Rosselli, Archivio Rosselli, Turin, C 957, http://www.archiviorosselli.it/User.it/index.php?PAGE=Sito–it/archivio–inventario3&start=0&arch–id=1547&arch–id–1=1676, accessed 21 June 2013.

[94] R. Sarti, 'La democrazia radicale: uno sguardo reciproco tra Stati Uniti e Italia', in Ridolfi, *La democrazia radicale*, 133–58 at p. 150; G. Angelini, *Nazione, democrazia e pace tra ottocento e novecento*, Milan 2012, 62.

[95] S. Pozzani, 'L'ultima organizzazione di Mazzini: l'Alleanza Repubblicana Universale', *Archivio Trimestrale: Rassegna Storica di Studi sul Movimento Repubblicano* vii/2 (Apr.–June 1981), 291–8.

[96] Smith, *Radical artisan*, 156–7; E. Barsotti, 'Difendere la grande repubblica: Mazzini, Saffi e la guerra civile americana, *Il pensiero mazziniano* lxvii/2 (2012), 82–139.

[97] On Mazzini's antipathy towards the US see J. Rossi, *The image of America in Mazzini's writings*, Madison 1954, 5, 14. See also A. Kőrner, 'Barbarous America', in A. Kőrner, N. Miller and A. I. P. Smith (eds), *America imagined: explaining the United States in nineteenth-century Europe and Latin America*, Basingstoke 2012, 125–59 at pp. 134–5, and P. Gemme, *Domesticating foreign struggles: the Italian Risorgimento and antebellum American identity*, Athens–London 2005, 31–2.

Distrustful of Mazzini's republican plots, Garibaldi put his trust once again in the Piedmontese monarchy in order to head an expedition to liberate Rome from the French. He was betrayed, however, by the king, and his troops suffered defeat twice, in Aspromonte in 1862, and at Mentana on 3 November 1867. The defeat at Mentana was a watershed: it clearly defined the democrats' opposition to Italy's liberal government.[98] After the battle, Victorian radicals, whose hopes had been briefly raised by Garibaldi's military intervention, when seeking to support the representatives of Italian democracy would be drawn increasingly towards those Italian leaders operating outside the parliamentary system.

Significantly, these men were democrats who had been in exile in England. Saffi, who had initially entered the Italian parliament as part of the so-called 'loyal-opposition', resigned in 1864 and would refuse to enter parliament again, although elected in 1866, 1874 and 1887. He could not bring himself to swear the oath of loyalty to the king once the hope of an imminent republican nation had vanished with the liberation of Rome.[99] Like Saffi, Federico Campanella, also previously an exile in London, left parliament in 1866.[100] Amongst other republicans who had been exiled in London (apart from Rosalino Pilo, who had died in Sicily in 1860) was Quadrio, whose militancy was expressed through his editorship of the democratic press, and who had opposed the monarchical parliamentary institution all along, and Alberto Mario – whose political activity was concentrated outside parliament too, in Lendinara, where he focused on energising workers' associations and promoting co-operation. A notable exception was Francesco Crispi, who despite having been an exile in London, took readily to the parliamentary arena, drifting into Mordini's pragmatic camp: Mazzini would be quick to condemn his ex-disciple, in 1865, as 'unfair and ungrateful'.[101] Crispi's defection and the breach between the two men would be doubly damaging to Mazzini, as it would contribute towards corrupting his doctrine of 'nation', giving it nationalistic overtones which Mazzini promptly recognised as alien, insidious and dangerous.[102]

Back in England, Mazzini's republican programme was attracting new followers due to the political discontent which was simmering between 1866 and 1867, when anti-monarchism was an undercurrent in reform agitation and found explicit expressions at branch levels in the Reform League, in 1868. As Anthony Taylor has affirmed, once radical franchise grievances

---

98 Riall, *Garibaldi*, 351.

99 Saffi to F. Dagnino, *L'Emancipazione*, 28 Nov. 1874.

100 A. Scirocco, 'Campanella, Federico', *DBDI*.

101 G. Mazzini, *Scritti politici*, ed. A. Comba and T. Grandi, Turin 1972, 955, quoted in Angelini, *Nazione*, 62. On Crispi see C. Duggan, *Francesco Crispi: from nation to nationalism*, Oxford 2002.

102 On Crispi's English exile see Duggan, *Crispi*, ch. vi, and at pp. 265–71 for Crispi's breach with Mazzini. See also Angelini, *Nazione*, 62–71.

had been addressed, some anti-monarchical discontent still remained.[103] Both English and Italian republicans constituted a political minority within their respective nations, yet both took advantage of the development of new forms of sociability which helped educate and recruit new members: workers' associations, co-operative societies and republican clubs. Republicans voiced their political opinions through their official organs: in Italy, with Quadrio's *Unità Italiana*, in England with Bradlaugh's *National Reformer*. These papers spoke in unison when reporting news concerning Mazzini. Italy, which Linton had hailed in *The English Republic* in 1851 as the foreign country which was 'keeping the Eve of the Republic', and, indeed, 'preparing for the Republic' while 'Young England' was 'idle', was now being ruled by what W. E. Adams defined, through the pages of the *National Reformer*, as a 'worthless king'.[104] Vicarious republicanism was a unifying element amongst discontented Victorian radicals and the blunders of the Italian king were an easy target which did not necessarily translate into open opposition to the monarchy in Britain. On the latter issue English republicans were often divided amongst themselves: on Italy, however, they could agree, as by damning continental despotism some of them might also be invoking 'the superiority of the British mixed monarchy'.[105]

Tyrannicide and Rome

As ever frustrated with the performance of the Italian king and convinced of the 'virtue of tyrannicide', W. E. Adams, in 1867, was agitated.[106] Mindful of the impact of his anonymous publication, *Tyrannicide: is it justifiable? –* which had rendered him a celebrity by default in 1858 – and angered by the continuing intervention of France in supporting the pope's temporal power, Adams resolved to write another pamphlet.[107] United by ideological kinship to his London publisher, Edward Truelove, Adams regularly provided *Newcastle Weekly Chronicle* readers with informed and critical commentary on the political situation in Italy.[108] Yet, in his letters to his publisher, Adams poured out not only his anti-monarchical feelings, but his deepest reservations about Garibaldi's chosen policy. Truelove was a trusted friend: a secularist and Owenite, he had been charged in 1858, after publishing Adams's

103 Taylor, 'Down with the crown', 61–2.

104 'Republican organisation, and Young England', *English Republic* (1851), 364; 'The fall of Gaeta', NR, 23 Feb. 1861, 5–6 at p. 6.

105 This point was made by Claeys with regard to the 1850s British republicans' support for continental causes: 'Mazzini', 231.

106 'The virtue of tyrannicide', AP, AIISH, 0211/1995/0797.

107 Hawkes to Holyoake, n.d., FH, MRM, 15.

108 See the article following the defeat of Mentana: 'The end of the Roman insurrection: who has gained by it?', NWC, 9 Nov. 1867.

Tyrannicide: is it justifiable?. He was also a loyal Mazzinian, having baptised his son with the name of Mazzini in 1849.[109] Addressing him, Adams wrote in his letter: 'For my part I am mostly indignant, not to say, only indignant, with that monster of depravity whom Garibaldi was foolish enough to install in Naples and Sicily. If the Italians ought to attack anybody at all it is their own king. I sincerely hope they will do it.'[110]

Critical and disparaging comments on Garibaldi's chosen path were not unusual at this time in exchanges between Mazzinians. General De Rohan, the American Mazzinian who had supplied Garibaldi with ships and had masterminded with Holyoake the expedition of a British Legion to help liberate Italy, in writing to Saffi, in 1863, lamented that confusion now reigned in Italy, as it had indeed before, 'under that child Garibaldi'.[111] Saffi himself had referred to Garibaldi as the *'eroe bambino'* ('the child hero') in a letter written in the same year.[112] Yet, when written by a self-declared apologist of tyrannicide like W. E. Adams, strong words against both Garibaldi and the king carried some weight.[113] Events accelerated after Mentana, as Garibaldi's new attempt to liberate Rome was halted by the French, with the collusion of Victor Emmanuel. It was then that W. E. Adams resolved to publish a new pamphlet, *Bonaparte's challenge to tyrannicides by the author of 'Tyrannicide: is it justifiable?'*, heavy with accusations against Italy's 'licentious king' and his 'extravagant executive', that is the government of Urbano Rattazzi. Once his publisher, Truelove, had ensured that there would be no risk of being exposed to legal proceedings, Adams promised personally to bear the expenses.[114]

News of the pamphlet spread within radical circles. Linton advised Adams to delete the term 'Tyrannicide' from the title; Bradlaugh offered unreserved praise and hastened to order one hundred copies to distribute in Sheffield and Halifax; Truelove enquired of Adams which radical bookshops in Newcastle should be contacted for distribution 'before the Philistines' would be upon them.[115] The publisher also promised to announce the immi-

---

[109] *Reasoner*, 14 Nov. 1849, 305–7.

[110] Adams to E. Truelove, 25 Oct. 1867, AP, AISSH, 0211/1995/1518; 0211/1995/1516.

[111] W. De Rohan to Saffi, Turin, 11 Apr. 1863, FS, BCAB, ii/16/1, 53.

[112] Saffi, 20 Feb. 1862, quoted in *Ricordi*, vii. 310–12.

[113] As a republican Adams could refer to the authority of Milton's writings to justify such acts. Regicide could by justified when it was not driven by fanaticism, but by 'cleare judgement' and carried out conscientiously and rationally: John Milton, *The tenure of kings and magistrates*, quoted in M. Dzelzainis, 'Anti-monarchism in English republicanism', in M. V. Gelderen and Q. Skinner (eds), *Republicanism: a shared European heritage*, i, Cambridge 2002, 27–42 at p. 40.

[114] *'Bonaparte's challenge to tyrannicides by the author of 'Tyrannicide: is it justifiable?'*, 'A suppressed pamphlet', 1867; Adams to Truelove, n.d. [1867], AP, AISSH, 0211/1995/1522.

[115] Adams to Truelove, n.d. AP AISSH, 0211/1995/1610; Bradlaugh to Adams, n.d. AP, AISSH, 0211/1995/1623.

nent printing of the pamphlet at the next meeting of the 'Northern Reform League', where he envisaged that he would have the chance 'to speak to some "advanced minds"'.[116] The news of the pamphlet had also come to the attention of Thomas Allsop, who had been implicated in the Orsini affair; he wrote to Adams in the hope of receiving a copy.[117]

All this came to an abrupt halt when Truelove received Adams's telegram telling him that publication must be halted.[118] A tip-off from 'two intimate friends', one of whom was Bradlaugh, had alerted Adams to the fact that the much contested Conspiracy Bill, which had quietly come into effect in 1861, guaranteed prosecution.[119] While resigned to being silenced, Adams was frustrated at his own impotence. To Truelove he wrote: 'Besides it is no use whatever ... <u>After all assassination is a thing to be done, not to be talked about</u> [sic].' In a final recommendation he added: 'I don't care to advise anybody to do what I am not prepared to do myself: but if anybody you know who has no family to make a coward of him cares to dare the Government and to defy the law he may reprint as much of the pamphlet he pleases.'[120] As was the case for many Italian Risorgimento patriots, the private and the public spheres, domestic duty and civic virtue, collided in this northern friend of the Italians.[121]

In 1870 the fall of Napoleon III would immediately be linked by W. E. Adams to the end of French interference in Italy.[122] Joy in announcing this to the readers of the *Newcastle Weekly Chronicle* was however mitigated by the news that Mazzini had been arrested: he would not be released from the Gaeta prison until Rome, no longer protected by the French, had been entered by the troops of the Italian monarch on 20 September. Writing to Caroline Stansfeld Mazzini would deem Italy, united by the monarch, and not the 'people', as only the 'ghost' and 'caricature' of the nation that he had dreamed of.[123] His morale was at a low ebb. As he had written in the summer to Emilie Ashurst Venturi he felt 'wrecked and lost' and judged that the end had come for him: 'Finis Josephi', he wrote to her.[124] He was therefore 'astonished' to find that in England John Morley's *Fortnightly Review* had published a letter of his in its entirety, an achievement for which

---

116 Truelove to Adams, Nov. 1867, AP, AISSH, 0211/1995/0135.

117 Allsop to Adams, 24 Nov. 1867, AP, AISSH, 0211/1995/0156.

118 Adams to Truelove, n.d., telegram, AP, AISSH, 0211/1995/1534.

119 'Bonaparte's challenge to tyrannicides', NR, 24 Nov.1867.

120 Adams to Truelove, 1867, AP, AISSH, 0211/1995/1539.

121 See P. Ginsborg, 'Romanticismo e Risorgimento: l'io, l'amore e la nazione', in Banti and Ginsborg, *Storia d'Italia*, 5–67, and M. Bonsanti, 'Public life and private relations in the Risorgimento', unpubl. PhD diss. London 2008.

122 Ironside, 'Collapse of the French empire', NWC, 20 Aug. 1870.

123 Mazzini to Stansfeld, 13 Sept. 1871, SEI xci. 201.

124 Mazzini to Venturi, Genoa, June 1870, SEI lxxxix. 253. On Mazzini's last years see G. Angelini, *L'ultimo Mazzini: un pensiero per l'azione*, Milan 2008.

Emilie Ashurst Venturi was held entirely responsible.[125] He was probably also entirely unaware of the support that he was still being lent by the northern press. In May 1869 Adams had thundered from the pages of the *Newcastle Weekly Chronicle*:

> It was not ... for such a Government as that which now dominates Italy – a Government which is destitute at once of virtue, of vigour and of patriotism – that Mazzini conspired and Garibaldi fought. They had hopes of giving their country not to a family and a class, but to the people who inhabit it. And these hopes they have not even yet abandoned. The millions of Italy, says Mazzini, are yet uncontaminated. They at least will do justice to the virtue and patriotism of the Republican party.[126]

Adams's description of the 'millions' of 'uncontaminated' Italian republicans was powerful: against these people the Italian monarchy was waging 'a war against thought'. 'Doubtless' he told his readers, 'they have some reason to dread the Republican Apostolate. But the Republic is inevitable.'[127]

Mazzini's last years and Victorian republicans

The faith that Adams still placed in Mazzini's vision for Italy would find expression in the 1870s and 1880s in the support given by other Victorian radicals to the initiatives championed by Italian Mazzinians. Such evidence undermines Morelli's unchallenged view that his English friends' 'Patriotic offering to Mazzini, in aid of the national apostolate', in February 1866, was a last, generous, 'farewell'.[128] Undoubtedly, the 'Patriotic offering' received substantial attention from the press, not least because John Stuart Mill was one of the signatories. However, this was not a seal, but one of the many signs which highlighted the long connection between Victorian and Italian Mazzinians. This would continue to find expression for decades to come.[129]

Mazzini indeed persisted in advocating from the pages of English papers his conviction that 'the false route' onto which 'new-born-Italy had been led

---

125 Mazzini to Venturi, Genoa, June 1870, *SEI* lxxxix. 253.

126 Ironside, 'Political letters – Joseph Mazzini', *NWC*, 29 May 1869.

127 *NWC*, 20 Aug. 1870.

128 'Patriotic offering to Joseph Mazzini, in aid of the National Apostolate – translation – Address to the people of Italy', Faenza, 5 May 1865, TWAS, CP, A867; 'Patriotic offering to Joseph Mazzini – To the Council of Direction of the Association for Progress', London, Feb. 1866, CP, A873. See also Morelli, *L'Inghilterra di Mazzini*, 211–17. The sum amounted to £521 2s. 7½d: E. Morelli, 'L'azione di Mazzini in Inghilterra per l'Italia', *Il Risorgimento*, special issue (1973), 31.

129 See *The English Leader*, 17 Mar. 1866, quoted in T. Raffaelli, 'Alcune note sulla raccolta di fondi a favour di Giuseppe Mazzini in Inghliterra (1865–66)', *BDM* ii (1988), 179–82

by corrupt and incompetent leaders' needed to be redirected. In March 1871 British readers could still witness Mazzini's resolve to continue to battle for Italy's republic in what was to be his last article for the *Fortnightly Review*.[130] Here 'Joseph Mazzini' acknowledged that the 'political education' of his countrymen was 'less advanced' than he had hoped. The message to his British friends was that Italians still needed to be educated, a task which he would help to undertake by launching on the anniversary of the Roman Republic (9 February) another newspaper, *La Roma del Popolo*.[131] This paper, which would be published by men who believed in a republican programme for Italy, was to benefit from a £10 contribution from John McAdam, £25 from Joseph Cowen, and £100 from Peter Taylor with further subscriptions from the Nathans, the Stansfelds, William Shaen and the Ashursts.[132] Its administrator, Ernesto Nathan, was also a young Englishman, recently arrived in Rome, where he was to settle.[133] The paper relied on a continuing close connection with English and American subscribers: subscription details given to its London readers specified that the distributors in the capital were D. Lama and J. Tancioni.[134] Yet subscriptions were coming in 'very slowly' and by September, with only 2,000 subscribers, the paper was in deficit.[135]

Between 1871 and 1872, while Mazzini was concerning himself with the political education of the Italians, republican organisations were spreading in Britain. At the root of the surge in the republicanism was the establishment of the Paris Commune on 4 September 1870, coupled with the queen's increasing isolation from her public duties since being widowed and her request for a larger annuity and a substantial dowry for her daughter – issues which were brought to the British public's attention by Peter Taylor and Charles Dilke.[136]

A first republican club in Birmingham, founded in February 1871, was followed by more clubs mushrooming all over England – in Newcastle, Jarrow, Middlesbrough, South Shields, Nottingham, Sheffield, Northampton and London, where the club was headed by Bradlaugh. By 1873 seventy-five more clubs had sprouted up, concentrated in regions with a renowned radical tradition such as the west Midlands and the North-East, with memberships

---

[130] G. Mazzini, 'Italy and the Republic', *Fortnightly Review*, 1 Mar. 1871, 289.

[131] Mazzini's 'Italy and the Republic', as published in the *Fortnightly Review*, reproduced the programme of *La Roma del Popolo*.

[132] Mazzini to Venturi, 10 Feb. 1871, *SEI* xc. 276–7; Mack Smith, *Mazzini*, 215; A. Levi, *Ricordi della vita e dei tempi di Ernesto Nathan* (1927), ed. A. Bocchi, Pisa 2006, 33. On the paper see L. Ravenna, *Il giornalismo mazziniano*, Florence 1939.

[133] Levi, *Ricordi*, 33.

[134] Mazzini to Venturi, 13 Mar. 1871, *SEI* xc. 309.

[135] Mazzini to Venturi, 25 Feb. 1871, *SEI* xc. 289–91; Mazzini to Stansfeld, 13 Sept. 1871, *SEI* xci. 206.

[136] F. D'Arcy, 'Charles Bradlaugh and the English republican movement (1868–78)', *HJ* xxv/2 (1982), 367–83 at p. 371.

reaching 5,000 to 6,000 – double the mid-century figures – and with 'thousands of people' attending republican meetings across the country.[137] Republican clubs were a form of sociability which had an educational function while also providing opportunities for convivial meetings and the consumption of radical literature.

The interpretation of 'republicanism' that these clubs embraced – resting on approval for the Paris Commune and support for 'red republicanism' – was a far cry from Mazzini's definition of the term. His ultimate political goal was to overthrow despotism: in this sense, the terms 'republic' and 'democracy' were 'virtually synonymous' for him.[138] William Roberts underlined that while Mazzini's ideas profoundly influenced English republicans, Mazzini 'did not openly espouse the cause of English republicanism'.[139] Indeed, while he warmly welcomed the republican revival of the early 1870s he struggled in being associated with it. Addressing this issue in a letter to Emilie Ashurst Venturi, he wrote: 'I see the growing of public opinion in England towards republicanism and feel glad and interested; but how I have done something towards it is a mystery.'[140] As William Roberts and others have indicated, in regarding British institutions as unique in their stability, Mazzini, like Tocqueville, had come to accept by the early 1860s 'that the British might be the one exception to his republican ideal'.[141] The more moderate republicans, who disapproved of the events in France, were therefore more likely to be in harmony with Mazzini, who condemned the Commune as the manifestation of the 'convulsive agonies of a suicidal people' who had lost their 'moral sense'.[142] Mazzini's condemnation of the Commune would indeed gain him some new followers in Britain, including the liberal Benjamin Jowett.[143]

The existence of what could be defined as 'undercurrents of republicanism' in Britain may account for the difficulties encountered by historians in defining British republicanism. Positions have become polarised, tending either to subsume popular radicalism within Gladstonian liberalism or, conversely, to affirm the uncompromising nature of the 'sustained political unrest' of British republicanism.[144] Such complexity is in line with the fact

---

[137] Prochaska, *The republic of Britain*, 109–10.

[138] Recchia and Urbinati, *Cosmopolitanism*, 10.

[139] Roberts, 'Mazzini's thought', 48.

[140] Mazzini to Venturi, 25 Apr. 1871, *SEI* cxi. 26–7.

[141] A. Tocqueville, *The Old Regime and the Revolution* (1856), ed. F. Furet and F. Mélonio, Chicago–London, 1998, 281. On the Anglo-Saxon model as an alternative to the French for European democrats see also Ridolfi, 'Visions of republicanism', 474, and Roberts, 'Mazzini's thought', 48.

[142] P. Pettit, *Republicanism: a theory of freedom and government*, Oxford 1999, 154.

[143] Mack Smith, *Mazzini*, 214.

[144] This definition echoes the title in Biagini and Reid, *Currents of radicalism*. The idea of different 'republicanisms' has become a familiar trope in contemporary debates: P. Zagorin, 'Republicanisms', *British Journal for History of Philosophy* xi/4 (2003), 701–14;

that there were a number of voices amongst Victorian republicans vying to claim Mazzini's political ideology as their own.

As Maura O'Connor has shown for the 1850s, English republicans could still 'selectively identify with those aspects of Mazzini' that best fitted 'their evolving political image'.[145] They were nevertheless keen to appropriate Mazzini as a charismatic figure and leader. Myth-founding Puritan heroes like Milton and Cromwell could be drawn from the English tradition; John Stuart Mill responded to some of their needs to vindicate constitutional representation; yet no contemporary thinker, other than what Biagini has defined as the 'English exile', could be associated with an uncompromising, militant faith in the idea of 'republicanism', whatever its reading might be.[146]

Mazzini was keen to receive fresh news on the movement in Britain and relied on Emilie Ashurst Venturi to identify a correspondent for the *Roma del Popolo* who would contribute a *résumé* on what were seen as the errors committed by monarchies at home and abroad.[147] He hoped that Peter Taylor would contribute to the paper not only financially, but intellectually, by writing about 'the prospects of the *radical* and even *republican* party in England'.[148] Yet he had no response from England and became increasingly frustrated.[149] By November 1871 he was writing to Emilie Ashurst Venturi:

> Is there really not a single English friend of mine to be found who will under-take to send me one or two letters concerning the progress of the republican ideas and Party in Great Britain? Giving names, different sections, spirit of each, importance, etc.? a sort of historical sketch with an idea at the top?[150]

While Mazzini's failure to recruit a correspondent for the *Roma del Popolo* might be read as a sign of his waning influence in England, as remarked upon by Morelli, this interpretation is not entirely convincing.[151] Although some sponsors, like Cowen, now seemed wary of Mazzini, there were other provincial republicans who still worshipped him. Emilie Ashurst Venturi, however, was not connected with them: it is no coincidence, for example, that she had refused to take an interest in W. E. Adams.[152]

The death of Mazzini, in March 1872, would graphically display the

---

D. Castiglione, 'Republicanism and its legacy', *European Journal of Political Theory* iv/4 (2005), 453–65 at p. 457; In his *'Down with the crown'* (p. 16) Taylor draws attention to the 'sustained political unrest' in the era of Gladstonian liberalism.

145 O'Connor, *Romance of Italy*, 66.

146 Biagini, 'Mazzini and anticlericalism', 145–66.

147 Mazzini to Venturi, 13 Mar. 1871, *SEI* xc. 313.

148 Mazzini to Venturi, July 1871, *SEI* xci. 111–14 at p. 114.

149 Mazzini to Venturi, 23 June 1871, *SEI* xci. 92.

150 Mazzini to Venturi, 6 Nov. 1871, *SEI* xci. 259–63 at p. 261.

151 Morelli, *L'Inghilterra di Mazzini*, 205.

152 Hawkes to Holyoake (n. d.), FH, MRM, 4.

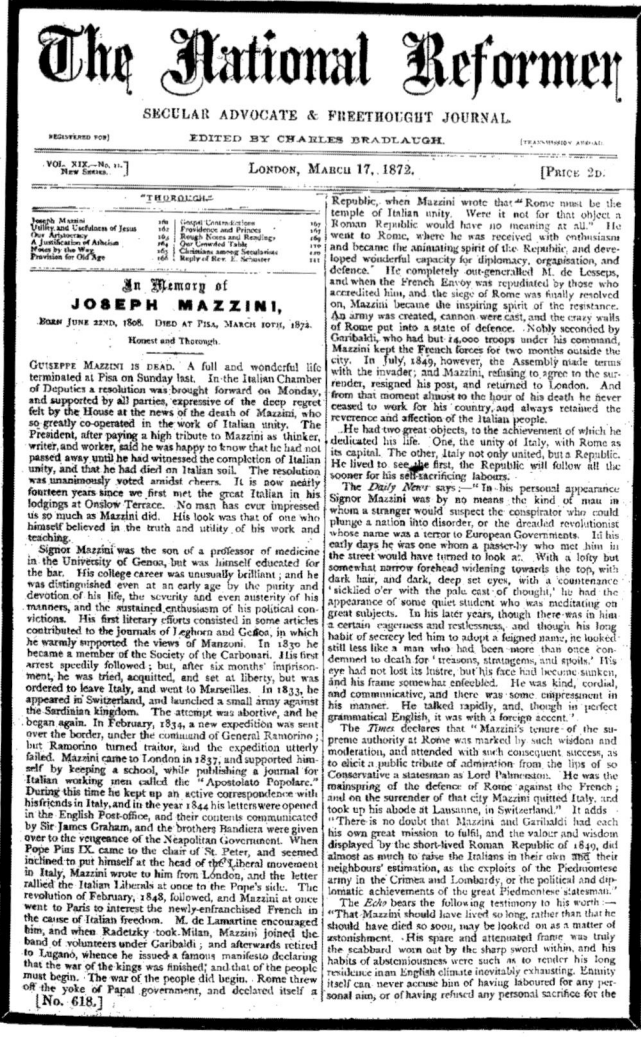

Fig. 5. 'Joseph Mazzini', *National Reformer*, 17 Mar. 1872.

high regard in which he was still held by Victorian republicans. Reacting to the news, *Reynolds's Newspaper*, unabashedly anti-monarchist, could not have spelled out its views more clearly.[153] The revealing opening lines – 'A great prophet has fallen' – were followed by a reflection on republicanism in England and Italy:

[153] On the antimonarchism of *Reynolds's Newspaper* see A. Taylor, '*Reynolds's Newspaper* opposition to monarchy and the radical anti-Jubilee: Britain's antimonarchist tradition reconsidered', *HJ* lxviii/167 (1995), 318–37.

Perhaps he (Mazzini) saw, but if he did he was too cautious to tell us so, that England was likely to follow in the wake of Italy and that the day might come when the exhaustion of our coal might also bring us to the exhaustion of our country, through debts contracted by a selfish aristocracy in foolish wars made against liberty. Italy is not fully emancipated; but the day of her deliverance is at hand. Royalty is getting a little unfashionable.... There will be another prophet in due time: for if Mazzini's life is done, his work is ready to be taken up by his successor, and that successor will appear ere long.[154]

The reflections of *Reynolds's Newspaper* included projections for the republican futures of both Italy and England; Italy, the readers were assured, was not far off the proclamation of the republic, a new republican leader would soon guide her to the realisation of Mazzini's dream, and England, it was anticipated, 'was likely to follow in the wake of Italy'. Italy's republican primacy was not in question; the only doubts aired were concerned with England's ability to follow suit.

Reynolds's Newspaper would pursue its antimonarchist rhetoric into the 1880s and 1890s, but, as Anthony Taylor has shown, increasingly it became a critique of the expensive window-dressing of royal festivals and jubilees rather than involving itself in political argument about social justice and equality.[155] Already by the mid-1870s torpor had replaced the popular enthusiasm of the early 1870s and the Republican League was struggling in its efforts to educate citizens in republicanism with only a few branches in Halifax, South Shields and Edinburgh remaining by the mid-1880s.[156] In Anthony Taylor's words, republicanism 'rumbled on in the *National Reformer*', which in 1872 had announced Mazzini's death as an occasion for universal republican mourning.[157] The front page was framed in black as a sign of official mourning, with the headline 'In memory of Mazzini, Honest and Thorough'. The *National Reformer's* homage underlined the 'two great objects' to which Mazzini had 'dedicated his life' (*see* Figure 5). While he had lived to see Italian unity, the Republic would follow 'all the sooner for his self-sacrificing labours'.[158]

The tone of the *National Reformer*, while slightly less confident of the imminence of Italy's republic, was not greatly dissimilar to that of *Reynolds's Newspaper* on the same occasion. Bradlaugh's paper also reported how English republican clubs had paid their tribute to the Italian prophet in London and throughout the country.[159] In recognisably Mazzinian tones the Tynemouth Republican Club expressed deep sympathy 'at the great and

---

154 'The death of Mazzini', *Reynolds's Newspaper*, 17 Mar. 1872.

155 Taylor, '*Down with the crown*', 125–8.

156 Royle, *Radicals, secularists and republicans*, 204–5.

157 Ibid. 206.

158 *NR*, 17 Mar. 1872.

159 *NR*, 24 Mar. 1872.

almost irreparable loss that the cause of Republicanism and humanity' had sustained 'not only in Europe, but in the whole of the civilized world'.[160]

While the official speeches in republican clubs formalised the recognition of the debt that Victorian radicals owed to Mazzini, the outpouring of grief and genuine admiration felt by W. E. Adams was most vividly expressed in the intimacy of the pages of his journal:

> The apostle of a new faith, he has left to the world an example of surpassing patriotism, to his country the duty of vindicating his memory and to the future a legacy of ideas which will fructify and bless the world. He was in advance of his time.... To few men has mankind ever been more unjust than to Mazzini. He is gone now. But his memory dear to all that value the great good characters of history, has now to be protected. For the rest the principles he taught and the eloquence he uttered will live as long as faith and language endure.[161]

It is difficult to believe that Italian Mazzinians would have felt any differently from this Victorian champion: protecting Mazzini's memory would soon become their mission. Pietro Finelli has shown how the 'myth' of Mazzini as a 'saint' rapidly grew within the confines of his native country.[162] Yet, when writing Mazzini's obituary for the *Newcastle Weekly Chronicle* W. E. Adams seemed to want to appropriate Mazzini as Britain's own. Comparing him with the wronged heroes of Britain's past he stated that 'The world was persistently unjust to Mazzini, as it was to Cromwell, as it still is to Paine. But posterity will do justice to the genius and the apostle.'[163] Posterity, in fact, would throw up new challenges to Mazzini's memory: in Italy his legacy would become increasingly contested. Not so in Britain, where Italian Mazzinians, who defended the democratic credentials of Mazzini's global vision, would be able to count on the lasting support of British radicals for decades to come.

Tributes to Mazzini were many in Britain: lengthy obituaries appeared in British papers of all political affiliations, testifying to the legacy which he left in his country of exile.[164] The *National Reformer*, in marking Mazzini's death as an occasion for universal republican mourning, had most vividly and publicly expressed the transnational significance of his teachings. Compared to such tribute, the announcement of Garibaldi's death, in 1882, was barely noticed in the inside pages of the paper. Ten years had elapsed; republicanism in England had passed its heyday by all accounts and Garibaldi remained the

---

[160] *NR*, 31 Mar. 1872.

[161] Adams journal, entry for March 1872, AP, AISSH, 0211/1995/1397.

[162] P. Finelli, 'E' divenuto un Dio: santità, patria e rivoluzione nel "culto di Mazzini", 1872–1905', in Banti and Ginsborg, *Storia d'Italia*, 665–97.

[163] 'Joseph Mazzini', *NWC*, 16 Mar. 1872, 4.

[164] Mack Smith, *Mazzini*, 226–9.

man who had turned his back on republican Italy: the *National Reformer* had possibly not forgotten this.

During the last decade of Mazzini's life, following the achievement of Italian unification, his reputation was not entirely eclipsed by Garibaldi's popularity in England. In fact the 'shock' of the monarchical turn gave way to manifold manifestations of discontent on the part of Victorian radicals whose loyalty to Mazzini's republican solution increased. Radical audiences and readers could find in the South and in the North of the country platforms of continuous support for the millenarian vision of a republican Italy. Indeed, the English 'left' not only responded in a critical way to Garibaldi's decision to hand Italy to Victor Emmanuel, but continued to harbour hopes that a republican solution to Italy's unity was imminent.

Frustration with the limited extension of the franchise following the 1867 Reform was succeeded in Britain by the resurgence of republicanism in the late 1860s and early 1870s, coinciding with the years of Mazzini's last battles. In the midst of Gladstonian popular liberalism 'Joseph Mazzini' enjoyed a status amongst republican clubs which has all too often been overlooked. The allegiance of Victorian radicals and their faith in Mazzini's imminent triumph in liberal Italy signified that Italian affairs were still followed with keen interest and hope by English radical newspapers. Moreover further support for Mazzini would be lent by the circle of Oxford intellectuals who had been introduced to Mazzini by Saffi. Such loyalty, while not as overt as the enthusiasm for Garibaldi, would prove to be particularly resilient in the coming years. Indeed, after his death Victorian Mazzinians would respond to Mazzini's last wish: to provide Italians with the education that they lacked so that they could address those issues which were central to Italy's nation-building effort: citizenship and universal suffrage.

5

Education, Democracy and International Policy: the Legacy of Exile, 1870–1882

'The science of international politics is actually simpler and less difficult than one might be led to think, as long as one relies on a few principles all derived from religion and the idea of Duty.'[1]

The European 'laboratory of democracy' which took shape in the context of the circulation of ideas shared by *Risorgimento* exiles in London was reorganised in new forms of transnational exchanges once the exiles had returned home.[2] As new challenges surfaced on Europe's geo-political landscape, Victorian radicals who had contributed to the 'making of Italy' would contribute to the 'making of Italians' by renewing ties with Italy's democrats who now gathered together in new forms of sociability. Maurizio Isabella's studies on the first generation of Italian exiles have shown how border-crossing of both people and ideas was an integral part of Risorgimento transnational perspectives.[3] This chapter focuses on how the experience of exile had important effects after political unification had been achieved and the exiles had largely returned home, highlighting how contacts between Victorian radicals and former *émigré* democrats endured, embracing the nation-building phase. The *long durée* of links between proponents of radical democracy confirms what has been claimed by Neville Kirk and others: a 'conventional understanding' that transnational ties are further substantiated by their 'degree of endurance', and can last for generations.[4]

In addressing *Fortnightly Review* readers for the last time Mazzini reiterated his 'unshaken republican faith', announcing that thereafter the 'Italian republican apostolate' and the Italian question would be inextricably linked to the education of the Italians.[5] His newly-founded paper, *La Roma del*

---

[1] G. Mazzini, 'Principles of international politics', abridged in Recchia and Urbinati, *Cosmopolitanism*, 227.

[2] Ridolfi, *La democrazia radicale*, p. ix; Isabella, *Risorgimento in exile*; Bertini, *La democrazia europea*.

[3] Isabella, *Risorgimento in exile*, and 'Exile and nationalism: the case of the Risorgimento', *EHQ* xxxvi/4 (2006), 493–520.

[4] N. Kirk, D. M. MacRaild and M. Nolan, 'Introduction: transnational ideas, activities, and organisations in labour history 1860s to 1890s', *LHR* lxxiv (2009), 221–32 at p. 225.

[5] G. Mazzini, 'Italy and the Republic', *Fortnightly Review*, 1 Mar. 1871, 289–309 at pp. 289–90.

Popolo, would also devote its pages to questions of international policy and to the mounting tide of socialism in Europe. Through the paper, which was to be his last venture, Mazzini observed developments in Italian and international policy with apprehension: the growing influence of anarchists in Italy, of socialists in France, and, moreover, the emerging nationalist rhetoric in Europe which followed the Franco-German war. Writing to Emilie Ashurst Venturi, in April 1871, Mazzini confessed to 'occasional fits of discouragement' due to the 'diffused desecration of names and ideas' which was evident in Bismarck's neo-imperialist rhetoric and in Crispi's repackaging of the meaning of nationalism.[6] Writing in October 1871 in *Roma del Popolo*, Mazzini denounced the 'confusion' of meanings between 'the sacred word' of 'nationality' and 'mean, jealous, hostile nationalism'.[7]

After Mazzini's death, his faithful followers would endeavour to counter the corrupting influence of Crispi's nationalistic policy by carrying on the apostolate of their 'Teacher'. Italian Mazzinians took on three main challenges: educating the Italians into the values of citizenship; continuing the apostolate of democratic republicanism in the face of the spread of socialist ideologies; and upholding Mazzini's idea of the positive – not aggressive – *esprit de nationalité*, in the context of international relations.[8] Within these three areas – education, republicanism and international order – this chapter focuses on how the transnational connections between Victorian and Italian Mazzinians were reaffirmed. Victorian Mazzinians supported financially and morally the Italian republicans in their struggle to educate Italian workers and affirm democracy in liberal Italy. Moral support took the form of public denunciations, letters of encouragement and the dissemination of information: these were all signs of radical Victorians' endorsement of Mazzini's legacy within the tradition of radical democracy in Europe. Italian democrats took strength from such transnational connection, and, indeed, returned the favour at times of international crisis.

The longevity of these Anglo-Italian entanglements was a legacy of exile. This was mostly due to the traces left by Mazzini during his long residence in England, but it was also the result of the influence that some of his Italian followers had exercised on Victorians who had either met them or had read their writings. Within the strict circle of Italian exiled democrats, faithful to their 'Teacher' and immune to the nationalistic shift promoted by Crispi, two men in particular left signs of their passage: Saffi, whose legacy in Oxford was strongly felt, and Maurizio Quadrio, an intransigent republican who had equally left his mark in London. By focusing on the trust that Victorian Mazzinians put in the Italian republicans' resolve to continue the 'apostolate' in liberal Italy this chapter offers an alternative view to the inter-

---

6   Mazzini to Venturi, 9 Apr. 187, quoted in Angelini, *Nazione*, 71.
7   G. Mazzini, 'Nazionalismo e nazionalità', *La Roma del Popolo*, 26 Oct. 1871.
8   Angelini, *Nazione*.

pretation recently offered by Danilo Raponi, who claimed that, once Italy was unified, the British 'delegated to Garibaldi the implementation of the measures which they thought were most important for the new independent country'.[9] Such a view stresses the distancing and disengagement of British liberal-conservatives with regard to a unified Italy; yet the entanglements of Victorian radicals with republicans in liberal Italy were more complex and long-lasting.

The liberation of Rome in 1870, which brought the pope's temporal power to an abrupt end, added a further dimension to the views of British observers on the prospects for a religious revival in Italy. Historians focusing on exchanges between the British and the Italians during the nation-building phase have highlighted the continued interest displayed by British Protestants in religious and moral reform in Italy.[10] The study of the 'Protestant Risorgimento', first highlighted by Giorgio Spini in his seminal study, was extended to an analysis of missionary activities in post-unification Italy, and indeed to a study of the proselytising initiatives which continued after the 'Roman question' had been resolved in 1870.[11] In the aftermath of the collapse of the pope's temporal power, however, the impetus for proselytising greatly diminished: on the one hand other concerns, particularly the challenges brought to the Church of England by the rise in secularism, became a greater priority in Britain;[12] on the other, the imperialist, 'civilizational perspective' which had buoyed up Evangelicals and missionaries of various Protestant denominations, gave way to a sense of the inadequacy of the Italians' character, whose main 'vice' was deemed to be their indifference to civic virtue.[13]

A study of Victorian Mazzinians' perspective on Italians shows, however, that such views were by no means unanimous: on the contrary, what clearly emerges from this analysis is that these men and women were not disillusioned with regard to the Italians' unredeemable 'national character'.[14] Indeed, Victorian Mazzinians who still believed in the exile's vision of the 'Third Rome', had faith in the ability of Italian republicans to carry out

---

[9] Raponi, 'Gran Bretagna', 151.

[10] For the focus on government relations in this period see the works of Owain Wright.

[11] Spini, *Risorgimento e protestanti*, and *Italia liberale e protestanti*; Raponi, 'Religious reformation and national unity'; M. P. Sutcliffe, 'Residenti anglicani inglesi: una sfida per il vescovo di Gilbilterra', in Maghenzani, *Il protentastesimo italiano nel Risorgimento*, 265–76. Studies on the pre-unification period include S. Matsumoto-Best, *Britain and the papacy in the age of revolution, 1846–51*, Woodbridge 2003; De Leonardis, *L'Inghilterra e la questione romana*; Blakiston, *The Roman question*; and C. T. McIntire, *England against the papacy, 1858–61*, Cambridge 1983.

[12] J. P. Parry, 'Nonconformity, clericalism and "Englishness": the United Kingdom', in Clark and Kaiser, *Culture wars*, 152–80.

[13] Raponi, 'Risorgimento e virtù civiche', 113–25 at p. 125.

[14] On the Italians' 'national character' see S. Patriarca, *Italian vices: nation and character from the Risorgimento to the republic*, Cambridge 2010

Mazzini's educational mission in liberal Italy. Such enduring trust was the result of the many links which existed between British and Italian Mazzinians. While Christopher Duggan has acknowledged that 'Mazzini's flame was kept burning by a small group of devotees' – Quadrio, Mario, Campanella, Nathan, Saffi' – he did not underline that all these men were closely connected with England, by having been exiled in London or Oxford (Quadrio, Saffi, Campanella), by their hybrid Anglo-Italian nationality (Nathan) or by marriage to Englishwomen devoted to Italy's cause (Saffi, Mario).[15]

The connection between Mazzinian discipleship and transnational encounters is one that has recently come to the attention of scholars interested in the history of emotions and gender studies. It has been highlighted by Ros Pesman, who focused on the history of love and intimacy across borders, and by Anne Summers in her study of women's transnational networks.[16] A further related area has encompassed the study of Italian Mazzinians' efforts to support Josephine Butler in her campaign against the Contagious Diseases Acts in liberal Italy.[17] This chapter complements such work by extending the field of research to the enduring ties between Victorian Mazzinians and republican exiles who had returned home.[18]

Victorian perspectives on the 'Mazzini schools'

Quadrio's legacy of exile was most powerfully expressed in his links with the Nathan family.[19] As an exile in London, he had taught the Nathan children from a tender age: their manifestations of loyalty to Mazzini would be manifold in the years to come. Their father, Meyer Moses Nathan, was a naturalised Englishman; their mother, Sara, was Italian in origin. Sara Nathan, who had met Garibaldi, Mazzini and Holyoake during the revolutionary years, had been known as one of the most ardent supporters of the Italian cause, regularly opening her house in Middleton Square to Italian exiles in London and to all 'patriots of democracy'.[20] The family were bankers at Cornhill in London and generously contributed towards the revolutionary enterprises.

---

[15] Duggan, 'Giuseppe Mazzini', 198.

[16] Pesman, 'The marriage of Giorgina Saffi and Aurelio Saffi'; Summers, 'British women', 187–209. See also R. Pesman, 'Mazzinian discipleship: Sara Nathan and Jessie White Mario', *Spunti e ricerche* xxi (2007), 33–50.

[17] On this topic see *Women's History Review,* special issue, xvii/2 (2008).

[18] On the portrayal of Italian women in liberal Italy by Mazzinian British emancipationists see Sutcliffe, 'Italian women in the making'.

[19] On the close relationship that the Nathans had with Maurizio Quadrio from the early days of his exile see Pelosi, *Della vita di Maurizio Quadrio*, and Levi, *Ricordi*, 10–11.

[20] Isastia, *Storia di una famiglia*, 1–70; Levi, *Ricordi*, 10. See also G. J. Holyoake, 'The Bologna Congress: golden days in Florence', *Co-operative News* xix/3 (Dec. 1888).

The Nathans' loyalty, very valuable to Mazzini during his life, would be just as precious after his death.

In 1872 Mazzini had chosen Quadrio as editor in Rome of the newly established organ of the Italian workers' societies, the *Emancipazione*, which was intended to provide for the material and moral education of Italian workers.[21] Mazzini's followers on both sides of the Channel were familiar with his last admonitions: prior to demanding political rights Italian workers would need to be educated, both in literacy and – crucially – in 'citizenship'.[22] Mazzini's death would test the resolve of English Mazzinians to follow his lead and support his followers in educating the Italians.

In the aftermath of Mazzini's death, the *Emancipazione* came to be at the centre of a debate on how best to commemorate the 'Teacher'. The proposal for a subscription fund to erect a monument in Rome, put forward by the working men's societies, was countered by Ernesto Nathan. While welcoming the erection of a statue to Mazzini in Genoa, his birthplace, Nathan suggested that it would be more appropriate to found in Rome a popular educational institute in Mazzini's name, to include evening classes, mobile libraries and a reading room. This would better respond to Mazzini's own idea that educating workers constituted the breeding ground for 'association'.[23]

Ernesto Nathan's suggestion was gracefully received, but the subscriptions to the school and to the monument ran parallel, with most of the money going to the latter. Significantly, if the subscription for the 'Mazzini School' succeeded, this was due to 'Mazzini's English friends', alerted by Sara Nathan.[24] Contributions came from Oxford, where Saffi had taught. Here the news of Mazzini's death had saddened not only the Master of Balliol, Benjamin Jowett, who had met Mazzini not long before to discuss matters of religion and materialism, but also some of Jowett's disciples and other known Oxford admirers of Mazzini.[25] On 24 August 1872 a list of names of English subscribers was published in the *L'Emancipazione* (*see* Table 2). The total sum received, converted into 546.75 lira, was more than half the amount

---

[21] On *L'Emancipazione* see A. Scirocco, 'Maurizio Quadrio e l'*Emancipazione*', in *Atti del secondo convegno su Mazzini e i mazziniani dedicato a Maurizio Quadrio*, Pisa 1978, 244–78.

[22] Duggan, *Crispi*, 370; G. Mazzini, 'Italy and the Republic', *Fortnightly Review*, 1 Mar. 1871, 289–309.

[23] E. Nathan to the Commissione Direttiva delle Società affratellate, *Il Dovere*, 30 Mar. 1872; Mazzini to G. Lamberti [1842], *SEI* xxiii. 77–8. On Mazzini's dislike of building monuments to the dead rather than using the money to build schools and hospitals see also Mack Smith, *Mazzini*, 230.

[24] R. Ugolini, 'L'educazione popolare di orientamento mazziniano a Roma: la famiglia Nathan e la Scuola "Giuseppe Mazzini" in trastevere', in *L'associazionismo mazziniano*, Rome 1982, 125.

[25] Mack Smith, *Mazzini*, 214. See also B. Jowett to F. Nightingale, Oxford, 8 Feb. 1871, in E. V. Quinn and J. M. Prest (eds), *Dear Miss Nightingale: a selection of Benjamin Jowett's letters (1860–93)*, Oxford 1987, 205.

Table 2
Subscriptions to the *Istituto Mazzini* in Rome,
received from Oxford and Cambridge

Oxford	
Revd B. Jowett	£ 1.10
T. H. Green	£ 1.00
Lewis Nettleship	£ 5.00
F. R. Sturgis	£ 1.00
A. C. Bradley	£ 2.00
N. Moor	£ 1.00
C .A. Macaulay	£ 1.10
F. M. Brown	£ 0.50
E. Myers	£ 5.00
Cambridge	
A T. Myers	£ 2.00

Source: *L'Emancipazione*, 17, 24 Aug. 1872.

collected, sufficient for plans for a Mazzinian educational institute in Rome to get underway. [26]

As the list of English subscribers shows, in the aftermath of the collapse of the pope's temporal power, Mazzini's intellectual sympathisers were still prepared to devote substantial contributions to building the new nation. In fact, it may be argued that subscribers to the 'Mazzini School' testify to the continuing faith of some English Mazzinians in 'Joseph Mazzini's' vision of a 'Third Rome'. As Mazzini had reiterated in the programme of the *Roma del Popolo*, reproduced by the *Fortnightly Review* in March 1871, the Roman Empire had imposed unity through force; the Rome of the popes through religious authority; the Rome of the people would give – once the Italians were 'nobler than they are now' – 'a Unity of civilization accepted by the free consent of the nations for Humanity'.[27] The new-born Italy, cradle of a new humanist civilisation, would lead the way in the emancipation of

---

[26] *L'Emancipazione*, 17, 24 Aug. 1872.

[27] Mazzini's idea of the 'Third Rome' was familiar to English readers: Mazzini reiterated the concept in his writings published in the *Fortnightly Review*. See, for example, his article 'Italy and the Republic', 1 Mar. 1871, at p. 292 and the article by J. Stansfeld, 'Mazzini on the Eastern question', trans. G. Mazzini and E. A. Venturi, *Fortnightly Review* (April 1877), xxi/124, 559–61. The idea of the 'Third Rome' was first elaborated by Mazzini in *Foi et avenir* (1835), *SEI* vi. 293–358.

Europe.[28] In such a context the subscription list of August 1872 appears in all its significance. Unlike all previous British fundraising activities for Italy, which were spurred by the unresolved 'Roman Question', this subscription shows that at least some of the English retained an interest in the educational progress of the Italians in a unified, reformed, liberal Italy, regardless of proselytising ambitions.

It was the social consciousness of these Oxford intellectuals which impelled them to provide, in Jowett's words, a 'means of giving the best education to the best intelligences in every class of Society'.[29] Indeed, Ernest James Myers, a poet and a contributor to the 'Mazzini School' became secretary of the London Society for the Extension of University Teaching; Bradley, also a generous contributor to the school in Rome, became in later years a keen supporter of the Workers' Educational Association. T. H. Green, who also responded to the Nathans' appeal, counted amongst his pupils Arnold Toynbee, the founder of the university settlement, Toynbee Hall, and was a leading light in civic idealism and social work.[30] These men's decision to subscribe to the 'Mazzini School' in Rome suggests that their social reforming, educational principles extended beyond national boundaries. Indeed, their donations may be seen as a manifestation of the multifarious facets of Victorian 'liberal internationalism', as described by Duncan Bell. Among its proponents was a miscellaneous collection of radicals and idealists.[31]

The decision of these progressive Englishmen to fund the 'Mazzini School' in Rome indeed points to a perceived convergence of ideals between them and the exile, which widened the circle of Mazzini's English followers beyond the Nonconformist, Unitarian supporters described by Biagini. Indeed Christopher Harvie has also shown that the Italian exile was 'venerated most by T. H. Green and his disciples at Oxford'.[32] Stuart Jones has equally stressed that Mazzini's 'Balliol followers' were liberal Anglicans:[33] and the connection between liberal Anglican ideals and Mazzini's thought goes some way towards explaining the intellectual triggers which could have motivated these men to subscribe to the Mazzini School. Their decision to fund an educational institution in Italy is also revealing in the context of recent

---

[28] A useful description of the concept of the 'Third Rome' is in G. Salvemini, *Mazzini*, London 1956.

[29] Jowett to J. Russell, 27 Oct. 1867, quoted in P. Hinchliff and J. Prest, 'Jowett, Benjamin (1817–93)', *ODNB*.

[30] M. Richter, 'T. H. Green and his audience: liberalism as a surrogate fate', *Review of Politics* xviii/4 (1956), 444–72.

[31] Bell, *Victorian visions*, 9.

[32] Harvie, The lights of liberalism, 104.

[33] H. S. Jones, 'The idea of the national in Victorian political thought', *EJPT* v/1 (2006), 12–21 at p. 18.

debates focusing on the relationship between 'civilisation' and nationalism in British intellectual thought.

Rebutting postcolonial and postmodern accusations that mid-Victorians regarded the Anglo-Saxon race as 'demonstrably supreme' and was already 'permeated with organic concepts of race and nation', Peter Mandler has argued that in British political thought the 'ladder of civilisation' 'remained the dominant metaphor' and therefore 'biological racism and organic nationalism' were inhibited.[34] This perspective implied 'a more or less uniform human structure' rather than a 'nationally differentiated' humanity: the 'civilizational perspective remained potentially universal, available to all people'.[35] Embracing this concept, which Mandler attributed to British liberalism alone, Jones argued that such ideas were not quintessentially British: quoting Maurizio Viroli, he contended that for Mazzini too 'nationhood' was 'a bridge towards a universal fraternity' and that his idea of 'civilisation' and 'humanity' was perfectly in tune with a distinctive trait which defined Victorian liberalism: it was devoid of nationalist connotations.[36] Indeed the contributions of liberal Anglicans to the 'Mazzini School' need to be read as a manifestation of a conscious awareness on the part of progressive Oxford liberals of the ideological convergence which drew together the exile's admirers across national boundaries. Their reading of his legacy was in sharp contrast with the pernicious tendency, emerging in Italy, which aimed to appropriate Mazzini's doctrine within a nationalist discourse.

Within a year of the founding of the school, weekly evening classes had been organised and Quadrio was put in charge of the delivery of lectures. The educational initiative proved difficult to run, however. Well-meaning speakers were inadequately trained for the purpose.[37] Moreover, the school, where the *Duties of man* was read and explained, was unsurprisingly unwelcome to the government, which regarded republican Mazzinians as 'the principal "red" threat'.[38] Until it closed in 1882 the school was the object of police reports.[39] What is clear from them is that the classes were moderately frequented and that the students were overwhelmingly middle-class.

---

[34] C. Hall, 'The nation within and without', in C. Hall, K. McClelland and J. Rendall (eds), *Defining the Victorian nation: class, race, gender and the Reform Act of 1867*, Cambridge 2000, 179–233. See also C. Hall, *White, male and middle-class: explorations in feminism and history*, Oxford 1992, and Mandler, '"Race" and "nation"', 224–44. As Mandler has indicated these postcolonial interpretations were strongly influenced by H. Bhabha, *Nation and narration*, London 1990.

[35] Mandler, '"Race" and "nation"', 226.

[36] Jones, 'The idea of the national', 13; M. Viroli, *For love of country: an essay on patriotism and nationalism*, Oxford 1997, 145.

[37] Nathan to White Mario, 25 Mar. 1873, JWM, MCRR, 430/22. Speaking in public was for Quadrio a 'duty' that was 'very painful': *Ricordi*, 48.

[38] Davis, *Conflict*, 92.

[39] For the entire duration of the school – eleven years – ministers alerted the head of the Police Headquarters to keep it under police surveillance. See *Questura di Roma*, bundles

Despite the difficulties, Mazzinians strove to reach a wider audience: Giorgina Craufurd Saffi, whose faith in Mazzini's guiding principle of education was also informed by her knowledge of educational institutes in Britain, wrote about political education in the new republican Roman paper, *Il Dovere*, launched by the Nathans in 1877.[40] On 18 March 1877 the paper reported that she had delivered a speech to a working men's society, suggesting the introduction of dividends which could be used to equip a library with the best books; mobile libraries were beginning to appear amongst workers' societies throughout Italy, but it was the moralising quality of the books purchased that Giorgina Craufurd Saffi was keen to ensure.[41]

Notwithstanding the regular interference of the authorities, which hampered the opening of new educational institutions, Sara Nathan devoted her energies for a decade to promoting the opening of reading rooms, schools and mobile libraries throughout the country, aided by Quadrio. Other Mazzinians – Vincenzo Brusco Onnis and Giulia Pezzi – opened Mazzini schools in Milan and in the north of Italy.[42] In London a new Mazzini School for Italian immigrants was also established, which was run by three Italians.[43] British readers were kept abreast of these developments by the reports which appeared in radical papers. In 1876 the *Examiner* reported that Mazzini's works, collected by Saffi, were circulating in working men's societies and Mazzini schools.[44] Another paper which kept readers informed on the progress of the Mazzini schools was the *Englishwoman's Review*. With Caroline Ashurst Biggs (1840–89) as one of its co-editors, the paper strove to follow signs of the progress of democracy in Italy, highlighting any positive indications of emancipation amongst Italian women.[45] In 1878 the paper gave a detailed account of the spread and nature of Mazzinian associations, writing that

---

6, 17, 20, and *Prefettura di Roma*, bundles 141, 157, 195, Archivio di Stato, Rome, quoted in Ugolini, 'L'educazione popolare', 128 n. 18.

[40] On *Il Dovere* see G. Monsagrati, 'Modelli dell'intransigentismo repubblicano: il gruppo romano del *Dovere*', in *L'associazionismo mazziniano*. On Giorgina Craufurd Saffi see Gazzetta, *Contributo*.

[41] *Il Dovere*, 18, 19 Mar. 1877.

[42] Quadrio to Nathan, 9 Oct. 1872: Ugolini, 'Nove lettere di Maurizio Quadrio nell'archivio Nathan', in *Atti del secondo convegno*, 358–79 at pp. 367–8. On the Mazzini schools see Luigi Ambrosoli, 'Appunti per una ricerca su problemi dell'istruzione e della cultura popolare in Maurizio Quadrio e nei Mazziniani dopo l'unità', in *Atti del secondo convegno*, 354–64.

[43] Nathan to V. Brusco Onnis, 27 Sept. 1876, Nathan papers, Domus Mazziniana, Pisa, DIIg58/63.

[44] 'Variorum Notes', *Examiner*, 18 Mar. 1876.

[45] Caroline Ashurst Biggs's mother, Mathilda Ashurst Biggs, had been an intimate friend of Mazzini. For a more detailed analysis of the role played by Caroline Ashurst Biggs as editor of the *Englishwoman's Review* see Sutcliffe, 'Italian women in the making'.

It would be difficult to overestimate the effect that [Mazzini's teachings on the emancipation of women] has had in the last twenty years in all the associations which in Italy correspond to our Mechanics' Institutes, Working Men's Unions and Free Schools. In these, succeeding writers, patriots and philanthropists, have echoed Mazzini's words, and taught according to their ability the equal duties, rights and responsibilities of women and men till it is becoming a portion of the creed which the party of progress in Italy has adopted from its great leader.[46]

On the fifth anniversary of Mazzini's death, in 1877, the *Englishwoman's Review* reported that demonstrations in honour and memory of the 'apostle' had been held 'in every town' by working men's societies, with messages being sent by both men's and women's associations. Working women's associations had paid tribute to Mazzini, acknowledging that the 'freedom of women, politically, socially and civilly' was 'as necessary a part of the national emancipation as the freedom of men'.[47]

In the Mazzini schools, education was considered to be linked to 'citizenship', understood as consciousness of duties as well as rights. As Brusco Onnis wrote in the first issue of the weekly paper *Libertà e Associazione* in 1873, in order for education to be effective individuals needed to experience freedom of conscience, a necessary condition for each one to perform their duties and exercise their rights.[48] Such debates, which emerged in the republican papers, provided an important political platform in anticipation of the educational reforms introduced by the Coppino Law in 1877. As the campaign for electoral reform got underway, in 1879, the link between education, 'citizenship' and the extension of suffrage could be ignored no longer.

Italy's tortuous path towards democracy: the radical gaze

Italian republicans were at the forefront of the campaign for electoral reform, yet their progress was slow. The difficulties which they encountered were many: on the one hand the government was suspicious of their activities, on the other 'internationalists' (socialists and anarchists) put forward an alternative agenda which was difficult to absorb within the republican programme. In the context of an increasingly complicated political landscape the allegiance of Victorian radicals was a balm: as Italian republicans were hounded by repressive government measures and were denied platforms to protest, they were determined to bring the battles fought by Saffi's circle to the attention of the British, challenging the indifference of the official press to the news coming from the democratic camp. Saffi was referred to

---

46 'Past and present Italian women', *Englishwoman's Review*, 15 May 1878.
47 'Foreign notes and news', *Englishwoman's Review*, 14 Apr. 1877.
48 *Libertà e associazione*, 9 Feb, 1873, quoted in Ambrosoli, 'Appunti', 352.

by Holyoake as the man who had 'succeeded his great friend in representing the Republican principle with similar refinement, force and fidelity'. He was known in Victorian radical circles for having retained 'many English friends' and supporters.[49]

The revolutionary climate which had come out of the experience of the Paris Commune created tensions and fears of 'internationalist' forces in Italy. In the Bologna region, Bakunin's ideology had found a significant following. Italian republicans, traditionally well represented there, were aware of the insurrectionary aims of 'internationalists', and while determined not to be drawn into an alliance, they succeeded in playing an important role in averting the escalation of violence.[50] The power that republicans held in these negotiations – a veritable 'state within the state' – had however alienated the government authorities, which in 1874, having been informed of a republican meeting with 'internationalists' at Villa Ruffi in Rimini, ordered the arrest of everyone involved, including Saffi and twenty-eight of his associates.[51]

Victorian radicals strove to draw international attention to the injustice of the arrests, championing the Italian republicans' cause and battling to bring their cases to the attention of the British press. This proved to be no easy task. The bias of the British press in presenting the news from Italy would be clearly felt by radicals who endeavoured to find a platform for their condemnations. They drew their information from the Italian republican papers – including the *Roma del Popolo*, and l'*Emancipazione*, both directed by Quadrio, and *Il Dovere*, the Roman republican paper owned by the Nathan family – for which the years between 1872 and 1876 were important. Victorian radicals complained that in the 'English press a sort of "conspiracy of silence"' had surrounded the arrests of the republicans. Saffi's brother-in-law, Edward Craufurd, who had just lost his seat as radical MP for Ayr Burghs, had done all he could – but only the 'liberal papers' had reported anything and 'with scarcely any success'.[52] Craufurd did however manage to have a correspondence published in the *Scotsman* and Jessie White Mario had written to the *Daily News*.[53] The *Examiner* too had related the Villa Ruffi episode, alerting English radicals to the abuses that republicans in liberal Italy were experiencing, particularly as elections were approaching.[54] The impression of inadequate reporting was however confirmed by Karl Blind, who, writing

---

[49] Ridolfi, 'Visions of republicanism, 475; Holyoake, *Sixty years*, i. 91; *Examiner*, 11 Sept. 1875.

[50] On the strong presence of republicans in this area see M. Ridolfi, *Il partito della repubblica: i repubblicani in Romagna e le origini del Pri nell'Italia liberale, 1872–95*, Milan 1989.

[51] On this see also Gazzetta, *Contributo*.

[52] W. Ashurst to Saffi, Florence, 30 Nov. 1874, FS, BCAB, ii/16/1, 79.

[53] Saffi to White Mario, Perugia, 14 Sept. 1874, JWM, MCRR, 430/41/1.

[54] 'Saffi's arrest', *Examiner*, 21 Nov, 1874.

from London to Saffi with regard to 'such a glaring act of injustice', was especially aggrieved by the fact that, in his opinion, even 'English "advanced Liberal" papers gave reports ... which violated every rule of fair play'.[55]

Although accounts of the background to the arrests were slow to reach and circulate in Britain, Saffi was able to relay in detail the history of the events in a pamphlet written in English, which he sent to William Ashurst the following year. While Saffi thought that it was now too late for the account to be made public – as it would be 'of no use for the general reader' – the *Examiner*, in 1875, chose to draw the attention of its readers to 'a remarkable pamphlet, *The Association in the Romagna and the Arrests in Villa Ruffi*', which was an outline of 'contemporary Democracy in Italy and of the arbitrary system of the government with which the advanced popular party' had 'to contend'.[56]

Saffi's close links with Victorian radicals meant that he was able to supply them with his reading on what he defined as the 'real motive of the arrest', namely, the 'desire of revenge on the part of the government for the part taken by the republican party in quelling the tumults at the time of the corn riots and re-establishing order'.[57] Maintaining social order had been a challenging task since the conservative government (*Destra Storica*) had introduced the grist tax in 1869. Discontent amongst the peasantry had been widespread and the conciliatory language of Mazzinians had struggled to keep revolutionaries at bay.

In 1876 the victory of the Italian Left (*Sinistra Storica*) initially raised hopes amongst radicals and republicans that the democratic reforms which they had promoted would soon be realised. In Lombardy, where the radicals were becoming established as a considerable force, the Milan democratic organ, *Il Secolo*, welcomed the new government unreservedly. Yet, only a year later, the formation of a more radical wing of the Left (*Estrema*), grouped around Bertani, Giovanni Bovio and Felice Cavallotti, indicated an element of dissatisfaction with Agostino Depretis's new government's policy, a frustration which was destined to grow in the following years, but which Victorian radicals did not immediately notice.[58] Guided, by Bertani, who had declared his opposition to Saffi's policy of fighting from outside the parliamentary arena, *Estrema* advanced a new generation of political leaders, like Cavallotti and Bovio, whose names were unfamiliar to Victorian radicals: they called themselves Italian Radicals. They were to be important protagonists in the coming years, which saw a renewed impetus for democratic reform, in political representation, education and taxation.

---

[55] Blind to Saffi, London, 24 Dec. 1874, FS, BCAB, ii/16/1, 80.

[56] *Examiner*, 11 Sept. 1875.

[57] Saffi to White Mario, Perugia, 14 Sept. 1874, JWM, MCRR, 430/41/1.

[58] G. De Caro, 'Giovanni Bovio', and A. Galante Garrone, 'Felice Cavallotti', *DBDI*, 552–9, 794–803.

In some respects at least the *Sinistra Storica* did deliver the reforms that Italian democrats and Victorian radicals had been striving for. In 1877 the introduction of the Coppino Law brought in reforms to the Italian educational system which appeared bolder than those enshrined in Gladstone's 1870 Elementary Education Act: this had responded with moderation to demands for a secular education by ensuring that Christian education was none the less embedded in the reformed institutions. This had happened despite a vigorous campaign in favour of a national education system, promoted by the National Education League. Most prominent within this movement were supporters of Mill's ideas and radical Nonconformist civic activists. Birmingham, which was at the centre of the agitation had seen George Dawson champion the cause of civic education, inspired by his admiration for Mazzinian 'civic republicanism'.[59] Replacing the religious catechism with the 'rights and duties of man and citizen', as the Italians had done with the Coppino Law, was a much bolder step.

Electoral reform in Italy was another sign of progress: it managed to extend the 1882 electorate to over two million males; the 1867 Reform Act in Britain had brought the number of those qualified to vote to just below that figure. As Ottavio Barié affirmed, 'taking into account the respective populations', the difference between the two countries was not great, 'particularly when considering the varying degrees of .... political experience of the two people'.[60] Britain, however, was only two years away from another electoral reform promoted by Gladstone, the 1884 Reform Act which would further expand the franchise to electors in the rural areas.

Positive developments in Italy in 1882 did not escape radical Victorian observers. Indeed, *Reynolds's Newspaper* reported on recent political achievements in Italy with admiration mingled with forlorn yearning for similar moves in Britain. According to its reports, the Italian prime minister, Depretis, understood the needs of his 'fellow-country-men and the business of statesmanship in its highest and best sense'. The objects of his government were summed up as 'granting to the people the greatest possible liberty, the development of the internal resources of the country, the education of the people and the prudent expenditure of *public money* [sic]'. In the context of a critical disdain for Britain's expansionist policies, the radical paper showed its awareness that the Italian democratic-radical movement had the opportunity to become a major political force in the 1880s:

> These are the legitimate ends of statemanship, be the form of government what it may, monarchical or republican. In Italy, since the Left have had the chief control of affairs, every male has been given a vote who has reached the years of discretion and who can pass a simple educational test equivalent

---

[59] Parry, *The politics of patriotism*, 268.

[60] Barié, 'Il radicalismo inglese', 126. Barié also refers to the 'varying degrees of evolution of the two people'.

to what we know as the three R's; the people have been given a national system of education; taxes have in great many instances been reduced on the necessaries of life such as salt and grist; the nation has been kept out of all foreign disputes and wars, large or small; and all the business of the country has been done in broad day, in sight of all the people.[61]

Indeed, a number of achievements that were highlighted by *Reynolds's Newspaper* were evidence of the political pressure that democrats had succeeded in exercising on society through associations and educational institutes. Their influence had been felt both at the level of educational reform, in 1877, and at the level of electoral reform, in 1882. The link that had been established between primary education and voting, on one side, and the introduction of compulsory elementary schooling, on the other, was seen by the democrats as the best guarantee of obtaining universal suffrage.[62] Furthermore, Mazzinian associations continued to provide a playground for workers' political education which included a widening sense of the meaning of 'citizenship'. Readers of the radical paper, the *Shield*, were kept abreast of the progress made by Italian republicans: even minor events, like a newly-formed Republican Club in Urbania, which had been named 'The Sara Nathan Association', were reported – as the title adopted seemed particularly 'significant of the republican virtues' which were spreading in liberal Italy.[63]

Meanwhile, however, new clouds were appearing on the horizon. Even the widening of the electoral base to include the working-classes could not empower Italian republicans, as their unwavering resolve to refuse to swear the oath of allegiance to the king continued to exclude them from parliament.[64] Moreover, the formation of the Workers' Party (*partito operaio*) in 1882 was to deplete greatly the ranks of the Italian democrats, depriving them of the opportunity to become a major popular force, 'able to emulate .... Gladstonian liberalism', according to Ridolfi.[65] Among the increasing difficulties experienced by republicans and democrats alike, the enlargement of the electorate – and the fear of the potential strengthening of the radicals – gave way to malpractice in the form of political agreements aimed at shoring up the moderate camp. From 1883 onwards such practices become

[61] 'Foreign and English statemanship', *Reynolds's Newspaper*, 15 Oct. 1882.

[62] R. Romanelli, 'Alla ricerca di un corpo elettorale: la riforma del 1882 in Italia e il problema dell'allargamento del suffragio', in P. Pombeni (ed.), *La trasformazione politica nell'Europa liberale, 1870–90*, Bologna 1986, 171–207 at p. 197.

[63] 'Popular gratitude in Italy', *The Shield*, 14 Oct. 1882. The news was taken from the republican paper, *Il Dovere*.

[64] A. Comba, 'I repubblicani alla ricerca di un'identità', in *Mazzini e i repubblicani*, Turin 1976, 474.

[65] Ridolfi, *Il circolo virtuoso*, 285.

engrained within the political system, a phenomenon which came to be known as *trasformismo*.[66]

International politics and Mazzini's 'prophecy'

The rosy picture of Depretis's government, displayed in the pages of *Reynolds's Newspaper*, neglected to address important recent changes in Italy's foreign policy. Following the unpopular decision of the Italian Foreign Minister at the Congress of Berlin (1878) not to advance any claims in the negotiations for a peaceful solution to the Eastern Question, a wave of nationalist outrage swept through the country, triggered by international recognition of French ambitions to expand into Tunisian territories. Responding to the public mood, Depretis had signed, in May 1882, a pact of Triple Alliance with Austria and Germany, in a display of anti-French sentiment. Italian radicals objected to the pact on a variety of grounds. Saffi, like many other democrats, saw in the alliance with Austria a betrayal of *Risorgimento* ideals as well as the government's abandonment of further claims to the eastern territories (*terre irredente*) which were perceived by Mazzini's followers and others as historically Italian;[67] Cavallotti rejected the anti-French stance out of loyalty to the French republican tradition; Bovio, like all radicals, came to loathe an alliance which would be 'ruinous to Italy, as entailing upon her continuous expenditure in armaments'.[68] Indeed, after signing the Triple Alliance Italy would claim to be in a good position to flex its muscles in Africa, where the disastrous battle of Dogali would take place in 1887.

Such international mayhem might have been avoided. At least this was the view of the Victorian radical MP James Stansfeld when, in April 1877,

[66] Beales and Biagini define *trasformismo* as a phenomenon 'which from the late 1870s systematically weakened the opposition and prevented the consolidation of a clear-cut party divided by merging the centre-right and centre-left in fluid coalitions': *The Risorgimento and the unification of Italy*, London 2002, 112. See also Galante Garrone, *I radicali*, 214–15, and Cammarano, *Storia dell'Italia liberale*, 91–8.

[67] Mazzini wrote that the territories 'from Fiume along the Eastern shore of the Adriatic as far as the river Boiano' were provinces bound to the Italians by 'historic tradition, affinity of language, and ties of affection'. This eastern boundary had been defined since Dante had included Pula within Italy in the *Divine Comedy* (*Inferno* ix.113). English readers were aware of Mazzini's claims: Stansfeld, 'Mazzini on the Eastern question', and G. Mazzini, 'International policy' (1871), trans. E. A. Venturi, *Fortnightly Review* xxi/124 (Apr. 1877), 559–61, 567–79 at pp. 573–3. Political explanations of Dante's *Divine Comedy* were not unusual during the Risorgimento: Gabriele Rossetti also associated Dante's free thought and anti-papalism with national resurgence. See 'Rossetti on the anti-papal spirit of Italian Classics', *Edinburgh Review* lx (1832), 531–51. See also Mclaughlin, 'Introduction: the centrality of Dante'.

[68] 'The opposition of Italian radicals to the Triple Alliance', *Pall Mall Gazette*, 20 June 1891.

he chose to publish an article entitled 'Mazzini and the Eastern Question'.[69] In the midst of an international crisis, he urged *Fortnightly Review* readers to draw counsel from Mazzini's 'prophecies' on world order. In republishing two of Mazzini's essays, 'Slavonian letters', originally written for the *Italia del Popolo* in 1857, and 'International policy', written for the *Roma del Popolo* in 1871, Stansfeld drew attention to Mazzini's vision and admonitions regarding global policy. As Stefano Recchia and Nadia Urbinati have recently argued, Mazzini's essay on international political thought showed him to be 'one of the leading pioneers of modern liberal internationalism, or democratic Wilsonianism'. It called for 'the pursuit of a principled foreign policy, centred on ideas of non-aggression' as 'a matter of moral duty' and 'international cooperation', and called for Italy's initiative in securing international peace.[70]

As Stansfeld explained to his readers, Mazzini believed that every nation had 'a mission in the world's organisation and progress'. Republican Italy, which had arisen 'in the name of national right', would have as its 'mission' 'the permanent and peaceful organization of Europe'. Monarchical Italy, however, would never see or fulfil such a mission.[71] According to Mazzini, liberal Italy had no sense of its goal in the context of humanity and therefore its foreign policy rested on the 'expedients' of its ministers, devoid of 'moral rule'. The true objective of Italy should be to make herself 'the centre and soul of a league composed of the minor European states, bound together by a common compact of defence against the possible usurpations of any of the greater powers'. Such league of *national unities, possibly intermixed with free Confederations* [sic] ... would constitute a material force of sixty-four millions of men, bound together by a common pact of independence and liberty', able to break down the tyranny of the Austrian Empire and the Turkish Empire in Europe.[72] In Mazzini's view, republican Italy's role in inspiring the Slavonian national movement would be crucial. As he stated, 'The Rome of the people, of the Italian nation, believing in progress, in the collective life of humanity, and in the division of labour among the peoples, is bound to unite them all as fellow-workers in the enterprise and be their help and guide.'[73]

Quoting Mazzini, Stansfeld stressed the 'absolute character of Mazzini's prophecies', but did not comment on his nationalist claims that the Eastern shore of the Adriatic, from Fiume to the river Boiano, was still an unre-

---

69 Stansfeld, 'Mazzini on the Eastern question'.

70 Mazzini's 'International policy' (1871) is reproduced in abbreviated form in Recchia and Urbinati, *Cosmopolitanism*, 224 n. 1, but all the following citations are drawn from the unabridged version as published in the *Fortnightly Review*, and disseminated to Victorian readers.

71 Mazzini, 'International policy', 576–7.

72 Ibid. 573, 576–7.

73 Ibid. 572.

deemed part of Italy.[74] As another article which appeared in the *Fortnightly Review* in 1933 perceptively highlighted, nationalism and democracy in nineteenth-century Europe were perceived as having 'an essential, almost mystical link', and Mazzini, 'the typical European hero of nineteenth-century radicalism', was unequivocally regarded by Victorians, Stansfeld included, as 'both nationalist and democrat'.[75]

Stansfeld was most struck, instead, by Mazzini's ideas on 'the mission of Europe towards Asia'.[76] As Recchia and Urbinati have argued, a 'civilising' perspective in relation to Asia was a common trope of nineteenth-century liberalism, and Stansfeld's admiration for Mazzini's suggestion confirms this view. Indeed, the similarities that have been noted by Stuart Jones between the 'flexible' and 'adaptive' 'civilising ladder' attributed by Peter Mandler to British liberal thought and Mazzini's own vision of the world seem particularly appropriate when attempting to understand the convergence of views on Asia between a Victorian radical, like Stansfeld, and Mazzini. The 'civilising mission' was neither 'racialised' nor 'nationalised', as 'civilisation' was universally encompassing.

Regardless of the embrace of a positive *esprit de nationalité*, and rejection of the destructive emerging *esprit de nationalisme* by transnational Mazzinians, European governments were busily carving up boundaries according to a world order dictated by the logic of power, not by the principle of self-determination.[77] By 1882 changes in the political climate were under way across the whole of Europe. Italian democrats – including republicans and members of the *Estrema* – were as keen observers of the foreign policy of other nations as Victorian radicals were of the Italian government's external relations.

Although the changes to Italy's foreign policy had seemingly escaped *Reynolds's Newspaper*, other radical observers were better informed, and indeed more perplexed. It was thus that James Bryce, in October 1882, while travelling in Italy, wrote to Saffi, in the hope of meeting him in Forlì. Bryce was rekindling an old acquaintance: Saffi had taught him Italian at Oxford decades before, initiating him into the spirit of the Risorgimento.[78] Bryce started his letter by expressing the wish that he had not been forgotten; yet the purpose of the contact was not one of nostalgia. As he explained, he was now professor of Roman Law at Oxford and an MP in the House of Commons, and it was in the latter capacity that he was 'very anxious to know' what Saffi thought of 'the present aspects of politics' in his new country

---

[74] Ibid. 573–4. See n. 68 above.

[75] J. Hallett, 'Nationalism: the world's bane', *Fortnightly Review* (June 1933), 694–702 at pp. 694–5.

[76] Stansfeld, 'Mazzini on the Eastern question', 561.

[77] Angelini, *Nazione*.

[78] Fisher, *Life of James Bryce*, 51.

and in France.[79] The encounter took place a few days later, and, while we can only surmise the commentary that Saffi would have furnished on the present state of affairs, it is clear that Bryce was satisfied with the meeting, as he wrote to his Italian mentor: 'although I had known you comparatively little at Oxford, I have never ceased to have the warmest admiration and reverence for you and those few other leaders to whom Europe as well as Italy owes so much'.[80]

The attitude of Italian democrats towards the government's new strong foreign policy and expansionist ambitions had been clear from the early months of the negotiations which would lead to the signing of the Triple Alliance. Anti-Austrian feelings sprang out of memories of the tyranny that Italians had endured, of the revolutions fought and the sacrifices borne to achieve a free, united nation. In this context the role played by Britain during the Risorgimento had not been forgotten. Indeed, on Sara Nathan's death, in March 1882, the commemorative speech by Antonio Fratti, delivered in the presence of Alberto Mario, provided the opportunity for Italian democrats to appeal to Britain and Italy to join hands – 'close in sincere friendship' – and counter 'those who dream of the Holy Alliance and have forgotten the bruises produced by the Austrian whip'.[81] The speech had commemorative overtones, ones which celebrated the principles of liberalism and democracy for which the Italians had fought with the support of radicals and liberals in Britain.

Yet Victorian radicals had little to celebrate with regard to the policy of their present government. Although Gladstone's cabinet was supposedly liberal, and indeed included that well-respected representative of the English tradition of liberalism, John Bright, fear of the power of the Land League in Ireland had led Gladstone to adopt 'draconian' measures in February 1881.[82] Reacting to the news, Jessie White Mario had written from Italy a fierce attack on Gladstone's government for the Newcastle Daily Chronicle. She congratulated the men and women of Newcastle who had stood up for the rights 'even of Irishmen, to liberty'. That the article was entitled 'A Mazzinian view of Mr. Gladstone', suggests that Northern readers were not only familiar with Mazzini's name, but equated him with standing up for the rights of all oppressed people.[83] The presence of John Bright in Gladstone's cabinet was alluded to as an inexplicable incongruence.

Another incident would soon render John Bright's position in the cabinet untenable: Lord Seymour's decision to bomb Alexandria in Egypt in 1882. As

---

[79] Bryce to Saffi, Venice, 1 Oct, 1882, FS, BCAB ii/16/1, 106.

[80] Bryce to Saffi, Venice, 15 Oct, 1882, FS, BCAB ii/12/4, 97.

[81] 'Conferenza commemorativa in onore di Sarah Nathan alla Sala Dante', Il Dovere, 12 Mar. 1882.

[82] M. R. D. Foot, The Gladstone diaries, January 1881– June 1883, x, Oxford 1990, p. ci.

[83] Jessie White Mario, 'A Mazzinian's view of Mr. Gladstone', Newcastle Daily Chronicle, 16 Feb. 1881.

the Italian paper, *Il Dovere*, was quick to report, Bright, acting as spokesman for the 'public conscience', had resigned and was heading a protest against the 'shameful politics' of the British government.[84] In a display of transnational democratic solidarity the Italian paper hailed men of principle across national boundaries, stating that 'Bright in England, Clemenceau in France, the Republican Societies in Italy raise their voice in protest to affirm the downtrodden principle of nationality and the sentiment of humanity.'[85]

Mazzinians responded to the crisis by joining protesting democrats across the nations. Indeed, the *Circolo Mazzini* of Genoa, after denouncing Lord Seymour's actions, drew up an appeal in the name of Genoese democrats which was readily dispatched to none other than Bright. The gesture was a display of European democratic solidarity in the midst of the nationalistic frenzy which was sweeping through the continent and Britain. Bright accused Gladstone's cabinet of embracing what he regarded as an illiberal and uncivilised policy. Grateful for the letter of support received from Genoa, Bright on 25 August 1882, sent a warm reply to the *Circolo Mazzini*, which reiterated his reasons for distancing himself from his colleagues. Bright closed his letter with a few words of hope, asserting that, despite the difficulties, the cause of peace would 'progress and triumph'. Bright's reply gave heart to the editors of *Il Dovere*: it showed that, despite the common accusation of aggressive policy which the British press directed towards the Italian government, the Italian people were recognised as standing for the principles of nationality and justice. Indeed, they would not hesitate to side with the oppressed in international conflicts, even when a people was deemed to be '*barbarian* [*sic*]' and the other side was strong and feared.[86]

It may seem somewhat surprising that the *Circolo Mazzini* should take it upon itself to write such a high profile letter. Yet it is likely that its members were still feeling the giddy after-effects of the recent media attention that they had attracted. The year 1882 had been a busy one for the Genoese *Circolo Mazzini*. A decade after his death, a monument to Mazzini had been set up in his home town, generating plenty of commotion and publicity. The Italian authorities had been wary and vigilant on the day, as Saffi had come to deliver a resounding speech in memory of the revered man and in honour of the republican ideal. According to Saffi the ceremony had been attended by at least 150,000 people. That there were few monuments to Mazzini in liberal Italy, compared to the many to Victor Emanuel and Garibaldi, rendered the inauguration momentous.[87] The occasion did not escape

---

[84] 'La causa del "fellah"', *Il Dovere*, 30 July 1882.

[85] Ibid.

[86] 'La risposta di un uomo grande', *Il Dovere*, 19 Sept. 1882.

[87] M. Finelli, 'Mazzini in Italian historical memory', *JMIS* xiii/4 (2008), 486–91 at p. 488.

Victorian Mazzinians, 'gratefully remembered' on the day.[88] William Shaen had sent a contribution, acknowledged by the *Circolo Mazzini*, which in return dispatched four commemorative medals and an album.[89]

Moreover, another important contribution had come from England. This was both a homage to the late Italian patriot and a testimony to the resilient loyalty of Victorian Mazzinians. As the statue of Mazzini was erected in 1882 in Genoa, Algernon Swinburne had given it transnational visibility by composing his 'Lines on the monument of Giuseppe Mazzini',[90] a eulogy which would resonate amongst Mazzinians in Britain and Italy, where Saffi ensured its circulation by translating it into Italian.[91] The language was embellished with the romantic tones of patriotism: the country as 'mother divine', the man as 'Angelo' – a term which was regularly employed by English Mazzinians when referring to him. The poem, which opened with the words 'ITALIA' and closed with the words 'Mazzini's name', indicated, in no uncertain terms, that Mazzini, and no other, was the 'father of the nation':

> 'Lines on the Monument of Giuseppe Mazzini (1882)', by
> Algernon Charles Swinburne
>
> ITALIA, mother of the souls of men,
> Mother divine,
> Of all that served thee best with sword or pen,
> All sons of thine,
> Thou knowest that here the likeness of the best
> Before thee stands;
> The head most high, the heart found faithfullest,
> The purest hands.
> Above the fume and foam of time that flits,
> The soul, we know,
> Now sits on high where Alighieri sits
> With Angelo.
> Not his own heavenly tongue hath heavenly speech
> Enough to say
> What this man was, whose praise no thought may reach,
> No words can weigh.
> Since man's first mother brought to mortal birth
> Her first-born son,
> Such grace befell not ever man on earth

---

[88] 'A Genova: l'inaugurazione del monumento', *Il Dovere*, 19 Sept. 1882; Saffi to W. Shaen, 2 July 1882, FS, BCAB, ii/16/1, 105.

[89] Saffi to Shaen, 2 July 1882, FS, BCAB, ii/16/1, 105; 'Il monumento', *Il Dovere*, 2 July 1882; 'L'albo e la medaglia per Mazzini', *Il Dovere*, 23 July 1882.

[90] A. C. S., *A midsummer holiday, and other poems* (1884), Charleston 2009, 66–8.

[91] Saffi to Dott. Bassini, 'Nota su A. C. Swinburne: per il giornale "La Patria", 1884, *Ricordi*, xiii. 196.

As crowns this one.
Of God nor man was ever this thing said,
that he could give
Life back to her who gave him, whence his dead
Mother might live.
But this man found his mother dead and slain,
With fast sealed eyes,
And bade the dead rise up and live again,
And she did rise.
And all the world was bright with her through him:
But dark with strife,
Like heaven's own sun that storming clouds be-dim,
Was all his life.
Life and the clouds are vanished: hate and fear
Have had their span
Of time to hurt, and are not: he is here,
The sunlike man.
City superb that hadst Columbus first
For sovereign son,
Be prouder that thy breast hath later nurst
This mightier one.
Glory be his for ever, while his land
Lives and is free,
As with controlling breath and sovereign hand
He bade her be.
Earth shows to heaven the names by thousands told
That crown her fame,
But highest of all that heaven and earth behold
Mazzini's name.

As Mazzini's death, in 1872, inaugurated the years of his contested legacy, Victorian Mazzinians unequivocally placed him within the pantheon of the defenders of European democracy. A decade later, as the inauguration of Mazzini's monument in Genoa was welcomed by Italian democrats as an occasion for national unity, English Mazzinians joined in the celebrations.[92]

As nationalist, expansionist and jingoistic policies became increasingly manifest in Europe, Mazzinians across national boundaries exchanged messages condemning the aggressive and warmongering steps taken by individual governments, whether it was Stansfeld condemning the Triple Alliance in unison with Italian democrats, the *Circolo Mazzini* reaching out to John Bright in condemning the bombing of Alexandria, or Bryce asking for clarity from Saffi on Crispi's foreign policy. Victorian observers, whether radicals or progressive liberals, looked to Mazzini's legacy in order to counter the 'mean, jealous, hostile nationalism', which he had described in one if his last,

[92] For the 'cult of Mazzini' and the uniting of Italian democrats around his memory see Finelli, "'É divenuto un Dio'".

164

alarmed writings.[93] Liberal Anglicans joined radicals in celebrating Mazzini's legacy, as they recognised that, unlike the 'internationalist' message, which was rooted in 'class', Mazzini's doctrine rested on the 'genuine *cosmopolitanism of nations'*.[94]

Mazzini's legacy remained a benchmark for late nineteenth-century Victorians, whether radical or liberal. His teachings and 'prophecies' with regard to world order confirmed them in their allegiance to what Mazzini had defined as the positive *esprit de nationalité*, the antithesis to the *esprit de nationalisme*. The latter, as Peter Mandler has cogently argued, Victorians rejected as it was neither part of nineteenth-century liberalism nor part of the logic of the 'civilisational ladder' which qualified British intellectual thought. Indeed, it is the parallel between the tenets of mid-Victorian progressive liberalism and Mazzini's thought which helps to explain the Oxford social reformers' tribute to his legacy, which was also displayed in their subscriptions to the 'Mazzini School'.

Liberal Anglicans, concerned with the question of education in society and devoted to the burgeoning university extension movement in Britain did not hesitate to cross national boundaries to promote and fund education amongst Italian workers and 'humanity' as a whole. Many of them called themselves Mazzinians. As the establishment of a secular educational institution in East London, Toynbee Hall, would soon show, their commitment to education for the people was non-denominational and divested of Protestant missionary imperatives. Inspired by Swinburne's verses and buoyed up by the news of the inauguration of a statue dedicated to Mazzini in Genoa, East London adult learners would soon embark on co-operative travels to Italy unencumbered by the Italian stereotypes that had blurred the gaze of *Grand Tour* travellers before them.[95]

---

[93] G. Mazzini 'Nazionalismo e nazionalità', *La Roma del Popolo* xxxv, 26 Oct. 1871.

[94] Recchia and Urbinati, *Cosmopolitanism*.

[95] T. Okey, *A basketful of memories: an autobiographical memoir*, London 1930, 66.

6

'Co-operative Tours' as Transnational Education of Citizens, 1886–1890

'What part of education is left for Co-operators to appropriate? The answer I would give is the education of the citizen.'[1]

The late 1880s were years of transition for Italy. Important protagonists of the *Risorgimento* had died and the Left was looking for new leadership.[2] While the *Estrema* found new guidance in the radical Lombard, Cavallotti, the continuous absence from the parliamentary arena of a republican like Saffi – who, once again elected, refused to take the parliamentary oath in 1887 – created a vacuum which enabled Crispi to take centre stage. Frustration and alienation as a result of Depretis's *trasformismo* had led many Italians to believe that a 'strong man' was needed: Crispi would provide just that. The period between 1887 and 1891 was in fact a time when political boundaries were reassessed and redrawn, as the high expectations of the forces of democracy came to measure themselves against the surreptitious changes which would eventually reveal in Crispi a duplicitous character, the 'turncoat' of democracy. Speaking in the name of all radicals Cavallotti, while rallying all democrats around an anti-Crispi manifesto for the 1890 elections, would accuse Crispi in parliament of being as deceitful a friend to them, as he had once been to Mazzini.[3]

This chapter explores early forms of Victorian 'co-operative travel' in the years of what Fulvio Cammarano defined as the 'Crispinian euphoria' of 1887–90.[4] By framing the experience of 'co-operative travel' in the context of the buoyant rhetoric which surrounded the new prime minister this chapter creates a deeper understanding of the context in which those first tours took place. More broadly, it focuses on the role that co-operative travel played in shaping mentalities beyond national boundaries, drawing together co-operators, social reformers and adult learners of different classes, regions and nations to share principles of democracy which transcended parochial interests. Just as the tradition of the *Grand Tour* had privileged classical Italy

---

[1] A. Toynbee, *Education of co-operators*, Manchester 1882 (?).

[2] Agostino Bertani, who had guided the democrats from 1878, died in 1886. Depretis died in 1887.

[3] Cammarano, *Storia dell'Italia liberale*, 133–5.

[4] The term 'euforia crispina' is borrowed from from Cammarano: ibid. 104–29.

as an educational playground for the cultured classes, liberal Italy became in the late 1880s the destination for social reformers and adult learners keen to observe the progress of a nation in the early throes of democracy: the 'education of the citizen', which the Mazzinian Arnold Toynbee had ascribed to co-operation, had therefore a transnational dimension which would find expression in the experience of co-operative travel to Italy.

When evaluating the positive responses of Victorian radicals to Crispi's first government, the ambiguity of this period needs to be taken into account: in the early days Crispi's political position was neither clear to Italian democrats, nor, consequently, and maybe inevitably, to the British audience. Indeed, in the context of English Mazzinians, Crispi's most adamant and most steadfast admirer was Jessie White Mario who not only worked for his paper *La Riforma*, but was a close and intimate friend. In the three decades between Crispi's participation in the 'expedition of the Thousand' in 1860, and the mid-1890s, Jessie White Mario carried on an assiduous and friendly correspondence with 'Don Ciccio', which was only brought to a halt by her sudden, late, brutal realisation that the friend whom she had trusted had betrayed all that Mazzini stood for – and had turned into a politician whom she disliked.[5]

In view of her important role as a disseminator, as a militant journalist writing for newspapers in Italy, but also in Britain and America, Jessie White Mario may be seen as one of the figures who contributed significantly to constructing an image of Crispi which was presented to progressive readers abroad.[6] Like other democrats, Jessie White Mario joined the chorus celebrating Crispi's arrival in 1887. She felt the that the 'evils' which had gathered during Depretis's government (particularly 'corruption of the moral sense') would be remedied by Italy's new premier: he would build on some of the advance that the Left (*Sinistra Storica*) had indeed made – extended manhood suffrage, no more imposed paper currency, an army drafted from citizens – and introduce new reforms. She did not anticipate Crispi's colonial expansion in Ethiopia. Indeed, in a letter to the Italian historian, Pasquale Villari, written in 1887, she confessed that Crispi was the living person whom she had most praised in her recent book about Bertani. Significantly, in 1901, when writing Crispi's obituary, she would add that if he had died at the end of his first government – before his imperialist aspirations had turned into 'megalomania' – he would have done so at his peak.[7] That for so

---

5   White Mario to Crispi, 6 Feb. 1887, JWM, MCRR, 656/47/6 (n.d. but c. 1992), MCRR, 656/48/9.

6   In her article in the *Newcastle Daily Chronicle* White Mario confidently addressed the readers as if they were conversant with Mazzini's doctrine: 'A Mazzinian's view of Mr Gladstone', 16 Feb. 1881.

7   Stefano Iacini, one of the last representatives of the 'Destra Storica' was the first to use the term 'megalomania' when referring to Crispi: *Pensieri sulla politica italiana*, Florence 1889, quoted in R. Vivarelli, *Italia 1861*, Bologna 2013, 85 n. 33.

long Jessie White Mario was lulled into a false sense of security and faith in Crispi's unquestionable credentials as a Risorgimento democrat was pivotal in defining the perspectives of radical readers abroad.[8]

Furthermore, in the mid-1880s the overriding rhetoric in Europe was that a strong policy was a good omen; indeed, in Britain too the radical unionist Joseph Chamberlain had told the conservative Arthur Balfour that his sort of radicalism favoured a strong and imperial government.[9] In addition, if from 1887 Crispi had ostentatiously displayed his aim to expand into Ethiopia and the horn of Africa, he had also shown great willingness to affirm Anglo-Italian friendship by signing a formal treaty – something which Salisbury, who sought to contain Crispi's belligerence, had rebuffed.[10]

Within this international context the Toynbee Hall travellers first set off to Italy, for many years the destination of the English elites.[11] Case studies demonstrate how the rhetoric of European democracy and 'humanity' provided Victorian co-operators and adult learners with a mental map which informed their experience of 'foreign' encounters, allowing them to transcend conventional 'picturesque', 'orientalist' readings of the Italian 'character', allegedly deeply seated in the cultural imagination of traditional *Grand Tour* consumers and more recent bourgeois 'tourists'.[12] Arguably, 'co-operative travellers' most closely mirrored the image of the 'Tourist in search of knowledge', which Anthony Trollope aspired to be, yet, as James Buzard has shown, never remotely attained. Such a figure was described in Trollope's *Travelling sketches* as somebody who

> Looks into municipal matters wherever he goes, learning all details as to mayors, aldermen and councilors [sic], as to customs, duties of provisions, as to import duties on manufactures, as to schools, convents and gaols, to scholars mendicants and criminals. He does not often care much for the scenery.[13]

---

[8] White Mario to P. Villari, 21 Nov. 1887, quoted in R. Certini, *Jessie White Mario una giornalista educatrice tra liberalismo inglese e democrazia italiana*, Florence 1998, 150–1. There is an extensive and lucid analysis of Jessie White Mario's views on liberal Italy and the Italian Left in the introduction to Biagianti, *La 'nuova Italia'*.

[9] This is quoted in R. Harcourt Williams (ed.), *Salisbury-Balfour correspondence* (Balfour Record Society, 1988), 137.

[10] Duggan, 'Gran Bretagna e Italia nel Risorgimento', 777, and *Crispi*, 567.

[11] For an overview of the topic see also M. P. Sutcliffe, 'The Toynbee Travellers' Club and the transnational education of citizens, 1888–90', *History Workshop* lxxvi (Autumn 2013), 137–59.

[12] For the changing definitions of 'tourist' and traveller' in the nineteenth century see Buzard, *The beaten track*, 18–79. For a critical assessment of early nineteenth-century British travellers see Porter, '"Bureau and barrack"', 407–33. More generally see Moe, *The view from Vesuvius*, and O'Connor, *Romance of Italy*.

[13] J. Buzard, 'Portable boundaries: Trollope, race and travel', *Nineteenth Century Contexts* xxxii (2010), 5–18 at p. 8.

Imbued with Mazzinian principles, consumers of 'co-operative tours' would scour the Italian social-political landscape in search of signs of a budding Mediterranean democracy. Indeed, some might even have been looking for the precursors of Mazzini's 'Third Rome'.

In the late 1880s skilled workers, clerks and teachers reached Italy on 'co-operative tours' either because invited to co-operative congresses or because they took part, as adult learners, in 'educational pilgrimages' organised by English Mazzinians. By focusing on the experience of Victorian 'co-operative travel', this chapter is designed to modify some of the conventional readings on the 'English', Italy and travel. By taking a two-directional approach in the analysis of 'co-operative travel' it also aims to blur the orientalist schema within which encounters between Victorians and Italians are conventionally univocally framed. The 'co-operative tours' undertaken by Italian co-operators who visited England's stores are therefore also taken into consideration.

Finally, a few words on definitions: the variety of initiatives which came under the common denomination of 'co-operative tours' has been here classified within three loose typologies of travel. The first type of 'co-operative tour' refers to the travels which were brought about by the congresses convened by the 'co-operative international': traces of these trips to Italy can be found not only in the official addresses of delegates, but also in the vivid accounts written by Holyoake for the *Co-operative News*. In such an internationalist context, the rhetoric expressed in the speeches of the English delegates was evocative of a long connection with Italy, expressed in the memory of the 'fathers of the nation' and in the English co-operators' millenarian expectations of Italy's renewal. The second type of 'co-operative tour', which was defined as a 'journey of learning', includes the itineraries undertaken by Italian co-operators in search of models of co-operation in Britain. The third typology of 'co-operative tour' also defines what has been described as an 'educational pilgrimage' around Italy, undertaken by English adult learners who saw in the progress of Italian co-operatives one of the many signs of a young democracy coming of age.[14]

Co-operative congresses, co-operative friendships

The autumn of 1886 saw the delegates of the Central Co-operative Board, Edward Vansittart Neale and George Holyoake, arrive in Milan to attend

---

[14] Born out of the tragedy of the First World War, similarly-inspired initiatives were later backed by supporters of the Workers' Travellers Association and others, including J. J. Mallon, head of Toynbee Hall: S. Barton, *Working-class organisations and popular tourism, 1840–1970*, Manchester 2005, 157–8.

the First Congress of Italian Co-operators.[15] It was a momentous occasion for establishing goals of co-operation in Italy as delegates from associations, Milanese deputies and co-operators from a spectrum of European nations congregated.[16] The one significant absentee was Saffi, who sent his best wishes from Forlì. The congress was extensively reported by Jessie White Mario in her correspondence with the *Nation*.[17] The northern industrial city of Milan had emerged as the driving force for workers' co-operation, and its official organ, the newly-founded *La Cooperazione Italiana*, had gone so far as to liken the city to Halifax, due to the co-operative 'miracles' that it had achieved.[18]

Holyoake returned to England impressed by the progress of co-operation in northern Italy, writing an account of it in a letter to Lady Tennyson.[19] Francesco Viganò, president of the Comitato Centrale delle Società Operaie, and well-known as the 'father of Italian co-operation', Carlo Romussi, vice-president and director of the Milanese democratic paper *Il Secolo*, Luigi Buffoli, secretary, and Ugo Rabbeno, representing the *Giornale degli economisti* could be seen at this point as the spokesmen for co-operative progress in Italy. Their names appeared on the editorial board of the *La Cooperazione Italiana* – from January 1887 the voice of co-operation.[20] Significantly, the first issue of the paper reported on the front page an address by Viganò and one by Neale – closely followed by a few words from Holyoake, who had pointedly announced at the closing banquet: 'Now you have a united Italy – strive to have a united industry.'[21]

Neale's long address, published in the *Cooperazione Italiana*, was far from simple well-wishing; it had the genuine tones of Christian Socialism which blended so closely with the Mazzinian rhetoric of 'humanity'. No nation, no race could be excluded from the common good, but to Italy was ascribed an even greater role: with a clear reference to Mazzini's vision of the 'Third Rome', Neale underlined how England had drawn from imperial Rome the

[15] For a lively and amusing description of Holyoake's train journey around Milan see McCabe, *Life of Holyoake*, 191–2.

[16] Other international representatives included M. Fougerousse from France and Ed Pietet from Switzerland: 'Cronaca Milanese: il congresso dei cooperatori', *Il Secolo*, 9–10 Oct. 1886. For a detailed account of the congress see R. Zangheri, G. Galasso and V. Castronovo, *Storia del movimento cooperativo in Italia, 1886–1986*, Turin 1987, 74–87.

[17] Saffi to the Comitato, 'Il primo Congresso dei cooperatori italiani', Forlì, 17 Sept. 1886, Saffi, *Ricordi*, xiii. 193; J. White Mario, 'The Co-operative congress in Milan', *The Nation*, 16 Oct. 1886, reported in Biagianti, *La 'nuova Italia'*, 165–70.

[18] 'Lo sviluppo della cooperazione', *La Cooperazione Italiana* (Aug. 1887).

[19] The friendly relations which he initiated with the Milanese co-operators were renewed yearly: each Christmas Holyoake received the typical *panettone* from them: McCabe, *Life of Holyoake*, ii. 199.

[20] Carlo Romussi (1847–1913) was one of the most coherent representatives of radical democracy in Italy. The Romussi Archive, in Milan, is indexed in the catalogue in S. Massari, *Carlo Romussi (1847–1913): inventario dell'archivio*, Turin 2007.

[21] McCabe, *Life of Holyoake*, 192.

light of ancient civilisation and from Christian Rome the light of the great religion of 'humanity'. Italy, with its 'genius for unity', was therefore destined to play a great part in the propaganda of the 'Gospel of Work'. Indeed, by ascribing to Italy the mission which Mazzini had envisaged for Britain, Neale wished the Italy of the future to show herself 'worthy of the high place in the history of humanity reserved to that nation which, by first practising the great principles which constitute the internal life of co-operation', would 'guide humanity on that path of complete civilization, where progress and poverty [would] cease to walk hand in hand'.[22]

Neale's appeal is remarkable as it closely mirrors Mazzini's projected plan for republican Italy, where association and duty were the prime constituents of the new civic religion which the 'Third Rome' was supposed to embrace as a model for humanity as a whole. The deference to Mazzini is however particularly striking when coming from an English co-operator, as it suggests that Italy, rather than England, might be the beacon nation, able to guide all other nations. Indeed, this attitude towards Italy's powers of self-regeneration and for guiding humanity had been expressed four decades earlier by Linton in the pages of the *English Republic*.[23]

Despite the messianic speech of the English co-operator, Milanese consumers of co-operative literature could be in no doubt as to which nation was leading the way in co-operation: the co-operative organ was steeped with news reporting on co-operative congresses throughout England, which Italian co-operators, whenever possible, travelled to attend. Indeed, in 1888, Ugo Rabbeno, author of books on the progress of co-operation, joined Neale, Holyoake and other delegates at a congress in Dewsbury.[24] Biographies of Neale and Holyoake appeared in *Il Secolo* and *La Cooperazione Italiana*, as did short biographical sketches of English working-class parliamentary candidates, all patently constituting models to emulate.[25] These included the stonemason Henry Broadhurst, coalminers Thomas Burt, William Abraham, B. Pickard and Charles Fenwick, from Newcastle, who cited Mazzini amongst his favourite authors.

Interest in the progress of co-operation in England fuelled the desire to learn more about its co-operative stores: in June 1889 Luigi Buffoli was able to realise his 'greatest desire', setting off on a 'journey of learning' through England.[26] Funded by an educational grant provided by the *Unione Coopera-*

---

22 Wansittart [sic] Neale, 'Ai cooperatori d'Italia', *La Cooperazione Italiana*, 1 Jan. 1887.

23 *English Republic* (1851), 287–8.

24 Ugo Rabbeno, *La cooperazione in Inghilterra*, Milan 1885, and 'Il Congresso cooperative inglese', *La Cooperazione Italiana* (July 1888).

25 'Un apostolo della cooperazione', *Il Secolo*, 10–11 Oct. 1886; 'Un altro apostolo della cooperazione', *Il Secolo*, 11–12 Oct. 1886; 'Edoardo Vansittaert Neale', *La Cooperazione Italiana* (Feb. 1889); 'I sette deputati operai inglesi', *La Cooperazione Italiana* (Nov. 1888).

26 He was accompanied by Domenico Sommariva and Achille De Simoni: 'Un viaggio cooperativo in Inghilterra', *La Cooperazione Italiana* (Sept. 1889).

tiva of Milan, Buffoli left the city by train heading straight to Manchester to visit Neale at the Central Co-operative Board and to survey the Wholesale Co-operative Society;[27] he then visited Rochdale, where he signed the visitors' book, and other co-operatives in Oldham, Leeds, Halifax, Huddersfield, Liverpool, London and Brighton, where Buffoli was finally welcomed by the legendary Holyoake.[28]

The ageing English co-operator had only recently returned from the second Italian Co-operators' Congress in Bologna which he and Neale had attended in 1888. Holyoake, who was in communication with Saffi and Jessie White Mario, both clearly *au courant* with the development of co-operation in Italy, had noted approvingly that in Bologna a co-operative society had devoted 20 per cent of its profits to education, adding that[29]

> Where the reader shall learn that there is a Store without an Intelligence Fund – with no News-room, no Library, no Lecture-hall, he may conclude there is no conception that Co-operation is training in the principles of business, which has honesty for the basis, equity for its aim, and intelligence as its ground of interest in it. In Italy, where they see most things at once, in France, which has propagandism in its blood, there is growing up a consistent conception that intelligence in a store is an investment that yields high interest.[30]

'Co-operative education', however, had a particular meaning for Holyoake, as it was meant to prepare co-operative members for the main objective: 'social citizenship' – implying active participation in society – and, indeed, what Holyoake referred to as 'companionship'.[31]

Embarking on a 'co-operative tour' to Bologna, Holyoake had found 'companionship' and more, both making and rekindling friendships. Having departed with Neale from Charing Cross, he arrived in Bologna to be greeted by two well-known figures of Italian co-operation, Viganò, now eighty-two years old, and Saffi, who had made it from Forlì and was able to translate and deliver Holyoake's address to the congress.[32] The speech, which was rich in references to the 'founding fathers' of Italy, was reported in the local *Resto del Carlino* and in *L'Emancipazione*, the republican paper which had once been

---

[27] Details on both great institutions of English co-operation had been published in 'Il magazzino cooperativo centrale in Inghilterra', *La Cooperazione Italiana* (July 1887).

[28] 'Un viaggio cooperativo in Inghilterra', *La Cooperazione Italiana* (June 1889; Jan. 1890).

[29] Holyoake to White Mario, 23 Sept. 1888, George Jacob Holyoake Archive, Bishopsgate Institute, Holyoake, 1/8. See also Holyoake, *Sixty years*, i. 91.

[30] G. J. Holyoake, *The Co-operative Movement to-day*, London 1912, 85.

[31] Idem, *Essentials of co-operative education*, Manchester 1898, 7.

[32] 'The Bologna Congress I', *Co-operative News*, 3 Nov. 1888, 1110; 'The Bologna Congress II', *Co-operative News*, 10 Nov. 1888, 1121.

edited by Quadrio and had been re-established, in 1886, under the editorship of Felice Albani.[33]

Neale and Holyoake were struck by the fact that the congress delegates were mostly members of the educated classes, but considered – with what Ibn Warraq might refer to as the 'pathological niceness of liberals' – that in both Italy and France the educated classes took part in congresses 'in the interest of the people', while 'in England' they did not 'in an equal degree show patriotic, public or social concern for working class co-operation'.[34] The warm relations between Holyoake and the delegates were reaffirmed over informal speeches at the official banquet, where Holyoake was addressed by the president of the People's Bank (*banca popolare*), Luigi Luzzatti, amicably referring to the English co-operator as 'a good republican, and under certain justifiable circumstances, possibly a revolutionist'.[35]

Holyoake's daughter, Emilie, travelling with her father as a member of the English Women's Co-operative Guild (WCG), took a particular interest in the congress.[36] The aim of the WCG was to encourage women – often regular workers in co-operative stores – to hold their own meetings, discussions and reading groups, addressing issues of education and citizenship in the spirit of co-operative sisterhood. Indeed, the centrality of education within the co-operative vision drew women to cross the line of the 'separate spheres' as they responded to their duty of raising young co-operators in the spirit of active citizenship. Amongst the readings recommended by the WCG were titles such as *The citizen reader* and, significantly, *The co-operative traveller abroad*.[37]

In 1888, when Emilie Holyoake, as treasurer of the WCG, attended the Bologna Congress, membership in Britain had grown to more than 1,400 women in over 40 branches. Thanks to Emilie's participation in the Bologna congress the commitment of a WCG member to women's education and citizenship had the chance to stretch beyond the national boundary. Once in Bologna, not only did Emilie make enquiries which she felt would benefit the guild at home, but she entertained the idea of promoting the establishment of a similar Co-operative Guild in Italy – reaching out to Italian women workers in a way that was reminiscent of the appeal to transnational sister-

---

33 A. Comba, 'La base repubblicana dal 1889 al 1893 nell' "Emancipazione" di Felice Albani', in *L'associazionismo mazziniano*, 99–117.

34 Warraq, *Defending the West*, 273–96; 'The Bologna Congress III', *Co-operative News*, 17 Nov. 1888, 1145–6.

35 'The Bologna Congress IV', *Co-operative News*, 24 Nov. 1888, 1169.

36 The WCG had been formed in 1883 thanks to Alice Acland's initiative: the Aclands were both heavily committed to the education of citizens and to the progress of co-operation. A. H. D. Acland, Alice's husband, held educational classes for co-operators at Toynbee Hall.

37 *The Women's Co-operative Guild: outline of work*, Manchester 1893, John Johnson collection, Bodleian Library, Oxford, 'co-operation', box 3.

hood which had been published in her father's *Reasoner* decades earlier.[38] Emilie's current interest, however, also reflected the emancipatory concerns aired in the articles published in Caroline Ashurst Biggs's *Englishwoman's Review*, where the news of Italian women workers' associations in Romagna was welcomed.[39]

For Holyoake and Neale the 'co-operative tour' was also an opportunity to visit old and new friends. At Saffi's house in Forlì, amongst wine presses, vineyards and wagon-loads of grapes drawn by white oxen, evenings were spent relaxing with the family, singing and sharing reminiscences of those who had perished to free Italy and celebrating those who were still 'taking a parlous part in the struggle', all the while living 'in honour'.[40] Saffi had been tested by his latest experience of the *Sinistra Storica*, by the news of the signing of the Triple Alliance and by Depretis's imperialist policy in Abyssinia, which had ended in military defeat in 1887: in his letters to his wife Giorgina one reads the desolation with which he witnessed how Italy was being 'profaned'.[41] Yet, in his encounter with Holyoake, Saffi also spoke with optimism of some aspects of Italy's economy – namely, the vital role that the traditional association between landlord and labourer in the *metayer* system (*mezzadria*) played in Tuscany, and its mixed application in Lombardy. Holyoake returned inspired, writing in the *Co-operative News* that 'There is no social question in Tuscany, and there would be none in England were the *metayer* system to be applied to manufacturers.'

During his visit to the town of Bologna, Holyoake was also alert to any signs of progress which he could relate to co-operative readers at home: he paid a visit to the Azzoguidi Topographical Society of Co-operative Printers of Bologna and visited the great exhibition in town, on which he commented that 'there were notable educational features excelling anything we have seen in English exhibitions'.[42] Arguably, Holyoake's observations were a measure of how the 'orientalist' gaze of *Grand Tour* travellers and later tourists was absent from the inquisitive mind of a visiting co-operator.

Thanks to a letter of introduction supplied by Emilie Ashurst Venturi, Holyoake had also been able to meet for the first time at the Bologna Congress, Ernesto Nathan, whose mother, Sara, he had known since the early revolutionary struggles. The meeting led to an invitation to the Nathans' 'imposing' villa in Antella, near Florence, where portraits of Mazzini, Saffi and Armellini were framed in three panels on the wall. 'Golden days' in

---

[38] Ibid; *Reasoner*, 15 Sept. 1852, 14, 215. On the guild see M. Llewlyn Davies, *The Women's Co-operative Guild, 1883–1904*, Kirkby Lonsdale 1904.

[39] 'Italy', *Englishwoman's Review*, 15 Aug. 1876.

[40] 'The Bologna Congress V', *Co-operative News*, 3 Dec. 1888, 1234–5.

[41] Saffi to Craufurd Saffi, Bologna, 10 Mar.1887, FC, BCAB, ii/14/2, 38. On the use of the religious lexicon by democrats after Mazzini's death see Finelli, 'È divenuto un Dio'.

[42] 'The Bologna Congress IV', 1169. Sismondi had famously celebrated Tuscany's rural order (*metayer*) as the best heritage of the communal past and antidote to rural capitalism.

Florence ensued, thanks to the generosity of Ernesto, who treated his guests to a memorable visit.[43] Yet, despite the inevitable pleasure which came with visiting Italy in style, Holyoake and Neale 'never lost sight of co-operation'. In Rome they were made aware of a plan to establish a store modelled on the Rochdale plan and they visited the editor, Felice Albani.[44] They then travelled on to Lendinara to visit Jessie White Mario whose promotion of co-operation in Italy was well-known to them due to the articles that she published in the *Newcastle Daily Chronicle*.[45] From Venice they finally set off for Milan, where they were met at the station by friends of the co-operative store: they visited the offices of the Unione Cooperativa and Carlo Romussi's office at the *Secolo*.[46]

The tour undertaken by the two ageing co-operators was marked by an enduring spirit of transnational 'social citizenship' which was by no means peculiar to them: it was one of the traits which defined 'co-operative travel'. However, 'co-operative travel' was not confined to congress delegates and senior co-operators for in these same years it would also be offered to a handful of adult learners. This stemmed from an experiment in affordable travel led by a group of social reformers residing at Toynbee Hall, one of the many educational institutions which had been set up in the capital, following the establishment of the pioneering Working Men's College in 1854.

Toynbee Hall

In 1872 the Working Men's College had suffered a major setback due to the death of its principal and main founder, the Christian Socialist Frederic Maurice. His death had closely followed that of Mazzini. Reflecting on the sudden deaths of both men, John Stuart Mill remarked in a letter to his friend John Cairnes that 'One mourns to see persons of the highest worth, and who were individually centres of important influences, passing away one after another. The best consolation is that the best part of their work was done; and the influence of their lives will still be continued by their memory.'[47]

Indeed, Maurice's legacy remained thanks to the new energy which his followers would inject into the college, ensuring that it would be a beacon for other educational institutions. In the case of Mazzini, it was not long

---

[43] 'The Bologna Congress V', 1234–5. On the Nathan family see Isastia, *Storia di una famiglia.*

[44] 'The Bologna Congress VI', *Co-operative News*, 15 Dec. 1888, 1249.

[45] 'The Bologna Congress VII', *Co-operative News*, 22 Dec. 1888, 1273.

[46] 'The Bologna Congress VIII', *Co-operative News*, 29 Dec. 1888, 1313.

[47] J. S. Mill, *Letter to J. Cairnes*, 6 Apr. 1872, *Collected works*, xvii, London 1996, 1879–80.

before his English admirers were to take on the challenge of securing his legacy by continuing his 'apostolate' within the adult education and the co-operation movements. Unlike in Italy, where such a task would come to be disputed by interested parties, ready to recast the exile's message to suit their political agendas, in England it was Victorian progressives alone who kept Mazzini's flame burning.[48] London would be particularly well served by one of T. H. Green's students, Arnold Toynbee, who candidly affirmed that 'Mazzini is the true teacher of our age.'[49]

Since T. H. Green had taught his audiences that 'active citizenship and reform' equated to religious fulfilment, teaching adult learners had become akin to a mission in Oxford.[50] Before long, Green's 'listeners and readers' had set off on educational enterprises 'to the East-End of London, and the industrial cities of the North, to the Workers' Extension Movement and the Workers' Educational Association, to the Christian Socialist Union, and the Charity Organization Society'.[51] Such institutions were a direct consequence of the university reform movement, which endorsed the universities' active role in addressing urban problems.[52] In conjunction with the London East End vicar, Samuel Barnett, Arnold Toynbee set out to create the conditions for collaboration between London workers and Oxford educators, leading to the establishment of a residential institution: the university settlement, 'Toynbee Hall', appropriately named after its main inspiration.[53]

Drawn towards marrying education and social reforms, Arnold Toynbee had influenced his own disciples by further developing the principles of Christian Socialism in the name of active citizenship. Founded in 1885, Toynbee Hall welcomed adult learners who 'had not religion or politics in common' and 'could hold views and join parties at their discretion'. By 1890 there were over a thousand students and sixty residents. During the early years the main direction of the institute was determined by the Revd Samuel Barnett and Bolton King. The latter, drawn from Oxford as one of the principal teachers, was resident tutor at Toynbee Hall for the first eight years.[54]

---

48 On Mazzini contended see Finelli, '"É divenuto un Dio"'. There is a wealth of material on the later historiography. For an introduction to the topic see Balzani, 'Il problema Mazzini'; Finelli, 'Mazzini in historical memory'; and Levis Sullam, *L'apostolo a brandelli*.

49 King, *Life of Mazzini*, 149. On T. H. Green's veneration for Mazzini see also Harvie, *The lights of liberalism*, 104.

50 Richter, 'T. H. Green and his audience', 467.

51 Ibid. 470.

52 A. Ockwell and H. Pollins, 'Extension in all its forms', in M. G. Brock and M. G. Curthoys (eds), *The history of the University of Oxford*, vii/2, Oxford 2000, 670.

53 S. Meacham, *Toynbee Hall and social reform, 1880–1914: the search for community*, New Haven–London, 1987.

54 J. J. Mallon, 'Toynbee Hall past and present', *Toynbee Travellers*, LMA, A/TOY/21/14; R. B. King, J. D. Browne and E. M. H. Ibbotson, *Bolton King practical idealist*, Warwickshire 1978, 7.

Only son of a Warwickshire squire of liberal convictions, Bolton King had been educated at Eton, before studying as an undergraduate at Balliol, where he came into contact with influential reformers, such as Benjamin Jowett and T. H. Green.

Barnett's interest in the co-operative movement ensured that Toynbee Hall residents grew increasingly familiar with the challenges facing workers and with their need to organise collectively. Barnett invited the Liberal MP Arthur Acland from Balliol to hold classes for London co-operators at the Hall: in Acland's view, the 'sole object' of co-operative education was to encourage 'thinking' rather than 'mere "cram"'.[55] As Standish Meacham indicated, increasingly thereafter 'the hall played host to groups of Co-operative mantle makers, cigar makers and the like'.[56] The subwarden at Toynbee Hall, Thory G. Gardiner (1884–9), was himself a staunch supporter of co-operation, which he considered to be at the heart of the principles held by all those frequenting Toynbee Hall.[57] Another important aspect of Barnett's vision was fostering cross-class fellowship between the Oxford teachers in residence and the adult learners. In Meacham's words, a 'machinery of connection' was created through a 'vast educational network of classes, clubs, organisations and projects'.[58]

The friendship which developed between Bolton King and Thomas Okey is a fortunate example of those connections which were able to bridge the class divide. Okey was a self-educated republican basket-weaver who had contributed to the *Republican*, the unofficial organ of the Land and Labour League (1870). His love of Italy and knowledge of Italian later gained him the first appointment to the prestigious Serena Chair of Italian in Cambridge in 1919.[59] At Toynbee Hall Okey taught Italian language and literature classes. Bolton King, who delivered a course on Italian history, imparted lessons not only on the past glories of the Italian Renaissance but also on current political and social conditions in Italy and the challenges of nation-building. Bolton King and Okey were both interested in the growing role of Italian workers; the emergence of co-operatives; the progress of Italian schools in the context of the educational reforms; and the challenges posed by the 'Southern Question'.

---

[55] On Arthur Acland's co-operative classes in the 1880s see Gurney, *Co-operative culture*, 34, 37. See also A. H. Dike Acland and B. Jones, *Working men co-operators: what they have done and what they are doing*, London 1889 edn, 150.

[56] Meacham, *Toynbee Hall*, 66.

[57] 'The party to East London friends [sic]', *Toynbee Record* (Dec. 1888), 30.

[58] Meacham, *Toynbee Hall*, 50.

[59] 'Un mazziniano inglese', *Il Secolo*, 30 June–1 July 1901; Okey, *A basketful*, 37. For details on the Land and Labour League see Harrison, *Before the socialists*, 218–43; on Okey see Limentani, 'Leone and Arthur Serena', 154–77. First established in 1919, the Serena chair has since been held by some of the most eminent figures in Italian studies.

Bolton King also introduced learners to Mazzini's doctrine. Soon a 'Mazzini Club' was established at Toynbee Hall.[60] More than a decade after his death, the memory of Mazzini was still vivid amongst Victorians: in 1883 a Branch of the National Secular Society had chosen Mazzini's thought as the topic for its Sunday Lectures.[61] Between 1886 and 1888 Bolton King also offered a course on Mazzini's doctrine as part of the Toynbee Hall Moral Philosophy evening classes.[62] In 1889 the course on Mazzini was still popular, and classes were held once a week during both spring and winter terms. Mazzini also figured in the 1889 Sunday lectures on 'Great Teachers' held at Toynbee Hall, where audiences averaged around a hundred people.[63]

The Toynbee Travellers' Club in Italy

It was during one of the meetings of the 'Mazzini Club' that a certain Mr Fergusson suggested organising 'a pilgrimage to Mazzini's tomb at Genoa'. This was to be the inspiration for the founding of the Toynbee Travellers' Club, which saw Bolton King and Okey make arrangements for the first expedition to Italy in the spring of 1888.[64] Recent studies edited by Vescovi and others have endeavoured to identify texts which 'reformulated the picturesque' beyond depictions in *Grand Tour* narratives of 'chaotic roads, dirty inns, stinky slums, crime and deprivation'.[65] The editors concluded that 'only a few Victorian writers' had tried to deconstruct and subvert such stereotypes of Italians – and these had little success in challenging national prejudices. When conventional *Grand Tour* narratives are brought together with the travelogues written by Toynbee Hall travellers, however, nineteenth-century English constructions of Italy and the Italians do acquire a more textured dimension.

The Toynbee Travellers' Club tours around liberal Italy were pioneering expeditions in more ways than one. If different categories of nineteenth-century travellers were united by a 'drive for "education and improvement" – of the self, one's own culture and the cultures encountered' – travelling adult learners were particularly well placed.[66] Initially, however, the tours were labelled by the English press as a new form of 'cheap travelling', as the organisers had managed to secure both half-price rail-fares through the

---

[60] Okey, *A basketful.*

[61] *Reynolds's Newspaper*, 24 June 1883.

[62] W. Picht, *Toynbee Hall and the English settlement movement*, London 1914, 38.

[63] *Toynbee Record*, 2, 3 (Dec. 1889), 27.

[64] Okey, *A basketful*, 66. See also J. D. Browne, 'The Toynbee Travellers' Club', *History of Education* xv/1 (1986), 11–17.

[65] Vescovi, Villa and Vita, *The Victorians and Italy*, 9.

[66] R. Dickinson and E. Sdegno, 'Introduction: nineteenth-century travel and cultural education', *Nineteenth Century Contexts* xxxii (2010), 1–4 at p. 4.

continent and preferential entry to museums and galleries in Italy. Indeed, the 'emigrantish flavour' found in the printed advice distributed to the Toynbee travellers – which recommended carrying 'soap, spirit-stove and kettle, japanned cup and saucer, large water-bottle, opera glass and coloured spectacles, needles, threads and buttons' – was a source of journalistic amusement.[67]

The items recommended for the 'Toynbee *bagage*' revealed that this was no luxury *Grand Tour*.[68] In fact, the travelling party was part of an 'educational expedition', connected with the Whitechapel centre for the University Extension Society, which Toynbee Hall had become.[69] In spring 1888 a total of eighty-one men and women set off on the first tour, destined for Florence: nearly all of them were 'innocent of foreign travel'. They were chiefly Board School teachers and the lower grades of civil servants, who had attended during the winter of 1887–8 intensive courses on Italy, its history, art, literature and language at Toynbee Hall.[70] Participants in the first expedition – easily recognised by the red-bound Baedekers, which they 'each fondly grasped' – gathered at Liverpool station. As recorded in the travel logbook, 'the train moved off amid the cheers and jeers of the crowds', 'owing to the sensational announcements of the evening papers'. According to a small boy who witnessed the scene, they had all come to see "'Petticoat Lane off to the Continent'".[71] The event certainly made headlines: indeed, the following year, when more Toynbee Hall travellers set off for Venice, their departure was even reported in provincial papers.

More than just popular tourism, the excursion to Italy of the Toynbee travellers exhibited the defining elements of a 'pilgrimage'. Capturing the spirit in which the journey unfolded, Dame Henrietta Barnett – wife of the Revd Samuel Barnett and a committed social reformer herself – described the expedition as a '17 days … co-operative tour'.[72] Unlike other 'cheap travels', which would steadily grow in number, the 'tours' organised by Bolton King and Okey included pilgrimages to places which were a testimony to Italy's budding democracy. In contrast with the traditional pilgrimages of English Catholics to Rome and with the official 'patriotic pilgrimage' staged with celebratory monarchical pomp by the Italian authorities around the tomb of King Victor Emmanuel II in 1884, the Toynbee Hall pilgrims – travelling representatives of the adult education movement – followed itineraries which targetted the symbols affirming the republican, democratic identity

67 'Cheap Travelling', *Birmingham Daily Post*, 22 Apr. 1889.

68 Ibid.

69 'Toynbee Hall', *Daily News*, 18 Apr. 1889.

70 Okey, A *basketful*, 67.

71 Logbook of the expedition to Florence, 1888, LMA, A/TOY/12/1.

72 S. Koven, 'Barnett, Dame Henrietta Octavia Weston (1851–1936)', ODNB. See also 'Points from letters', *The Times*, 2 June 1930.

of liberal Italy. In 1889 'good Mazzinites' could not pass Genoa without giving 'a loving thought to the greatest patriot' and a visit to Milan could not be complete without paying respects to the progress of the Cooperative Society's work in the most representative city of Italian democrats.[73] While artistic masterpieces and architectural beauty were admired during the expeditions, the organisers of the Toynbee tours searched beyond what James Buzard defines as the 'aesthetic effect of a foreign culture as a co-ordinated picture or *mise-en-scène*', long privileged by the traditional cultured traveller: it was the soul of the new Italy that they were pursuing.[74]

The state of elementary education particularly interested the Board School teachers, a category which had included Englishwomen since 1870 (*see* Figure 6).[75] A tour of Venice, in 1889, was not complete without a visit to the Communal School of Burano. The same could be said of the trip to Siena, in 1890, where one of the appointed guides, J. Chase Scargill, noted in the logbook:

> Being an educational party, we must show our sympathy with the educators of our hosts as we visit them at school. Much to the delight of the Sienese youngsters we crowd into their white-washed rooms under the plaster busts of King Humbert by which each class is guarded. One of our numbers – a London teacher – says: The classes were small, held in separate rooms and appeared in excellent order.... A thing that surprised us was the salaries paid to the Teachers: we were informed that one lady after 27 years' service received a sum equal to £40 a year. No payment by results. Inspector thought it would be a good thing if there were.[76]

The reference to King Humbert's bust guarding the young Italians drew attention to the symbolism of monarchical patriotism which was being carefully orchestrated in the new nation.[77] The Toynbee travellers were in fact witnessing what was seen as one of the most delicate aspects of nation-building: the education of the Italians and the national *incivilimento* (civilising) of the new Italy. As Raymond Grew pointed out, 'Education was the panacea. In the first years of the new nation, remarkably able ministers of education devoted themselves to that cause, despite inadequate budgets,

---

[73] Logbook of the expedition to Siena, Perugia and Assisi, 11 Apr. 1890, LMA, A/TOY/012/002, 17; 'From Whitechapel to Venice', *Pall Mall Gazette*, 11 May 1889.

[74] Buzard, *The beaten track*, 10.

[75] On this see P. Hollis, *Ladies elect: women in English local government, 1865–1914*, Oxford 1989.

[76] 'From Whitechapel to Venice'; logbook of Siena, Perugia and Assisi expedition, 11 Apr. 1890, LMA, A/TOY/012/002, 39–40.

[77] On this topic see C. Brice, *Monarchie et identité nationale en Italie (1861–1900)*, Paris 2010.

Fig. 6. School Board teacher on the Tuscan Tour, 1890. (Toynbee Hall Papers, London Metropolitan Archives, Corporation of London).

schools, and teachers.'[78] Significantly, Edmondo De Amicis's *Heart*, an Italian schoolboy's journal, had been published in Italy in 1886. It was a resounding success: it was reprinted numerous times and was even published in English in 1887. While its tone was undoubtedly pro-monarchy, its international success demonstrates that the question of Italian education attracted a transnational readership.

Bolton King's impressions of Italian society were measured against his desire to witness the progress that was being made. Writing in the logbook of the tour to Florence, in 1888, he commented that 'when we remember how recently Italian unity has been secured one can feel but little doubt

[78] R. Grew, 'Culture and society, 1796–1896', in Davis, *Italy in the nineteenth-century*, 224.

that it is the <u>coming democracy of the Mediterranean</u> [*sic*]'.[79] A survey of the press unsurprisingly found in the democratic Milanese paper, *Il Secolo*, 'the paper that strikes one as the greatest power in the country', 'the Italian *Pall Mall*' ... and indeed 'a paper much in advance of our conventional Morning dailies'.[80] The comparison with the *Pall Mall Gazette* was significant: at the time of the tour W. T. Stead, its new editor, was raising the paper's profile by publishing inflammatory denunciations of the dire poverty and destitution in the East End. Similarly, in Italy, the well-respected *Il Secolo* had come to be the voice of Milanese democracy, often referred to as the 'workers' gospel'. Indeed, during the 1882 elections the paper had facilitated workers' access to the vote by providing information on how to enrol on the electoral lists. By 1883 it had started a moral campaign against the institutional malpractices introduced in the cabinet by Depretis.[81]

In the summer of 1887 the fall of Depretis's government and the arrival of Crispi had been welcomed by *Il Secolo* – and in almost every quarter – as the end of a period of decadence and an opportunity for new 'broad-ranging proposals for reform'.[82] Crispi had made clear his intolerance of the Vatican – something which pleased the well-informed Toynbee travellers. Writing in the travelogue in 1888, Bolton King noted that 'It is the struggle against the educational programme for Signor Crispi, the brilliant Italian Premier, that seems to lead to the strained relations between Church and State.'[83] Indeed, Crispi's defiance of the pope had come to both national and international attention early on. Already in 1885 Crispi had spearheaded a campaign to erect a monument dedicated to Giordano Bruno in Rome. One of the 'martyrs of free thought', Bruno, who had been condemned to death by the Inquisition, was a symbol of defiance against the authority and tyranny of the Catholic Church. Mazzinians across national boundaries associated him with anticlericalism and anti-Catholicism. It is not surprising that the international committee which supported erecting the monument included three English admirers of Mazzini: Swinburne, Stansfeld and Brad-laugh.[84] The Toynbee Hall travellers' buoyancy at the announcement of the new premier therefore seemed justified: free from the tyranny of the pope, Italy would embrace progress. Moreover, the travellers had been 'assured by

---

[79] Logbook of Florence expedition, 137, LMA, A/TOY/12/1.

[80] Ibid.

[81] L. Barile, *Il secolo, 1865–1923: storia di due generazioni della democrazia lombarda*, Milan 1980, 104–11.

[82] 'Il successore di Depretis', *Il Secolo*, 1 Aug. 1887. The translation is in Duggan, *Crispi*, 494.

[83] Logbook of Florence expedition, LMA, A/TOY/12/1, 141.

[84] For a detailed analysis of Crispi's support for the monument as a defiant gesture towards the Vatican see L. Berggren and L. Sjöstedt, *L'ombra dei grandi: monumenti e politica monumentale a Roma, 1870–95*, Rome 1996. For the English supporters see the appendix at p. 277.

observers upon whose competence and impartiality every reliance' could be placed, that equally in Naples, Rome and Turin the men were 'practically all agnostics' – though it was recognised that the women were 'clerical', as their education was 'still much neglected'.[85]

With Samuel Barnett as president, Okey as treasurer and Bolton King as secretary, the early years of the Toynbee Hall tours could not fail to chart an itinerary of Italy which was also a pilgrimage to the symbols of Italy's democratic achievements and goals. However, the credentials of the Club in seeking to understand the complexity of Italy's social conditions were further strengthened by the honorary membership of Pasquale Villari – the author of the famous *Lettere meridionali*, which had inspired a groundbreaking investigation into Sicilian society during the government of the *Sinistra Storica*.[86] In 1890 Villari was in fact made vice-president of the Toynbee Travellers' Club. The role played by Villari in Italy in the context of the emerging 'Southern Question' has been described by Nelson Moe as inaugurating 'a new intellectual function: that of the Meridionalist, the writer, from northern or southern Italy, who endeavours to provide a representation of the South to the nation's elites, especially in the North'.[87] However, the presence of Villari's name amongst the honorary members of the Toynbee Travellers' Club suggests that he also intended his audience to be transnational. In aiming to reach a wider audience Villari was assisted by Jessie White Mario whose extensive writings on social conditions, education and co-operation in Italy were sent to the *Nation*.[88] Villari also shared his views with another English friend, John Stuart Mill, who believed that there was 'a most encouraging mental activity amongst the (unfortunately too narrow) educated class in Italy'.[89]

In meeting the Toynbee travellers Villari saw a further opportunity to illustrate and explain to external observers the problems which had emerged

---

[85] Logbook of Florence expedition, LMA, A/TOY/12/1, 141.

[86] Pasquale Villari, *Le lettere meridionali ed altri scritti sulla questione sociale in Italia*, Turin 1885. For a recent, sensitive and measured biography of Pasquale Villari see R. Drake, 'Meridionalismo, the crisis of liberalism and the advent of Marxism in post-Risorgimento Naples', *European Legacy* ix/4 (2004), 481–502. For an earlier historiographical critique of the 'meridionalisti' on both sides of the Atlantic see J. Morris and R. Lumley, *The new history of the Italian south*, Exeter 1997, and Moe, *The view from Vesuvius*, 237.

[87] N. Moe, 'The emergence of the southern question in Villari, Franchetti, and Sonnino', in Schneider, *Italy's southern question*, 61.

[88] Villari himself had originally encouraged Jessie White Mario to carry out her survey of the slums of Naples and their correspondence is evidence of a long friendship and communality of intents: Certini, *Jessie White Mario*, 63 (and see the appendix for transcripts of the correspondence between Pasquale Villari and Jessie White Mario, found in the Biblioteca Apostolica Vaticana). On the involvement of English ladies in education in Naples after 1861 see Albisetti, 'Education for the poor Neapolitan children', 632–52.

[89] J. S. Mill to P. Villari, 28 Feb. 1872, *Collected works*, xvii: http://oll.libertyfund. org/?option=com_staticxt&staticfile=show.php%3Fperson=21&Itemid=28.

in Italy since unification: as he pointedly put it, 'while you are seeing the monuments and art of old Italy, it may be worth your while to observe how the new Italy has struggled from the old'.[90] On 8 April 1888 the Toynbee travellers gathered around the illustrious professor to hear his address on 'The social condition of Italy'; he explained that although he had lived many years in Florence he was from the South and proceeded to explain the link which he had established between brigandage in the South of Italy and poverty. In Villari's view southern peasants, who had been rich in corn and wine before the arrival of the railways, had been left in misery, and 'civilisation' had 'proved to the poor people of Italy not a blessing but a curse'. The Toynbee travellers also learned how in the North the spread of *pellagra* – a disease of poverty – had had devastating effects on peasant incomes, while conditions in Naples were compared to the worst slums of London's East End, a reality which the London 'pilgrims' could adequately picture. Villari's famous moral outcry was thus rehearsed before the English audience in his final appeal to them: 'Moral purpose should accompany us from the moment we wake up to the moment we sleep; so shall we have a noble ideal to help the moral health of the South.'[91]

Grand Tours and 'co-operative tours': a comparison

Villari's encounter with a group of English visitors was possibly less unusual than it may seem. According to John Pemble, Villari was the only Italian whom Elizabeth Barrett Browning had met socially in 1853, despite living in Florence 'more or less as a recluse' for many years.[92] Yet, while more sociable British residents in Florence were known to have opened their houses to liberal writers and intellectuals before 1870, 'this bond of sympathy' is largely reckoned to have become 'redundant' 'after the victory of the liberal cause'. Indeed, according to John Pemble, after 1870 the lines of communication between British visitors and natives were closed down. [93]

What Pemble terms one of the 'essential ingredients' of British aristocratic and bourgeois life abroad was aloofness, the desire to avoid dealings with locals – a distance which increasingly applied also to 'tourists' chaperoned by Cook's Travels: the Italians and the English would make 'no friendships' and for Victorian and Edwardian travellers the 'revolution in transport' had 'failed as a force for greater international harmony and communication'.[94]

---

[90] P. Villari, 'The social condition of Italy', Florence 1888: logbook of Florence expedition, LMA, A/TOY/12/1.

[91] Ibid.

[92] Pemble, *Mediterranean passion*, 262.

[93] Ibid. For similar views see also O'Connor, *Romance of Italy*, and Porter, 'Bureau and barrack'.

[94] See Boxall papers, quoted in Pemble, *Mediterranean passion*, 261, 274.

Indeed, Frederic Harrison, who had met Saffi's revolutionary republican friends on his 1859 tour around Italy, wistfully commented in 1887 that 'We go abroad, but we travel no longer. We see nothing really of the people among who we sojourn. We never touch their lives. They are not even our caterers or our servants. We lodge in sham Grand Hotels.'[95]

Indeed, when returning from their first tour, the Toynbee travellers shared some of these concerns. Bolton King noted that 'we carried with us our Toynbee topics and our ordinary English interests much as if we had gone to Brighton or Southend ... hence ... in this way the tour was not so useful educationally.'

Lessons however were learnt. If the hotels chosen had given no opportunity to 'learn more about the Italian social and political problems', small *pensioni* off the beaten track would serve such purposes better.[96] Therefore, on the expedition to Siena, Perugia and Assisi, organised in 1890, the travellers were divided into seven groups of eight, each with a guide. The hotels, allocated to separate groups, were intentionally small and not frequented by English tourists. The aim was to provide the opportunity for encounters and exchanges with Italians. A stop-off in Sestri Levante (Liguria), 'unaccustomed to have its solitude invaded wholesale', was an easy introduction to local hospitality: 'the population escorted the strangers to the inn' and 'manifested along the way a keen interest which was fully reciprocated'.[97] Touching incidents along the way left lasting impressions, which the group guide, J. Chase Scargill, recorded:

> Few things in Italy perhaps impress the Teutonic Londoner more favourably than the graceful courtesy, the complete absence of vulgarity in all ranks of these children of the South. The hotel porter and the cameriera [chambermaid], the artisan at work in his dark cavernous shop open to the street, the casual inhabitant of whom you ask the way, the Contadina in great flapping Tuscan straw hat, each and all will go out of their way to render any small service, in no servile spirit but with a dignified politeness which is very fascinating.[98]

The 'civilised' decorum noticed in Italians of all ranks was prized according to the hierarchy of values of 'respectable' lower- and middle-class Victorians. The 1890 expedition to Tuscany counted fifty-seven travellers, twenty-seven men and thirty women. According to the *Pall Mall Gazette* the teachers were mostly from the East End.[99] If 'the sight of men and cities' was valu-

95 F. Harrison, *Memories and thoughts*, London 1906, 249.
96 Logbook of Florence expedition, LMA, A/TOY/12/1.
97 Logbook of Siena, Perugia and Assisi expedition, LMA, /TOY/012/002, 17–20.
98 Ibid. LMA, /TOY/012/002, 31.
99 'Pall Mall Gazette Office', *Pall Mall Gazette*, 23 Apr. 1890.

Fig. 7. Toynbee Hall travelling women and man, 1890. (Toynbee Hall Papers, London Metropolitan Archives, Corporation of London).

able and deemed 'to make teaching more real and human' – in the words of the *Toynbee Record* – H. H. Asquith, Liberal MP, and Ernest Hart, a leading medical journalist, felt strongly that travellers drawn from different classes and categories should also benefit from the opportunity to travel.[100] The two men therefore joined forces to offer an £8 scholarship to be awarded by the Toynbee Committee to an artisan without sufficient means to join the Tuscan tour.[101]

As railways increased people's mobility, amateur photographers were able to record landscapes and peoples beyond national boundaries: the Toynbee travellers were said to have returned from the Venice tour in 1889 with around 2,000 photographs which illustrated what was termed 'contempora-

[100] 'School teachers in Switzerland', ibid. 6 Oct. 1889; 23 Apr. 1890.
[101] 'The Toynbee Travellers' Easter trip', ibid. 4 Mar. 1890.

neous posterity'.[102] 'Photographs and Pictures, especially of foreign travel' were in demand at Toynbee Hall, and the Education Committee made an appeal for donations in 1888.[103] In 1890, on the travellers' return from the trip to Tuscany, a selection of travel photos, collected in an album, was displayed at Toynbee Hall. In September, visitors to an open day were invited to browse around the university settlement, familiarise themselves with the activities and admire exhibits which included the Toynbee Travellers' Club photos.[104] Some of the impressions of Italy gathered by the Toynbee travellers during their tour thus managed to reach a wider audience in the East End.

The surviving snapshots of the 1890 tour around Siena, Perugia and Assisi help to form a clearer impression of the Toynbee travellers' 'gaze', as they encountered new peoples and landscapes (*see* Figure 7). Split up in small groups, they were able to mingle with Italians, learn about their crafts, enquire about their earnings and exchange friendly gestures with men, women and children (*see* Figure 8). The photographs of Italian peasants were equally indicative of the mind-set of the observers: these portraits were not constructed around orientalist bucolic scenes – showing 'lazy', 'carefree' Italians, at rest or dancing barefoot. Here men were captured as working men, one for example in front of a church carrying his implements to work the land (*see* Figure 9), another in a long working apron, surrounded by his family, all of them wearing shoes (*see* Figure 10). Okey, who was chaperoning the travellers around, was constantly taking notes which were to stand him in good stead years later when writing about Italy (*see* Figure 11).[105] Contacts made during the 'co-operative tours' would help him and Bolton King build an accurate social picture of *fin-de siècle* Italy.

Not only therefore, did co-operative travellers shun the typical aloof-ness described by Pemble, but they engaged with their Italian hosts. When Holyoake and Neale travelled to the Co-operators' Congresses in Milan and Bologna, and when Bolton King and Okey organised the first trips to Italy, friendships with Italians were forged and reaffirmed. Villari secured close links with the Toynbee Travellers Club, and the exchanges between English and Italian co-operators were long-lasting. Holyoake visited Viganò in his villa near Monza, Saffi in Forlì, then Nathan near Florence.[106] Buffoli, for his part, was happy to visit both Neale in the North and Holyoake in Brighton once he had crossed the Channel. The visit of the Toynbee travellers to the Milan co-operative was a further sign that the English guests were taking an interest in Italian social progress and were keen to form transnational ties amongst workers: the common culture of co-operation had indeed the poten-

---

102 'Toynbee Travellers', *Toynbee Record* (June 1889), 107.

103 *Toynbee Record* (Nov. 1888), 10.

104 *Daily News*, 20 Sept. 1890.

105 B. King and T. Okey, *Italy today*, London 1901.

106 McCabe, *Life of Holyoake*, ii. 192.

Fig. 8. Meeting local weavers in S. Gimignano, 1890. (Toynbee Hall Papers, London Metropolitan Archives, Corporation of London).

tial to transcend national boundaries. Singling out the Milan co-operators was also evidence that Bolton King and Okey were well informed as to the main drivers of democracy in Italy: the commentary about *Il Secolo* which appeared in the Toynbee travel logbook testified to a deep understanding of political allegiances in the country being visited.

If religious loyalties, as noted by Pemble, traditionally contributed towards maintaining the divide between travellers and hosts, this was unlikely to be the case amongst the Toynbee travellers. Pemble underlined how the British, with their 'special churches, special priests, special rituals and special cemeteries' were an inward-looking spiritual community of patriotism.[107] British Catholics were 'generally speaking, no closer to the Mediterranean

---

[107] On the blurring of boundaries between the assumed stark divisions between English Anglicans and Italian Catholics see Sutcliffe 'Residenti anglicani inglesi'.

Fig. 9. Tuscan peasant with implement, 1890. (Toynbee Hall Papers, London Metropolitan Archives, Corporation of London).

people'.[108] Yet 'co-operative travel' was distinguished by other traits: adult learners were often from a Nonconformist background, Mazzinians were frequently Unitarian, and one of the known characteristics of the Toynbee Hall learners was their not having a religion in common.[109] If anything, free thought and secularism may have more easily defined some of them, as the spreading of agnosticism amongst Italians seemed to be easily the trait that they were most keen to celebrate.

Moreover, the visits to primary schools and the respectful comparisons which were made by School Board members between the educational systems of the two countries demonstrate that the Toynbee travelling teachers had

[108] Pemble, *Mediterranean passion*, 271–2.
[109] J. J. Mallon, 'Toynbee Hall past and present', LMA, A/TOY/21/14.

Fig. 10. Tuscan family, 1890. (Toynbee Hall Papers, London Metropolitan Archives, Corporation of London).

no difficulty in identifying with social groups abroad – something which, according to Pemble, was a problem for bourgeois tourists.[110] Indeed, the commentary on one 'lady' teacher's salary was an indication of the English women teachers' sympathy for their poorly paid Italian colleagues, a sign of transnational empathy and possibly even co-operative 'sisterhood', which had similarly linked Emilie Holyoake to Italian women workers when imagining a women's co-operative guild in Italy. Posing in a photo with Italian peasant women, an English lady traveller was immortalised, smiling at her Italian 'sisters', showing a willingness to reach beyond cultural differences through the spiritual kindness born of shared 'humanity' (*see* Figure 12).

It is therefore not surprising that when the Toynbee travellers returned to their dwellings, they were proud to be holidaying in small hotels which were

[110] Pemble, *Mediterranean passion*, 263.

190

Fig. 11. Thomas Okey, taking notes on the Tuscan Tour, 1890. (Toynbee Hall Papers, London Metropolitan Archives, Corporation of London).

entirely frequented by 'natives'.[111] It was the 'citizens' of liberal Italy, as much as the country's art and monuments, in whom they were interested. The Kodak snapshots collected during the 1890 tour provide some evidence of the attitudes of some Toynbee Hall travellers towards Italians: families, peasants, women, children, beggars and workers, the people of liberal Italy were immortalised with the realism of the *Macchiaioli* painters rather than the voyeurism of the orientalist gaze – also a paradigm for representing southern Europeans.[112]

[111] Logbook of Siena, Perugia and Assisi expedition, LMA, A/TOY/012/002.

[112] See Moe, *View from Vesuvius*. On orientalist representations of the South of Italy see J. Dickie, *Darkest Italy*, New York 1999. As Anna Ottani Cavina has argued the *Macchiaioli* painters depicted Tuscan towns and countryside 'without grandeur and hyperbole', but with the 'piercing observation of everyday, provincial subjects': 'The landscape of the Macchiaioli: a path towards the modern', *JMIS* xviii/2 (2013), 225–231 at p. 228.

Fig. 12. A woman traveller among Tuscan women, 1890. (Toynbee Hall Papers, London Metropolitan Archives, Corporation of London).

Ten years later, while writing *Italy today*, Thomas Okey and Bolton King would devote numerous pages to analysing the rural economy of liberal Italy and the progress made by peasants: rather than relying on the use of well-worn clichés, the authors concurred that while the agricultural classes of Italy were exceedingly diverse, what qualified them was the 'accumulated labour of industrious generations': from the 'patient Italian' building olive and vine terraces on the Riviera, to the Sorrento peasant who had made lemon-gardens out of bare limestone cliffs. Lombardy too had been 'laboriously irrigated'.[113] The authors pointed out that the *mezzadria* was a traditional form of 'co-partnership' – a term much celebrated in the late 1880s within the co-operative movement (and at Toynbee Hall) as an alternative

---

[113] King and Okey, *Italy today*, 256.

to socialism. Despite the fact that the state had neglected him, the Italian peasant had 'been working out his own salvation' through the growth of co-operation and education: co-operative dairies (*latterie sociali*) , which had started in 1872, were spreading, together with the network of village banks (*casse rurali*) and co-operative syndicates.[114] In the north 'the shortcomings of Parliament' had only 'stimulated self-help', and travelling schools (*cattedre ambulanti*) were also multiplying.[115] Italian peasants, who, according to a well-established historiography, had not taken part in the insurrections or indeed the culture of the Risorgimento, emerged in the Toynbee Hall pictures as the face of the new liberal Italy. Despite economic problems in some regions, which would trigger transatlantic migration, they, as new Italians, were regarded as striking evidence of the progress that had been made.[116]

On Edward Said's own admission, orientalist readings never quite fitted visual images drawn from 'popular culture'.[117] Insofar as Kodak snap-shots taken by adult learners may qualify as 'popular culture', the pictures undoubtedly reveal as much about the photographer's 'eye' as they do about the subject portrayed – an 'eye' which, unlike the often-quoted orientalist 'gaze', viewed the Italians in the making as 'citizens' of a new democracy. If historians of northern Europeans' travel – from Buzard to Moe – liberally borrowing from Said's paradigm, applied Gramsci's *hegemonic* theory to the experience of travel and encounters between elite travellers and locals in Italy, the case studies illustrated here show that the orientalist narrative – if not completely flawed, when read within the confines of Europe – was at least only a partial representation of nineteenth-century English travellers bound for Italy.[118] The inappropriateness of applying orientalist readings to 'popular culture' seems particularly relevant when analysing the records left by Toynbee Hall travellers.

Indeed, if, as Maura O'Connor observed, 'travel made ... English middle-class men and women more self-conscious about their Englishness', as Italy was represented as the 'romanticized and feminized *other*' compared to civi-lised England, 'co-operative travellers' – 'armed with kettle, japanned cup

---

[114] Ibid. 187–91.

[115] Ibid. 183–8.

[116] Despite the phenomenon of emigration, according to Bolton King and Okey, the growth of co-operation and education had resulted in wheat yields quadrupling around Bergamo, and new work becoming available for Italians, who were now keen to return from the Atlantic to their villages: ibid. 191.

[117] J. M. Mackenzie, *Orientalism*, Manchester–New York 1995, 14. See also 'Interview', in Sprinker, *Edward Said*, 246.

[118] See Buzard, *The beaten track*, 15, and Moe, *View from Vesuvius*. Contemporary critiques of the orientalist edifice have indeed argued that Said's construction is to be considered flawed in all its applications, including in the analysis of 'high culture'. See Warraq, *Defending the West*, and Irwin, *For lust of knowing*.

and saucer' – saw encounters with different cultures as an opportunity to smile at their own ways:[119]

> Some of our party while waiting seized the opportunity for making tea. What a site [*sic*] for the natives! They gathered around in a semicircle and watched the proceedings most curiously, an occasional smile crossing their brown faces at some of the expedients of the cooks.[120]

On a surprisingly cold day the Toynbee travellers had the chance of an even closer encounter. As Chase Scargill wrote, 'the old Italian women were very willing to let us warm our hands at their *scaldinos*'.[121] Indeed, Toynbee travellers' humanity seemed to furnish some of them with the ability to connect with Italians, overcoming cultural barriers far better than the *Grand Tour* travellers, who had travelled to Italy for many decades before them.

The level of authenticity of some of the exchanges noted among the variety of 'co-operative tours' examined brings into question whether Gramsci's theoretical construct of hegemony, applied by some historians as an interpretative paradigm for the educated elites' experience of southern travel, may constitute an adequate tool for the analysis of working-class forms of travel to Italy, led by educators and social reformers. Indeed, within Gramsci's theoretical framework it is not so much the concept of hegemony but rather that of organic intellectuals which may provide a paradigm for the interpretation of the role of the Toynbee Hall 'co-operative tour' guides. Bolton King and Okey were both defined by their desire to challenge hegemonic ideas and by their ability to mix culture with practical life. Okey, an apprenticed artisan, had become an intellectual through adult education; Bolton King, a 'practical idealist', combined his intellectual rigour with running a co-operative experiment in Warwickshire.[122]

Both men's political engagement was expressed most significantly in their commitment to social improvement in Britain, demonstrated by their work at Toynbee Hall, and further evidenced by Bolton King's decision to stand as a Liberal candidate in Stratford-upon-Avon in 1901.[123] All this could be seen as reflecting the 'agency' of organic intellectuals acting within the 'cultural power and party formation' of their nation'.[124] However, Bolton King and Okey also shared a commitment to the transnational dimension

---

[119] O'Connor, *Romance of Italy*, 2, 4.

[120] Logbook of Siena, Perugia and Assisi expedition, LMA, A/TOY/012/002, 44.

[121] Ibid.

[122] King, Browne and Ibbotson, *Bolton King*.

[123] For a discussion on the meanings of 'organic intellectuals' in Gramsci see C. Borg, J. Buttigieg and P. Mayo, *Gramsci and education*, Oxford 2002, 307–12. Bolton King, Browne and Ibbotson, *Bolton King*; 'Un Mazziniano inglese', *Il Secolo*, 29 June–30 July 1901.

[124] Borg, Buttigieg and Mayo, *Gramsci and education*, 308.

of 'humanity' born out of Mazzinian inspiration, which was expressed in their desire to support Italians through the nation-building phase of liberal Italy: orientalist paradigms could hardly be applied to either the Toynbee Hall 'co-operative tours' or indeed to the co-operative visits of Holyoake and Neale.

The resolve of female co-operative travellers to investigate the progress of Italian women in education and co-operation complemented the Toynbee travellers' interest in the long process of 'making Italians'. Indeed, it may be said that the evidence of these women's 'agency' colours the narrative surrounding feminised support for the long *Risorgimento* beyond the familiar circle of the bourgeois English ladies associated with the Muswell Hill brigade, and beyond those women whose commitment to Italy was closely associated with their passion for Italian men.[125] The examples of Emilie Holyoake and that of the travelling School Board teachers of Toynbee Hall indicate that at least some working women showed a keen interest in the opportunities that liberal Italy might offer to their Italian sisters, retaining an unusually long-term commitment to the progress made by female Italian citizens. The celebration of Sara Nathan's life in an obituary published in 1882 in the 'liberal and feminist' *Englishwoman's Review*, noted by Anne Summers as a surprisingly late tribute to an Italian woman, may only be adequately understood if read in this larger context.[126] Just as English women co-operators at home were inching towards a small degree of control and leadership in driving educational issues within co-operatives, women embarking on 'co-operative travel' abroad extended their desire for empowering women through education to citizenship beyond the national boundary.[127]

Optimism amongst Victorian female emancipationists about the progress of Italian women was partly gleaned from the encouraging news on Italy disseminated by Caroline Ashurst's Biggs's paper, the *Englishwoman's Review*. More generally, such optimism was influenced by the peculiar buoyancy of the years between 1887 and 1890, most aptly defined by Cammarano as the period of 'Crispinian euphoria'. When the Toynbee travellers referred to Crispi as 'the brilliant Italian Premier' they were no less deceived by the progressive traits in his policy than the Milanese democrats of *Il Secolo*, who had celebrated Crispi's arrival in government, or indeed Jessie White Mario, whose correspondence had fed radical papers. Indeed, it may be said that Victorian radicals were united with those Italian democrats whose programme they upheld when supporting Crispi, the 'turncoat' of democracy. Yet the man, according to Cavallotti's belated accusations, had not only deceived Mazzini and all Italian democrats, but, since joining Mordini's

---

[125] On this topic see Summers, 'British women and cultures of internationalism', 192–5.

[126] Ibid, 192.

[127] Only in 1884 were the first English women elected to an educational committee of co-operators.

camp, had turned his back on all the lofty idealism of Italian republicanism. British progressives, who had shared the hopes of exiled democrats, would soon learn to draw a distinction between Mazzini's 'nation' and Crispi's nationalism. They would do so unequivocally.

Finally, one last word about these remarkable – if not intrepid – Toynbee travellers. What was possibly most striking in them were the traits of 'co-operative travel' which most set them apart from more familiar 'excursionists': much more than the Toynbee '*bagage*' remarked upon as the party set off from London's East End, what qualified these travellers was their education in the fraternal and sisterly spirit of democracy. According to Jacques Derrida, 'Democracy has seldom represented itself without the possibility of at least that which always resembles … the possibility of *fraternization*.'[128] Co-operation, defined by Holyoake as 'organised brotherhood', in its transnational dimension had the ability to broaden minds in a way that proved elusive to aristocratic *Grand Tour* travellers and later bourgeois 'tourists', whose mental horizons often 'contracted as their physical horizons widened'.[129] Instead, these travellers were guided by the values of 'association' in 'humanity'. As an avowed Mazzinian co-operator educated at Toynbee Hall, W. H. Brown, affirmed at the end of 1914 that the greatest value of the co-operative movement was that it created 'an atmosphere of kindly endeavour', one which recognised that 'Peace' was the 'password to Prosperity' and that 'War wounds Victor and Victim'.[130] Yet it was only after the First World War had torn Europe apart that the pacifist discourse of co-operators would find explicit realisation in the Co-operative Holiday Association, where the value of travel as a way to deepen workers' knowledge of other European people would acquire, for a brief time new, powerful resonance.[131]

[128] J. Derrida, *The politics of friendship*, London–New York 2005, p. viii.
[129] Quoted in Massari, *Carlo Romussi*, 1; Pemble, *Mediterranean passion*, 274.
[130] W. H. Brown, *The case of co-operation in peace and war*, Stratford 1914, JJC, 'co-operation', box 2.
[131] Barton, *Working-class organisations*, 157–8.

Conclusion

'But is there not a voice, not yet completely silenced in Italy, that bids us hope for better things – a voice that calls to us from a forsaken tomb on the slopes of Staglieno?'[1]

The 'popular Risorgimento' in transnational perspective

In focusing on the 'long connection' between Victorian radicals and Risorgimento democrats this book has questioned established historical views on the relationship between the 'English' and Italy, showing the limits of the 'official history' and adding a transnational dimension to the 'popular Risorgimento' narrative. By taking into account the views of Victorian republicans on Italy's constitutional monarchy the 'myth' that all the 'English' were satisfied with Cavour's pincer movement and the victory of the moderates has been challenged. In other ways too this study has unscrambled the traditional narrative, questioning how representative of the nation's 'people' were the 'English' analysed by the dominant Risorgimento historiography. Socially, this book has shifted the perspective from the educated classes to the adult education movement; chronologically, it has pushed the boundaries of conventional periodisation beyond the revolutionary phase of the Risorgimento by including the nation-building years; geographically it has highlighted the role played by the English 'peripheries' rather than the decision-makers in Whitehall, setting off from the northern industrial provinces and terminating in London's East End.

It has been argued that the 'long connection' of transnational democracy which linked Britain and Italy – from the early mechanics' institutes and co-operative stores in Lancashire and Yorkshire to the Mazzini Schools and the Co-operative Congresses in liberal Italy – was an intricate geo-political web which had its core in the diaspora of the Risorgimento democrats and the legacy that they left behind. Within this network of informal groups 'Joseph Mazzini' had been pivotal in providing Victorian 'common readers' – unencumbered by readings on the decadence of the Italian 'character' and free from orientalist stereotypes of travel – with the opportunity to imagine Italy as a nation constructed along new paradigms.[2]

---

[1] Mazzini was buried in the cemetery at Staglieno: G. O. Griffith, 'Mussolini, Mazzini and humanity', *Congregational Quarterly* xiv/1 (1936), 9–17 at p. 17.

[2] Duggan, 'Giuseppe Mazzini', 187.

By investigating Mazzini's following in provincial England, as well as around the margins of the capital, the 'peripheries' have been included within the discourse on Europe's connections of democracy, by-passing the 'centre' often equated with the official narrative of diplomacy and partial to the compromises of Italian moderates. Moreover, by taking into account forms of sociability, such as working men's associations, educational institutes and the organs of the democratic press, which acted as their mouthpiece, this analysis has contributed to bringing to the surface previously ignored connections of radical democracy which ran on into the nation-building phase. In doing so the 'losers' of the Risorgimento have been given some transnational resonance.

Indeed, thanks to the experience of exile, Mazzini's republican dream had been shared across national boundaries. Such a dream was based on the belief that Italy, as a newly-formed nation, could draw on its established tradition of free thought. Mazzinians were confident that Italy had the potential to provide a civic model for society, defined by republican institutions modelled on the peninsula's medieval communes and organised according to a novel system of production based on association and harmonious relations between classes. Within the nation, universal suffrage would be granted to educated 'citizens', aware of their duties as well as their rights. By bestowing upon Italy the role of beacon nation, radical Victorian self-improvers and educated middle-class Mazzinians understood the heroic struggle towards liberty of the Risorgimento and the glorious memory of Italy's republican past as good omens for the future.

Victorian Mazzinians did not, however, interpret the claims that the exile made for the 'Third Rome' as an assertion of national or nationalist superiority: they understood that Mazzini's principle of national determination for Italy was equally applicable to all other nations. Mazzini's nineteenth-century Victorian readers unequivocally identified his vision with political and social legitimacy based on the regulatory ideas of democracy and humanity, not aggressive nationalism. Indeed, Mazzini's vision of 'humanity' – defined as the orderly association of nations able to ensure global 'progress' – gave new hope to different groups: Victorian co-operators, robbed of Owen's millenarian expectations, as well as former, crest-fallen Chartists and die-hard internationalist republicans, inspired by the myth of the Roman Republic.

Moreover, Mazzini's ideal also inspired progressive social reformers – whether Nonconformist, liberal Anglican or secularist – who read Mazzini's vision for 'humanity' according to the religious rhetoric which imbued and permeated both Victorian culture and Mazzini's texts. Anticlericalism (understood as an attack on the powerful religious hierarchy) and anti-Catholicism equally provided these disparate groups with a common denominator. Mazzini's language of individual 'duty' and cross-class 'association' in society spoke to Nonconformists as well as liberal Anglicans whose sense of public duty led them to establish a secular educational institution, Toynbee Hall.

Indeed, the echo of Mazzini's passage was long-lasting amongst secularists. In the mid-1850s Mazzini had welcomed Holyoake's desire to promote his writings in the secular *Reasoner*, on condition that his divergence from atheist positions was made clear: the secular movement had since embraced Mazzini's ideals and continued to promote his global vision of democracy and peace into the late nineteenth century. Increasingly familiar with the debates on the meaning of 'citizenship' and often guided by the nineteenth-century ideal of the 'ladder of civilisation', all Victorian Mazzinians understood the ideas of 'liberty' and 'association' as inextricably linked to the exile's concept of 'nation', an ideal which, as Mandler has argued, was untainted by nationalist or racist connotations in British culture. It was this reading of Mazzini which also reached the adult learners of Toynbee Hall.

Mazzini's long-term vision for Italy enabled Victorian radicals to weather the disappointment of Italy's monarchical turn. Indeed, some of them continued for decades to follow the political events which unfolded in unified Italy. They were often well-informed of the antidemocratic measures which liberal Italy's governments took against Italian Mazzinians and voiced their protest – although they were largely ignored by the official press and by the British government.[3] Despite the difficulties, Mazzinians in Britain continued to look upon Italy with hope, after 1861 trusting in the progress of the 'budding democracy'. Even in 1889, despite the news of Crispi's increasingly belligerent policy, the *Co-operative News* chose to dwell upon the promising advances that the Italian co-operatives were making and to downplay the government's aggressive anti-French policy. On 2 February it wrote:

> In co-operative affairs Italy is visibly progressing. When once the national finances are put on sound footing, this country will be distinguished chiefly by the vigour of its popular institutions. France will watch with sympathy this civilizing tendency, and if the great political wirepullers will refrain from interference, the two nations will save their gunpowder, and will offer each other only good examples.[4]

This book has argued that Victorian radicals who opposed imperialistic and jingoistic manifestations at home were equally keen to identify the positive signs of emerging democracies abroad, and particularly in Italy. Not only within the co-operative movement, but also in the wider context of the adult education movement, Mazzini continued to be hailed as one of the leading lights of democracy and association: in the mid-1890s the London Society for the Extension of University Teaching included Mazzini's teachings in its lecture on co-operation.[5]

3   *Examiner*, 11 Sept. 1875.
4   'Co-operation in Italy', *Co-operative News*, 2 Feb. 1889.
5   H. J. Rose, *Syllabus of a course of twelve lectures on social and industrial England since 1750*, Cambridge 1894, 24.

Despite the optimistic forecasts of Victorian co-operators, liberal Italy was changing at a pace that 'the coming democracy of the Mediterranean' was finding difficult to control. Crispi had long abandoned not only the republican camp but the democrats, and by 1890 he was ruling the country to the sound of colonial expansionism and a tough line against the Left.[6] Meanwhile Saffi, whose 'romantic spiritualism' had taken hold on Victorian anti-utilitarian idealists, was pursuing Mazzini's ambition of reclaiming for Italy the north-eastern 'unredeemed territories', according to the ambiguous principles of 'democratic interventionism' whose insidious rhetoric would soon be co-opted by Italian expansionists.[7] In domestic policy Saffi was also struggling: it was becoming increasingly difficult to overcome republicans' internal divisions over whether to operate inside or outside the parliamentary system. In fact, Saffi looked more and more to America as the republican model which Italy should follow.[8]

On the eve of the elections in 1890 the emergence onto the Milanese scene of the increasingly influential socialists forced republicans to seek a compromise democratic manifesto – the so-called *Patto di Roma* – which was devised to counter Crispi's political leadership. The programme had the full support of *Il Secolo*. Yet the 1890 elections were a bitter defeat for the democrats, with a poor turn-out (53 per cent), the smallest since 1870, and an unequivocal victory for the moderate camp.[9] In Laura Barile's words, the 'highest hopes' that the 1890 elections had kindled amongst Italian radicals were dashed and a sense of decline ensued.[10]

In the throes of this crisis the news of Saffi's serious illness worried all republicans. Jessie White Mario, whose life continued to be devoted to the education of Italians and to the progress of co-operation in Italy, wrote to Holyoake that[11] 'the last of the "makers of Italy" are passing one by one' – a great sadness for those who had 'shared their work'.[12] A measure of how weary Jessie White Mario had become may be gleaned by the fact that she refused the offer made to her by Cowen, in 1890, to write her autobiography

---

[6] Duggan, *Crispi*, 589.

[7] On democratic interventionism and the Mazzinian party, formed in 1900, see Sarti, *Mazzini*, 227. In 1919 the Fiume expedition, organised by the nationalist Gabriele D'Annunzio to reclaim the 'unredeemed territories' north of the Adriatic, included a number of Mazzinians, according to E. Lodolini, 'L'organizzazione del partito mazziniano italiano in Italia e all'estero agli inizi del secolo XX', *RSR* xli (1954), 398–403 at p. 403. See also his 'Mediterraneo, Adriatico, intervento nella politica del partito mazziniano italiano (1900–18), *RSR* xxviii (1951), 473–86.

[8] G. Spadolini, *I repubblicani dopo l'unità, 1871–90*, Florence 1980, 60. On Saffi and America see also Ridolfi, 'Visions of republicanism', 475, and Barsotti, 'Difendere la grande repubblica', 82–139.

[9] Barile, *Il secolo*, 191.

[10] Ibid. 187–92 at p. 192.

[11] J. White Mario, 'Poets and co-operatives', *Nation*, 13 Sept. 1888.

[12] White Mario to Holyoake, Mantua, 22 Feb. 1890, HP, HHM, 3221, MM/96636/8.

by giving 'an account of her own adventures ... to appear in instalments' in the *Newcastle Weekly Chronicle*.[13] Her customary enthusiasm for celebrating the achievements of the Italian Risorgimento was no doubt also frustrated by the slow progress of social reforms in Italy.[14]

Without their leader Italian republicans rapidly developed an 'identity crisis'.[15] As Saffi was buried, Mazzini's legacy was the subject of a political controversy which was played out in parliamentary debates. Crispi's desire to ascribe to Mazzini the unifying role of patriotic 'father of the nation' contrasted notably with the increasingly deep political divisions which were afflicting Italian society. Indeed, Crispi's attempts to appropriate the language of 'nationality' and 'mission' according to the tenets of 'biological racism' and organic nationalism alarmed many Italian democrats who condemned his policies.[16] Crispi's approval of the erection of a marble monument to Mazzini in Rome equated more to the attempted taming of the spirit of a republican who had never reconciled himself to the Italian monarchy.[17] Indeed, the monument project could be seen as an attempt to 'freeze' or 'archive' Mazzini forever.[18]

The legacy of the long connection

While Mazzini's legacy became increasingly contested in Italy, the tie between Victorian radicals and Risorgimento democrats loosened. Saffi's death, in 1890, broke the primary transnational connection of the generation of men and women who had shared the emotions of 'making Italy' and the challenges of 'making the Italians'. As this book has shown, in the aftermath of Mazzini's death, Saffi had been the main point of reference for both Italian and Victorian Mazzinians. The friendships formed during the years of

13 CP, TWAS, E436, 78.

14 J. White Mario, 'The patrimony of the poor in Italy', *Nation*, 20 Feb. 1880.

15 Comba, 'I repubblicani alla ricerca di un' identità', 486.

16 See the extract from the powerful speech delivered by Napoleone Colajanni on the centenary of Mazzini's birth, in 1905, reported in Finelli '"E divento un Dio"', 693. The migration from Mazzini's concept of 'civil religion', rooted in the Jacobin principles of liberty and equality, to the Fascist cult and sacralisation of the nation is described in E. Gentile, *Il culto del littorio: la sacralizzazione della politica nell'Italia fascista*, Bari 1993.

17 The erection of Mazzini's statue was a much contended question in monarchical Italy: it was not resolved until 1949, when the statue was unveiled. On this occasion an ageing British co-operator, W. H. Brown, travelled to Italy to honour the exile's memory: Sutcliffe, 'Mazzini's transnational legacy'. With regard to the debate over erecting Mazzini's statue as a national monument see J. C. Lescure, 'Les Enjeux du souvenir: le monument national à Giuseppe Mazzini', *Revue d'histoire moderne et contemporaine* x/1–2 (1993), 177–201, and Duggan, 'Giuseppe Mazzini', 219–20.

18 M. Finelli, 'Nuovi percorsi della storiografia mazziniana', in S. Bonanni (ed.), *Pensiero e azione Mazzini nel movimento democratico italiano e internazionale*, Rome 2006, 565–9.

exile and the familial ties with the Crauford family, had ensured that Saffi's link with Victorian radicals remained strong for decades. Since resigning as deputy in the Italian government in 1866 he had become a beacon for extra-parliamentary Italian republicanism and democracy. His battles, his defeats, his arrests, had enhanced the international visibility of Italian democrats struggling with censorship and policing: all this was due to the personal and political integrity for which Saffi was known in Britain.

On the other side of the Atlantic, Americans too had looked to Saffi as the new leader of Italian republicanism. As Sarti has underlined, the religious and spiritual inspiration of Mazzini's thought had facilitated the reception of his writings within the Anglo-Saxon world, not only in Britain but also in America.[19] While Mazzini's project for a 'Universal Republican Association' had not found sufficient American support in the mid-1860s, the importance of establishing a web of republican allegiance across the Atlantic made headway after his death.[20] In the late 1880s an American journalist, Theodore Stanton, approached Saffi about summarising the current outlook for republicanism in Italy in an article to be published in 'a score of the leading newspapers'.[21] Saffi's name was well known in America and on his death Jessie White Mario wrote an obituary in the *Nation*.

The news of Saffi's death, however, somehow did not reach the secretary of the newly-established Pan-Republic Congress, O. McDowell. On 29 July 1891 McDowell addressed a letter to Saffi notifying him that he had been elected a member of the General Committee in charge of a Pan-Republican Congress. This was to be held in the United States, and thereafter every five years 'in some centre in the republican world'. The letter was evidence that Mazzini's legacy of democratic idealism was still felt amongst republicans across continents.[22] Saffi, had he lived, might still have provided the Pan-Republican Congress with a direct transatlantic connection with the 'apostle'. However Saffi was dead, and could not be replaced. Indeed, as the exiles of the Risorgimento who had endeavoured to build Italy's democracy died one by one, the new generation of Italian republicans appeared divided, disbanded and had lost direction.[23]

Yet an echo of the 'long connection' of transnational democracy remained. Bolton King, who had met democrats in Milan whilst chaperoning Toynbee travellers, continued to maintain links with Italian kindred spirits. Indeed,

---

[19] Sarti, 'La democrazia radicale', 133–57 at p. 141.

[20] See J. Rossi, *The image of America in Mazzini's writings*, Madison 1954, 137–48. More broadly on this topic see D. Fiorentino and M. Sanfilippo, *Le relazioni tra Stati Uniti e Italia nel periodo di Roma capitale*, Rome 2008.

[21] T. Stanton to Saffi, Paris, n.d., *c.* 1888, FS, BCAB, ii/16/1, 164.

[22] O. McDowell to Saffi, 29 July 1891, FS, BCAB, ii/27/2, 51.

[23] Spadolini, *I repubblicani dopo l'unità*, 68–75; Comba, 'I repubblicani alla ricerca di un'identità', 485–6; Galante Garrone, *I radicali*, 269; M. Tesoro, *I repubblicani nell'età giolittiana*, Florence 1978.

it was his intimate understanding of Italy's political and social challenges which enabled him to co-author *Italy today* in 1901, a book which endeavoured to explain liberal Italy's fragile political equilibrium at the turn of the century.[24] Bolton King's knowledge of Italian society was always closely connected with his desire to rekindle what he saw as the Anglo-Italian connection: this was clearly stated in his *History of Italian unity* (1899) and in the articles that he published in various reviews.[25] Holyoake too, faithful to the struggles of the Risorgimento, strove to maintain friendly relations with Italian co-operators and democrats. In 1899, in the political crisis that followed the bloody repression of the Milanese strikes, he sent a heartfelt message of support to Romussi on his release from prison (*see* Figure 13).[26]

If Italian Mazzinian democrats could still count on the moral support of Anglo-Saxon radicals and liberals, this was because Mazzini's intellectual memory was untarnished in Britain and the transatlantic world.[27] Indeed, his visionary understanding of the essential democratic constituents of global order was still celebrated in Britain, in 1912, where W. T. Stead in the *Review of Reviews*, wished that Italy might withdraw from the Triple Alliance, embrace the 'peace *entente*' and, once and for all, 'seize her opportunity' to assist the Slavs, in fulfilment of Mazzini's 'prophecy'.[28] Mazzini's wish to liberate the Slavs had been closely linked to his desire to connect with neighbouring peoples whose lands Dante, whom he considered the nation's precursor and bard, had once regarded as Italian. Mazzini's vision on Italy's mission in the Adriatic sometimes led to discordant interpretations amongst Italians.[29] English readers, however, were familiar with this Mazzinian rhetoric: adult learners too, especially those who had read Carlyle, and those who knew John Ruskin and Dante Gabriel Rossetti from their work at the Working Men's College, had learned about Dante's national vision for Italy,

[24] 'Un mazziniano inglese', *Il Secolo*, 29 June–30 July 1901.

[25] B. King, *A history of Italian unity*, London 1912. For a full bibliography of Bolton King's articles see F. Matassa, *L'Italia nella storiografia dell'otto-novecento*, Rome 2011.

[26] Romussi, like many democrat journalists, was arrested in 1899, following the Milanese protests: Holyoake to C. Romussi, 'Biglietto da visita', 5 June 1899, doc. 2862, Archivio Romussi, Milan.

[27] On the global legacy of Mazzini, including its uses and abuses in the wider world, see Bayly and Biagini, *Mazzini*.

[28] W. T. Stead, 'The progress of the world', *Review of Reviews* (Dec. 1912), 601–30 at p. 610.

[29] In 1918, when the rhetoric of Italy's 'mutilated victory' in the First World War fired Italian nationalists to make claims on the Istrian territories Mazzini's rhetoric would be appropriated in a display of the public use of history. On the divergent positions of democrats like Gaetano Salvemini, and nationalists, see A. Ghisleri, 'L'Istria italiana e le Alpi Giulie secondo Mazzini', in *Italia e Jugoslavia: La Voce*, Florence 1918. On the polarised positions see A. Frangioni, *Salvemini e La Grande Guerra: interventismo democratico, wilsonismo, politica delle nazionalità*, Soveria Mannelli 2011, 176–8.

One who has never ceased to be interested in you and has sent you messages of honour and hope Congratulates you on being free again

June 5 1899 George Jacob Holyoake
Eastern Lodge Brighton, England

ARCH.
ROMUSSI

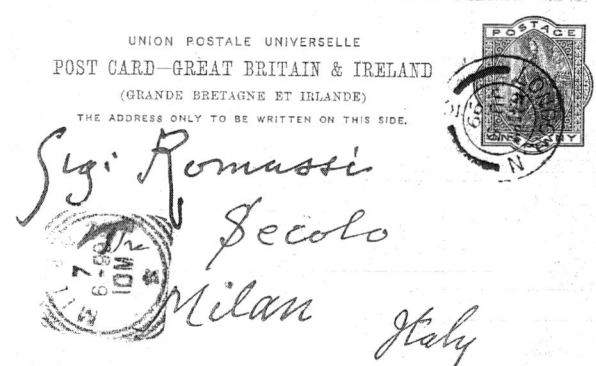

UNION POSTALE UNIVERSELLE
POST CARD—GREAT BRITAIN & IRELAND
(GRANDE BRETAGNE ET IRLANDE)
THE ADDRESS ONLY TO BE WRITTEN ON THIS SIDE.

Sig. Romussi
Secolo
Milan Italy

Fig. 13. Card from G. J. Holyoake to Carlo Romussi on his release from prison, 1899. (Archivio Romussi, Milan).

which would one day be free from the papal tyranny.[30] On the other side of the Atlantic Mazzini's popularity as an icon of global freedom and democracy also endured: in the aftermath of the First World War, Woodrow Wilson

[30] Ruskin celebrated Dante's moral and intellectual qualities in *The stones of Venice*, amply distributed amongst Working Men's College students. Dante Gabriel Rossetti, who taught at the college, showed his admiration for Dante in his paintings. For Carlyle Dante was emblematic as the 'hero as poet'.

famously welcomed the opportunity to realise Mazzini's project for a 'cosmo-politanism of nations', by seeking to secure a peaceful global order.[31]

In Italy, conversely, Mazzini's legacy would be chequered – even dissonant, and could not be passed from one generation to the next uncontaminated by Crispi's nationalism. One of the side effects of the implosion of liberalism during the *fin de siècle* crisis was the refashioning and appropriation of Mazzini's thought by aggressive nationalists. Italy's 'long Risorgimento', as suggested by Gilles Pécout, encompassed a period which lasted until 1922, with the *fin de siècle* crisis developing between the 1890s and the subsequent establishment of the fascist dictatorship;[32] the appropriation of Mazzini as the prophet of fascism mirrored this crisis chronologically, spanning Crispi's leadership to the offshoots of Giovanni Gentile's final distortion of the exile's message.[33]

Such appropriation introduced in Italy a division between those who claimed to be Mazzini's followers, feeding a long historiography on the uses and misuses of the exile's writings which has not yet abated. Indeed, Mazzini's memory also fell prey to political revisionism, which, as the well-respected Italian scholar, Angelo Del Boca, has recently pointed out, during the last decade has not spared any of the great questions in Italy's national history.[34] While Roberto Vivarelli conceded that the link between the exile's 'religion of the nation' and fascism may have eluded Mazzini's 'intentions', Simon Levis Sullam claimed to identify the recognisable 'ideological nucleus' of an 'authoritarian' policy in Mazzini's writings, peppered with an 'irrationalistic' style.[35] Similarly, Mazzini's imagined 'nation', interpreted by Alberto Banti as a racial community descending from blood ties – rather than from an inclusive tradition of free thought – fuelled the historiographical controversy.[36]

---

[31] N. Urbinati, 'The legacy of Kant: Giuseppe Mazzini'cosmopolitanism of nations', in Bayly and Biagini, *Mazzini*, 32–5; Roberts, 'Mazzini's thought', 72.

[32] G. Pécout, *Il lungo Risorgimento: la nascita dell'Italia contemporanea, 1770–1922*, Milan 1999. On the chronological definition of the *fin de siècle* crisis see also F. Gaeta, *La crisi di fine secolo e l'età giolittiana*, Turin 1982.

[33] G. Gentile, *I profeti del Risorgimento italiano*, Rome 1923. The essays were first published in a series of articles in 1919. See Levis Sullam, *L'apostolo a brandelli*, 77.

[34] A. Del Boca, *La storia negata: il revisionismo e il suo uso politico*, Vicenza 2009, 9. On the political use of some 'anti-myth' ingredients by the Northern League and the southern separatist movement see S. Patriarca, 'Unmaking the nation? Uses and abuses of Garibaldi in contemporary Italy', *Modern Italy*, special issue, x/4 (2010), 467–83.

[35] Vivarelli, *Italia, 1861*, 63–4; Levis Sullam, 'L'apostolo a brandelli', p. xi.

[36] A. M. Banti, *L'onore della nazione: identità sessuali e violenza nel nazionalismo europeo dal XVIII secolo alla Grande Guerra*, Turin 2005, 156. The debate on Mazzini's legacy was particularly heightened on the 150th anniversary of the unification of Italy. See G. Galasso, 'Non si può accusare Mazzini se il paese smarrisce l'identità', *Corriere della Sera*, 10 Dec. 2010. Divergent views on the concept of nationalism in Risorgimento Italy, expressed by A. M. Banti and M. Viroli, are summarised in 'L'idea di patria ieri e oggi', Bari 2011 (http://www.laterza.it/index.php?option=com_content&view=article&id=378:lid, accessed 20 June 2013).

In this context, the question of Mazzini's identity and legacy in Italy became increasingly contested: indeed it was framed by Balzani as a 'problem'.[37]

Unravelling this would prove challenging. In the hands of nationalists and imperialists, the so-called historical rights of nations could fuel expansionist wars, countering Mazzini's vision that it was the duty of all free nations to unite in the association of humanity. The Anglo-Saxon world had no problem in understanding Mazzini's message of democracy.[38] Indeed, as the American scholar, David G. Rowley powerfully expressed it, 'nationalism in Mazzini's hands was a demand for democracy'.[39] According to Michele Finelli, failing to acknowledge this has led Italians to 'struggle collectively to come to terms with Mazzini's legacy and image'.[40]

Yet, recognising this tension should not lead us to draw a black-and-white dichotomy between Mazzini's memory in Italy and that of the Anglo-Saxon world, as Duggan has argued. Indeed such geographical polarisation of 'divergent legacies' risks effacing the tradition of Mazzinian democracy which ran through the twentieth century within the Italian antifascist resistance, a tradition also displayed in the rekindling of transnational connections between Italian democrats and post-Victorian British Mazzinians.[41]

While it is indeed true that Mazzini's legacy was contested in Italy, it was not wholly appropriated by nationalists and fascists: embracing such geographically polarised discourse risks overshadowing not only the Saffis, the Quadrios and the Nathans, but also the new generation of liberal intellectuals gathering around the movement *Giustizia e Libertà*, underplayed by Duggan as an 'elitist' movement.[42] It is possible that Duggan's discounting of the role played by the Rosselli brothers may be explained in the context of the revisionist critique of fascist historiography. Yet, as Sergio Luzzatto has underlined, such a historiography, which promotes the demystification of the resistance, has also given way to the wholesale liquidation of the ideological and ethical relevance of antifascist protagonists.[43]

As Gwilym O. Griffith witnessed Italy plunge into the darkest years of fascism, his thoughts went back to Mazzini, whom he hailed as the 'prophet

---

[37] Balzani, 'Il problema Mazzini'. See also Levis Sullam, *L'apostolo a brandelli*.

[38] On this I take a different view from Roland Sarti who wrote that 'works written by non-Italians reflected different concerns': *Mazzini*, 235. Griffith directly engaged with the problem of the appropriation of Mazzini by the Fascist rhetoric.

[39] Rowley, 'Mazzini'

[40] Finelli, 'Mazzini in Italian historical memory', 486–91 at p. 487.

[41] Duggan, 'Giuseppe Mazzini', 194, 205. For the endurance of the democratic Mazzinian tradition in the early twentieth century see Frangioni, *Salvemini*.

[42] Ibid. 199.

[43] S. Luzzatto, *La crisi dell'antifascismo*, Turin 2004, 74. For the origins of the historiographical revisionism of the Italian resistance see Claudio Pavone's groundbreaking work *A civil war: a history of the Italian resistance* (1991), New York 2013.

of modern Europe'.[44] Formed in late Victorian Britain, 'second generation' Mazzinians like Griffith (b. 1882) and Bolton King (b. 1860) showed their allegiance to Mazzini's vision for Italy in their support for Italian antifascists.[45] Their correspondences and encounters with Mazzinians like Carlo Rosselli and Gaetano Salvemini had a peculiar connotation: they had roots in a shared vision of 'democracy' and 'humanity' which was also a legacy of Mazzini's exile.[46]

Bolton King had come across Mazzini's readings in reformed Oxford; Griffith, from a less privileged background, had read his writings in the Birmingham Free Library. It was here that, in 1899, the seventeen-year old Griffith, who would become a Congregationalist pastor, devoured six volumes of Mazzini's essays in 'the great silent reading room', as part of his journey of self-improvement.[47] Bolton King and Griffith would later write notable biographies of Mazzini.[48] As 'second generation' Mazzinians they were part of a much larger group in Britain, including co-operators, Labour and 'Lib-Lab' supporters. Mazzini, who had enthused Victorian radicals, had left a lasting legacy within the English 'Left'. This was reflected by a survey amongst Labour Leaders published in the *Review of Reviews* in 1906 which referred to the Italian exile as one of the authors who had most deeply influenced them.[49] It is not surprising that Carlo Rosselli's project of 'liberal-socialism' would closely mirror the Labour model.[50]

In fascist Italy, the task of restoring Mazzini to his proper place fell to Gaetano Salvemini and the Rosselli brothers. Salvemini, an antifascist Mazzinian, recognised the dangers of his doctrine in preaching the religion of national right: Mazzini's teachings, in order to respond to the spirit of his wider vision, should not be read to the letter, he claimed, but be interpreted and adapted in the light of contemporary challenges and threats. As Salvemini told a packed audience of youngsters in the provincial town of Warwick, in 1926, combating the pernicious tendencies of nationalists meant, if anything, being 'more Mazzinian than Mazzini'.[51]

[44] Griffith, *Mazzini*, and 'Mussolini'.

[45] 'Second generation' Mazzinians did not witness Italy's struggles for unity. Bolton King was born in 1861 and died in 1937, only a few months before the exiled Rosselli brothers were assassinated by Fascist emissaries.

[46] Salvemini, who had fled from imprisonment in Florence, and Bolton King both spoke about Mazzini at the King's High School in Warwick in 1926: see appendix 2 below.

[47] G. O. Griffith, 'Mazzini and the great apostolate: a Welsh tribute', BDM (1965), 5–16 at p. 10.

[48] Idem, *Mazzini*; King, *The life of Mazzini*.

[49] As quoted in Rose, *The intellectual life*, 41–2.

[50] Nadia Urbinati (ed.), *Liberal socialism*, Princeton 1994.

[51] *Warwick & Warwickshire Advertiser & Leamington Gazette*, 20 Mar. 1926, 6: see appendix 2 below.

His audience understood: the local paper hailed Salvemini as the 'modern Mazzini'.[52]

As a historian, Nello Rosselli spearheaded studies on Mazzini's labour politics.[53] His brother, Carlo, who called for a thorough study of the 'democratic Risorgimento' from the pages of *Giustizia e Libertà* in 1935, was also a stalwart defender of the Mazzinian articulation of democracy. His own clandestine antifascist movement, forced to operate underground or from abroad, was modelled on the democratic organisational network which Mazzini had coordinated as a Risorgimento exile and through which he reached out to Italians in Paris who were outside the intellectual milieu.

British Mazzinians denounced the abuses suffered by antifascists under Mussolini. On 16 October 1929 Bolton King published a letter in the *Manchester Guardian* denouncing the imprisonment of the 'student and writer', Nello Rosselli, whose only crime was being related to 'a critic of the government', Carlo Rosselli. As Bolton King wrote to Carlo Rosselli himself, he had to 'put it very mildly', as both 'the government and the English press' felt the need to 'humour' Mussolini at this time.[54] Less ambiguous was Bolton King's condemnation of the fascist regime in 1931, when, following the arrest of most of the leading members of the antifascist *Giusitizia e Libertà*, he wrote a lucid account of the rise and dangers of the fascist regime, *Fascism in Italy*: Carlo Rosselli managed to have the book translated in a clandestine edition so that it could be distributed to young Italians in Italy.[55]

Carlo Rosselli and Salvemini were well aware of the value of maintaining their connection with British Mazzinians at this sensitive time. Not only did they retain close ties with Bolton King, but they also both corresponded with Griffith: indeed, their intellectual exchanges helped Griffith better to define his understanding of some aspects of Mazzini's thought, in view of his publication of the biography of the Italian exile.[56] Just as fascists were claiming Mazzini as their own, the intellectual reading of Mazzini's vision as an important building block for global democracy was therefore also being shared across national boundaries.[57] In 1936 Griffith's article, 'Mussolini,

---

[52] See appendix 2 below.

[53] His book, *Mazzini e Bakunin.*, was published in 1927.

[54] King to C. Rosselli, Warwick, 21 Oct. 1929, papers of the late Ms Joane Brown, private collection.

[55] Fifty copies of the Italian translation on India paper, together with antifascist leaflets, were dropped on Rome by Lauro De Bosis on 3 October 1931. De Bosis, who had met Salvemini in the United States, flew on to his death: King, *Il fascismo in Italia*, A copy of the translation of Bolton King's book, with an introduction signed by *Giustizia e Libertà*, is held at the Biblioteca Centrale Nazionale in Rome.

[56] T. Grandi, 'Lettere di Carlo Rosselli e Gaetano Salvemini intorno al "Mazzini" di G. O. Griffith', *BDM* (1959), 2–11.

[57] For a sympathetic review of G. O. Griffith's book on Mazzini see G. Salvemini, 'Mazzini's visions', *Saturday Review*, 8 July 1933, 694.

Mazzini and humanity', published in the *Congregational Quarterly*, was the indignant response from across the Channel to the fascist appropriation of the 'Teacher' as prophet of fascism.[58]

Taking the long view on Mazzini's legacy and the complex network of transnational democratic connections within which it was situated may provide a new opportunity to take stock, to assess from a global perspective the role that the memory of Mazzini the exile played in the fight against fascism in Italy and in Europe, rather than in the theoretical underpinning of the fascist dictatorship. Undeterred by the confusion of meanings that some of Mazzini's rhetoric had engendered in a nation in crisis, second-generation British Mazzinians had no qualms in recognising fellow Mazzinians as anti-fascists: indeed, their personal exchanges with the founders of *Giustizia e Libertà* were the late vestiges of a meaningful, long line of transnational encounters of men and women who for decades unequivocally understood Mazzini's vision as the bedrock of European democracy and global peace.[59]

[58] Grandi, 'Lettere', 2–11; Griffith, 'Mussolini' and 'Mazzini's letter to Mussolini', *The Christian World* (1942), quoted in Grandi, 'Lettere'. See Bolton King's letter on the Rosselli brothers in the *Manchester Guardian*, 16 Oct. 1929.

[59] After the war Federico Chabod's lecture series, published as *L'idea di nazione* (Bari 1965), connected Mazzini's idea of patriotism with the pursuit of liberty.

APPENDICES

APPENDIX 1

Henry Gilpin, *Mazzini*[1]

Thou of the pensive brow, the troubled heart;
Dreamer of Italy! The man who stood
In the Eternal City, 'mid the throng,
A soldier and a patriot; breathing words
That told of freedom and he glorious cause,
Thy words of truth and fire are bearing fruit,
The dream of noble hearts hath found a voice
And arms to fight for what a dreamer dreamed.

Thou pioneer of freedom! But for thee
A Garibaldi ne'er had taken arms,
Or found the hearts that throbbed for Italy,
Thou, the dreamer deemed, hast proved to be
A John the Baptist to prepare the way
For Italy's Messiah! Let the crown,
The fadeless crown, whose laurels never die,
Encircle too that high and massive brow,
Wrinked and care-worn in the holy cause
Of freedom and of right.

The advocates of right and truth's advance
Are always counted dreamers; but their dream
Will have its full fruition. Even in nature,
The little seeds that kindly have sown,
Would never promise the sublime result,
That shows our native oak with spreading brnaches
The king that rules the forests of our land.
And though immortal man! E'en from thy youth,
Hast spread the seed of freedom's holy tree,
And now a giant oak it spreads around
The shadow of its branches.

Dreamer no more! The sacred Cause of life,
Hath proved the dream in truth and sanctity,
God is love! and is the God of freedom.
Awake once more to gladness, children, ye
Who are the image of the parent God;
Of whom He said of such His kingdom are,
Lift up little hands and learn to bless,

---

[1]   FH, MRM, 18/128.

E'en in the gladness of your childhood's joy,
Your two deliverers.

Bright daughters of the land of cloudless skies,
Undertaken now by tyranny and gloom,
Sing a new song of triumph and love,
Those eyes that wept upon the blighted flowers
Tears for your long lost country, let them now
Smile with a new found light; a change has come.
The dreamer and the worker who have made
That early dream of sunshine to be true,
Have trod their destined path, and now once more,
The classic land is free.

Sing the new song of triumph! Chains no more
Shall manacle the genius of thy land,
But, in the light of freedom and its strength,
Thy sons and daughters, sun-bright Italy,
Shall learn to love and to rejoice once more,
And praise the God of freedom and of love.

Thy dream was in the darkness of the night,
When gloomy clouds encompassed every star;
Yet thy soul's strength made darkness into light,
And looked beyond the clouds where angels are.
They ushered thee the dream, and bade thee wake,
To a new presence in thy soul unknown,
That made thee live and struggle for its sake,
And breath for freedom and for it alone.

Nobly the cause has triumphed in thy hands,
God's pioneer! His dreamer!

No. 14, Market Street, Newcastle (1861?), Henry Gilpin

A Modern Mazzini: Italian Historian at Warwick. Professor Salvemini's Lecture²

Professor Salvemini, Italy's greatest living historian, honoured Warwick, and particularly the King's High School on Friday last week, when he lectured to a large audience on Mazzini, the apostle of Italian unity and independence Professor Salvemini is the modern Mazzini; he suffered imprisonment in Florence last year because of his political opinions, and he too, is working for a new order in Europe.

Mr Bolton King M.A., Mazzini's biographer and author of the History of Italian Unity presided at the lecture and also spoke on Mazzini.

'It is a great honour for us', said Mr Bolton King, opening the address, 'to have here Professor Salvemini to talk to us. We welcome him for two reasons. Firstly because he is a great historian, one of the most distinguished of modern historians, with world-wide fame. Secondly because he is a great patriot. He has not been afraid to risk his life, comfort and position in order to protest against the ruffianism which now takes the place of government in Italy. I am sure that his fellow countrymen will hail him home as one of the men who had the courage to express opinions which they most share, but few dared to express (…).'

Mazzini's two theories
'It is with much emotion that I speak of Mazzini before the man to whom Italy owes the finest biography of Mazzini', began Professor Salvemini, 'but at the same time I feel that the presence of Mr Bolton King is a good omen, and I thank him for the honour he does me in taking the chair. And I thank Miss Doorly for having given me the opportunity of speaking at the High School to an audience of youth on a subject that is dear to me.'

Professor Salvemini then proceeded to speak of how Mazzini preached two theories: the right of every nation to form a political union, independent of all foreign domination, and the duty of all free nations to unite in the association of humanity.

The first, he said, had been entirely realised. Fifty years after Mazzini's death the political map coincides almost exactly with his vision of Europe. But in this Europe that in its important features so closely resembles the Europe of Mazzini, he would seek in vain for the features of the new humanity of which he was the prophet. The recognition of national rights of unity had given neither peace nor unity to Europe as a whole. The continent had been disorganised, instead of

---

² *Warwick & Warwickshire Advertiser & Leamington Gazette*, 20 Mar. 1926, 6.

being reorganised, by the triumph of nationality – even the principle of nationality itself was threatened with shipwreck.

Professor Salvemini showed how the abuse of the principle would create wars, which would cause further wars, the ultimate result being the breakdown of national states. Just as Mazzini's vision of national unity had been laughed at by 'practical men' of that day, their direct successors, the 'practical men' of the present day, were laughing at the larger vision of nations in association for humanity. Seventy years ago Mazzini said that wherever there was unity of language or territorial continuity, sooner or later arose a national sentiment. Once formed that sentiment becomes a prominent force in history, and it cannot altogether be stifled. But the 'practical man' in Mazzini's time saw no possibilities in this sentiment, and it was condemned to die. Yet Italy achieved national unity.

Europe as a nation[3]
'Let us turn to the practical man of our time', continued the Professor. For illustration he referred to peace problems following the Great War, such as that of Austria-Hungary, which, experience has proved, was only to be solved on Mazzinian lines. Half Mazzini's theory has been realised; half remains to be achieved – the fusion of Europe into a free nation. 'We are right in refusing to be satisfied, and we should be wrong if we allow ourselves to be discouraged', said Professor Salvemini. Mazzini's ideas had pointed to the true solution of post-war problems, and the second part of this theory must be applied to prevent war. After the next war victorious countries would be as devastated, depopulated, and impoverished as the vanquished, and strife would result in the complete rout of our civilization.

Even more easily now than in the past national sentiments, disassociated from international feeling, could become malicious, in the same way that religious feeling disassociated from charity, had led to atrocities being committed in the name of God. That religious sentiment had not vanished but had become purer and nobler from the teaching of great spirits of humanity. National feeling too, did not tend to disappear, but was capable of growth in nobleness and purity. Nationalists and Imperialists of all countries proclaim that it is lost labour to seek to discipline national sentiment to something higher. But the future was dependent more than anything on the will of those working for that end.

'*Of course we must review our whole system of ideas if Mazzini is to guide us*,' continued the Professor. 'The ideal of a man like Mazzini can never be reduced to formulae to be repeated, but he defined it with marvellous clarity. In Europe divided up amongst the dynasties Mazzini visualised almost every one of the new nations which were to be. But his vision was weakened by a great lack and a great illusion.' That lack was that he saw Europe as countries divided by artificial boundaries. With the exception of Spain and Italy there were no natural divisions. Where, for example, could be placed the line between German national territory and that of Poland? What national frontier divides Roumanians from the Magyars? Moreover, few nationalities form a compact mass over the territory. Groups of one nationality mixed with groups from other countries.

---

[3] The italic below is mine.

Another factor to be considered was that during the last century large numbers of people from all countries had moved to different parts of the world. Natural frontiers did not make nations. Geographers divided by mountain ranges and natural features; the frontiers since were a matter of human will. *In the nineteenth century Mazzini's mistake, in visualising neighbouring groups, each seeking extension at the cost of the other, could be understood, but it could not be countenanced now.*

'We Mazzinians'

Professor Salvemini further developed the idea of nationalism as opposed to international feeling. *He showed how so-called historical rights were a most dangerous cause of war.* Then there was the possibility of struggle between ruler and people. *To all these problems Mazzini's theory afforded no solution* – one might even logically say suggest an inhuman solution [*sic*]. Mazzini affirmed that each nation must maintain itself immune from invasion. By this could be meant as the extermination of all alien groups. The rights of minorities should be protected against what might be the oppression of sectarian majorities.

'*We Mazzinians of to-day must be more Mazzinian than Mazzini*', said the Professor, proceeding to speak on the solution of the problem. They must recognise the importance of reconciling the absolute independence of the nations with international union. *They wanted the League of Nations to be furnished with all legal powers so that it could impose its weight on international relations as the need arose.*[4]

Statesmen today were too closely concerned with the present to see the future. They must look with clear eyes at the practical difficulties to avoid fatal errors. From Mazzini's absolute concentration on a single idea they could learn the virtue of knowing how to wait because of the faith in their hearts. *For the man who sought to follow Mazzini's ideal of sacrificing service, Mazzini was no longer dead but alive, working with that man, urging him on, and righting him in the hours of discouragement, and still urging him on in the hour of defeat.*[5]

---

[4]   Democratic interventionists of Mazzinian ilk, such as Salvemini, originally interpreted the First World War as the 'Fourth Risorgimento War', by means of which the 'unredeemed territories' of Istria and/or Dalmatia should be reclaimed for Italy. Salvemini, following Mazzini, believed that Istria, with its majority Italian population, would go to Italy and was surprised by the solution to the Adriatic boundary put forward by the League of Nations and confirmed by the peace treaty, in 1919. As the claims on the 'unredeemed territories' rapidly escalated into the aggressive nationalist rhetoric of Italy's 'mutilated victory', Salvemini, however, realised the dangers of appropriations, which rigidly applied Mazzini's national ideals. He therefore turned towards the peaceful internationalism promoted by Wilson, whose democratic reading of Mazzini was in line with Salvemini's own views. On Salvemini and the League of Nations see Frangioni, *Salvemini e La Grande Guerra*.

[5]   The link which Salvemini traced between Mazzini's ideal of European and global democracy and antifascism was underlined by the 'Modern Mazzini's' concluding remarks.

Bibliography

Unpublished primary sources

Amsterdam, International Institute of Social History
W. E. Adams papers
Adams journal, reel 1,
AP, 0211/1995/0217; 0211/1995/0220; 0211/1995/0603; 0211/1995/0618; 0211/0647; 0211/1995/0666; 0211/1995/0797; 0122/1995/0902; 0122/1995/1299
Adams journal, reel 2
AP, 0211/1995/0135; 0211/1995/1397; 0211/1995/1516; 0211/1995/1518; 0211/1995/1522; 0211/1995/1534; 0211/1995/1539; 0211/1995/1610; 0211/1995/1623
A. Herzen papers
32

Bologna, Bibilioteca Comnunale dell'Archiginnasio
Fondo Saffi
FS, i/16/1, 35; ii/1, 53; ii/12/4, 97; ii/14/2, 38–56; ii/16/1, 15; ii/16/1, 16; ii/16/1, 23; ii/16/1, 29; ii/16/1, 35; ii/16/1, 53; ii/16/1, 55; ii/16/1, 79; ii/16/1, 80; ii/16/1, 105; ii/16/1, 106; ii/16/1, 164; ii/27/2, 57; ix/87/3

Connecticut, private collection
Papers of the late Ms Joane Browne
Uncatalogued letters

Harvard, Houghton Library
Linton papers
WL Eng. 180

London, Bishopsgate Foundation and Institute
George Jacob Holyoake Archive
1/8; 11

London, British Library
Gladstone papers
MSS 44386, 44531

London, London Metropolitan Archives, Corporation of London
Toynbee papers
A/TOY/12/1; TOY/012/002; A/TOY/21/14

Manchester, Co-operative Archive, Holyoake House
Holyoake papers
HP 28, 863, 1376, 3221
HP, HHM, 28
MM/96636/2, 8

Milan, Archivio Giangiacomo Feltrinelli
Fondo Linton, FL 1, 30/5; 2, 72/4

Milan, Archivio Romussi
2862

Milan, Museo del Risorgimento
Fondo Curatulo 338/ 666; 365/2599; 441
Fondo Holyoake 3/33; 4/11; 12/63; 15; 18/28; 79, 80

Newcastle-upon-Tyne, Newcastle University, Special Collections
Cowen tracts 31 7, 50–5

Newcastle-upon-Tyne, Tyne and Wear Archives Service
Cowen papers
CP, A8, A176, A212, A247, A361, A366, A423, A469, A479, A481, A484,
    A487, A492, A506, A574–86, A627, A648, A649, A650, A867, A873, A882
C1519, C1531
E436, 78
Box 16 (19) viii

Oxford, Bodleian Library
John Johnson collection
'co-operation', boxes 2, 3

Pisa, Domus Mazziniana
Nathan papers
DIIg58/63

Rome, Museo Centrale del Risorgimento
Carte Jessie White Mario
JWM 430/22; 430/41/1; 656/47/6; 656/48/9

Turin, Archivio di Stato
Lettere Ministri Esteri, Gran Bretagna
GB 10

Turin, Fondo Nathan-Rosselli, Archivio Rosselli
C 957 3

Printed primary sources

Newspapers and periodicals
L'Apostolato Popolare
Athenaeum
Birmingham Daily Post
Cooper's Journal
Co-operative News
La Cooperazione Italiana
Corriere della Sera
Daily Chronicle
Daily News
Il Dovere
L'Emancipazione
The English Republic
Englishwoman's Review
Era
The Examiner
Fortnightly Review
Glasgow Herald
Herald of Co-operation and Organ of the Redemption Society
Herald of Redemption
Howitt's Journal
Hull Packet and East Riding Times
Illustrated London News
Jersey Independent
Leader
Leeds Mercury
Leeds Times
L'Homme
Literary Examiner
Liverpool Mercury
Lloyds Newspaper
Manchester Time and Gazette.
Morning Chronicle
Movement
Nation
The National Reformer
Newcastle Daily Chronicle
Newcastle Weekly Chronicle

The Northern Daily Express
Northern Liberator
The Northern Star
The Northern Tribune
Pall Mall Gazette
The People's Journal
The People's Paper
Il Popolo d'Italia
Preston Guardian
Punch
Reasoner
Reynolds's Newspaper
Reynolds's Political Instructor
La Roma del Popolo
Il Secolo
Sheffield Free Press
The Shield
The Times
Warwick & Warwickshire Advertiser & Leamington Gazette
The Westminster and Foreign Quarterly Review/The Westminster Review

Contemporary books and articles

Acland, A. H. D. and B. Jones, *Working men co-operators: what they have done and what they are doing*, London 1889

A. C. S., *A midsummer holiday, and other poems* (1884), Charleston 2009

Adams, W. E., 'Republican organisation, and Young England', *English Republic* (1851), 364

—— 'The fall of Gaeta', NR, 23 Feb. 1861, 5–6

—— *Memoirs of a social atom*, London 1903

[Adams, W. E.], Bonaparte's challenge to tyrannicides by the author of 'Tyrannicide: is it justifiable?, unpubl. pamphlet 1867

Address of the Council of the People's International League, London 1847

Anon, *The Women's Co-operative Guild; outline of work*, Manchester 1893

—— *Two hundred and fifty good books for co-operative libraries*, Manchester 1894

Armstrong, C., *Pilgrimage from Nenthead*, London 1938

Baines, E., *The social, educational and religious state of the manufacturing districts*, London–Leeds 1843

Cagnacci, C., *Giuseppe Mazzini e i fratelli Ruffini*, Porto Maurizio 1893

Carlyle, T., *On heroes, hero worship and the heroic in history*, London 1840

—— *Past and Present*(1843), Berkeley–Los Angeles–London 2005

Cooper, T., *Life of Thomas Cooper*, London 1872

De Tocqueville, A., *L'Ancien Régime et la révolution*, Paris 1860

—— *The Old Regime and the revolution*, ed. F. Furet and F. Mélonio, Chicago–London 1998

Fisher, H. A. L., *Life of James Bryce, Viscount Bryce of Dechmont*, i, London 1927

Gentile, G., *I profeti del Risorgimento italiano*, Rome 1923

Hallett, John, 'Nationalism: the world's bane', *Fortnightly Review* (June 1933), 694–702

Harrison, F., *Memories and thoughts*, London 1906

—— *Autobiographic memoirs*, London 1911

Hole, J., 'Mr. Mazzini and Communism, no. I', *Herald of Co-operation and Organ of the Redemption Society* 10 (Oct. 1847), 73–4

—— 'Mr. Mazzini and Communism, no. II', *Herald of Co-operation and Organ of the Redemption Society* 11 (Nov. 1847), 81–3

—— *'Light, more light!' On the present state of education*, London 1860

Holyoake, G. J., *Self-help by the people: the history of co-operation in Rochdale: the Society of Equitable Pioneers, 1844–1857*, London 1867

—— *Sixty years of an agitator's life*, London 1893

—— *The jubilee history of the Leeds Industrial Co-operative Limited from 1847 to 1897 traced year by year*, Manchester 1897

—— *Essentials of co-operative education*, Manchester 1898

—— *Bygones worth remembering*, London 1905

—— *The Co-operative Movement to–day*, London 1912

Howitt, W., 'Letters to the working men of England', *People's Journal* xxv, 20 June 1846, 338–42

Hudson, W. J., *The history of adult education: in which is comprised a full and complete history of the mechanics' and literary institutions*, London 1851

Ireland, A., *Recollections of George Dawson and his lectures in Manchester*, Manchester 1882

King, B., *Essays by Joseph Mazzini*, London 1894

—— 'England and Italy', *Macmillan's Magazine* lxxxii (July 1900)

—— *The life of Mazzini*, London 1903

—— *A history of Italian unity*, London 1912

—— *Il fascismo in Italia*, Rome 1931

—— and T. Okey, *Italy today*, London 1901

—— and T. Okey, *L'Italia d'oggi*, Bari 1904

Knight, W. A., *Memoir of John Nichol*, Glasgow 1896

Linton, W., *English Republic*, London 1851–4

—— *European republicans: recollections of Mazzini and his friends*, London 1892

Llewlyn Davies, M., *The Women's Co-operative Guild, 1883–1904*, Kirkby Lonsdale 1904

McCabe, J., *Life and letters of George Jacob Holyoake*, London 1908

Mazzini, G., 'I collaboratori della Giovine Italia ai loro concittadini' (1832), *SEI*. iii. 27–74

—— 'Faith and the future' (1835), in King, *Essays by Joseph Mazzini*, 23–101

—— 'Les Patriotes et le clergé' (1835), *SEI*, vi. 162–208

—— 'De la Mission de la presse périodique' (1836), *SEI* vii. 237–65

—— 'Agli italiani, e specialmente agli operai italiani' (1840), *SEI*. xxv 3–20

—— 'Italy, Austria and the pope', *Northern Star*, 19 July; 27 Sept. 1845

—— 'Thoughts upon democracy, no. IV', *People's Journal* lii, 26 Dec. 1846, 361

—— 'Thoughts upon democracy in Europe, no. V', *People's Journal* lviii, 6 Feb. 1847, 79–81

—— 'Thoughts upon democracy in Europe, no. VI', *People's Journal* lxviii, 17 Apr. 1847, 219–22

—— *The pope and the nineteenth century*, London 1850

—— 'The duties of man', *English Republic* (1851)

—— *Two letters to the people of England on the war*, London 1855

—— *Mazzini's letters to Daniel Manin*, London 1856

—— *The late Genoese insurrection defended*, London 1858

—— *The Italian question and the republicans*, London 1861

—— 'Italy and the republic', *Fortnightly Review*, 1 Mar. 1871, 289

—— 'Nazionalismo e nazionalità', *La Roma del Popolo*, 35, 26 October, 1871

—— 'International policy' (1871), trans. E. A. Venturi, *Fortnightly Review* xxi/124 (Apr. 1877), 567–79

Morley, J., *Recollections*, London 1917

Nettleship, R. L., *A memoir of Thomas Hill Green*, London 1906

Okey, T., *A basketful of memories*, London 1930

Orsini, F., *Memoirs and adventures*, London 1857

—— and C. Bonavino, *Memorie politiche, con un'appendice per Ausonio Franchi*, Lugano 1860

'Patriotic offering to Joseph Mazzini – To the Council of Direction of the Association for Progress', London 1866

Picht, W., *Toynbee Hall and the English settlement movement*, London 1914

Rabbeno, U., *La cooperazione in Inghilterra*, Milan 1885

Rose, H..J. *Syllabus of a course of twelve lectures on social and industrial England since 1750*, Cambridge 1894

Saffi, A., *Ricordi e scritti (1849–57)*, Florence 1848–19

Salvemini, G., 'Mazzini's visions', *Saturday Review*, 8 July 1933, 694

Stansfeld, J., 'Mazzini on the Eastern question', trans. G. Mazzini and E. A. Venturi, *Fortnightly Review* xxi/124 (Apr. 1877), 559–61

Stead, W. T., 'The progress of the world', *Review of Reviews* (Dec. 1912), 601–30

Swinburne, A. C., *A midsummer holiday, and other poems* (1884), London 2009

—— *Ode to Mazzini, the saviour of society, liberty and loyalty*, London 1913

Toynbee, A., *Education of co-operators*, Manchester 1882 (?).

Villari, P., *Le lettere meridionali ed altri scritti sulla questione sociale in Italia*, Turin 1885

—— 'The social condition of Italy', Florence 1888

Welford, R., *Men of mark 'twixt Tyne and Tweed'*, London 1895

White Mario, J., *Giuseppe Dolfi*, Florence 1883

—— *The birth of modern Italy*, London 1909

Official documents

Hansard Parliamentary Debates

The National Petition (30 May–12 July 1839)

Letter-Opening Affair (14 June 1844–May 1845)

Greco-Conspiracy (Mar. 1864)

Published primary sources

Black, F. G. and R. M. Black (eds), *The Harney papers*, Assen 1969

Blakiston, N. (ed.), *The Roman question: extracts from the dispatches of Odo Russell from Rome (1858–1870)*, London 1962

Della Seta, U., *Giuseppe Mazzini pensatore: le idee madri*, Rome 2011

Edizione nazionale: scritti editi ed inediti di Giuseppe Mazzini, Imola 1906–90

Foot, M. R. D. (ed.), *The Gladstone diaries*, Oxford 1968–94

Fyfe, J. (ed.), *Autobiography of John McAdam (1806–1883)*, Edinburgh 1980

Garibaldi G., *Epistolario*, Rome 1973–2002

Ghisalberti A. M. (ed.), *Lettere di Felice Orsini*, Rome 1936

Harcourt Williams, R. (ed.), *Salisbury-Balfour Correspondence* (Balfour Record Society, 1988)

Hudson, D., *Munby, man of two worlds: the life and diaries of Arthur J. Munby (1828–1910)*, London 1972

Levi, A., *Ricordi della vita e dei tempi di Ernesto Nathan* (1927), ed. A. Bocchi, Pisa 2006

Mayper N. and R. Sarti (eds), '*Dear Kate: lettere inedite di Giuseppe Mazzini a Katherine Hill, Angelo Bezzi e altri italiani a Londra (1841–1871)*, Soveria Mannelli 2011

Mazzini, G., 'The duties of man' (1841–60), in Recchia and Urbinati, *Cosmopolitanism*, 80–107

—— 'Concerning the fall of the Roman Republic (1849)', in Recchia and Urbinati, *Cosmopolitanism*, 208–12

—— 'From a revolutionary alliance to the United States of Europe' (1850), in Recchia and Urbinati, *Cosmopolitanism*, 132–5

—— 'Principles of international policy' (1871), abridged, in Recchia and Urbinati, *Cosmopolitanism*, 224–40

—— *Edizione nazionale: scritti editi ed inediti*, ed. M. Menghini, Imola 1906–90

Mill, J. S., *Collected works*, London 1996

Mordini, A., 'Osservazioni sopra una nuova organizzazione in Italia presentate nel giugno 1852', in Galante Garrone, *I radicali in Italia*, 30–1

Quinn E. V and J. M Prest (eds), *Dear Miss Nightingale: a selection of Benjamin Jowett's letters, 1860–93*, Oxford 1987

Recchia S. and N. Urbinati (eds), *A cosmopolitanism of nations: Giuseppe Mazzini's writings on democracy, nation building, and international relations*, Princeton 2009

Richards, E. F. (ed.), *Mazzini's letters to an English family, 1844–54*, London–New York 1920

Rossetti, G., 'Rossetti on the anti-papal spirit of Italian Classics', *Edinburgh Review* lx (1832), 531–51

Saffi, A., 'Religion in Italy', *Westminster and Foreign Quarterly Review*, 1 Oct. 1853

White Mario, J., 'The Co-operative Congress in Milan', *The Nation*, 16 Oct. 1886, in Biagianti, *La 'nuova Italia'*, 165–70.

Works of reference

Baylen, J. O., and N. Gossman (eds), *Biographical dictionary of modern British radicals*, II: *1830–1870*, Brighton 1984; III, *1870–1914*, Hemel Hempstead 1988

Brake, L. and M. Demoor (eds.), *Dictionary of nineteenth-century journalism*, Ghent–London 2009

Caravale, M. (ed.), *Dizionario biografico degli italiani*, Rome 1960–

Mathew, H. C. G. and B. Harrison (eds), *Oxford dictionary of national biography*, Oxford 2004; online edn L. Goldman

Secondary sources

Albisetti, J. C., 'Education for the poor Neapolitan children: Julie Schwabe's nineteenth-century secular mission', *History of Education* xxxv/6 (2006), 632–52

Allen, J., '"Resurrecting Jerusalem": the late Chartist press in the north-east of England, 1852–9', in Allen and Ashton, *Papers for the people*, 168–89

—— *Joseph Cowen and popular Tyneside radicalism, 1829–1900*, Monmouth 2007

—— 'Northern Liberator', *DNCJ*, 458–9

—— 'English Republic', *DNCJ*, 204

—— and O. R. Ashton (eds), *Papers for the people: a study of the Chartist press*, London 2005

Altick, R. D., *The English common reader: a social history of the mass reading public, 1800–1900*, Chicago 1957

—— *Punch: the lively youth of a British institution, 1841–1845*, Columbus [1997]

Altschuler, S. B., 'National Reformer (1860–91)', *DNCJ*, 439

Ambrosoli, L., 'Appunti per una ricerca su problemi dell'istruzione e della cultura popolare in Maurizio Quadrio e nei Mazziniani dopo l'unità, in *Atti del secondo convegno*, 354–64

Anderson, B., *Imagined communities: reflections on the origins and spread of nationalism*, London–New York 1991

Angelini, G., *L'ultimo Mazzini: un pensiero per l'azione*, Milan 2008

—— *Il Risorgimento democratico: tra unità e federazione*, Milan 2011

—— *Nazione, democrazia e pace tra ottocento e novecento*, Milan 2012

Antoniucci, R., '"He had the English manner": Giuseppe Mazzini tra le pagine dei romanzieri vittoriani', in Q. Marini, G. Sertoli, S. Cedrino and L. Cavaglieri, *L'officina letteraria e culturale dell'età mazziniana, 1815–70*, Novi Ligure 2013, 113–28

Arisi Rota, A., *I piccoli cospiratori: politica ed emozioni nei primi mazziniani*, Bologna 2010

—— and R. Balzani, 'Discovering politics: action and recollection in the first Mazzinian generation', in Patriarca and Riall, *The Risorgimento revisited*, 77–97

Ascoli, A. R. and K. V. Hennenberg (eds), *Making and remaking Italy: the cultivation of national identity around the Risorgimento*, Oxford–New York 2001

Ashley, S. A, *Making liberalism work: the Italian experience, 1861–1914*, Westport 2003

Ashton, O., 'The mechanics' institute and radical politics in Cheltenham Spa (1834–1840)', *Cheltenham Local History Society Journal* ii (1984), 25–8

—— *W. E. Adams: Chartist, radical and journalist (1832–1906)*, Whitley Bay 1991

—— and P. A. Pickering, *Friends of the people: uneasy radicals in the age of the Chartists*, London 2002

—— 'Newcastle Weekly Chronicle', *DNCJ*, 446–7

—— R. Fyson and S. Roberts (eds), *The Chartist legacy*, Monmouth 1999

Ashton, R., *Victorian Bloomsbury*, New Haven 2012

L'associazionismo mazziniano, Atti dell'Incontro di studio (Ostia 13–15 Nov. 1976), Rome 1982

Atti del secondo convegno su Mazzini e i Mazziniani dedicato a Maurizio Quadrio, Pisa 1976

Bacchin, E., ' "Italy for the Italians": l'opinione pubblica britannica di fronte al Risorgimento (1859–60)', *Annali della Scuola normale superiore di Pisa* ii/2 (2010), 463–88

—— 'Il Risorgimento oltremanica: nazionalismo cosmopolita nei meeting britannici di metà Ottocento', *Contemporanea: rivista di storia dell'800 e del 900* xiv (2011), 173–203

Bagatin, P. (ed.), *Tra Risorgimento e nuova Italia: Alberto Mario un repubblicano federalista*, Florence 2000

Baioni, M., 'Miti di fondazione: Risorgimento democratico e Repubblica', in M. Ridolfi, (ed.), *Almanacco della repubblica: storia d'Italia attraverso le tradizioni, le istituzioni e le simbologie repubblicane*, Milan 2003, ch. v

Balzani, R., 'Il problema Mazzini', *Ricerche di storia e politica* ii (2005), 159–72

—— and A. Varni, 'L'influenza della tradizione cristiana nella formazione del pensiero di Giuseppe Mazzini', *Annali di storia dell'esegesi* i (1992), 191–200

Banti, A. M., *L'onore della nazione: identità sessuali e violenza nel nazionalismo europeo dal XVIII secolo alla Grande Guerra*, Turin 2005

—— *La nazione del Risorgimento: parentela, santità e onore alle origini dell'Italia unita*, Turin 2006

—— and M. Meriggi, 'Introduzione', *Quaderni Storici* lxxvii (1991), 357–9

—— and P. Ginsborg (eds), *Storia d'Italia*, Turin 2007

Barié, O., 'Il radicalismo inglese nel primo decennio dell'Italia unità', *RST* ix (1965), 117–40

Barile, L., *Il Secolo, 1865–1923: storia di due generazioni della democrazia lombarda*, Milan 1980

Barsotti, E., 'Difendere la grande repubblica: Mazzini, Saffi e la guerra civile americana, *Il pensiero mazziniano* lxvii/2 (2012), 82–139

Barton, S., *Working-class organisations and popular tourism (1840–1970)*, Manchester 2005

Baylen J. O. and J. B. Brown, 'Arnold Toynbee (1852–83)', *DMBR* iii. 815–17

Bayly, C. A. and E. Biagini, 'Introduction', in their *Mazzini*, 1–7

—— (eds), *Giuseppe Mazzini and the globalisation of democratic nationalism*, Oxford 2008

Beales, D., *England and Italy (1859–60)*, London 1961

—— 'Garibaldi in England: the politics of Italian enthusiasm', in J. A. Davis and P. Ginsborg (eds), *Society and politics in the age of the Risorgimento*, Cambridge 1991, 184–216

—— and E. F. Biagini, *The Risorgimento and the unification of Italy*, London 2002

Behagg C., 'An alliance with the middle class: the Birmingham Political Union and early Chartism', in J. Epstein and D. Thompson, *The Chartist experience: studies in working-class radicalism and culture, 1830–60*, London 1982, 58–86

—— 'Attwood, Thomas (1783–1856)', *ODNB*

Belchem, J., 'Republicanism, popular constitutionalism and the radical platform in early nineteenth-century England', *Social History* vi/1 (1981), 1–32

—— 'Britishness, asylum-seekers and the northern working class: 1851', *Northern History* xxxix (2002), 59–74

Bell, D., *Victorian visions of global order: empire and international relations in nineteenth-century political thought*, Cambridge 2007

Berggren L. and L. Sjöstedt, *L'ombra dei grandi: monumenti e politica monumentale a Roma (1870–95)*, Rome 1996

Bersohn, 'The Examiner', *DNCJ*, 211

Bertini, F., *La democrazia europea e il laboratorio risorgimentale italiano (1848–60)*, Florence 2007

Bhabha, H., *Nation and narration*, London 1990

Biagianti, I., *La 'nuova Italia' nelle corrispondenze americane di Jessie White Mario*, Florence 1999

Biagini, E., *Liberty, retrenchment and reform: popular liberalism in the age of Gladstone, 1860–80*, Cambridge 1992

—— *Gladstone*, London 2000

—— 'Neo-Roman liberalism: "republican" values and British liberalism, c. 1860–75', *History of European Ideas* xxix (2003), 55–72

—— 'Radicalism and Liberty', in P. Mandler, *Liberty and authority in Victorian Britain*, Oxford 2006, 101–25

—— 'Mazzini and anticlericalism: the English exile', in Bayly and Biagini, *Mazzini*, 145–66

—— 'Citizenship and religion in the Italian constitutions, 1796–1849', *History of European Ideas* xxxvii/2 (2011), 211–17

—— 'The politics of Italianism: *Reynolds's Newspaper*, the Indian mutiny, and the radical critique of liberal imperialism in mid-Victorian Britain', in T. Crook, R. Gill and B. Taithe (eds), *Evil, barbarism and empire: Britain and abroad c. 1830–2000*, Basingstoke 2011, 99–125

—— and A. J. Reid (eds), *Currents of radicalism: popular radicalism, organised labour and party politics in Britain, 1850–1914*, Cambridge 1991

Bianco, M., 'La democrazia di William Lovett', *Il pensiero mazziniano* lxvii/3 (2012), 9–18

Blakiston, N., 'Garibaldi's visit to England in 1864', *Il Risorgimento* xvi (1964), 133–43

—— *Inglesi e italiani nel Risorgimento*, Catania 1973

Boase, G. C., 'Hadfield, Charles, *ODNB*

Bocchi A. and C. Palazzolo (eds), *Giuseppe Mazzini e John Stuart Mill*, BDM, special issue, I/1 (2004)

Bolton King, R., J. D. Browne, and E. M. H. Ibbotson, *Bolton King practical idealist* (Warwickshire Local History Society occasional paper ii, 1978)

Bonanni, S., *Pensiero e azione: Mazzini nel movimento democratico italiano e internazionale*, Rome 2006

Bonsanti, M., 'Amore familiare, amore romantico e amor di patria', in Banti and Ginsborg, *Storia d'Italia*, 127–52

Bord, J., *Science and Whig manners: science and political style in Britain, ca. 1790–1850*, Basingstoke 2009

Borg, C., P. Buttigieg and P. Mayo, *Gramsci and education*, Oxford 2002

Borutta, M., 'Anti-Catholicism and the culture of war in Risorgimento Italy', in Patriarca and Riall, *The Risorgimento revisited*, 191–213

Brake, L. and M. W Turner, 'The Reasoner', *DNCJ*, 532

Brand, C. P., *Italy and the English romantics: the Italianate fashion in early nineteenth-century England*, Cambridge 1957

Brice, C., *Monarchie et identité nationale en Italie (1861–1900)*, Paris 2010

Briggs, A., *Victorian people: a reassessment of persons and themes (1851–67)*, Harmondsworth 1965

—— (ed.), *Chartist studies*, London–Basingstoke 1977

Brilli, A., *Un paese di romantici briganti: gli italiani dell'immaginario del grand tour*, Bologna 2003

—— *Il viaggio in Italia: storia di una grande tradizione culturale*, Bologna 2008

Brown, W. H., 'Mazzini ispira i cooperatori britannici', *Bollettino della Domus Mazziniana* (1956), 11–16

Browne, J. D., 'The Toynbee Travellers' Club', *History of Education* xv/1 (1986), 11–17.

Burgess G. and M. Festenstein (eds), *English radicalism, 1550–1850*, Cambridge 2007

Burn, W. L., *The age of equipoise: a study of the mid-Victorian generation*, New York 1964

Buzard, J., *The beaten track*, Oxford 1993

—— 'Portable boundaries: Trollope, race and travel', *Nineteenth Century Contexts* xxxii (2010), 5–18

Cammarano, F., *Storia dell'Italia liberale*, Bari 2011

Campanella, A., 'Joseph Cowen, Garibaldi e Mazzini', *NRS* i–ii (1966), 201–18

Cannadine, D., *G. M. Trevelyan, a life in history*, London 1992

Carter, N., 'Hudson, Malmesbury and Cavour: British diplomacy and the Italian question, February 1858 to June 1859', *HJ* xl/2 (1997), 389–423

—— 'Hudson, Sir James (1810–85)', *ODNB*

Castelli, A., *L'unità d'Italia: pro e contro il Risorgimento*, Rome 1997

Castiglione, D., 'Republicanism and its legacy', *European Journal of Political Theory* iv/4 (2005), 453–65

Cecchinato, E., *Camicie rosse: i garibaldini dall'unità alla grande guerra*, Rome–Bari 2007

—— and M. Isnenghi, 'La nazione volontaria', in Banti and Ginsborg, *Storia d'Italia*, 697–720

—— and M. Isnenghi (eds), *Gli italiani in guerra: conflitti identità, memorie dal Risorgimento ai nostri giorni*, i, Turin 2008

Certini, R., *Jessie White Mario: una giornalista educatrice tra liberalismo inglese e democrazia italiana*, Florence 1998

Chabod, F., *L'idea di nazione*, Bari 1965

Chaney, E., *The evolution of the Grand Tour: Anglo–Italian cultural relations since the Renaissance*, London 2000

Chase, M., 'Republicanism: movement or moment', in D. Nash and A. Taylor (eds), *Republicanism in Victorian society*, Stroud 2000, 35–50

—— 'Building identity, building circulation: engraved portraiture and the *Northern Star*', in Allen and Ashton, *Papers for the people*, 25–53

—— *Chartism: a new history*, Manchester–New York 2007

—— and I. Dyck, (eds), *Living and learning: essays in honour of J. F. C. Harrison*, Aldershot 1996

Claeys, G., 'Mazzini, Kossuth, and British radicalism, 1848–54', *JBS* xxviii/3 (1989), 225–21

—— Citizens and saints: politics and anti-politics in early British socialism, Cambridge 1989

—— Imperial sceptics: British critics of empire (1850–1920), Cambridge 2010

Clark, C. and W. Kaiser (eds), Culture wars: secular-Catholic conflict in nineteenth-century Europe, Cambridge 2003

Clark, J. C., D., 'Religion and the origins of radicalism in Britain', in Burgess and Festenstein, English radicalism, 241–84

Cole, G. D. H., A century of co-operation, Manchester 1945

Collini, S., R. Whatmore and B. Young, History, religion and culture: British intellectual history, 1750–1950, Cambridge 2000

Colls, R., The identity of England, Oxford 2002

—— and P. Dodd (eds), Englishness, politics and culture, 1880–1920, London 1986

Comba, A., 'La base repubblicana dal 1889 al 1893 nell' "Emancipazione" di Felice Albani', in L'associazionismo mazziniano, 99–117

—— 'I repubblicani alla ricerca di un'identità', in Mazzini e i repubblicani, Turin 1976, 457–513

Condren, C., 'Afterword: radicalism revisited', in Burgess and Festenstein, English radicalism, 313–14

Conti, F., 'I riflessi del viaggio di Garibaldi in Inghilterra: la sinistra fiorentina fra opposizione e alternative di governo', RST xxviii (1982), 219–36

Conti Odorisio, G., 'Giuseppe Mazzini ed Harriet Martineau: un'amicizia possibile', in Bocchi and Palazzolo, Giuseppe Mazzini e John Stuart Mill, 71–100

—— 'Giuseppe Mazzini: dai diritti dell'uomo alla religione dell'umanita', in Mastellone, Mazzini e gli scrittori politici, i. 117–29

Cragoe, M. and A. Taylor (eds), London politics, 1760–1914, London 2005

Croce, B., 'Avvertenza', in Bolton King and Okey, L'Italia d'oggi, pp. v–viii

Cunningham, H., 'Jingoism in 1877–78', VS xiv (1971), 429–53

—— 'The language of patriotism', History Workshop xii/1 (1981), 8–33

—— The challenge of democracy: Britain, 1832–1918, Harlow 2001

Curatulo, G. E., Garibaldi e le donne, Rome 1913

D'Agnillo, R., 'Now in happier air': Arthur High Clough's "Amours de voyage" and Italian republicanism', in Vescovi, Villa and Vita, The Victorians and Italy, 99–112

D'Amelia, M., La mamma, Bologna 2005

D'Arcy, F., 'Charles Bradlaugh and the English republican movement, 1868–78', HJ xxv/2 (1982), 367–83

Davis, J. A., 'Garibaldi and England', History Today xxxii (1982), 21–6

—— Conflict and control: law and order in nineteenth–century Italy, London 1988

—— Naples and Napoleon: southern Italy and the European revolutions, 1780–1860, Oxford 2006

—— 'The many English lives of Giuseppe Garibaldi', in S. Bonanni (ed.), Garibaldi: cultura e ideali, Rome 2008, 339–62

—— 'L'immagine di Cavour in Inghliterra', in U. Levra (ed.), Cavour, l'Italia e l'Europa, Bologna 2011, 225–40

—— (ed.), Italy in the nineteenth century, Oxford 2000

De Caro, Gaspare, 'Giovanni Bovio', DBDI , 552–9

De Leonardis, M., L'Inghilterra e la questione romana, 1859–70, Milan 1980

Degli Innocenti, M., Garibaldi e l'ottocento: nazione, popolo, volontariato, associazione, Manduria 2008

Del Boca, A., *La storia negata: il revisionismo e il suo uso politico*, Vicenza 2009

Del Cornò, A., 'Un ritrovato giornale mazziniano: "Il Pellegrino"', in *Le fusa del gatto: libri, librai e molto altro*, Siena 2013, 191–208

Della Peruta, F., *Mazzini e i rivoluzionari Italiani: Il "partito d'azione", 1830–45*, Milan 1974

—— *L'Italia del Risorgimento*, Milan 1997

—— (ed.), *Giuseppe Mazzini e i democratici*, Milan–Naples 1969

—— (ed.), *Scrittori politici dell'ottocento: Giuseppe Mazzini e i democratici*, Milan–Naples 1969

Demoor, M., 'Athaeneum', *DNCJ*, 26–8

Derrida, J., *The politics of friendship*, London–New York 2005

Di Porto, B., 'La visione internazionale di Aurelio Saffi', *BDM* xxvii (1981), 227–41

—— *Storia del Patto di Fratellanza: movimento operaio e democrazia repubblicana (1860–93)*, Rome 1982

Dickie, J., *Darkest Italy*, New York 1999

Dickinson R. and E. Sdegno, 'Introduction: nineteenth-century travel and cultural education', *Nineteenth Century Contexts* xxxii (2010), 1–4

Dillane, F., 'Chapman, John', *DNCJ*, 107

Drake, R., 'Meridionalismo, the crisis of liberalism and the advent of Marxism in post-Risorgimento Naples', *European Legacy* ix/4 (2004), 481–502

Duggan, C., *Francesco Crispi: from nation to nationalism*, Oxford 2002

—— 'Gran Bretagna e Italia nel Risorgimento', in Banti and Ginsborg, *Storia d'Italia*, 777–96

—— 'Giuseppe Mazzini in Britain and Italy: divergent legacies, 1837–1915', in Bayly and Biagini, *Mazzini*, 187–210

—— 'Il culto dell'uno dal Risorgimento al fascism', in S. Soldani (ed.), *L'Italia alla prova*, Milan 2011, 41–64

Dzelzainis, M., 'Anti-monarchism in English republicanism', in M. V. Gelderen and Q. Skinner (eds), *Republicanism: a shared European heritage*, i, Cambridge 2002, 27–42

Epstein J. and D. Thompson (eds), *The Chartist experience: studies in working-class radicalism and culture, 1830–60*, London 1982

Figes, O., *Crimea: the last crusade*, London 2010

Finelli, M., *Il 'prezioso elemento': Giuseppe Mazzini e gli emigrati italiani nell'esperienza della scuola italiana di Londra*, Verucchio 1999

—— 'Nuovi percorsi della storiografia mazziniana', in S. Bonanni (ed.), *Pensiero e azione Mazzini nel movimento democratico italiano e internazionale*, Rome 2006, 565–9

—— 'Mazzini in Italian historical memory', *JMIS* xiii/4 (2008), 486–91

Finelli, P., '"É divenuto un Dio": santità, patria e rivoluzione nel "culto di Mazzini" (1872–1905)', in Banti and Ginsborg, *Storia d'Italia*, 665–97

Finigan, L., *The life of Peter Stuart the Ditton doctor*, London 1920

Finn, M., *After Chartism*, Cambridge 1993

Fiorentino, D. and M. Sanfilippo, *Le relazioni tra Stati Uniti e l' Italia nel periodo di Roma capitale*, Rome 2008

Flick, C., *The Birmingham Political Union and the movements for reform in Britain, 1830–39*, Hamden 1978

Foot, M. R. D. *The Gladstone diaries, January 1881–June 1883*, Oxford 1990

Frangioni, A., *Salvemini e La Grande Guerra: interventismo democratico, wilsonsimo, politica delle nazionalità*, Soveria Mannelli 2011

Fraser, H., *The Victorians and Renaissance Italy*, Oxford 1993

Freitag, S. (ed.), *Exiles from European revolutions: refugees in mid-Victorian England*, New York–Oxford 2003

French, A., *Art treasures in the North: northern families on the Grand Tour*, Norwich 2009

Fruci, G., 'Il sacramento dell'unità nazionale: linguaggi, iconografia e pratiche dei plebisciti risorgimentali (1848–70)', in Banti and Ginsborg, *Storia d'Italia*, 567–605.

Funaro, L. E., 'Il viaggio di Garibaldi in Inghilterra e la crisi della democrazia italiana dopo l'unità', *SS* vii (1966), 129–57

Fyfe, J., 'Scottish volunteers with Garibaldi', *Scottish Historical Review* lvii (1978), 168–81

Gaeta, F., *La crisi di fine secolo e l'età giolittiana*, Turin 1982

Galante Garrone, A., *I radicali in Italia, 1849–1925*, Milan 1978

—— 'Felice Cavallotti', *DBDI*, 794–803

—— 'Non si può accusare Mazzini se il paese smarrisce l'identità', *Corriere della Sera*, 10 Dec. 2010

Gasparini, L., 'Una nuova fonte di documenti sul movimento mazziniano nei rapporti coi patrioti inglesi, e specialmente con G. J. Holyoake', *RSR* iv (1933), 767–79

Gazzetta, L., *Contributo alla storia del mazzinianesimo femminile*, Milan 2003

Gemme, P., *Domesticating foreign struggles: the Italian Risorgimento and antebellum American identity*, Athens–London 2005

Gentile, E., *Il culto del littorio: la sacralizzazione della politica nell'Italia fascista*, Bari 1993

Gerwarth, R., 'Introduction: hero cults and the politics of the past: comparative European perspectives', *EHQ* xxxix/3 (2009), 381–7

—— and L. Riall, 'Fathers of the nation? Bismarck, Garibaldi and the cult of memory in Germany and Italy', *EHQ* xxxix/3 (2009), 388–413

Ghisleri, A., 'L'Istria italiana e le Alpi Giulie secondo Mazzini', in *Italia e Jugoslavia: La Voce*, Florence 1918

Gilley, S., 'The Garibaldi riots of 1862', *HJ* xvi/4 (1973), 697–732

Ginsborg, P., *Daniele Manin and the Venetian revolution of 1848–49*, Cambridge 1979

—— 'Il mito del Risorgimento nel mondo britannico: "la vera poesia della politica"', *Il Risorgimento* xliii/1–2 (1995), 385–99

—— 'Romanticismo e Risorgimento: l'io, l'amore e la nazione', in Banti and Ginsborg, *Storia d'Italia*, 5–67

Gleason, J. H., *The genesis of Russophobia in Great Britain: a study of the interaction of public opinion*, Cambridge 1950

Gosden, P. H. J. H., *The Friendly Societies in England, 1815–75*, Aldershot 1961

Gossman, N. J., 'Republicanism in nineteenth-century England', *International Review of Social History* vii (1962), 553–74

Gottardi, M. (ed.), *Fuori d'Italia: Manin e l'esilio*, Venice 2009

Grandi, T., 'Lettere di Carlo Rosselli e Gaetano Salvemini intorno al "Mazzini" di G. O. Griffith', *BDM* (1959), 2–11

Grew, R., 'How success spoiled the Risorgimento', *JMH* xxxiv/3 (1962) 239–53

—— A sterner plan for Italian unity, London 1963

—— 'Culture and society, 1796–1896', in Davis, Italy in the nineteenth century, 206–34

Griffith, G. O., Mazzini: prophet of modern Europe, London 1932.

—— 'Mussolini, Mazzini and humanity', Congregational Quarterly xiv/1 (1936), 9–17

—— 'Mazzini and the great apostolate: a Welsh tribute', BDM (1965), 5–16

Grugel, L. R., 'G. J. Holyoake', DMBR ii. 242–4

Gurney, P., 'George Jacob Holyoake: socialism, association, and co-operation in nineteenth-century England', in S. Yeo (ed.), New views on co-operation, London–New York 1988, 52–72

—— 'A higher state of civilization and happiness', in F. V. Holthoon and M. V. d. Linden, Internationalism in the Labour movement, ii, Leiden 1988, 543–64

—— 'The middle-class embrace: language, representation, and contest over co-operative forms in Britain, c. 1860–1914', VS xxxvii/2 (1994), 253–86

—— Co-operative culture and the politics of consumption in England, 1870–1930, Manchester 1996

Hall, C., White, male and middle-class: explorations in feminism and history, Oxford 1992

—— 'The nation within and without', in C. Hall, K. McClelland and J. Rendall (eds), Defining the Victorian nation: class, race, gender and the Reform Act of 1867, Cambridge 2000, 179–233

Harrison, J. F. C., A History of the Working Men's College, London 1954

—— Social reform in Victorian Leeds: the work of James Hole, 1820–95, Leeds 1954

—— Learning and living (1790–1960): a study in the history of the English education movement, London 1961

—— 'Chartism in Leeds', in Briggs, Chartist studies, ch. iii

—— 'Chartism in Leicester', in Briggs, Chartist Studies, ch. iv

Harrison, R., Before the socialists: studies in labour and politics, London 1965

Harvie, C., The lights of liberalism: university liberals and the challenge of democracy, 1860–86, London 1976

Hearder, H., Italy in the age of the Risorgimento, London 1983

—— Cavour, New York 1994

Hennock, E.P., Fit and proper persons: ideal and reality in nineteenth-century urban government, London 1973

Hewitt, M., An age of equipoise? Re-assessing mid-Victorian Britain, Aldershot 2000

—— 'Hole, James (1819/20–95)', ODNB

—— 'Why the notion of Victorian Britain does make sense', VS xlviii/3 (2006), 395–438

Hinchliff, P. and J. Prest, , 'Jowett, Benjamin (1817–1893)', ODNB

Hobsbawm, E., 'The tramping artisan', Economic History Review iii (1951), 299–320

—— and J. W. Scott, 'Political shoemakers', in E. Hobsbawm, Worlds of labour: further studies in the history of labour, London 1984, 103–30

Hollis, O., Ladies elect: women in English local government, 1865–1914, Oxford 1989

Hostetter, R., The Italian socialist movement: origins, 1861–82, New York–London–Toronto 1958

Howe, A., '"Friends of moderate opinions": Italian political thought in 1859 in a British Liberal mirror', *JMIS* xvii/5 (2012), 608–11

Hudson, P., *The industrial revolution*, London 2004

Hugman, J., '"A small drop of ink": Tyneside Chartism and *the Northern Liberator*', in O. Ashton, R. Fyson and S. Roberts, *The Chartist legacy*, Monmouth 1999, 24–47

Humpherys, A., 'People's Paper', *DNCJ*, 489–91

—— and L. James (eds), *G. W. W. Reynolds: nineteenth-century fiction, politics and the press*, Aldershot 2008

Irwin, R., *For lust of knowing: the orientalists and their enemies*, London 2006

Isabella, M., 'Italian exiles and British politics before and after 1848', in Freitag, *Exiles*, 59–87

—— 'Exile and nationalism: the case of the Risorgimento', *EHQ* xxxvi/4 (2006), 493–520

—— 'Mazzini's internationalism in context', in Bayly and Biagini, *Mazzini*, 37–58

—— 'Emotions, rationality and political intentionality in patriotic discourse', *Nations and Nationalism* xv/3 (2009), 396–401

—— *Risorgimento in exile: Italian emigrés and the liberal international in the post-Napoleonic era*, Oxford 2009

—— 'Garibaldi, re di Londra', *Il Sole 24 Ore*, 28 Feb. 2010

—— 'Il movimento risorgimentale in un contesto globale', in Roccucci, *La costruzione dello stato-nazione*, 87–107

—— 'Review article: rethinking Italy's nation-building 150 years afterwards: the new Risorgimento historiography', *Past & Present* ccxvii/1 (2012), 247–68

Isastia, A., *Storia di una famiglia del Risorgimento: Sarina, Giuseppe, Ernesto Nathan*, Turin 2010

Isnenghi, M., 'Il mito di Garibaldi', in M. Ridolfi (ed.), *Giuseppe Garibaldi: il radicalismo democratico e il mondo del lavoro*, Rome 2008, 159–61

Jackson, D. M., '"Garibaldi and the pope!" Newcastle's Irish Riot of 1866', *North East History* xxxiv (2001), 48–82

Janz, O. and L. Riall, 'Introduction: the Italian Risorgimento: transnational perspectives', *Modern Italy*, special issue xix/1 (2014), 1–4

Jones, H. S., 'The idea of the national in Victorian political thought', *EJPT* v/1 (2006), 12–21

Kirk, N., D. M. MacRaild and M. Nolan, 'Introduction: transnational ideas, activities, and organisations in labour history 1860s to 1890s', *LHR* lxxiv/3 (2009), 221–32

Kørner, A., 'Barbarous America', in A. Kørner, N. Miller and A. I. P. Smith (eds), *America imagined: explaining the United States in nineteenth-century Europe and Latin America*, Basingstoke 2012, 125–59

Koven, S., 'Barnett, Dame Henrietta Octavia Weston (1851–1936)', *ODNB*

Lancaster, B., *Radicalism, co-operation and socialism: Leicester working-class politics, 1860–1906*, Leicester 1987

Laurent, J., 'Science, society and politics in late nineteenth-century England: a further look at mechanics' institutes', *Social Studies of Science* xiv/4 (1984), 585–619

Laven, D., 'Mazzini, Mazzinian conspiracy and British politics in the 1850s', *BSM* ii (2003), 267–82

Lescure, J. C., 'Les Enjeux du souvenir: le monument national à Giuseppe Mazzini', *Revue d'histoire moderne et contemporaine* xl/2 (1993), 177–201

Levis Sullam, S., '"Dio e il popolo": la rivoluzione religiosa di Giuseppe Mazzini', in Banti and Ginsborg, *Storia d'Italia*, , 401–22

—— *L'apostolo a brandelli: l'eredità di Mazzini tra Risorgimento e fascismo*, Bari 2010

Limentani, U., 'Leone and Arthur Serena and the Cambridge Chair of Italian: 1919–34', in McLaughlin *Britain and Italy*, 154–77

Limiti G., (ed.), *Il mazzinianesimo nel mondo*, Pisa 2011, ii–iv

Lodolini, E., 'Mediterraneo, Adriatico, intervento nella politica del Partito Mazziniano italiano (1900–1918)', xxviii (1951), 473–86

—— 'L'organizzazione del partito mazziniano italiano in Italia e all'estero agli inizi del secolo xx', *RSR* xli (1954), 398–403

LoPatin-Lummis, N., *Political unions, popular politics and the Great Reform Act of 1832*, New York 1999

Lovett, C., *The democratic movement in Italy, 1830–76*, Cambridge, MA 1982

Lupo, S., *L'unificazione italiana: mezzogiorno, rivoluzione, guerra civile*, Rome 2011

Luzzatto, S. *La crisi dell'antifascismo*, Turin 2004

Lyttelton, A., 'Creating a national past: history, myth and image in the Risorgimento', in A. R. Ascoli and K. V. Hennenberg (eds.), *Making and remaking Italy: the cultivation of national identity around the Risorgimento*, Oxford–New York 2001, 27–73

—— 'Sismondi, il mondo britannico e l'Italia del Risorgimento tra passato e presente', in L. Pagliai and F. Sofia (eds), *Sismondi e la nuova Italia*, Florence 2011, 145–80.

—— 'Sismondi, the republic and liberty: between Italy and England, the city and the nation', *JMIS* xvii/2 (2012), 168–82

Mack Smith, D., 'Garibaldi e l'Inghilterra', *NA* cxvii (1982), 415–32

—— *Cavour and Garibaldi, 1860*, Cambridge 1985

—— 'Gli inglesi e l'amore per l'Italia', *NA* cxxi (1986), 144–53

—— *Mazzini*, New Haven–London 1994

—— 'Britain and the Italian Risorgimento', in McLaughlin, *Britain and Italy*, 13–31

McAllister, A., *John Bull's Italian snakes and ladders*, Newcastle-upon-Tyne 2007

—— '"A pair of naked legs and a ragged scarf": an overview of Victorian discourses in Italy', in Vescovi, Villa and Vita *The Victorians and Italy*, 19–43

McIntire, C. T., *England against the papacy (1858–61)*, Cambridge 1983

Mackay, D., 'Joseph Cowen e il Risorgimento', *RSR* li (1964), 5–26

Mackenzie, J. H., *Orientalism*, Manchester–New York, 1995,

McKibbin, R., *Classes and cultures: England, 1918–51*, Oxford 1998

McLaughlin, M., 'Introduction: the centrality of Dante', in McLaughlin *Britain and Italy*, 1–12

—— (ed.) *Britain and Italy from romanticism to modernism: a Festschrift for Peter Brand*, Oxford 2000

McWilliam, R., 'Reynolds's Political Instructor', *DNCJ*, 540

Maghenzani S. (ed.), *Il protestantesimo italiano nel Risorgimento: infleunze, miti, identità*, Turin 2012

Maidment, B., 'Punch', *DNCJ*, 517–19

Manacorda, G., *Il movimento operaio italiano attraverso i suoi congressi*, Rome 1953

Mandler., P., ' "Race" and "nation" in mid-Victorian thought', in Collini, Whatmore and Young, *History, religion and culture*, 224–44

—— *The English national character: the history of an idea from Edmund Burke to Tony Blair*, London–New Haven 2006

—— and S. Pedersen (eds), *After the Victorians: private conscience and public duty in modern Britain*, London 2005

Marazzi, M., *Il romanzo risorgimentale di Giovanni Ruffini*, Florence 1999

Mares, D., 'Transcending the metropolis: London and provincial popular radicalism, c. 1860–75', in M. Cragoe and A. Taylor (eds), *London politics, 1760–1914*, London 2005, 121–43

Massari, S. (ed.), *Carlo Romussi (1847–1913): inventario dell'archivio*, Turin 2007

Mastellone, S., *Il progetto politico di Mazzini: Italia–Europa*, Florence 1994

—— *Storia della democrazia in Europa*, Turin 2003

—— *Mazzini scrittore politico in inglese: democracy in Europe, 1840–55*, Florence 2004

—— 'La "social philosophy" di John Stuart Mill e la "educative democracy" di Giuseppe Mazzini', in Bocchi and Palazzolo, *Giuseppe Mazzini e John Stuart Mill*, 7–27

—— *Mazzini e Linton: una democrazia europea (1845–55)*, Florence 2007

—— 'Mazzini's International League and the politics of the London Democratic Manifestos, 1837–50', in Bayly and Biagini, *Mazzini*, 93–104

—— *La nascita della democrazia in Europa: Carlyle, Harney, Mill, Engels, Mazzini, Schapper: addresses, appeals, manifestos (1836–55)*, Florence 2009

—— 'Garibaldi e i "red republicans", in A. M. L. Del Grosso (ed.), *Garibaldi nel pensiero politico europeo*, Florence 2010, 33–6

—— (ed.), *Mazzini e gli scrittori politici europei (1837–57)*, Florence 2005

Matassa, F., *L'Italia nella storiografia dell'otto-novecento*, Rome 2011

Mathew, H. G. C., *Gladstone (1809–74)*, Oxford 1986

Matsumoto-Best, S., *Britain and the papacy in the age of revolution, 1846–51*, Woodbridge 2003

—— 'Palmerston and Italy', in D. Brown and M. Taylor (eds), *Palmerston studies*, ii, Southampton 2007, 79–96

Meacham, S., *Toynbee Hall and social reform, 1880–1914: the search for community*, New Haven–London 1987

Meriggi, M., 'Il Risorgimento rivisitato: un bilancio', in Roccucci, *La costruzione dello stato-nazione*, 39–57

Moe, N., *The view from the Vesuvius*, Berkeley 2006

—— 'The emergence of the southern question in Villari, Franchetti, and Sonnino', in Schneider, *Italy's southern question*, 51–76

Monsagrati, G., 'Casaccia Felice', *DBDI*, 39–41

—— 'Fabrizi Nicola', *DBDI*, 803–13

—— 'Modelli dell'intransigentismo repubblicano: il gruppo romano del *Dovere*', in *L'associazionismo mazziniano*, 27–96

—— 'Alle prese con la democrazia: Gran Bretagna e U.S.A. di fronte alla Repubblica Romana', in *La Repubblica Romana*, 279–306

—— 'La Repubblica Romana del 1849', in Ridolfi, *Almanacco della repubblica*, 84–96

—— 'Nella morsa delle potenze: la politica estera della Repubblica Romana', in C. Cipolla (ed.), *Il sogno di Garibaldi*, Milan 2013, 79–90

Montale, B., *La Confederazione operaia genovese e il movimento mazziniano in Genova dal 1864 al 1892*, Pisa 1960

Mordini, A., 'Osservazioni sopra una nuova organizzazione in Italia presentate nel giugno 1852', in Galante Garrone, *I radicali in Italia*, 30–2

Morelli, E., G., *Mazzini in Inghilterra*, Florence 1938

—— *L'Inghilterra di Mazzini*, Rome 1965

—— 'L'azione di Mazzini in Inghilterra per l'Italia', *Il Risorgimento*, special issue (1973), 25–32

—— *Mazzini, quasi una biografia*, Rome 1984

Morgan, S., 'Historicizing celebrity', in *Celebrity Studies* i/3 (2010), 366–8

Morris, J. and R. Lumley, (eds), *The new history of the Italian South*, Exeter 1997

Morris, R. J., *Class, sect and party: the making of the British middle class, Leeds, 1820–50*, Manchester–New York 1990

Morton, G., B. de Vries and R. J. Morris, *Civil society, association and urban places: class, nation and culture in nineteenth-century Europe*, Farnham–Burlington, VT 2006

Mussell, J., 'Leader', *DNCJ*, 351

Nabulsi, K., 'Patriotism and republicanism in the "oath of allegiance" to Young Europe', *EJPT* v/1 (2006), 61–70

Nash, D. and A. Taylor, (eds), *Republicanism in Victorian society*, Stroud 2000

Natalini, G., *Storia della Repubblica Romana del quarantanove*, Rome 2000

Neville, K., *Change, continuity and class: labour in British society, 1850–1920*, Manchester 1998

Nicosia, A., 'Sismondi e Mazzini', in Mastellone, *Mazzini e gli scrittori politici*, ii. 291–8

O'Connor, M., *The romance of Italy and the English political imagination*, Basingstoke 1998

—— 'Civilizing southern Italy: British and Italian women and the cultural politics of European nation building', *Women's Writing* x/2 (2003), 253–68

O'Gorman, F., *The Cambridge companion to Victorian culture*, Cambridge 2010

Ockwell A. and H. Pollins, 'Extension in all its forms', in M. G. Brock and M. G. Curthoys, *The history of the university of Oxford*, vii/2, Oxford 2000, 661–88

Onnis, P., 'Battaglie democratiche e risorgimento in un carteggio inedito di Giuseppe Mazzini e George Jacob Holyoake', *RSR* xxii (1935), 883–927

Ottani Cavina, A., 'The landscape of the Macchiaioli: a path towards the modern', *JMIS* xviii/2 (2013), 225–31

Packe, M., *The bombs of Orsini*, London 1957

Parry, J., 'Nonconformity, clericalism and "Englishness": the United Kingdom', in Clark and Kaiser, *Culture wars*, 152–80

—— *The politics of patriotism: English liberalism, national identity and Europe, 1830–86*, Cambridge 2006

Passerini, L., *Europe in love, love in Europe*, New York, 1999

Patriarca, S., 'Indolence and regeneration: tropes and tensions of Risorgimento patriotism', *AHR* cx/2 (2005), 380–408

—— *Italian vices: nation and character from the Risorgimento to the republic*, Cambridge 2010

—— 'Unmaking the nation? Uses and abuses of Garibaldi in contemporary Italy', *Modern Italy* special issue x/4 (2010), 467–83

—— and L. Riall (eds), *The Risorgimento revisited: nationalism and culture in nineteenth-century Italy*, Basingstoke 2012

Pavone, C., *A civil war: a history of the Italian resistance* (1991), New York 2013

Pécout, G., *Il lungo Risorgimento: la nascita dell'Italia contemporanea, 1770–1922*, Milan 1999

—— 'International volunteers and the Risorgimento: introduction', *JMIS* xiv/4 (2009), 413–26

Pelosi, S., *Della vita di Maurizio Quadrio*, Sondrio 1921

Pemble, J., *The Mediterranean passion: Victorians and Edwardians in the South*, Oxford 1987

Pesman, R., 'Mazzini in esilio e le inglesi', in I Porciani (ed.), *Famiglia e nazione nel lungo ottocento italiano: modelli, strategie, reti di relazioni*, Rome 2006, 55–82

—— 'Mazzinian discipleship: Sara Nathan and Jessie White Mario', *Spunti e ricerche* xxi (2007), 33–50

—— 'The marriage of Giorgina Saffi and Aurelio Saffi: Mazzinian nationalism and the Italian home', in L. Baldassar and D. Gabaccia (eds), *Intimacy and Italian migration: gender and domestic lives in a mobile world*, New York 2010, 25–35

Pettit, P., *Republicanism: a theory of freedom and government*, Oxford 1999

Pfister, M., *The fatal gift of beauty: the Italies of British travellers: an annotated anthology*, Amsterdam–Atlanta 1996

—— and R. Hertel, *Performing national identity: Anglo-Italian cultural transactions*, Amsterdam–New York 2008

Pichetto, M. T., 'John Stuart Mill', in Mastellone, *Mazzini e gli scrittori politici*, i. 1–28

Pine-Coffin, R.S., *Bibliography of British and American travel in Italy to 1861*, Florence 1974

Pinto, C., '1857: conflitto civile e guerra nazionale nel mezzogiorno', *Meridiana* lxix (2010), 171–200

—— 'La rivoluzione discipinata del 1860: cambio di regime ed elite politiche nel mezzogiorno italiano', *Contemporanea* 1 (2013), 39–68

Pocock, J. G. A., *The Machiavellian moment: Florentine political thought and the Atlantic republican tradition*, Princeton 2003

Polonsky, R., 'Is this not paradise?', *Times Literary Supplement*, 9 Sept. 2011

Porter, B., *The refugee question in mid-Victorian Britain*, Cambridge 1979

—— '"Bureau and barrack": early Victorian attitudes towards the continent', *VS* xxvii/4 (1984), 407–33

Pozzani, S. 'L'ultima organizzazione di Mazzini: l'Alleanza Repubblicana Universale', *Archivio Trimestrale: Rassegna Storica di Studi sul Movimento Repubblicano* vii/2 (Apr.–June 1981), 291–8

Pozzi, R., 'Mazzini e il Sansimonismo', in Limiti, *Il Mazzinianesimo nel mondo*, iv. 33–48

Price, R. N., 'The Working Men's Club movement and Victorian social reform ideology', *VS* xv/2 (1971), 117–47.

Prochaska, F., *The republic of Britain, 1760–2000*, London 2000

Prothero, I. 'Chartists and political refugees', in Freitag, *Exiles*, 209–33

Raffaelli, T., 'Alcune note sulla raccolta di fondi a favour di Giuseppe Mazzini in Inghliterra (1865–66)', *BDM* ii (1988), 179–82

Ralli M., 'Dolfi Giuseppe', *DBDI* , 451–62

Raponi, D., 'Religious reformation and national unity: British Protestants and Italy, 1860–1870', in R. Crone, D. Gange and K. Jones, *New perspectives in British cultural history*, Newcastle-upon-Tyne 2007, 78–89

—— 'An anti–Catholicism of free-trade? Religion and the Anglo–Italian relations of 1863', *EHQ* xxxix/4 (2009), 633–52

—— 'Gran Bretagna', in F. Cammarano and M. Marchi (eds), *Il mondo ci guarda: l'unificazione italiana nella stampa e nell'opinione pubblica internazionali, 1859–61*, Florence 2011, 141–52

—— 'Risorgimento e virtù civiche: riflessioni dei protestanti britannici sull'identità nazionale italiana, 1861–75, in Maghenzani, *Il protestantesimo italiano*, 113–25

Ravenna, L., *Il giornalismo mazziniano*, Florence 1939

Reidy, D. V., 'Panizzi, Gladstone, Garibaldi and the Neapolitan prisoners', *Electronic British Library Journal* (2005), 1–15

Remedi, A. G., 'Casareto Antonio', *DBDI*, 180–2

La Repubblica Romana nel movimento europeo tra il 1848 e il 1849, RSR, special issue lxxxvi (1999)

Riall, L., 'Garibaldi: the first celebrity', *HT* (2007), 57–8

—— *Garibaldi: invention of a hero*, New Haven–London 2007

—— 'The politics of Italian romanticism: Mazzini and the making of a nationalist culture', in Bayly and Biagini, *Mazzini*, 167–86

—— *Risorgimento: the history of Italy from Napoleon to nation-state*, London 2009

—— 'Martyr cults in nineteenth-century Italy', *JMH* lxxxii/2 (2010), 255–87

Riccardi, C., 'Sconfitte critiche del Risorgimento: il moto letterario in Italia di Mazzini', in Q. Marini, G. Sertoli, S. Cedrino and L. Cavaglieri, *L'officina letteraria e culturale dell'età mazziniana, 1815–1870*, Novi Ligure 2013, 65–74

Richter, M., 'T. H. Green and his audience: liberalism as a surrogate fate', *Review of Politics* xviii/4 (1956), 444–72

Ridley, J., *Garibaldi*, London 2001

Ridolfi, M., *Il partito della repubblica: i repubblicani in Romagna e le origini del Pri nell'Italia liberale (1872–95)*, Milan 1990

—— *Il circolo virtuoso: sociabilità democratica, associazionismo e rappresentanza politica nell'ottocento*, Florence 1992

—— 'Visions of republicanism', *JMIS* xiii/4 (2008), 468–79

—— (ed.), *Almanacco della repubblica: storia d'Italia attraverso le tradizioni, le istituzioni e le simbologie repubblicane*, Milan 2003

—— (ed.), *La democrazia radicale nell'ottocento europeo: forme della politica, modelli culturali, riforme sociali*, Milan 2005

Roberts, S., 'The later career of Thomas Cooper (c. 1845–55)', *Leicester Archaeological Historical Society Transactions* lxiv (1990), 62–72

—— *The Chartist prisoners: the radical lives of Thomas Cooper (1805–92) and Arthur O'Neill (1819–96)*, Oxford 2008

Roberts, W., *Prophet in exile: Joseph Mazzini in England, 1837–68*, New York 1989

—— 'Mazzini's thought in the development of British culture, politics and society', in Limiti, *Il mazzinianesimo nel mondo*, i. 3–75

Roccucci, A. (ed.), *La costruzione dello stato-nazione*, Rome 2012

Romanelli, R., 'Alla ricerca di un corpo elettorale: la riforma del 1882 in Italia e il problema dell'allargamento del suffragio', in P. Pombeni (ed.), *La trasformazione politica nell'Europa liberale, 1870–90*, Bologna 1986, 171–207

—— 'Political debate, social history and the Italian *borghesia*: changing perspectives in historical research', *JMH* lxiii/4 (1991), 717–39

Romani, R., 'Political thought in action: the moderates in 1859', *JMIS* xv/5 (2012), 593–607

Rose, J., *The intellectual life of the British working classes*, New Haven–London 2001

Rosselli, C., 'Discussione sul Risorgimento': *Giustizia e Libertà*, 26 Apr. 1935, in Castelli, *L'unità d'Italia*, 40–6

Rosselli, N., *Mazzini e Bakunin: dodici anni di movimento operaio in Italia, 1860–72*, Turin 1967

Rossi, J., *The image of America in Mazzini's writings*, Madison 1954

Rothney, J., 'La società degli amici d'Italia e la nuova riforma', *RSR* xlviii/1 (1961), 21–58

Rowley, D. J., 'Giuseppe Mazzini and the democratic logic of nationalism', *Nations and Nationalism* xviii/1 (2012), 39–56

Royle, E., 'Mechanics' institutes and the working classes, 1840–60', *HJ* xiv/2 (1971), 305–21

—— *Victorian infidels: the origins of the British secularist movement, 1791–1866*, Manchester 1974

—— *The infidel tradition from Paine to Bradlaugh*, London 1976

—— *Radicals, secularists and republicans: popular freethought in Britain (1866–1915)*, Manchester 1980

—— *Robert Owen and the commencement of the millennium: a study of the Harmony Community*, Manchester 1998

—— 'Bradlaugh, Charles (1833–91)', *ODNB*, 197–8

—— and J. Walvin, *English radicals and reformers: 1760–1848*, Lexington, KY 1982

Rudman, H. W., *Italian nationalism and English letters: figures of the Risorgimento and Victorian men of letters*, London 1940

Russi, L., 'L'Inghilterra di Pisacane', in Mastellone, *Mazzini e gli scrittori politici*, ii. 313–30

Sabetti, F., *Civilization and self-government: the political thought of Carlo Cattaneo*, Lanham 2010

Salvemini, G., *Mazzini*, London 1956

Sandrock K. and O. J. Wright, *Locating Italy: East and West in British-Italian cultural transactions*, Amsterdam–New York 2013

Sarti, R., *Mazzini: A life for the religion of politics*, Westport 1997

—— 'Giuseppe Mazzini e la tradizione repubblicana', in Ridolfi, *Almanacco della repubblica*, 56–67

—— 'La democrazia radicale: uno sguardo reciproco tra Stati Uniti e Italia', in Ridolfi, *La democrazia radicale*, 133–58

—— 'L'apostolo a brandelli: l'eredità di Mazzini tra Risorgimento e fascismo', review, *JMIS* xvi/4 (2011), 555–7

Schaff, B. (ed.), *Exiles, emigrés and intermediaries: Anglo–Italian cultural relations*, Amsterdam–New York 2010

Schneider, J. (ed.), *Italy's southern question: orientalism in one country*, Oxford 1998

Schoyen, A.R., *The Chartist challenge: a portrait of George Julian Harney*, London–Melbourne–Toronto 1958

Schwegman, M.,'Amazons in Italy: Josephine Butler and the transformation of the Italian female militancy', *Women's History Review* xvii/2 (2008), 173–8

Scirocco, A., 'Campanella, Federico', *DBDI*, 365–71

—— *I democratici italiani da Sapri a Porta Pia*, Naples 1969

—— 'Maurizio Quadrio e *L'Emancipazione*', in *Atti del secondo convegno* , 244–78

Sellers, I., 'Dawson, George', *ODNB*, 554–6

Sestan, E., 'De Boni Filippo', *DBDI* , 396–405

Shannon, R., 'David Urquhart and the Foreign Affairs Committees', in P. Hollis (ed.), *Pressure from without in early Victorian England*, London 1974, 239–61

Shirley, M., 'Reynolds's Weekly Newspaper', *DNCJ*, 540–1

Smith, F. B., 'British Post Office espionage, 1844', *HS* xiv/54 (Apr. 1970), 189–203

—— *Radical artisan: W. J. Linton, 1812–97*, Manchester 1973

Soldani, S., 'Il Risorgimento delle donne', in Banti and Ginsborg, *Storia d'Italia*, 183–224

Southall, H., 'Mobility, the artisan community and popular politics in early 19th century England', in G. Kearns and C. W. J. Withers (eds), *Urbanising Britain: essays on class and community in the nineteenth century*, Cambridge 1991, 103–53

Spadolini, G., *I repubblicani dopo l'unità (1871–90)*, Florence 1980

Spini, G., *Risorgimento e protestanti*, Turin 1998

—— *Italia liberale e protestanti*, Turin 2002

—— 'Mazzini e la dimensione religiosa della democrazia', in Limiti, *Il mazzianiesimo nel mondo*, iv. 249–58

Sprinker, M., *Edward Said: a critical reader*, Oxford 1992

Stedman Jones, G., *Languages of class: studies in working-class history (1832–1982)*, Cambridge 1983

Steedman C., *Labours lost: domestic service and the making of modern England*, Cambridge 2009

Summers, A., 'Introduction: the Internationalist Abolitionist Federation', *Women's History Review* xvii/2 (2008), 149–52

—— 'British women and cultures of internationalism, c. 1815–1914', in D. Feldman and J. Lawrence (eds), *Structures and transformations in modern British history*, Cambridge 2011, 187–209

Sutcliffe, M. P., 'Volontari garibaldini inglesi: escursionisti in Sicilia: volontari inglesi a seguito di Garibaldi', in A. Garibaldi Jallet and A. Lazzarino Del Grosso (eds), *Garibaldi: orizzonti mediterranei*, La Maddalena 2009, 217–38

—— 'Negotiating the "Garibaldi moment" in Newcastle-upon-Tyne (1854–61)', *Modern Italy*, xv/2 (2010), 129–44

—— 'W. E. Adams: un mazziniano inglese di provincia', in M. Di Napoli and G. Monsagrati (eds), *Mazzini compagno di vita*, Pisa 2010

—— 'L'amore per Garibaldi: consumante passione o prodotto di consumo', in P. Morris, F. Ricatti and M. Seymour (eds), *Politica ed emozioni nella storia d'Italia*, Rome 2012, 53–70

—— 'Mazzini's transnational legacy amongst British co-operators (*ca.* 1885–1949)', *LHR* lxxvii/3 (2012), 267–88

—— 'Residenti anglicani inglesi: una sfida per il vescovo di Gilbilterra', in Maghenzani, *Il protentastesimo italiano*, 265–76

—— 'British red shirts: a history of the Garibaldi volunteers', in B. Collins and

N. Airelli (eds), *Transnational soldiers: foreign military enlistment in the modern era*, Basingstoke 2013, 202–18

—— 'Marketing "Garibaldi panoramas" in Britain (1860–64)', *JMIS* xviii/2 (2013), 232–43

—— 'The Toynbee Travellers' Club and the transnational education of citizens, 1888–90', *History Workshop* lxxvi (Autumn 2013), 137–59

—— 'Italian women in the making: re-reading the *Englishwoman's Review* (ca. 1871–89)', in N. Carter (ed.) *Britain, Ireland and the Italian Risorgimento*, Basingstoke 2014, forthcoming

Taylor, A., '*Reynolds's newspaper* opposition to monarchy and the radical anti-jubilee: Britain's antimonarchist tradition reconsidered', *HJ* lxviii/167 (1995), 318–37

—— 'Republicanism reappraised: anti-monarchism and the English radical tradition, 1850–1872', in J. Vernon (ed.), *Re-reading the constitution*, Cambridge 1996, 154–78

—— '*Down with the crown': British anti-monarchism and debates about royalty since 1790*, London 1999

Taylor, A. J. P., *The Italian problem in European diplomacy, 1847–9*, Manchester 1932

Taylor, B., *Eve and the New Jerusalem*, London 1983

Taylor, M., 'The old radicalism and the new: David Urquhart and the politics of opposition', in Biagini and Reid, *Currents of radicalism*, 23–44

—— *The decline of British radicalism, 1847–60*, Oxford 1995

—— 'Rethinking the Chartists: searching for synthesis in the historiography of Chartism', *HJ* xxxix/2 (1996), 479–95

—— 'Republics versus empires: Charles Dilke's republicanism reconsidered', in Nash and Taylor, *Republicanism*, 25–34

—— *Ernest Jones, Chartism and the romance of politics (1819–69)*, Oxford 2003

—— 'Urquhart, David (1805–77)', *ODNB*, 945–8

Tesoro, M., *I repubblicani nell'età giolittiana*, Florence 1978

Thompson, D., *The Chartists: popular politics in the industrial revolution*, New York 1984

Thompson, E. P., *The making of the English working class*, New York 1964

—— 'The peculiarities of the English', in his *The poverty of theory and other essays*, London 1978, 245–301

Todd, N., *The militant democracy: Joseph Cowen and Victorian radicalism*, Whitley Bay 1991

Trevelyan, G.M., *Garibaldi and the making of Italy*, London 1911

——'Englishmen and Italians: some aspects of their relations past and present' (1919), in his *Clio, a muse and other essays*, Freeport 1968, 104–23

—— *British history in the nineteenth century (1782–1901)*, London 1922

Turner, M. W. and L. Brake, 'The Reasoner', *DNCJ*, 532

Tylecote, M., *The mechanics' institutes of Lancashire and Yorkshire before 1851*, Manchester 1957

Ugolini, R., 'Nove lettere inedite dalla corrispondenza di Maurizio Quadrio nell'archivio Nathan', in *Atti del secondo convegno*, 358–79

—— 'L'educazione popolare di orientamento mazziniano a Roma: la famiglia Nathan e la Scuola "Giuseppe Mazzini" in Trastevere', in *L'associazionismo mazziniano*, 119–67

Ulin, D., 'Westminster Review', *DNCJ*, 672–3

Urry, J., *The tourist gaze: leisure and travel in contemporary societies*, London 2002

Urbinati, N., 'The legacy of Kant: Giuseppe Mazzini's cosmopolitanism of nations', in Bayly and Biagini, *Mazzini*, 11–35

—— (ed.), *Liberal socialism*, Princeton 1994

Usher, J., 'Okey, Thomas (1852–1935)', *ODNB*

Valiani, Leo, 'Interventi: atti del XIII congresso storico toscano', *RST* iv (1960), 227–8

Van Gelderen, M. and Q. Skinner, *Republicanism: a shared European heritage*, ii, Cambridge 2002

Vargo, G. and M. Chase, 'Northern Star', *DNCJ*, 459–60

—— '"Outworks of the citadel of corruption": the Chartist press reports the empire', *VS* liv/2 (2012), 227–53

Varouxakis, G., ' "Patriotism", "cosmopolitanism" and "humanity" in Victorian political thought', *EJPTheory* v/1 (2006), 100–18

Venturi, F., 'La circolazione delle idee', *RSR* xli (1954), 223–42

—— 'L'Italia fuori dall'Italia', in *Storia d'Italia: dal primo settecento all'unità*, iii, Turin, 1973, 987–1117

Vernon, J., *Politics and the people: a study in English political culture c. 1815–67*, Cambridge 1993

Vescovi, A., L. Villa and P. Vita, *The Victorians and Italy: literature, travel, politics and art*, Milan 2009

Viarengo, A., *Cavour*, Rome 2010

Vincent, A., 'Green, Thomas Hill (1836–82)', *ODNB*

Vincent, J., *The formation of the British Liberal party, 1857–68*, London 1966

Viroli, M., *For love of country: an essay on patriotism and nationalism*, Oxford 1995

Vivarelli, R., *Italia 1861*, Bologna 2013

Wanrooij, B. P. F, 'Josephine Butler and regulated prostitution in Italy, *Women's History Review* xvii/2 (2008), 153–71

Warraq, I., *Defending the West: a critique of Edward Said's orientalism*, Amherst-NY 2007

Webb, R. K., *The British working-class reader: literacy and social tension (1790–1848)*, London 1955

Weisser, H. G., 'Chartist internationalism: 1845–48', *HJ* xiv/1 (1971), 49–66

—— *April 10: challenge and response in England in 1848*, Lanham–London 1983

Williams, J., 'Abraham, William', *ODNB*

Wilson, A. N., *The Victorians*, London 2002

Windland, K., 'Garibaldi and the Welsh political imagination', in M. Cragoe and C. Williams (eds), *Wales and war: society, politics and religion in the nineteenth and twentieth centuries*, Cardiff 2007

Wolffe, J., *The Protestant crusade in Great Britain. 1829–1860*, Oxford 1991

Woolf, S., *L'Italia repubblicana vista da fuori*, Bologna 2007

Worden, B., 'The Victorians and Cromwell', in Collini, Whatmore and Young, *History, religion and culture*, 112–35

—— *Roundhead reputations: the English civil wars and passions of posterity*. London 2001, 215–95

Wright, O. J., 'British representatives and the surveillance of Italian affairs, 1860–70', *HJ* li/3 (2008), 669–87

—— 'Police "outrages" against British residents and travellers in liberal Italy (1867–77), *Crime Histories and Societies* xiv/1 (2010), 51–72

—— 'British foreign policy and the Italian occupation of Rome, 1870', *IHR* xxiv/1 (2012), 161–76

Yong, A. S., *Race and the nation in liberal Italy. 1861–1911: meridionalism, empire and diaspora*, New York 2006

Zagorin, P., 'Republicanisms', *British Journal for History of Philosophy* xi/4 (2003), 701–14

Zangheri, R., G. Galasso and V. Castronovo, *Storia del movimento cooperativo in Italia, 1886–1986*, Turin 1987

Unpublished theses

Bonsanti, M., 'Public life and private relations in the Risorgimento', Phd, London 2008

Darvill, P. A., 'The contribution of co-operative retail societies to welfare within the framework of the North East coast area', M. Litt., Durham 1954

Fyfe, J., 'Scotland and the Risorgimento', Phd, Guelph 1976

Mackay, D. F., 'The influence of the Italian Risorgimento on British public opinion', Phd, Oxford 1961

Windland, K., 'Garibaldi in Britain: reflections of a liberal hero', Phd, Oxford 2002

Electronic resources

http://www.archiviorosselli.it/User.it/index.php?PAGE=Sito–it/archivio–inventario3&start=0&arch–id=1547&arch–id–1=1676

Gale nineteenth-century newspapers and periodicals:

http://gale.cengage.co.uk/product–highlights/history/19th–century–british–library–newspapers.aspx

http://mlr.com/DigitalCollections/products/ukperiodicals/

'Mazzini's letters', London 1856: http://www.jstor.org/stable/60202125

The Carlyle Letters online: http://carlyleletters.dukejournals.org/

Collected works of John Stuart Mill online: http://oll.libertyfund.org/?option=com_staticxt&staticfile=show.php%3Fperson=21&Itemid=28

'L'idea di patria ieri e oggi', Bari 2011: http://www.laterza.it/index.php?option=com_content&view=article&id=378:lid accessed on 20 June 2013

Index